United States
SUPREME
COURT
EMPLOYMENT
CASES

Seventh Edition

Oakstone

Oakstone Legal & Business Publishing, Inc.
6801 Cahaba Valley Road
Birmingham, Alabama 35242-2627

Copyright © 2001 by Oakstone Legal & Business Publishing, Inc.
ISBN 1-931200-10-6
Printed in the United States of America

Library of Congress Cataloging-in-Publication Data

U.S. Supreme Court employment cases.
p.   cm.
Includes index.
ISBN 1-931200-10-6
1. Labor laws and legislation--United States--Digests. I. United
States. Supreme Court. II. Oakstone Publishing (Birmingham, Ala.)
III. Title: US Supreme Court employment cases.
KF3314.U8 2001
344.73'01'0264--dc20
[347.30410264]   93-22375
                                                                  CIP

Other Titles Published by Oakstone Legal & Business Publishing:

Deskbook Encyclopedia of American School Law
Students with Disabilities and Special Education
Private School Law in America
Deskbook Encyclopedia of American Insurance Law
Deskbook Encyclopedia of Public Employment Law
Deskbook Encyclopedia of Employment Law
U.S. Supreme Court Education Cases
Statutes, Regulations and Case Law Protecting Individuals with Disabilities
Federal Laws Prohibiting Employment Discrimination
Higher Education Law in America

TABLE OF CONTENTS

CHAPTER ONE
DISCRIMINATION

TABLE OF CONTENTS

TABLE OF CONTENTS

TABLE OF CONTENTS

TABLE OF CONTENTS

CHAPTER TWO
EMPLOYEE BENEFITS

TABLE OF CONTENTS

CHAPTER THREE
FREEDOM OF EXPRESSION

TABLE OF CONTENTS

TABLE OF CONTENTS

TABLE OF CONTENTS

CHAPTER FIVE
LABOR RELATIONS

TABLE OF CONTENTS

TABLE OF CONTENTS

TABLE OF CONTENTS

TABLE OF CONTENTS

TABLE OF CONTENTS

TABLE OF CONTENTS

TABLE OF CONTENTS

CHAPTER EIGHT
WORKERS' COMPENSATION

TABLE OF CONTENTS

INTRODUCTION

When legal issues are discussed, people invariably want to know how the United States Supreme Court has ruled on the particular issue in question. The inquiry is sometimes unanswerable because the Court does not rule on every legal issue which arises. It does, however, issue opinions in a great many specific areas. When the Court issues such an opinion, the precedent it sets is useful in establishing law in other areas. By the use of analogy, a Supreme Court ruling on a particular point may be used to create law in a similar area.

This volume examines employment cases in both the public and private sectors which have reached the Supreme Court. Certain issues, such as discrimination and labor relations, have been before the Court many times. Other issues have been litigated less frequently. However, virtually every Supreme Court case from the 1980s forward is included in this volume. In addition, a number of important older cases are summarized within. This book is a comprehensive and complete guide to employment law.

Steve McEllistrem, Esq.
Editorial Director
Oakstone Legal & Business Publishing

GUIDE TO THE USE OF U.S. SUPREME COURT EMPLOYMENT CASES

The organization of this volume is chronological by subject matter. Each chapter constitutes a particular subject matter area, further divided by subsets within that area. To examine a particular topic, find that area of the law in the table of contents or the index, and you will be directed to the cases which address that issue. If you start at the beginning of that subsection, you will see the development of the law in that area, up to the most recent Supreme Court cases. If you know the name, or part of the name, of a particular case, you can check either the table of cases or the Defendant-Plaintiff table of cases (which lists the cases alphabetically by the defendants' names).

The cases in this volume contain important legal precedents. Even cases like *Patterson v. McLean Credit Union*, Chapter One, which held that 42 U.S.C. § 1981 did not apply to post-contract formation discrimination—and which has been partially overruled by the Civil Rights Act of 1991—have not been completely overruled. It is also important to note that Supreme Court cases which are no longer recent can still have great legal importance; those which are relevant to legal issues confronting you must be considered.

This volume can be the starting point for researching employment law topics. With each case, a full legal citation is provided. From this citation, you can obtain the actual case opinion from any law library for scholarly research. To keep abreast of changes in employment law, your subscription to *Employment Law Report, Employment Discrimination Law Update* or *Public Employment Law Report* will provide you with easy-to-read case summaries in a style similar to that utilized in this text. The editors recommend that you use this volume in conjunction with other Oakstone Legal & Business publications so that you can compare recent state and federal court decisions with the Supreme Court precedents contained inside for a broad view of the entire employment law field.

ABOUT THE EDITORS

Steve McEllistrem is the editorial director of Oakstone Legal & Business Publishing. He is the co-author of *Federal Laws Prohibiting Employment Discrimination* and *Deskbook Encyclopedia of Employment Law*. He graduated *cum laude* from William Mitchell College of Law and received his undergraduate degree from the University of Minnesota. Mr. McEllistrem is admitted to the Minnesota Bar.

James A. Roth is the former managing editor of *Employment Law Report* and the co-author of *Statutes, Regulations and Case Law Protecting Individuals with Disabilities*. He is a graduate of the University of Minnesota and William Mitchell College of Law. Mr. Roth is admitted to the Minnesota Bar.

Patricia Grzywacz is the managing editor of Oakstone's education and employment products. She is the co-author of the deskbook *Students with Disabilities and Special Education*. Ms. Grzywacz graduated from Widener University School of Law and received her undergraduate degree from Villanova University. She is admitted to the Pennsylvania and New Jersey bars.

TABLE OF CASES

TABLE OF CASES

TABLE OF CASES

TABLE OF CASES

TABLE OF CASES

TABLE OF CASES

TABLE OF CASES

TABLE OF CASES

DEFENDANT - PLAINTIFF
TABLE OF CASES

DEFENDANT - PLAINTIFF TABLE OF CASES

DEFENDANT - PLAINTIFF TABLE OF CASES

T

T.L.O.; New Jersey v., 293
Tarkanian; NCAA v., 308
Teal; Connecticut v., 9
Terry; Local No. 391 v., 228
Thomas; North Star Steel Co. v., 245
Thomas; Peacock v., 95
Thomas; Perry v., 273
Thurston; Trans World Airlines, Inc.
   v., 47
Tilley; Mead Corp. v., 90
Todd; Jim McNeff, Inc. v., 200
Toledo; Gomez v., 177
Town & Country Electric, Inc.; NLRB
   v., 208
Trans World Airlines, Inc.; Zipes v., 79
Transp. Agency, Santa Clara County;
   Johnson v., 34
Transp. Agency, Santa Clara County;
   Johnson v., 34
Transp. Management Corp.; NLRB v., 193
Tuttle; City of Oklahoma City v., 153

U

U.S. Dep't of Agriculture; FLRA v., 249
U.S.; Brogan v., 287
U.S.; Hazelwood School District v., 8
U.S.; International Brotherhood of
   Teamsters v., 19
U.S.I. Film Products; Landgraf v., 86
Umbehr; Bd. of County Comm'rs,
   Wabaunsee County, Kansas v., 129
Unemployment Appeals Comm'n of
   Florida; Hobbie v., 310
United Air Lines, Inc.; Sutton v., 63
United Automobile, Aerospace and
   Agricultural Implement Workers of
   America, Intern. Union, Local 787;
   Textron Lycoming Reciprocating
   Engine Div., AVCO Corp. v., 222
United Food & Commercial Workers Union;
   NLRB v., 212
United Mine Workers of America; Carbon
   Fuel Co. v., 222
United Mine Workers of America, District
   17; Eastern Associated Coal Corp. v.,
   275
United Parcel Service, Inc.; Murphy v., 64
United States Postal Service; Bowen
   v., 304

United States; Lockheed Aircraft Corp.
   v., 317
United Transp. Union; Cuyahoga Valley
   Railway Co. v., 237
United Transportation Union; Reed
   v., 232
Updegraff; Wieman v., 133
Usery; National League of Cities v., 215

V

Verner; Sherbert v., 309
Veterans Administration; Irwin v., 72
Vinson; Meritor Savings Bank, FSB v., 37
Von Raab; National Treasury Employees
   Union v., 291

W

Waco; Mireles v., 174
Warren City School Dist., Migra v., 163
Washington Gas Light Co.; Thomas
   v., 320
Waters; Furnco Construction Corp. v., 19
Weber; United Steelworkers, Etc. v., 14
Western Line Consolidated School District;
   Givhan v., 124
White; Dougherty County Board of
   Education v., 281
White; Forrester v., 174
Wilander; McDermott International, Inc.
   v., 335
Wilks; Martin v., 12
Williams; Caterpillar Inc. v., 224
Winnebago County DSS; DeShaney
   v., 148
Wirtz; Maryland v., 214
Wisconsin Employment Relations Comm'n;
   Madison School Dist. v., 266
Wood; Bishop v., 299
Worthington; Icicle Seafoods, Inc. v., 218
Wyoming; EEOC v., 57

Y

Yeshiva Univ.; NLRB v., 268

Z

Zimmerman Brush Co.; Logan v., 74
Zipes; Independent Federation of Flight
   Attendants v., 84

CHAPTER ONE

Discrimination

I. RACE AND NATIONAL ORIGIN DISCRIMINATION

A. Scope and Standard of Proof

One of the most important Supreme Court cases in the area of civil rights is *Griggs v. Duke Power Co.*, where the Court held that Title VII forbids not only practices adopted with a discriminatory *motive*, but also those which have a discriminatory effect. Upon showing discriminatory effect, the burden shifts to the employer to prove that business necessity required the employment practice.

In *Griggs,* a group of black employees at a North Carolina power plant sued under Title VII of the Civil Rights Act of 1964, challenging their employer's requirement that employees possess a high school diploma or pass an intelligence test as a condition of employment in or transfer to jobs at the plant. Section 703 of the Act authorized the use of an ability test, so long as it was not intended or used to discriminate. The district court held that the employer's prior policy of racial discrimination had ended, and the U.S. Court of Appeals, Fourth Circuit, upheld that determination. The employees appealed to the U.S. Supreme Court.

The Supreme Court held that Title VII requires the elimination of artificial, arbitrary, and unnecessary barriers to employment that discriminate on the basis of race. If a practice excludes minorities and cannot be shown to be related to job performance, it is prohibited, even if the employer lacked discriminatory intent. Title VII does not preclude the use of testing or measuring procedures so long as they are demonstrably a reasonable measure of job performance. In this case, the procedures were not related to job performance. Therefore, they violated Title VII. The Court reversed the lower court decisions. *Griggs v. Duke Power Co.,* 401 U.S. 424, 91 S.Ct. 849, 28 L.Ed.2d 158 (1971).

The Supreme Court case that established the standard of proof for discrimination lawsuits is *McDonnell Douglas Corp. v. Green,* where the Court stated that an employee alleging discrimination must show that he or she belongs to a protected minority, has applied and is qualified for an available position, was rejected, and that the employer continued to seek applicants with the complainant's qualifications.

In this case, a black civil rights activist engaged in disruptive and illegal activity against his former employer as part of his protest that his discharge, and the employer's general hiring practices, were racially motivated. Soon after, the employer advertised for qualified personnel, but rejected the activist's reemployment application on the grounds of his illegal conduct. The activist filed a complaint with the Equal Employment Opportunity Commission (EEOC), claiming a Title VII violation. The EEOC found that there was reasonable cause to believe that the discharge violated § 704(a) of Title VII, which forbids discrimination against applicants or employees for protesting against discriminatory employment conditions. The activist eventually sued, and a federal district court ruled that his activity was not protected by § 703(a). The court dismissed the § 703 claim because the EEOC had made no finding with respect to that section.

The court of appeals affirmed, and also stated that § 703(a)(1), which prohibits discrimination in any employment decision, could also be used to make a viable claim. The employer sought review from the U.S. Supreme Court.

The Supreme Court held that a reasonable cause finding by the EEOC is not necessary in order for a party to raise § 703(a)(1) at trial. It further held that in a private, nonclass-action complaint under Title VII the complaining party has the burden of establishing a *prima facie* case, which can be satisfied by showing that he belongs to a racial minority, has applied and was qualified for a job the employer was trying to fill, was rejected, and the employer continued to seek applicants with the complainant's qualifications. Even though the employee had done this, the employer carried its burden in showing that it had a reason for rejecting the applicant. The Court remanded the case, but allowed the activist an opportunity to show that the employer's reason for refusal was simply a pretext for a racially discriminatory decision. *McDonnell Douglas Corp. v. Green*, 411 U.S. 792, 93 S.Ct. 1817, 36 L.Ed.2d 668 (1973).

In 1974, the Supreme Court held that an employee could seek a trial under Title VII after having submitted a claim of discrimination to arbitration. However, even though the arbitration was not binding, the arbitrator's decision could be introduced as evidence in the Title VII suit.

A company fired a black drill operator for producing too many defective or unusable parts. The employee filed a grievance under the collective bargaining agreement (CBA) in force, claiming racial discrimination. He also filed a complaint with the Colorado Civil Rights Commission. Following an arbitration hearing, conducted pursuant to the CBA, the arbitrator found that the discharge had been for cause. When the EEOC found no reasonable cause to believe Title VII had been violated, the employee brought suit in federal court. The court granted summary judgment to the company, holding that the employee was bound by the decision at the arbitration hearing. The U.S. Court of Appeals affirmed, and the case came before the U.S. Supreme Court.

The Supreme Court held that the employee's right to a new trial was not foreclosed by the prior submission of his claim to arbitration. Title VII was designed to supplement existing laws and instructions relating to employment discrimination. The right to sue in court was an independent right not precluded by arbitration. The Court also held, however, that the arbitrator's decision could be admitted as evidence against the employee in the Title VII suit. The Court reversed the lower courts' decisions. *Alexander v. Gardner-Denver Co.*, 415 U.S. 36, 94 S.Ct. 1011, 39 L.Ed.2d 147 (1974).

In *Albermarle Paper Co. v. Moody*, the Supreme Court held that employment testing which, although it appeared to be neutral on its face, was discriminatory against minorities, had to be justified by business necessity. The complaining party could then demonstrate that there were other less discriminatory means of achieving the same result available to the employer.

A group of black employees sued their North Carolina employer and the employees' union for Title VII violations. The major issues were the plant's seniority system, its program of employment testing, and backpay. The federal district court found that the employees had been locked in the lower paying job classifications and ordered a new system of plantwide seniority. The court refused to order backpay. It also refused to limit the plant's testing program, stating that the tests were job related. The employees appealed the backpay and employment issues and the court of appeals ruled in their favor. The plant appealed to the U.S. Supreme Court.

The Supreme Court held that if there is unlawful discrimination, backpay should only be denied for reasons that would not frustrate the purposes of Title VII. The absence of bad faith on the employer's part is not a sufficient reason for denying backpay. In this case, however, there was some question about the timing of the demand for backpay, so the issue would remain open on remand. With regard to employment testing, the Court stated that testing must be correlated with important elements of work or be relevant to the job. The testing in this case was defective because it failed to meet these standards. *Albemarle Paper Co. v. Moody*, 422 U.S. 405, 95 S.Ct. 2362, 45 L.Ed.2d 280 (1975).

In 1976, the Supreme Court stated that Title VII and 42 U.S.C. § 1981 apply to whites as well as to nonwhites in the private employment context. When policies are applied unevenly to different races, Title VII is violated, regardless of whether the class more heavily impacted is whites.

Two white employees of a transportation company were discharged for misappropriating cargo from one of the company's shipments. However, a black employee, charged with the same offense, was not terminated. After grievance proceedings were unsuccessful, the two employees sued the company and their union for discriminating against them by retaining the black employee while letting them go. A federal district court dismissed the complaint, finding that 42 U.S.C. § 1981 (which prohibits discrimination in the making and enforcement of contracts) did not apply to discrimination against whites, and that no valid claim had been stated under Title VII. The U.S. Court of Appeals affirmed, and the case came before the U.S. Supreme Court.

The Supreme Court held that both Title VII and § 1981 apply to whites as much as to nonwhites in the private employment context. While theft of cargo may warrant discharging an employee, such a policy must be applied evenly to both whites and nonwhites or Title VII is violated. Here, if all other things were equal, then the union and the company would have unlawfully discriminated against the employees—the union by shirking its duty to properly represent the employees, and the company by discharging only the white employees. Since the case should not have been dismissed, the Court reversed and remanded it. *McDonald v. Santa Fe Trail Transp. Co.*, 427 U.S. 273, 96 S.Ct. 2574, 49 L.Ed.2d 493 (1976).

In a 1977 employment discrimination case, the Court stated that
under Title VII employers accused of employment discrimination were
entitled to meet the complaining parties' evidence with their own evidence
to rebut an inference of discrimination.

A suburban St. Louis, Missouri, school district had a racial composition of
only 1.8 percent black teachers, compared to an area wide rate of 15.4 percent.
School principals in the suburban district had almost unlimited discretion in their
hiring policies. The district's attendance rate was only two percent black
compared to 50 percent black students in the nearby St. Louis city school district.
The U.S. government sued the suburban school district on the theory that the
district had a pattern or practice of racially discriminatory hiring practices. The
government based its case on statistical disparities, subjective hiring practices
and evidence from 55 unsuccessful black teaching applicants. The court ruled
that there was no pattern or practice of discrimination in the district's hiring
practices. It noted that the district had never operated a racially segregated dual
school system, and that the small percentage of black employees corresponded
with the small number of black students in the district. On appeal, the U.S. Court
of Appeals, Eighth Circuit, reversed the district court's decision ruling that
teacher-student ratios were irrelevant and that the correct comparison was
between the district's black employment rate and that of the local labor market.
The district petitioned to the U.S. Supreme Court, which granted certiorari.

The Court held that employment statistics were relevant in establishing a
pattern or practice of race discrimination under Title VII. However, the court of
appeals erroneously substituted its judgment for the district court's when it held
that the government had successfully proven its case. The court of appeals
should have permitted the district to meet the government's evidence with its
own evidence in rebuttal to contradict the evidence of employment discrimination.
Title VII was inapplicable to public employers until March 24, 1972, and
employers who used nondiscriminatory policies after that date were not in
violation of the Act despite prior transgressions. The district had hired progressively
more black teachers in years after 1972, making necessary a remand to the
district court for further findings consistent with the Court's opinion. *Hazelwood
School Dist. v. U.S.*, 433 U.S. 299, 97 S.Ct. 2736, 53 L.Ed.2d 768 (1977).

In *Gulf Oil Co. v. Bernard,* where a company sought to limit
communication between class action plaintiffs and potential class members,
the Supreme Court held that there would have to be sufficient grounds for
the imposition of such an order because such interference would hinder
the class plaintiffs.

An oil company and the EEOC entered into a conciliation agreement with
respect to alleged discrimination against black and female employees at a
refinery. The company began to notify potential discriminatees, offering
settlements in return for a full release. A group of black present and former
employees, and rejected applicants, then sued under Title VII. The company
sought an order to limit communications between the named plaintiffs and
potential class members who were not actual parties to the litigation. A federal

district court issued the order, requiring court approval before such communications could be made. The U.S. Court of Appeals reversed, holding that the order was an unconstitutional prior restraint on free speech in violation of the First Amendment.

The U.S. Supreme Court agreed that the district court had exceeded its authority in entering the order. Since the order interfered with class representatives' efforts to inform potential class members of the existence of the lawsuit against the company, and since it made it more difficult for class representatives to obtain information about the merits of the case, there would have to be sufficient grounds to impose the order. Here, the record did not reveal any such grounds. The Court affirmed the court of appeals' decision striking down the order. *Gulf Oil Co. v. Bernard*, 452 U.S. 89, 101 S.Ct. 2193, 68 L.Ed.2d 693 (1981).

An employer who granted special treatment to certain black candidates who passed a written examination for promotion could not use that as a defense in a lawsuit which alleged that the exam was discriminatory to blacks. An employer cannot discriminate against one part of a class of minorities while granting preferential treatment to another part of the class.

Black employees of a Connecticut state agency received provisional promotions to supervisor status. To attain permanent status, they had to participate in a selection process that required a passing score on a written examination. Fifty-four percent of black candidates passed, compared to 68 percent of the white candidates. The failing black employees sued, claiming a violation of Title VII. While the case was pending, the employer promoted 22.9 percent of the black candidates who passed the test, but only 13.5 percent of the white candidates. The employer argued that this was a complete defense to the suit. The district court agreed, but the U.S. Court of Appeals, Second Circuit, reversed. Appeal was then taken to the U.S. Supreme Court.

The Court held that the eventual hiring of a greater percentage of blacks did not preclude a Title VII lawsuit, nor was it a defense. The pass-fail barrier created a *prima facie* case of employment discrimination. The employer needed to show that the barrier was not an artificial, arbitrary or unnecessary barrier, but rather measured skills related to effective performance as a supervisor. No special treatment of part of a class could be used to justify discrimination against another part. The case was remanded for further proceedings. *Connecticut v. Teal*, 457 U.S. 440, 102 S.Ct. 2525, 73 L.Ed.2d 130 (1982).

The Supreme Court clarified in the following case that once the employer produces a legitimate nondiscriminatory reason for its action towards an employee, the burden falls on the employee to show that the stated reason for the action is a mere pretext.

A black Washington, D.C., post office employee was turned down for a promotion. Although he possessed the minimum qualifications necessary, the postal service selected a nonminority candidate. It asserted that he was not promoted because he had turned down several lateral transfers which would have broadened his postal service experience. He filed suit against the post office under Title VII, 42 U.S.C. § 2000e *et seq.*, claiming that he had been discriminated against by race. The federal district court ruled in favor of the postal service, but the court of appeals reversed. It held that the district court had erred in requiring the employee to offer direct proof of discriminatory intent.

On appeal, the U.S. Supreme Court noted that once the employee established a *prima facie* case that the postal service had discriminated against him, and the postal service had produced a legitimate, nondiscriminatory reason for not promoting him, the burden fell on the employee to show that the reason given for rejecting him was pretextual. However, it was not necessary for him to submit direct evidence of discriminatory intent. Rather, he merely had to persuade the judge that the postal service's reason was not the real reason for his rejection. Because the district court had used the wrong standard to determine whether the postal service was liable, the Court vacated the court of appeals' decision and remanded the case to the district court. *U.S. Postal Service Bd. of Governors v. Aikens*, 460 U.S. 711, 103 S.Ct. 1478, 75 L.Ed.2d 403 (1983).

A plaintiff in a Title VII suit need not prove discrimination with scientific certainty. The burden is just to prove discrimination by a preponderance of the evidence.

Certain black employees of the North Carolina Agricultural Extension Service and the United States sued the service in a federal district court, alleging a pattern and practice of racial discrimination in employment and provision of services. The district court found no pattern to certify the action as a class action, and further held that no individual discrimination had taken place. The U.S. Court of Appeals, Fourth Circuit, affirmed, and a further appeal was taken to the U.S. Supreme Court. The Supreme Court held that, under Title VII, the service had a duty to eradicate salary disparities between white and black workers that had their origin prior to the enactment of Title VII. Here, the employees had shown by a preponderance of the evidence that discrimination had occurred, even though they had not proven it with scientific certainty. Since it was more likely than not that discrimination had played a part in the salary discrepancies, the Court determined that the employees were entitled to the relief they sought. The Court thus affirmed in part and reversed in part, and remanded the case for a proper determination of damages. *Bazemore v. Friday*, 478 U.S. 385, 106 S.Ct. 3000, 92 L.Ed.2d 315 (1986).

In *Watson v. Fort Worth Bank and Trust*, the Supreme Court determined that a disparate impact (discriminatory effect) analysis could be applied to subjective employment criteria. Now an employee would no longer have to prove discriminatory intent on the part of the employer to successfully maintain a lawsuit under Title VII.

A Texas woman of African-American heritage was rejected in favor of white applicants for four promotions to supervisory positions in the bank where she worked. Rather than use specified standards in the selection process, the bank was relying on the subjective judgment of various white supervisors. The employee exhausted her administrative remedies, then brought suit against the bank in a federal district court, alleging violations of Title VII. The district court dismissed her claim, holding that she had not met her burden of proof that the bank had acted with the intent to discriminate against her personally. The U.S. Court of Appeals, Fifth Circuit, affirmed. The employee sought review from the U.S. Supreme Court. On appeal, she argued that the district court should have applied a disparate impact analysis to her claims. In other words, she would only have to show that the bank had adopted a facially neutral policy without a discriminatory motive which had the effect of discriminating against her. The Supreme Court held that, when analyzing subjective or discretionary employment practices, a court may, in appropriate cases, analyze the practice under the disparate impact approach. This would solve the problem of prohibited conduct caused by subconscious stereotypes and prejudices. The Court remanded the case for evaluation under the disparate impact approach. *Watson v. Fort Worth Bank and Trust*, 487 U.S. 977, 108 S.Ct. 2777, 101 L.Ed.2d 827 (1988).

The following case made clear that to show disparate impact, a plaintiff class must do more than rely on statistical evidence that a high percentage of nonwhites worked at unskilled positions while a high percentage of whites worked at skilled positions. The proper comparison is generally between the racial composition of the at-issue jobs and the racial composition of the qualified population in the relevant labor market.

Two companies operated salmon canneries in Alaska. The unskilled cannery jobs were filled predominately by nonwhites, and the skilled noncannery jobs were filled predominantly with white workers. A lawsuit followed in which a group of cannery workers alleged that various hiring and promotion practices were responsible for the separation of races in the work force, and that this disparate impact violated Title VII. The question of how to analyze the workers' claims eventually came before the U.S. Supreme Court.

The Supreme Court held that to make out a *prima facie* disparate impact case, the proper comparison is between the jobs at issue and the racial composition of the qualified labor market. Here, the case would have to be remanded for such a comparison. The Court then decided that if a *prima facie* case of disparate impact was shown, the employer would have to produce evidence of a business justification that is more than merely insubstantial for the employer's practice to be upheld as permissible. *Wards Cove Packing Co. v. Atonio*, 490 U.S. 642, 109 S.Ct. 2115, 104 L.Ed.2d 733 (1989). The Civil Rights Act of 1991 strengthened the standard from "business justification" to "business necessity," the standard enunciated in *Griggs v. Duke Power Co.,* and firmly placed the burden of proof on the employer to show the necessity for the adopted practice.

Nonparties to proceedings in which consent decrees are entered may challenge employment decisions taken according to the consent decrees.

In 1974, the NAACP and seven black persons entered into consent decrees with an Alabama city and a county personnel board. The decrees stated that the city and board had practiced discriminatory employment practices in violation of Title VII and other civil rights statutes. They mandated an extensive remedial plan, including annual hiring and promotional goals for black firefighters. A federal district court approved the decrees, which were then challenged by the city firefighters' labor organization in a reverse discrimination lawsuit. The court ruled against the firefighters' association and its decision was affirmed by the U.S. Court of Appeals, Eleventh Circuit. A second group of white firefighters then sued the city and board in a federal district court, claiming that they had been denied promotions in favor of less qualified blacks. The court dismissed their lawsuit, ruling that the city was required to promote blacks under the consent decree. The firefighters appealed to the Eleventh Circuit, which ruled in favor of the firefighters. It found that they had not participated in the consent decrees and were bringing independent racial discrimination claims. The court rejected the doctrine of impermissible collateral attack, which had been used by other U.S. circuit courts to immunize parties participating in consent decrees from reverse discrimination complaints by nonparties. The U.S. Supreme Court agreed to hear the appeal of both the city and a group of intervening black firefighters.

The Supreme Court noted that nonparties are not bound by judgments and decrees among parties to a lawsuit. Moreover, Rule 19(a) of the Federal Rules of Civil Procedure required mandatory joinder where parties to the lawsuit had inconsistent obligations to persons claiming an interest in the action. Litigants are presumed to know the nature and scope of their litigation, and they should bear the burden of bringing in additional parties when required. The Court rejected the argument that this burden would discourage civil rights litigation because of the perceived difficulty in identifying numerous adverse claimants. This difficulty was an effect of the broad remedial relief that resulted from consent decrees in racial discrimination cases. Parties seeking the aid of courts to change existing employment policies and employers were best able to bear the burden of identifying potentially affected third parties. The Supreme Court affirmed the court of appeals' decision. *Martin v. Wilks,* 490 U.S. 755, 109 S.Ct. 2180, 104 L.Ed.2d 835 (1989).

In 1993, the Court held that even though the trier of fact had rejected an employer's asserted reasons for discharging an employee, this did not mean that the employee was entitled to judgment as a matter of law. The employee still had the ultimate burden of persuasion as to whether the employer intentionally discriminated against him.

A Missouri halfway house employed an African-American correctional officer. After being demoted and ultimately discharged, the officer filed suit alleging that these actions had been taken because of his race in violation of Title VII. At trial, the federal district court found that the officer had established, by a preponderance of the evidence: 1) a *prima facie* case of racial discrimination; 2) that the employer had rebutted the presumption by introducing evidence of two legitimate nondiscriminatory reasons for its actions; and 3) that the employer's reasons were pretextual. However, the district court held that the employee had failed to carry his ultimate burden of proving that the adverse actions were racially motivated, and found for the halfway house. The employee then appealed to the U.S. Court of Appeals, Eighth Circuit. The Eighth Circuit reversed the decision of the trial court and held that the employee was entitled to judgment as a matter of law once he proved that all of the employer's proffered reasons were pretextual. The halfway house appealed to the U.S. Supreme Court.

The Supreme Court reinstated the district court's decision, stating that the judge's rejection of an employer's asserted reasons for its actions does not entitle a plaintiff to judgment as a matter of law. Under *McDonnell Douglas v. Green*, 411 U.S. 792, 93 S.Ct. 1817, 36 L.Ed.2d 668 (1973), once the employee established a *prima facie* case of discrimination, a presumption arose that the employer unlawfully discriminated against him, requiring judgment in his favor unless the employer came forward with an explanation. This presumption placed upon the employer the burden of proving that the adverse actions were taken for legitimate, nondiscriminatory reasons. However, the ultimate burden of persuasion remained at all times with the employee. The trier of fact was required to decide whether the employee had proven that the employer intentionally discriminated against him because of race. Accordingly, the Supreme Court upheld the district court's decision for the halfway house. *St. Mary's Honor Center v. Hicks*, 509 U.S. 502, 113 S.Ct. 2742, 125 L.Ed.2d 407 (1993).

On remand, the district court ruled against the officer, who appealed again to the U.S. Court of Appeals, Eighth Circuit. The court of appeals affirmed the district court and reiterated the Supreme Court's mandate that an appropriate factfinder must determine that the employer has unlawfully discriminated. The district court had determined that the officer's unfair treatment was because of personal animosity and was not race-related. The court affirmed the decision in favor of the employer. *Hicks v. St. Mary's Honor Center*, 90 F.3d 285 (8th Cir.1996).

B. Affirmative Action

In an effort to eradicate the discriminatory effect that test-taking had on blacks and Hispanics, the County of Los Angeles sought to use a random selection process to hire applicants. The county was ordered to undertake affirmative action efforts and eventually found a nonrandom, nondiscriminatory method.

In 1969, persons seeking employment with the Los Angeles County Fire Department were required to take a written examination as well as a physical test. Applicants were ranked according to their performance on the tests and selected for interviews on the basis of their scores. Those who passed the oral interviews were placed on a hiring-eligible list. Because blacks and Hispanics did poorly on the written exams, this method resulted in disparate impact (a facially neutral policy which has a discriminatory effect) on minority hiring. In 1972, the county administered a new test it had designed which was graded on a pass-fail basis solely to screen out illiterates. It then intended to select 500 passing applicants at random to interview. However, prior to doing so, the county was sued because its random selection process was violative of Civil Service regulations.

A hiring freeze was instituted, and as a result of the ensuing manpower shortage, the county next sought to use a prior graded test to meet the needs of the fire department. At this point, a class action suit was filed on behalf of present and future black and Mexican-American applicants in a federal district court. It was alleged that the hiring procedure violated 42 U.S.C. § 1981. The court found that violations had occurred and ordered affirmative action efforts. The court of appeals affirmed this decision, and the U.S. Supreme Court agreed to hear the case. However, by the time the case reached the Court, the district court had found an efficient and nonrandom way to screen applicants and increase minority representation in the fire department. Because the Supreme Court determined that a successful system was being used and the chances of reverting to the old invalidated system were now very slim, it held that the case should be dismissed on grounds of mootness. Accordingly, it dismissed the case. *County of Los Angeles v. Davis*, 440 U.S. 625, 99 S.Ct. 1379, 59 L.Ed.2d 642 (1979).

In 1979, the Court stated that even though Title VII prohibits race discrimination, not all private, voluntary affirmative action plans are invalid. The Court upheld a private affirmative action plan in the following case.

A union and a company entered into a collective bargaining agreement, which included an affirmative action plan designed to raise the percentage of black craftworkers in the company's plants to the percentage of blacks in the local labor force. After some junior black employees were selected for in-plant craft training programs over some senior white employees, a lawsuit was brought in federal district court, alleging that the affirmative action program was in violation of Title VII. The court held that the plan violated Title VII, and the U.S. Court of Appeals affirmed. The U.S. Supreme Court then granted certiorari.

The Court first stated that Title VII's prohibition against racial discrimination did not condemn all private, voluntary, race-conscious affirmative action plans. To do so would defeat the very purpose of Title VII. The Court then noted that the affirmative action plan in this case was permissible. It opened employment opportunities for blacks in areas that were traditionally closed to them and it did not unnecessarily trammel the interests of white employees. Finally, the Court stated that the plan was a temporary measure, designed only to eliminate a manifest racial imbalance. The Court reversed the court of appeals' decision and upheld the plan. *United Steelworkers, Etc. v. Weber*, 443 U.S. 193, 99 S.Ct. 2721, 61 L.Ed.2d 480 (1979).

The Supreme Court invalidated an affirmative action plan approved by a Michigan school board and teachers' association that enhanced minority teacher rights in the event of a layoff. The plan would have permitted layoffs of more senior whites in an attempt to preserve the racial balance of the teaching force.

White Michigan teachers sued their board of education for attempting to implement a collective bargaining agreement provision under which their seniority rights were impaired in favor of less senior minority teachers in the event of a layoff. They sued in a federal district court under the Equal Protection Clause and Title VII of the 1964 Civil Rights Act, as well as state law. The district court ruled that the importance of providing minority teachers as role models for minority students as a remedy for past societal discrimination justified the layoff provision. The U.S. Court of Appeals, Sixth Circuit, affirmed the district court's decision and the white teachers appealed to the U.S. Supreme Court. By a five to four vote the justices reversed the lower court decisions and held that the white teachers had been unfairly discriminated against in violation of the Equal Protection Clause. A total of six different opinions were filed in the case as the justices failed to agree on an appropriate standard of review for government affirmative action programs.

The majority opinion rejected the school board's argument that race-based layoffs were necessary to remedy the effects of societal discrimination. Clear and convincing evidence must be presented to prove that the government entity in question had engaged in past racial discrimination. Similarly, the Supreme Court rejected the role model justification for retaining minority teachers, because it would allow racially based layoffs long after they were needed to cure the ills of past discrimination. "Carried to its logical extreme, the idea that black students are better off with black teachers could lead to the very system the Court rejected in *Brown v. Board of Education....*"

The majority opinion held that even if the school board had sufficient justification for engaging in remedial or benign racial discrimination, laying off white teachers was too drastic and intrusive a remedy. While hiring goals and promotion policies favorable to minorities were acceptable under the Equal Protection Clause, the actual laying off of a certain race of employees was unconstitutional. "Denial of future employment is not as intrusive as loss of an existing job." The layoffs made by the school board were impermissible and the lower court rulings were reversed. *Wygant v. Jackson Bd. of Educ.*, 476 U.S. 267, 106 S.Ct. 1842, 90 L.Ed.2d 260 (1986).

In 1989, the Court held that an affirmative action plan in Virginia had to be narrowly tailored to achieve a compelling governmental interest. Since the plan could not pass this strict scrutiny, it had to be struck down.

The city of Richmond, Virginia adopted a plan requiring prime contractors awarded city construction contracts to subcontract at least 30 percent of the dollar amount of each contract to one or more minority business enterprises (MBEs). These were defined as businesses from anywhere in the country which were owned and controlled (at least 51 percent) by black, Spanish-speaking, Asian, Indian, Eskimo, or Aleut citizens. The plan purported to be remedial in nature, but no direct evidence was presented at the hearing prior to its adoption that the city had discriminated on the basis of race in letting contracts. After the sole bidder on a city contract was denied a waiver of the MBE requirement and lost its contract, it sued the city under 42 U.S.C. § 1983, alleging that the plan was unconstitutional under the Fourteenth Amendment's Equal Protection Clause. The federal court upheld the plan and the U.S. Court of Appeals, Fourth

Circuit, affirmed. The U.S. Supreme Court vacated and remanded for further consideration in light of *Wygant v. Jackson Board of Educ.,* 476 U.S. 267, 106 S.Ct. 1842, 90 L.Ed.2d 260 (1986). On remand, the court of appeals held that the plan violated the Constitution. The case again came before the U.S. Supreme Court.

The Court held that the city had failed to demonstrate a compelling governmental interest through evidence of past discrimination in the city's construction industry. It is not enough to generally assert that past discrimination has occurred. Next, the Court held that the plan was not narrowly tailored to remedy the effects of prior discrimination since it allowed minority entrepreneurs from anywhere in the country to obtain a preference over other citizens based solely on race. The lower court decision was affirmed. *City of Richmond v. J.A. Croson Co.,* 488 U.S. 469, 109 S.Ct. 706, 102 L.Ed.2d 854 (1989).

After *City of Richmond v. J.A. Croson Co.*, was decided, a similar affirmative action plan came before the Supreme Court. In this case, a Florida city asserted that the case was moot because the plan had been repealed and replaced by another plan. The Court held that the case was not moot and that an association had standing to challenge the city's plan.

A Florida city passed an ordinance requiring that it set aside 10 percent of all city contracts to be awarded to minority business enterprises (MBEs). Under the ordinance, a MBE was a business at least 51 percent owned by persons who were "black, Spanish-speaking, Oriental, Indian, Eskimo, Aleut or handicapped." Women-owned firms were also considered MBEs under the ordinance. The ordinance did not require "mathematical certainty" when designating contracts awarded to MBEs, but required that the city come as close as possible to ten percent. The ordinance provided that this be reduced in certain limited situations. An association of Florida construction firms sued the city in a U.S. district court alleging that the set asides provided by the ordinance violated the Equal Protection Clause of the Fourteenth Amendment. The district court entered summary judgment for the association. On appeal, the U.S. Court of Appeals, Eleventh Circuit, reversed, holding that the association lacked standing to bring suit. The association appealed to the U.S. Supreme Court. After the Supreme Court agreed to hear the case, the city repealed the ordinance and enacted a second ordinance which: 1) provided that only women and African-Americans were eligible for the set asides, 2) changed the set asides' percentage goals, and 3) provided "five alternative methods for achieving participation goals."

The city contended that the "challenged statutory language" had been repealed and therefore the case was moot. The Supreme Court disagreed, ruling that the ordinance had not been "sufficiently altered" to moot the present lawsuit. It declined to adopt a *per se* rule that all statutory changes, however insignificant, would moot a lawsuit. Next, the association argued that it had standing to challenge the ordinance. The Supreme Court agreed, noting that to have standing to challenge the ordinance the association had to demonstrate: "an injury in fact," a causal connection between the injury and the challenged conduct, and "a likelihood that the injury would be redressed by a favorable decision." Under the principles established in *Regents of Univ. of California v. Bakke*, 438 U.S. 265, 98 S.Ct. 2733, 57 L.Ed.2d 750 (1978), an individual denied an equal opportunity need not allege that he would have obtained the desired benefit absent the denial in order to have standing. Rather, the challenging party need only establish that he or she was denied an "opportunity to compete." Here, the denial of equal treatment with respect to the city contracts was sufficient to establish an injury. Further, the ordinance prevented the association from competing on an equal footing in its quest for a benefit. Since, absent the ordinance, the association members would have bid on the set aside contracts, and since a judicial decree would "redress the injury," the association had standing to challenge the ordinance. The holding of the appellate court was reversed. *Northeastern Florida Chapter of the Associated General Contractors of America v. City of Jacksonville*, 508 U.S. 656, 113 S.Ct. 2297, 124 L.Ed.2d 586 (1993).

In the following case, the Supreme Court reaffirmed the application of strict scrutiny to all racial classifications for federal, state and local governments. Moreover, the Court narrowed affirmative action program requirements to ensure a sufficiently detailed examination.

The Federal Lands Highway Division, part of the U.S. Department of Transportation, awarded a highway construction contract to a Colorado contractor. The contractor received additional compensation for hiring a subcontractor controlled by "socially and economically disadvantaged individuals." The highway division construed the relevant federal statute as containing a presumption that African-American, Hispanic, Asian-Pacific, Subcontinent Asian, Native American, and female individuals were socially and economically disadvantaged. The contractor rejected the low bidder on the subcontract, because it was not controlled by disadvantaged persons. The subcontractor filed suit in a federal district court, claiming that the race-based presumption violated its right to equal protection. The district court granted the U.S. government's motion for summary judgment, and the U.S. Court of Appeals, Tenth Circuit, affirmed. The subcontractor appealed to the U.S. Supreme Court.

The Supreme Court reversed the Tenth Circuit decision, ruling that the standard of review for federal, state and local governments should be strict scrutiny. Affirming the principles laid out in *City of Richmond v. J.A. Croson Co.*, 488 U.S. 469, 109 S.Ct. 706, 102 L.Ed.2d 854 (1989), the Court held that the Fifth and Fourteenth Amendments require that all racial classifications be narrowly tailored to further a compelling government interest. The Court rejected the government's plea for a less rigorous standard, ruling that only strict scrutiny would submit racial classifications to a sufficiently detailed examination. It noted that heightened scrutiny would "smoke out illegitimate uses of race by assuring that the legislative body is pursuing a goal important enough to warrant use of a highly suspect tool." The Court reversed and remanded the case to determine whether the use of the subcontractor compensation clauses could be properly described as compelling. *Adarand Constructors, Inc. v. Pena*, 515 U.S. 200, 115 S.Ct. 2097, 132 L.Ed.2d 158 (1995).

C. Relief

Title VII requires the courts to "make whole" victims of discrimination. In the following case, the applicants who had not been hired were not only entitled to jobs, but also to retroactive seniority to the date when they should have been hired.

A black over-the-road (OTR) truck driver applied for a job with a transportation company, but was not hired. He then brought a class action suit against the company and his union, alleging various racially discriminatory employment practices in violation of Title VII. After a trial, the federal district court found that the company had engaged in a pattern of discrimination. It ordered the company to stop its illegal practices and to notify class members of their right to priority consideration of OTR jobs. However, it declined to award backpay and seniority status retroactive to the date of application for unnamed members of the class. The U.S. Court of Appeals affirmed the order in part, but held that backpay should have been awarded. On further review, the U.S. Supreme Court held that unnamed members of the class should have been granted seniority in addition to being hired. To require an employer only to hire a class victim of discrimination falls short of the "make whole" purpose of Title VII. The only way to allow the victim of discrimination to obtain his rightful place in the hierarchy of seniority was to grant him seniority status retroactive to the date of application. The Court reversed and remanded the case. *Franks v. Bowman Transp. Co., Inc.,* 424 U.S. 747, 96 S.Ct. 1251, 47 L.Ed.2d 444 (1976).

A year after *Franks v. Bowman Transp. Co.,* the Court held that retroactive seniority could not be given to a date earlier than the effective date of Title VII. The Court also stated that a bona fide seniority system will not be held unlawful merely because it perpetuates pre-Title VII discrimination.

The United States sued a nationwide common carrier of motor freight, and a union representing a large group of the company's employees, claiming that the company engaged in a pattern of discriminating against blacks and Hispanics. The government claimed that the minority members were hired as local city drivers, a lower paying, and less desirable position than line drivers (long distance drivers). The government also claimed that the collective-bargaining agreements between the union and company "locked-in" the effects of racial discrimination, because a transferred city driver forfeited all seniority he had earned. The district court held that the union and company had violated Title VII and enjoined both from committing further violations thereof. The district court stated that the affected class of discriminatees included all minority members hired as city drivers at every terminal with a line-driver operation, whether or not they were hired before the effective date of Title VII. Stating that they had been injured to varying degrees, the court divided the affected class into three groups. The court of appeals rejected this approach, and review was sought from the U.S. Supreme Court.

The Supreme Court held that the government had successfully shown that discrimination had occurred. The Court also held that retroactive seniority may be awarded as relief for post-Title VII discriminatees, even if the seniority system agreement makes no provision for such relief. However, it stated that the union's conduct in agreeing to the seniority system did not violate Title VII. Employees who suffered only pre-Title VII discrimination were not entitled to relief, and no person could be given retroactive seniority to a date earlier than the Act's effective date. Therefore, the union's injunction was vacated. A bona fide seniority system does not become unlawful simply because it perpetuates pre-Title VII discrimination. The seniority system was made in good faith and applied to all members. Every post-Title VII minority member was entitled to relief unless the company could show that it did not discriminate. Non-applicants had to be allowed to prove that they should be treated as applicants and entitled to relief. They would have to show that they would have applied for a line-driver position, but for the discriminatory policy. *International Brotherhood of Teamsters v. U.S.*, 431 U.S. 324, 97 S.Ct. 1843, 52 L.Ed.2d 396 (1977).

Federal courts should not impose hiring methods on companies for the purpose of increasing minority employment until it has been shown that the employers have violated Title VII.

Three black bricklayers sought employment with a construction company. The company hired superintendents for specific jobs and let them hire their own work force. The superintendent involved in this case hired only one of the three applicants, and at a date much later than the application. The applicants sued, claiming a violation of Title VII. A federal district court dismissed the suit, holding that no discrimination had been proven. The U.S. Court of Appeals reversed, finding that a *prima facie* case had been made out, and that the company had not effectively rebutted it. The appellate court devised an "appropriate" hiring procedure for the company, and an appeal was taken to the U.S. Supreme Court.

The Court first agreed that the applicants had made out a *prima facie* case of discrimination. It then held, however, that the appellate court should not have imposed a hiring method to enable the company to consider more minority employees until a violation of Title VII was proven. Further, the company should have been allowed to offer statistics showing that its work force was racially balanced. While not conclusive, such evidence was one factor to be considered in determining whether discrimination was a motive in the hiring practices of the company. The Court reversed and remanded the case. *Furnco Construction Corp. v. Waters*, 438 U.S. 567, 98 S.Ct. 2943, 57 L.Ed.2d 957 (1978).

In 1983, the Court examined lawsuits brought by private plaintiffs under Title VI (which outlaws discrimination in programs which receive federal financial assistance). The Court held that only equitable relief was available in such lawsuits. To obtain money damages, plaintiffs would have to bring suit under 42 U.S.C. § 1983.

A group of black and Hispanic police officers challenged several written examinations administered by the city of New York, which were found to have a discriminatory impact and not to be job-related. Each officer was hired anyway, but later than similarly situated white officers. Then, when the police department laid off people on a "last-hired, first-fired" basis, the black and Hispanic officers were disproportionately affected by the layoffs. A federal district court granted relief to the officers under Title VI and Title VII. The U.S. Court of Appeals, Second Circuit, affirmed the relief granted by virtue of Title VII, but reversed as to Title VI.

On appeal to the U.S. Supreme Court, the Court first held that discriminatory intent was not an essential element of a Title VI violation. The Court then stated that only injunctive, noncompensatory relief could be recovered for a defendant's unintentional violation of Title VI where private plaintiffs were involved. This meant that private plaintiffs in such cases could not obtain money damages unless they could bring their suit under 42 U.S.C. § 1983 (where the defendant acts under color of state law). By suing under Title VI, which outlaws discrimination in programs that receive federal financial assistance, the plaintiffs would be limited to nonmonetary relief. *Guardians Ass'n v. Civil Service Comm'n of City of New York*, 463 U.S. 582, 103 S.Ct. 3221, 77 L.Ed.2d 866 (1983).

The Supreme Court held that a federal district court could not modify a layoff plan where the modification went beyond the terms of a consent decree because the effects of the modification were felt by employees who had not been parties to the lawsuit when the consent decree was entered.

A black firefighter challenged the hiring and promotion practices of the Memphis, Tennessee, Fire Department. Subsequently, a consent decree was entered into for the purpose of remedying the department's hiring and promotion practices with respect to blacks. After this occurred, budget deficits required a reduction of city employees. A federal district court entered an order for an injunction to prevent the fire department from following its seniority system in the impending layoffs. A modified layoff plan was approved, and some white employees with more seniority than black employees were laid off. In the challenge to this modification of the consent decree, the U.S. Court of Appeals affirmed the district court's modification.

On appeal to the U.S. Supreme Court, the Court held that the injunction was an invalid exercise of the district court's powers. Here, the modification went beyond the terms of the consent decree. Further, its effects were felt by the union and certain white employees who had not been parties to the suit when the consent decree was entered. Since this was not a valid Title VII remedial order, the Court reversed the court of appeals' decision and struck down the injunction. *Firefighters Local Union No. 1784 v. Stotts*, 467 U.S. 561, 104 S.Ct. 2576, 81 L.Ed.2d 483 (1984).

In 1986, six members of the Supreme Court agreed that a district court could, in appropriate circumstances, order preferential relief to individuals who were not the actual victims of race discrimination as a remedy for violations of Title VII.

A sheet metal workers union and its apprenticeship committee engaged in a continuing practice of discrimination toward black and Hispanic individuals for a number of years. After numerous court orders were unsuccessful in reversing the practice of the union, the Equal Employment Opportunity Commission (EEOC) initiated an action against the union under Title VII. The district court ordered the union to end its discriminatory practices, and established a 29 percent nonwhite membership goal (based on the percentage of nonwhites in the relevant labor pool in New York City). After several more court actions, the union was found guilty of civil contempt for disobeying earlier court orders. The court then imposed a fine on the union to be placed in a special fund for the purpose of increasing nonwhite membership in the union. The U.S. Court of Appeals affirmed, and the union appealed to the U.S. Supreme Court.

On appeal, the Supreme Court noted that Title VII allowed the kind of affirmative, race-conscious relief which the district court had ordered in this case. A court need not order relief only for actual victims of past discrimination, but can also order relief of a broader scope to satisfy the purposes of Title VII. The Supreme Court also found that the imposition of fines (and the special fund) was designed to coerce compliance and was thus a proper remedy for civil contempt. It affirmed the lower court decisions. *Local 28 of Sheet Metal Workers v. EEOC,* 478 U.S. 421, 106 S.Ct. 3019, 92 L.Ed.2d 344 (1986).

Race-conscious relief may by provided by consent decrees which involve court-approved voluntary agreements among parties.

An organization of black and Hispanic firefighters employed by the city of Cleveland filed a complaint against the city, charging it with discrimination on the basis of race and national origin in the hiring, assignment and promotion of firefighters in violation of Title VII. The firefighters' labor union was able to intervene in the suit, but it objected to the consent decree entered into between the organization and the city. The U.S. Court of Appeals upheld the decree as valid, and the union appealed to the U.S. Supreme Court.

The Court first noted that Title VII did not preclude entry of a consent decree which benefited individuals who were not the actual victims of the employer's discriminatory practices. Title VII prohibited a court from ordering the hiring or promotion of an individual who was refused employment or promotion for any reason other than discrimination. However, past discriminatory practices by an employer might justify relief for nonvictims of the same class in certain contexts. Next, the Court stated that since the consent decree was voluntary, there was no Title VII violation in the adoption of it by the parties and the court. Finally, the Court stated that the consent decree was valid even though the intervenor-union did not consent to it because the decree did not bind the union to do or not do anything. The Court affirmed the appellate court's decision. *Local No. 93, International Ass'n of Firefighters v. City of Cleveland,* 478 U.S. 501, 106 S.Ct. 3063, 92 L.Ed.2d 405 (1986).

The Supreme Court upheld a 50 percent promotion requirement for blacks to eradicate the discriminatory exclusion of blacks from certain

positions. This relief was justified by a compelling governmental interest and was narrowly tailored to achieve its purposes.

In 1972, a federal district court determined that the Alabama Department of Public Safety had systematically excluded blacks from employment as state troopers in violation of the Fourteenth Amendment and issued a hiring quota order. By the early 1980s, there were still no blacks who had been promoted to the rank of corporal. The district court determined that the test used for promotions had an adverse impact on blacks and ordered the department to promote at least 50 percent blacks to the rank of corporal if qualified black candidates were available. It also ordered the department to submit a realistic schedule for the development of promotional procedures for all ranks above the entry level. The United States appealed the order, asserting that it violated the Equal Protection Clause of the Fourteenth Amendment. The U.S. Court of Appeals affirmed the order and the question came before the U.S. Supreme Court.

The Supreme Court held that the one-black-for-one-white promotion requirement was permissible under the Fourteenth Amendment. There was a compelling governmental interest in eradicating the department's pervasive and continuing discriminatory exclusion of blacks. Further, the order provided for promotions only when openings were available and did not require gratuitous promotions. Also, the requirement could be waived if no qualified black troopers were available. Finally, the requirement was only a temporary measure and was contingent on the department's successful implementation of valid promotional procedures. Accordingly, the Court found that the requirement did not impose an unacceptable burden on whites and was thus constitutional. The Court affirmed the lower courts' rulings. *United States v. Paradise*, 480 U.S. 149, 107 S.Ct. 1053, 94 L.Ed.2d 203 (1987).

D. Other Considerations

1. 42 U.S.C. § 1981

Liability under 42 U.S.C. § 1981 may not be imposed absent intentional discrimination, whereas under Title VII, liability may be imposed where facially neutral policies have a discriminatory effect.

In contracts between a union and certain construction industry employers, an exclusive hiring hall was established. Also, the parties created an apprenticeship program between the union and several trade associations. After the union engaged in a pattern of intentional race discrimination with respect to the administration of the system, the state of Pennsylvania brought suit in a federal court under 42 U.S.C. § 1981 against the union, the employers, and the trade associations. The district court found that even though the employers and the trade associations had not intentionally discriminated against minority workers, they were nevertheless liable under § 1981 for the purpose of imposing an injunctive remedy. Because the hiring procedure had been delegated to the union (which had intentionally discriminated), the employers and the trade associations were liable under the doctrine of *respondeat superior* (vicarious liability). The U.S. Court of Appeals affirmed, and further appeal was taken to the U.S. Supreme Court.

The Supreme Court determined that liability could not be imposed under § 1981 without proof of intentional discrimination. Because the district court had not found any discriminatory intent on the part of the employers and the trade associations, they could not be vicariously liable for the union's acts. They did not control the union's activities, and no agency relationship existed. Further, the district court had improperly allocated to the employers and the trade associations a portion of the costs of the remedial decree. Without a supportable finding of liability, it did not have the power to do so. The Court reversed and remanded the case. *General Building Contractors Ass'n v. Pennsylvania*, 458 U.S. 375, 102 S.Ct. 3141, 73 L.Ed.2d 835 (1982).

After a court found that an employer had not systematically engaged in a discriminatory pattern of conduct toward certain employees, the Supreme Court determined that the employees were not precluded from bringing individual claims against the employer under 42 U.S.C. § 1981. It was possible that isolated cases of discrimination existed, and this could be litigated despite the earlier ruling.

The Equal Employment Opportunity Commission brought an action in a federal district court against the Federal Reserve Bank of Richmond, Virginia, alleging that one of the bank's branches had violated Title VII by engaging in discriminatory employment practices. Four black employees were allowed to intervene and received certification as a class. They then notified other class members who joined in the suit. The court found discrimination with respect to employees in certain specified pay grades, but not with respect to employees above those grades. The court denied other employees' motions to intervene because they were in the higher grades, and they then filed separate actions under 42 U.S.C. § 1981. The U.S. Court of Appeals, Fourth Circuit, reversed the district court's finding of discrimination in the class action and further determined that the judgment in the class action precluded the individual suits from being litigated.

The U.S. Supreme Court granted certiorari. The Court noted that, while the class members were bound by the judgment against them in the class action, they were not precluded from bringing individual claims against the bank. Even though it had not been shown that the bank had systematically engaged in a discriminatory pattern of conduct, the individuals might be able to show isolated cases of discrimination. The Court thus reversed the court of appeals' decision and allowed the individual claims. *Cooper v. Federal Reserve Bank of Richmond*, 467 U.S. 867, 104 S.Ct. 2794, 81 L.Ed.2d 718 (1984).

Part of the Civil Rights Act, as codified at 42 U.S.C. § 1981, states that "[a]ll persons ... shall have the same right to make and enforce contracts ... as is enjoyed by white citizens...." In 1987, the Court ruled that although originally intended to vindicate the rights of former slaves, § 1981 extended to persons of Arab ancestry and other ethnic groups as well.

A private college in Pennsylvania denied tenure to a professor it had employed under a one-year nonrenewable contract. The professor was a Muslim who was born in Iraq but was a U.S. citizen. He claimed that the college had refused to grant tenure on the basis of his national origin and religion in violation of state and federal civil rights laws, including § 1981. The professor sued the college in a federal district court, which dismissed many of the claims because they were too late to meet local statutes of limitations. The court also dismissed the § 1981 claim, ruling that the act did not extend to the professor. It ruled that § 1981, which forbids racial discrimination in the making and enforcement of any contract, does not reach claims of discrimination based on Arab ancestry. The court stated that Arabs were Caucasians, and that since § 1981 was not enacted to protect whites, an Arab professor could not rely upon the statute. The professor appealed to the U.S. Court of Appeals, Third Circuit. The appeals court affirmed the district court's decision that the professor's Title VII claim was untimely, but reversed its decision regarding the § 1981 claim. The college appealed to the U.S. Supreme Court, which agreed to review only the § 1981 claim.

In affirming the court of appeals' decision, the Supreme Court noted that although § 1981 does not use the word "race," the Court has construed the statute to forbid all racial discrimination in the making of private as well as public contracts. It observed that persons who might be thought of as Caucasian today were not thought to be of the same race at the time § 1981 became law. The Court cited several dictionary and encyclopedic sources to support its decision that for the purposes of § 1981, Arabs, Englishmen, Germans and certain other ethnic groups are not to be considered a single race. Based on the history of § 1981 the Court reasoned that Congress "intended to protect from discrimination identifiable classes of persons who are subjected to intentional discrimination solely because of their ancestry or ethnic characteristics." If the professor could prove that he was subjected to intentional discrimination because he was an Arab, rather than solely because of his place of origin or his religion, the lawsuit could proceed under § 1981. The court of appeals' decision in favor of the professor was affirmed and the case was remanded for trial. *St. Francis College v. Al-Khazraji*, 481 U.S. 604, 107 S.Ct. 2022, 97 L.Ed.2d 749 (1987).

Racial harassment relating to conditions of employment, as discussed in *Patterson v. McLean Credit Union*, was not actionable under 42 U.S.C. § 1981 because that statute was restricted in its scope to the making and enforcement of contracts. This decision led to the amendment by Congress of § 1981 to include "the making, performance, modification, and termination of contracts" in the phrase "make and enforce contracts." Thus, employees can use § 1981 to sue for damages as a result of discrimination that occurs after the contract has been formed.

A black woman was employed by a credit union as a teller and file coordinator for ten years. After being laid off, she filed suit against her employer in federal district court, alleging violations of 42 U.S.C. § 1981. She asserted that her employer had engaged in racial harassment during the employment relationship in violation of § 1981. Section 1981 gives all persons the same right to "make and enforce contracts" as white citizens have. The district court held that racial harassment was not actionable under § 1981, and the U.S. Court of Appeals, Fourth Circuit, affirmed. The employee petitioned the U.S. Supreme Court for review.

The Supreme Court held first that § 1981 applied to private as well as public contracts. However, it then stated that § 1981 did not apply to conduct which occurs after the formation of a contract and which does not impair the right of the complaining party to enforce established contract obligations. The racial harassment complained of here would be actionable under Title VII of the Civil Rights Act, but the employee could not seek relief under § 1981. *Patterson v. McLean Credit Union,* 491 U.S. 164, 109 S.Ct. 2363, 105 L.Ed. 2d 132 (1989). The Civil Rights Act of 1991 allows the application of § 1981 to post-formation conduct.

2. Seniority Systems

A requirement for permanent employment that is based on length of employment will probably pass constitutional muster. In the case below, a 45-week requirement for attaining permanent employee status was held to be a component of a valid seniority system.

A multi-employer brewery industry collective bargaining agreement accorded greater benefits, with respect to hiring and layoffs, to permanent employees than it did to temporary employees. To become a permanent employee, an employee had to work at least 45 weeks in a single calendar year. A black temporary employee of a brewing company filed a class action suit against the brewers association and several unions, alleging that the collective bargaining agreement's 45-week requirement operated to preclude him and members of his class from achieving permanent status. A federal district court dismissed the claim, and the U.S. Court of Appeals reversed. It held that the 45-week requirement was not a seniority system under Title VII (which allows differences in terms, conditions and privileges of employment which are not the result of an intent to discriminate).

On appeal to the U.S. Supreme Court, the Court found that the 45-week requirement was a component of a valid seniority system. Since it was based on length of employment rather than education standards, aptitude or physical tests, or other standards that give effect to subjectivity, it was valid and enforceable. The Court remanded the case so that the employee could try to show that the system was not bona fide or that the differences were the result of an intent to discriminate. *California Brewers Ass'n v. Bryant,* 444 U.S. 598, 100 S.Ct. 814, 63 L.Ed.2d 55 (1980).

In 1982, the Court held that bona fide seniority systems which were adopted after the effective date of Title VII and which merely had a discriminatory effect (as opposed to being intentionally discriminatory) were entitled to the immunity provided by § 703(h) of Title VII.

Prior to 1963, a tobacco company and a union engaged in overt race discrimination. However, discrimination continued even after that by means of a seniority system that segregated whites and blacks. In a lawsuit brought by the EEOC and a class of black employees, a federal district court held that the seniority system was not a bona fide seniority system. The U.S. Court of Appeals held that Congress intended the immunity accorded to bona fide seniority systems to run only to those which were in place at the time of Title VII's effective date. On appeal to the U.S. Supreme Court, the Court determined that the bona fide seniority system immunity was not limited to those systems in place before the adoption of Title VII. Section 703(h), which granted this immunity, did not make a distinction between pre- and post-act discrimination impact. Dissenting, Justice Brennan stated that the Court's holding meant that seniority plans adopted after Title VII became effective would not be subject to challenge under the disparate impact standard of *Griggs v. Duke Power Co.*, 401 U.S. 424, 91 S.Ct. 849, 28 L.Ed.2d 158 (1971). Thus, the employees challenging the seniority system would have to show more than discriminatory effect; they would have to show discriminatory intent. *American Tobacco Co. v. Patterson*, 456 U.S. 63, 102 S.Ct. 1534, 71 L.Ed.2d 748 (1982).

Likewise, in *Pullman-Standard v. Swint*, an otherwise valid seniority system in place prior to Title VII's enactment that was merely discriminatory in its *effect* on minorities was upheld.

In 1971, black employees at a manufacturing company in Alabama brought suit against the company and their union, alleging violations of the Civil Rights Act of 1964 under Title VII. Prior to 1965, the company had openly pursued a racially discriminatory policy of job assignments. A seniority system was adopted in 1954 that measured length of continuous service in a particular department. The lawsuit alleged that the seniority system violated Title VII. A federal district court judge found that the system was the result of "colorblind objectives" and that it did not foster discrimination. The U.S. Court of Appeals reversed, and the case reached the U.S. Supreme Court, which held that a showing of disparate impact alone was not sufficient to invalidate the seniority system if it did not have a discriminatory purpose. Here, the court of appeals had improperly reversed the district court. The question of whether the system was intended to discriminate was a question of fact that should have been left to the district court to resolve. The Court thus reversed the court of appeals' decision and remanded the case. *Pullman-Standard v. Swint*, 456 U.S. 273, 102 S.Ct. 1781, 72 L.Ed.2d 66 (1982).

II. SEX DISCRIMINATION

A. Sex Discrimination

Title VII of the Civil Rights Act also protects against sex discrimination. In a 1971 case, the Supreme Court held that if men with pre-school age children were hired by a company, then the company could not refuse to

hire women with pre-school age children. However, a bona fide occupational qualification can justify an otherwise discriminatory requirement.

A Florida woman sued a company under Title VII claiming that she had been denied employment because of her sex. The company refused to accept job applications from women with pre-school age children. The district court granted summary judgment to the company, noting that 70-75 percent of the applicants were women and 75-80 percent of those hired for the position were women. It reasoned that no question of bias was presented. The court of appeals affirmed. The U.S. Supreme Court granted review. The Court stated that § 703(a) of the Civil Rights Act of 1964 requires that persons of like qualifications be given equal employment opportunities irrespective of their sex. There cannot be one hiring policy for women and one for men. Only if the requirement was a bona fide occupational qualification reasonably necessary to the normal operation of the business, could it be justified. The Court remanded for full development of the issue. *Phillips v. Martin Marietta Corp.*, 400 U.S. 542, 91 S.Ct. 496, 27 L.Ed.2d 613 (1971).

An airline which refused to credit a returning employee with seniority from her earlier days with the company was held not to have violated Title VII despite the fact that it had forced the employee to resign in violation of Title VII. The Court determined that the seniority system in place was bona fide.

A flight attendant for an airline company was forced to resign in 1968 when she married. When the airline's policy of "single only" flight attendants was found to be violative of Title VII, it abated the policy. The flight attendant was rehired by the airline in 1972 as a new employee, without seniority from her days with the airline prior to 1968. She sued the company in a federal district court, alleging that, by refusing to credit her with pre-1972 seniority, the airline was guilty of a present, continuing violation of Title VII. The court dismissed the case, but the U.S. Court of Appeals reversed. The U.S. Supreme Court granted certiorari. The Supreme Court noted that the violation alleged by the flight attendant was not a continuing violation because she had not asserted that the seniority system in place discriminated against female employees or that it treated former employees who were discharged for discriminatory reasons differently from other former employees. Since the flight attendant had not shown intentional discrimination on the part of the airline, her claim for relief was barred. The Court held that it is permissible to treat employees differently according to a bona fide seniority system if the differences are not the result of intentional discrimination. The Court reversed the court of appeals' decision. *United Air Lines, Inc. v. Evans,* 431 U.S. 553, 97 S.Ct. 1885, 52 L.Ed.2d 571 (1977).

In *Dothard v. Rawlinson*, the Supreme Court held that height and weight restrictions were discriminatory against women. However, it allowed the employer to use sex as a bona fide occupational qualification because of the nature of the job.

An applicant for employment at an Alabama prison was rejected because she failed to meet its 120-pound weight requirement. The statute that established the weight requirement also established a minimum height of 5 feet 2 inches. She sued, challenging the requirements as establishing gender criteria for assigning correctional counselors to "contact" positions. A federal district court found for the applicant, noting that 40 percent of the female population, but only one percent of the male population, would be excluded by the requirements. The court rejected the employer's bona fide occupational qualification (BFOQ) defense, ruling that being a male was not a legitimate qualification.

The U.S. Supreme Court held that the district court was correct with regard to the finding of discrimination. The applicant had established a *prima facie* case of discrimination, which the employer failed to rebut. The Court noted that Title VII was an effort by Congress to remove artificial, arbitrary and unnecessary barriers to employment such as race and sex. The district court had committed no error in finding that the height and weight restrictions were discriminatory as applied to female applicants. The state had failed to justify the correlation between height (and weight) and strength or to show that height and weight were essential to job performance. However, the Court noted that a state regulation enacted after the commencement of the lawsuit was not a violation of Title VII. The regulation, which described prisoner contact jobs in male penitentiaries as too dangerous for women, was permissible as a measure of controlling inmates and safety at male prisons. The Court held that the state regulation outlined a BFOQ and reversed that part of the district court's judgment. *Dothard v. Rawlinson*, 433 U.S. 321, 97 S.Ct. 2720, 53 L.Ed.2d 786 (1977).

In the following case, the Supreme Court held that an employer could not require female employees to pay more into their pension funds than male employees, despite the fact that women live longer than men. This generalization could not be used to justify discrimination against individual women.

The Los Angeles Department of Water and Power required its female employees to make larger contributions to their retirement pension funds than male employees. Upon retirement, each employee eligible for monthly retirement benefits received an amount computed as a fraction of salary multiplied by years of service, funded entirely by their own contributions. The department justified the disparity in contribution by the use of mortality tables and experience that showed that females lived longer than males, necessarily increasing the average pension of retired females. The monthly pension contribution required of female employees was $14.84 higher than that of male employees. A group of aggrieved female employees filed a Title VII discrimination complaint against the department in a federal district court, seeking an injunction against the disparate contributions and a refund of their excess contributions. Meanwhile, the California state legislature enacted a law prohibiting municipal agencies from requiring higher contributions based upon sex. The department then amended its plan so that both sexes paid the same retirement contribution. The court granted the employees' motion for summary judgment on federal law grounds and ordered restitution of the excess funds. The department appealed to the U.S. Court of Appeals, Ninth Circuit, which affirmed the district court decision. The department appealed to the U.S. Supreme Court, which granted a writ of certiorari.

Before the Supreme Court, the department argued that the difference in required contributions was based upon mortality tables, which constituted a factor other than sex under the 1963 Equal Pay Act, and therefore was not unlawful discrimination. The Court held that while there was a legitimate basis in fact for the distinction drawn by the department, the distinction involved a generalization which was not true in each individual case. Not every individual female lived longer than every individual male. Because Title VII prohibited unlawful discrimination against any *individual* with respect to compensation, terms, conditions or privileges of employment, courts were required to focus on alleged discrimination against individuals and to disregard generalizations about classes of persons. The lower courts had correctly ruled that the distinction drawn by the department was unlawful discrimination based upon sex. However, the lower courts had inappropriately awarded restitution of excess contributions to the aggrieved female employees. The pension fund had taken the disparate contributions in the good faith belief that the mortality tables would justify them. Employers should be given time to adjust to the requirements of Title VII and there was no reason to penalize the funds and possibly jeopardize them for a good faith error. The Court remanded the case for proceedings consistent with its opinion. *City of Los Angeles Dep't of Water v. Manhart*, 435 U.S. 702, 98 S.Ct. 1370, 55 L.Ed.2d 657 (1978).

In an employment discrimination lawsuit filed under Title VII, the aggrieved party bears the burden of proving that the employer's refusal to hire is a pretext for unlawful discrimination.

In an employment discrimination case against a state college, a federal district court ruled that the college had discriminated against a professor on the basis of sex. The U.S. Court of Appeals, Fifth Circuit, affirmed the decision, ruling that Title VII of the 1964 Civil Rights Act, 42 U.S.C. § 2000e *et seq.*, required the college to prove absence of discriminatory motive. In a *per curiam* opinion, the U.S. Supreme Court held that this burden was too great. It ruled that in an employment discrimination case, the employer need only "articulate some legitimate, nondiscriminatory reason for the employee's rejection." In other words, the employee has the burden of proving that the reason for the employee's rejection was a mere pretext. The Court vacated the court of appeals' decision and remanded the case for reconsideration under the lesser standard. *Trustees of Keene State College v. Sweeney,* 439 U.S. 24, 99 S.Ct. 295, 58 L.Ed.2d 216 (1978).

In *Texas Dep't of Community Affairs v. Burdine,* the Court clarified the standard required for proving discrimination. After the employee states a *prima facie* case, and after the employer articulates a legitimate, nondiscriminatory reason for its action, the employee must prove that the reason proffered by the employer is a mere pretext for discrimination.

A Texas woman with several years experience in employment training was hired by the state's department of community affairs. She received one promotion, and subsequently applied for a supervisor's position, which she did not receive. The department then fired her in a staff reduction. However, it later rehired, transferred and promoted her, keeping her salary commensurate with what she would have received had she gotten the first promotion. She nevertheless sued the department in a federal district court, asserting that the failure to promote and the decision to terminate her were based on gender discrimination. The district court ruled for the department and she appealed to the U.S. Court of Appeals, Fifth Circuit, which held that she had not been discriminated against in the nonpromotion, but that she had been discriminated against in the termination. The department petitioned the U.S. Supreme Court for review.

The Supreme Court first stated that the employee had the burden of showing a *prima facie* case of discrimination, namely: that she belonged to a protected minority, she was qualified for the job, she was rejected despite her qualifications, and after her rejection the department continued to look at candidates with the same qualifications. The burden would then shift to the department to "articulate some legitimate, nondiscriminatory reason for the employee's rejection." If it was successful, the employee would then have to prove that the reasons given by the department were a pretext for discrimination. Because the court of appeals had not used this standard, the Supreme Court vacated its decision and remanded the case for a determination based on this. *Texas Dep't of Community Affairs v. Burdine,* 450 U.S. 248, 101 S.Ct. 1089, 67 L.Ed.2d 207 (1981).

The Supreme Court held that the prohibition in Title VII against sex-based wage discrimination was not limited to claims for equal pay for equal work. Even where a lawsuit could not be filed under the Equal Pay Act because of job differences, a Title VII lawsuit was not necessarily precluded. However, an employer may use the affirmative defenses set out in the Equal Pay Act when defending a Title VII suit.

Female guards at an Oregon county jail were paid substantially less than male guards at the same facility. The county eliminated the female section of the jail, transferred its prisoners to a neighboring county and terminated the employment of the female guards. The terminated guards sued the county in a federal district court under Title VII of the 1964 Civil Rights Act, 42 U.S.C. § 2000e *et seq.,* seeking back pay and alleging that they had been unlawfully paid unequal wages for substantially similar work as that performed by the male guards. The court held that the male guards supervised over ten times as many prisoners and did less clerical work than their female counterparts. It ruled that the females were not entitled to equal pay because they did not perform substantially similar work, and that the pay inequity was not attributable to sex discrimination. The court held that because the females had not met the standard of the 1963 Equal Pay Act, 29 U.S.C. § 206(d), no Title VII action was possible. The female employees appealed to the U.S. Court of Appeals, Ninth Circuit, which reversed, holding that alleged sex discrimination victims were entitled to Title VII protection. The county appealed to the U.S. Supreme Court.

The Court first noted that the case did not involve a comparable worth analysis, but was simply a sex discrimination case. It stated that the court of appeals had correctly ruled that Title VII wage discrimination claims could be brought in this situation, and that the female guards were not limited to remedies under the Equal Pay Act. Title VII by its terms barred sex-based wage discrimination but permitted differentials if such differentials could be justified under the Equal Pay Act. This included seniority, merit, quantity or quality of work or other bona fide factors. Title VII claims for sex-based wage discrimination were thus permissible. In this case, the county had evaluated the female guards' job worth at 95 percent of the male guards, yet had paid them only 70 percent as much. The court of appeals had correctly ruled that this presented a viable Title VII complaint for sex discrimination. *County of Washington v. Gunther*, 452 U.S. 161, 101 S.Ct. 2242, 68 L.Ed.2d 751 (1981).

Title IX of the 1972 Education Amendments, 20 U.S.C. § 1681 *et seq.*, prohibits gender discrimination in education programs and activities that receive federal financial assistance. Sanctions for noncompliance include termination of funding for specific future grants. In 1982, the Supreme Court ruled that Title IX's nondiscrimination requirements applied not only to students and academic policies, but to employment as well.

In 1975, the U.S. Department of Education issued regulations prohibiting gender-based employment discrimination in all federally-funded education programs. The regulations pertained to many employment practices including job classification and pregnancy leave. A tenured Connecticut public school teacher took a one-year maternity leave. The school, which received Title IX funds, refused to rehire her and she filed an administrative appeal, resulting in an education department request to investigate school district employment practices. The district refused the request for an investigation and sued the U.S. government in a federal district court, which granted an injunction against enforcing the nondiscrimination regulations. The court ruled that Title IX's nondiscrimination mandate applied only to discrimination practices against students and not to teachers and employment practices. The district court also rejected another Title IX complaint by a Connecticut public school guidance counselor who claimed that her school district gave her discriminatory work assignments and failed to renew her contract on the basis of her sex. The U.S. Court of Appeals, Second Circuit, consolidated the two cases and reversed the district court decisions. The U.S. Supreme Court granted certiorari.

The Court found no reason to limit Title IX to discrimination complaints by students alone. Section 901(a) of the statute broadly stated that "No person in the United States shall, on the basis of sex, be excluded from participation in, be denied the benefits of, or be subjected to discrimination under any education program or activity receiving Federal financial assistance...." An extensive review of the statute's legislative history revealed evidence that employment practices were within the scope of Title IX. The Court affirmed the appeals court's decision, although it rejected the court's attempt to expand potential funding termination beyond the particular program which was found to be in noncompliance. The Court remanded the case with instructions to apply the act to the cases, permitting funding termination on a program-specific basis only, if the records justified a finding of gender-based discrimination in a federally funded program. *North Haven Bd. of Educ. v. Bell*, 456 U.S. 512, 102 S.Ct. 1912, 72 L.Ed.2d 299 (1982).

In *Ford Motor Co. v. EEOC,* the Court held that applicants who had been offered unconditional employment after being discriminated against were only eligible for back pay up until the date of the offers.

Three women applied for "picker-packer" positions at an automobile company's warehouse, positions which no women had held before. The company hired three men instead, and a discrimination charge was filed with the Equal Employment Opportunity Commission (EEOC). The company later offered two of the women the job for which they had been turned down, but without seniority to the date of the applications. The women declined the offers. The EEOC then sued the company in a federal district court, which held that the company had violated Title VII. The court ordered the company to pay back pay from the date of the applications to the date of its order. The U.S. Court of Appeals affirmed the decision, and further appeal went to the U.S. Supreme Court. The Court held that an unconditional offer of employment will toll the continuing accrual of back pay liability under Title VII even if the employer does not offer seniority retroactive to the date of the alleged discrimination. Accordingly, for the two women who had been offered employment after they were initially rejected by the company, back pay was only due up until the time of the offer by the company. The Court reversed the lower courts' rulings, effectively requiring claimants to minimize their damages by accepting unconditional offers. *Ford Motor Co. v. EEOC*, 458 U.S. 219, 102 S.Ct. 3057, 73 L.Ed.2d 721 (1982).

If an employer provides benefits for its employees, it may not do so in a discriminatory manner. In the following case, the Supreme Court applied Title VII even though elevation to partnership status was not an "offer of employment."

A woman lawyer was hired by a law firm as an associate. She took the job because the firm apparently represented that she would make partner if her work was satisfactory. The firm decided not to make her a partner, maintaining its all-male partnership status. After filing a charge with the Equal Employment Opportunity Commission, the lawyer sued the firm (her employment had terminated when she did not make partner), alleging discrimination under Title VII. A federal district court dismissed the complaint on the ground that Title VII was inapplicable to the selection of partners by a partnership. The U.S. Court of Appeals affirmed, and the case came before the U.S. Supreme Court. The Supreme Court reversed the court of appeals, finding that the lawyer had stated a cognizable claim under Title VII. Where an employer provides its employees with benefits, it may not do so in a discriminatory manner. If it is a term, condition or privilege of employment, discrimination by the employer is unlawful. Further, even if elevation to partnership status is not an offer of employment, Title VII still applies to bar discrimination in such a context. The Court remanded the case for further proceedings. *Hishon v. King & Spalding*, 467 U.S. 69, 104 S.Ct. 2229, 81 L.Ed.2d 59 (1984).

In *Anderson v. Bessemer City*, the Supreme Court upheld a district court's discrimination ruling, and stated that the U.S. Court of Appeals had improperly re-examined the evidence. Since there was sufficient evidence to support the charge, the district court's ruling should not have been overturned.

A North Carolina city developed a new job for managing the city's recreational facilities. Four men and one woman composed the mayoral committee responsible for selecting an applicant. After considering eight applicants, the four men voted to hire a 24-year-old man who had recently graduated from college with a physical education degree. The sole female committee member voted to hire the only female applicant, a 39-year-old teacher with degrees in social studies and education. The female applicant filed a sex discrimination complaint under Title VII against the city, claiming that she had not been hired solely on the basis of her sex.

The federal district court in which the matter was filed held in the applicant's favor, finding that she had a broader range of experience than the male applicant. The court also held that the male committee members were biased against the female applicant and that one male committee person had stated that he would not have wanted his wife to perform the recreation director's job duties. There was also evidence that the committee had actively solicited male applicants but had made no attempt to recruit females. Finally, the reasons given for hiring the male applicant were pretextual. The city appealed to the U.S. Court of Appeals, Fourth Circuit, which reversed the lower court's decision. The applicant appealed to the U.S. Supreme Court, which held that the court of appeals had improperly weighed the district court findings by attempting to conduct a new evaluation of the evidence. There was sufficient evidence of sex bias and discrimination in the district court record and the court of appeals should not have denied relief to the applicant. The Court reversed the court of appeals' judgment. *Anderson v. Bessemer City*, 470 U.S. 564, 105 S.Ct. 1504, 84 L.Ed.2d 518 (1985).

In 1987, the Supreme Court held that an affirmative action plan that took sex into account as one factor in the hiring decision was valid. The plan was not a quota system, and it presented a case-by-case approach. Further, the Court reaffirmed its decision in *Steelworkers v. Weber*, 443 U.S. 193, 99 S.Ct. 2721, 61 L.Ed.2d 480 (1979) that an employer seeking to implement an affirmative action plan need not point to its own prior discriminatory practices, but need only point to a conspicuous imbalance in traditionally segregated job categories.

A California county transportation agency voluntarily adopted an affirmative action plan. The plan allowed the agency to consider, as one factor, the sex of an applicant in making promotions. The long term goal of the plan was to achieve a workforce whose composition reflected the proportion of women and minorities in the area labor force. When a road dispatcher position opened up, the agency promoted one of the qualified female applicants. A male employee who was passed over sued the agency in a federal district court. The court found that the woman had been selected because of her sex and invalidated the agency's plan. The court of appeals reversed this decision, and the man further appealed the case to the U.S. Supreme Court.

The Supreme Court held that the agency had appropriately taken the woman's sex into account as one factor in determining that she be promoted. It found that the agency plan was flexible and presented a case-by-case approach to effecting a gradual improvement in the representation of women and minorities in the agency. Thus, the plan was fully consistent with Title VII. Even though the male candidate had shown a *prima facie* case of discrimination on the part of the agency, the agency had shown a nondiscriminatory rationale for its decision, namely the affirmative action plan. Further, the Court noted that an employer need not point to its own prior discriminatory practices to justify its adoption of such a plan. It need only point to a conspicuous imbalance in traditionally segregated areas of employment. Since the plan had taken into account distinctions in qualifications to provide guidance, the agency had not merely engaged in blind hiring by the numbers. The Court affirmed the court of appeals' decision and upheld the affirmative action plan. *Johnson v. Transp. Agency, Santa Clara County,* 480 U.S. 616, 107 S.Ct. 1442, 94 L.Ed.2d 615 (1987).

The Supreme Court, in *Price Waterhouse v. Hopkins,* permitted discrimination if the employer could show that it would have made the same decision absent the discrimination. However, the Civil Rights Act of 1991 changes this result by prohibiting only certain injunctive relief, such as reinstatement.

A woman worked for a nationwide accounting firm as a senior manager and was proposed as a candidate for partnership. When she was refused admission as a partner, she brought suit against the firm in a federal district court under Title VII, charging that the firm had discriminated against her on the basis of sex in its partnership decisions. The district court found that the firm had discriminated against the manager, but held that it could avoid equitable relief if it could prove by clear and convincing evidence that it would have made the same decision in the absence of a discriminatory motive. The U.S. Court of Appeals, District of Columbia Circuit, affirmed, and noted that the firm could avoid all liability if it showed that it would have made the same decision without the discrimination (again, by clear and convincing evidence). The case came before the U.S. Supreme Court.

The Supreme Court held that under Title VII, the employer could avoid liability if it showed by a mere preponderance of the evidence that it would have made the same decision even if it had not taken the manager's gender into account. This preserved the employer's right to freedom of choice. The Court then reversed and remanded the case for a determination of whether the same decision would have been made absent the discrimination. *Price Waterhouse v. Hopkins,* 490 U.S. 228, 109 S.Ct. 1775, 104 L.Ed.2d 268 (1989). Under the Civil

Rights Act of 1991, if it is shown that discrimination is a contributing factor in the employment decision, then (assuming that the employer can show that it would have made the same decision absent the discrimination) courts will be prohibited from ordering certain injunctive relief—like reinstatement. However, money damages may still be available.

The Supreme Court stated that employers might be liable for punitive damages under Title VII even where an employee does not prove that the employer engaged in some extraordinarily egregious behavior. However, it also held that employers cannot be vicariously liable where managers act contrary to the employer's good faith efforts to comply with Title VII.

A male and a female employee who had both received "distinguished" performance ratings competed for a promotion. After she was rejected, the female employee sued for gender discrimination, claiming that the other candidate had been "pre-selected." A federal jury found discrimination and awarded the employee $52,718 in back pay. But the district court judge refused to allow the jury to consider punitive damages, and the employee appealed. The U.S. Court of Appeals, D.C. Circuit, affirmed, and the case reached the Supreme Court.

The Court noted that punitive damages could be awarded without a showing of egregious behavior independent of the employer's state of mind. Where the employer acts with malice or with reckless indifference to the employee's federally protected rights, punitive damages are a proper form of relief.

Punitive damages would not be warranted, the Court said, where the employer is unaware of the relevant federal prohibition, or where the employer discriminates with the distinct belief that the discrimination is lawful, such as where it reasonably believes a bona fide occupational qualification is satisfied. The Court also noted that an employer cannot be held vicariously liable under Title VII (for punitive damages) for the discriminatory decisions of its management employees where those decisions are contrary to the employer's good faith efforts to comply with the statute. *Kolstad v. American Dental Ass'n*, 527 U.S. 526, 119 S.Ct. 2118, 144 L.Ed.2d 494 (1999).

In a case decided late in the 2000-2001 term, the Supreme Court held that the Civil Rights Act of 1991 does not contemplate the inclusion of front pay as part of a compensatory damage award in federal anti-discrimination cases. Thus, an employee who prevailed against her employer in an employment discrimination case filed under Title VII was allowed to increase a $300,000 compensatory damage award for lost compensation represented by front pay.

A federal district court held that the employee was subjected to sexual harassment by co-workers and that supervisors were aware of the harassment. She took a medical leave of absence to obtain psychological assistance and was discharged for failing to return to work. The court awarded the employee more than $100,000 in back pay and benefits, more than $250,000 in attorneys' fees and $300,000 in compensatory damages, which represented the maximum amount under the 1991 act's limit for employers with more than 500 employees. The U.S. Court of Appeals for the Sixth Circuit affirmed the district court judgment, finding flagrant sex discrimination that the employer's managers and supervisors did not take adequate steps to prevent.

The employee appealed to the U.S. Supreme Court, arguing that her compensatory damage award had been improperly capped at $300,000 and that she was entitled to a further award representing "front pay." The Supreme Court explained that front pay is generally money awarded to an employee for lost compensation during the period between a judgment and reinstatement. Courts also order front pay as a substitute for reinstatement in cases where reinstatement is not possible.

The court stated that victims of sex discrimination have traditionally been entitled to remedies under Title VII such as injunctions, reinstatement, back pay, lost benefits and attorneys' fees. The Civil Rights Act of 1991 expanded traditional Title VII remedies to include compensatory and punitive damage awards. When read as a whole, the 1991 act was best interpreted as excluding front pay from the meaning of compensatory damages. Under that construction, front pay was not included in the statutory damage limit and the employee was entitled to a front pay award to supplement the $300,000 awarded by the district court. According to the Court, Congress sought to expand available remedies when amending the Civil Rights Act by permitting employees to recover compensatory and punitive damages, including front pay. The Court reversed the lower court decisions and remanded the case for further proceedings. *Pollard v. E.I. du Pont de Nemours & Co.*, ___ U.S. ___, 121 S.Ct. 1946, ___ L.Ed.2d ___ (2001).

B. Sexual Harassment

The Supreme Court has held that sexual harassment constitutes a form of sex discrimination protected by Title VII. Sexual harassment creates a hostile work environment and need not be sex-related; any form of harassment against an employee because of the employee's sex will be considered harassment.

A woman worked for a bank in various capacities over a four-year period. Her supervisor allegedly harassed her during this period, demanding sexual favors, and forcibly raping her on several occasions. When the employee took an indefinite sick leave, the bank discharged her. She then brought suit against the bank, claiming that she had been subjected to sexual harassment in violation of Title VII. On conflicting trial testimony, a federal district court ruled for the bank, finding that the bank did not have notice of any harassment, and that its policies forbade such behavior. The U.S. Court of Appeals reversed, and appeal was taken to the U.S. Supreme Court.

The Supreme Court first noted that sexual harassment is clearly a form of sex discrimination prohibited by Title VII. It then stated that while absence of notice of harassment will not necessarily shield an employer from liability, employers are not always liable automatically for sexual harassment by their supervisor employees. The Court determined that Congress intended agency principles to apply to some extent. The Court also held that it was not improper to admit into evidence the complainant's "sexually provocative speech and dress." Even though voluntariness in the sense of consent is not a defense to a sexual harassment claim, such information bears on the issue of whether the complainant has found particular sexual advances unwelcome. The Court affirmed the court of appeals' holding, and remanded the case. *Meritor Savings Bank, FSB v. Vinson*, 477 U.S. 57, 106 S.Ct. 2399, 91 L.Ed.2d 49 (1986).

Conduct can be actionable as "abusive work environment" harassment even where it does not seriously affect an employee's psychological well-being or lead the employee to suffer injury.

A Tennessee woman worked as a manager of a rental equipment company. The president of the company often insulted her because of her gender and frequently made her the target of unwanted sexual innuendoes. The employee subsequently quit and sued the company, claiming that the president's conduct had created an abusive work environment because of her gender. The federal district court found that, although this was a "close case," the president's conduct did not create an abusive environment because while some of the conduct would offend a reasonable woman, it was not so severe as to be "expected to seriously affect the manager's psychological well-being." The U.S. Court of Appeals, Sixth Circuit, affirmed and the manager appealed to the U.S. Supreme Court.

The Supreme Court reaffirmed the standard set forth in *Meritor Savings Bank v. Vinson*, 477 U.S. 57, 106 S.Ct. 2399, 91 L.Ed.2d 49 (1986), that "Title VII is violated when the workplace is permeated with discriminatory behavior that is sufficiently severe or pervasive to create a hostile environment." The Court noted that the standard required only an objectively hostile environment—one that a reasonable person would find hostile—as well as the victim's subjective perception that the environment was abusive. Further, the court held that the determination of whether the environment was hostile could only be reached by looking at all the circumstances, which include frequency, severity, whether the conduct was humiliating, whether it unreasonably interfered with the employee's performance, and the psychological harm to the victim. The court reversed and remanded the case with instructions for the trial court to consider the psychological harm to the victim as but one factor to be considered in looking at all the circumstances. *Harris v. Forklift Systems, Inc.*, 510 U.S. 17, 114 S.Ct. 367, 126 L.Ed.2d 295 (1993).

In 1998, the Supreme Court extended Title VII protections to same-sex harassment.

A Louisiana offshore service employed a roustabout to work on oil platforms in the Gulf of Mexico. He claimed that he was forcibly subjected to sex-related humiliating actions, assault and threats of rape by co-workers, including two employees with supervisory authority. When he complained to the employer's safety compliance clerk, the clerk did nothing and stated that he had also been subjected to abuse by the co-workers. Eventually, the roustabout quit and sued the employer in the U.S. District Court for the Eastern District of Louisiana, alleging sex discrimination in violation of Title VII of the Civil Rights Act of 1964. The court granted summary judgment to the employer, holding that the roustabout had no viable cause of action under Title VII since the harassment was caused by same-sex co-workers. The U.S. Court of Appeals, Fifth Circuit, affirmed the judgment and the roustabout appealed to the U.S. Supreme Court.

The Court stated that sex discrimination in the form of same-sex harassment that is so objectively offensive that it alters the conditions of employment is actionable under Title VII. The Court found no language in Title VII that bars a sex discrimination claim when the complaining party and alleged perpetrators are of the same sex, and it rejected the employer's assertion that allowing the claim would transform Title VII into a general code of workplace civility. The Court noted that not all verbal or physical harassment in the workplace is prohibited by Title VII, since it does not cover conduct that is not severe or pervasive enough to create an objectively hostile or abusive work environment. The Court reversed the lower court decisions and remanded the case. *Oncale v. Sundowner Offshore Services, Inc.*, 523 U.S. 75, 118 S.Ct. 998, 140 L.Ed.2d 201 (1998).

In the case below, the Supreme Court held that Title VII imposes vicarious liability on an employer for sexual harassment by supervisors.

An Illinois employee of a corporation alleged that she was subjected to constant *quid pro quo* sexual harassment from one of her supervisors, a mid-level manager who had the authority to hire and promote, subject to higher approval, but who was not considered a policymaker. The employee refused all of the supervisor's advances, but suffered no tangible retaliation and was even promoted once. Despite her knowledge of the employer's sexual harassment policy, she never complained to upper level management about the supervisor's behavior. The employee resigned and sued the employer in a federal district court alleging sexual harassment and constructive discharge in violation of Title VII of the Civil Rights Act of 1964. The district court granted the employer's motion for summary judgment and the U.S. Court of Appeals, Seventh Circuit, reversed. The U.S. Supreme Court granted review.

The Supreme Court held that Title VII imposes vicarious liability on an employer for actionable discrimination caused by a supervisor with authority over an employee. When a supervisor discriminates in the terms and conditions of a subordinate's employment, his actions draw upon his superior position over the subordinate. However, in cases where there is no tangible employment action taken against the employee, the employer may assert a two-pronged affirmative defense. First, the employer must prove that it exercised reasonable care to prevent and promptly correct any sexual harassment. Second, the employer must prove that the employee unreasonably failed to avail herself of any employer remedies or failed to avoid harm otherwise. However, the affirmative defense is not available to the employer when the supervisor's harassment culminates in a tangible employment action such as discharge or demotion. The Court remanded the case for further consideration in light of its holding. *Burlington Industries, Inc. v. Ellerth*, 524 U.S. 742, 118 S.Ct. 2257, 141 L.Ed.2d 633 (1998).

In a different case decided on the same day as *Ellerth*, the Supreme Court found a city vicariously liable for the creation of a hostile work environment.

A Florida woman worked as a lifeguard for a city. She had two male supervisors who controlled all aspects of her job, including work assignments and discipline. The lifeguard was subjected to severe and pervasive unwelcome touching, sexual comments, and other offensive behavior from the two supervisors. Although the city had a policy against sexual harassment, it completely failed to disseminate the policy to the lifeguard's department. Also, the policy did not assure that any harassing supervisors could be bypassed in registering complaints. The employee did not report this harassment to higher management, from whom she was completely isolated. She eventually resigned and sued the city in a federal district court alleging sexual harassment in violation of Title VII of the Civil Rights Act of 1964 and 42 U.S.C. § 1983. The district court found the city liable for the harassment. The U.S. Court of Appeals, Eleventh Circuit, reversed. Using the same holding as it did in *Ellerth,* the Supreme Court found the city vicariously liable for the hostile environment created by the lifeguard's supervisors. The Court reversed the court of appeals' decision and remanded the case for reinstatement of the district court decision. *Faragher v. City of Boca Raton*, 524 U.S. 775, 118 S.Ct. 2275, 141 L.Ed.2d 662 (1998).

The Supreme Court reversed a decision in favor of a school employee who claimed sexual harassment by male co-workers and retaliation by the district, finding she failed to show any causality between the alleged harassing incident and the allegedly retaliatory job transfer.

A school district employee met with two male co-workers to review psychological evaluation reports from job applicants seeking employment with the district. She alleged that during one meeting, her supervisor read from a report that one applicant had commented to a co-worker, "I hear making love to you is like making love to the Grand Canyon," and that the supervisor then said, "I don't know what that means." According to the complaining employee, the other employee responded, "Well, I'll tell you later," and then both male employees chuckled. The employee asserted that when she complained about this incident, she was transferred to another position in retaliation. The transfer took place 20 months after the alleged harassment.

A federal district court awarded summary judgment to the school district and the employee appealed. The U.S. Court of Appeals, Ninth Circuit, reversed, observing that the employee had a reasonable belief that the harassing incident violated Title VII and that the EEOC had issued a right-to-sue letter within three months of the job transfer, making summary judgment improper.

The U.S. Supreme Court accepted the school district's petition for review concerning the question of the employee's reasonable belief that a Title VII violation had occurred. It held that no reasonable person could have believed that the single incident giving rise to the lawsuit violated Title VII. Sexual harassment is actionable only if it is so severe or pervasive as to alter the conditions of the victim's employment and create an abusive working environment. According to the Court, simple teasing, offhand comments and isolated incidents that are not extremely serious will not amount to discriminatory changes in the terms and conditions of employment. In this case, the employee's job required that she review the offensive statement. She conceded that it did not upset her to read the written remark in the applicant's file. Significantly, the supervisor's comment and the male employee's response was at worst "an isolated incident" that could not remotely be considered serious under recent Supreme Court precedents.

The Court found "no causality at all" between the job transfer proposed by the school district and the employee's complaint. It noted that there must be a very close proximity in time between an employer's knowledge of an employee's protected conduct and an adverse employment action if this is the employee's only evidence of retaliation. The Court reversed the Ninth Circuit's judgment, in effect reinstating the district court's decision. *Clark County School District v. Breeden*, ___ U.S ___, 121 S.Ct. 1508, 149 L.Ed.2d 509 (2001).

C. Pregnancy Discrimination

In 1974, three teachers challenged school district rules which required them to take mandatory unpaid leaves of absence at specified times during and after childbirth. The Supreme Court held that the mandatory cut-off dates were arbitrary and bore no rational relationship to the state interest in continuity of instruction. Because the rules created an irrebuttable presumption of physical incompetency by pregnant teachers even where contrary medical evidence was present, the rules violated the Due Process Clause of the U.S. Constitution.

Two public school teachers in Ohio and one in Virginia brought lawsuits challenging their school districts' maternity leave of absence rules. The Cleveland, Ohio, school board rule required a pregnant school teacher to take unpaid maternity leave five months before the expected childbirth. The teacher could return to work at the next regular school semester following the date when her child attained the age of three months. The Chesterfield County, Virginia, school board rule required a teacher to take leave of absence four months before the anticipated childbirth with reemployment guaranteed no later than the first day of the school year following the date she was declared re-eligible. Both rules required a physician's written statement prior to reemployment. The teachers in this lawsuit challenged the constitutionality of the mandatory leave of absence rules.

The U.S. Supreme Court held that the rules of both school boards regarding leave of absence at mandatory and fixed time periods violated the Due Process Clause of the Fourteenth Amendment. The Court said that the arguments advanced by the school districts in defense of their rules, such as continuity of classroom instruction, physical inability of teachers to teach, and health of the teacher and unborn child contained arbitrary irrebuttable presumptions. The arbitrary fourth or fifth month maternity leave rules bore no rational relationship to the state interest in continuity in the classroom, and could work against continuity by requiring that leaves be taken in mid-semester even when the teacher could have finished the semester. The Court further held that the return to work provisions of the rules were valid with respect to physical examination before returning to work and the dates of reemployment. However, the Court struck down the Cleveland, Ohio, board's rule requiring teachers to wait for reemployment until the child was three months old. The Court found the rule in violation of due process because of the irrebuttable presumptions the rule contained bearing no rational relationship to any legitimate school interest. *Cleveland Bd. of Educ. v. LaFleur*, 414 U.S. 632, 94 S.Ct. 791, 39 L.Ed.2d 52 (1974).

The Court stated that an employer's disability benefits plan did not violate Title VII despite the fact that the plan failed to cover pregnancy-related disabilities. The Court determined that the benefits plan was merely less than all-inclusive and that this was acceptable. However, this case was overruled seven years later.

A company provided its employees with a disability plan that paid weekly nonoccupational sickness and accident benefits; however, the plan excluded disabilities arising from pregnancy. A group of women employees brought a lawsuit against the company, asserting that its policy constituted sex discrimination in violation of Title VII. A federal district court held for the employees, and the U.S. Court of Appeals affirmed. The company petitioned for a writ of certiorari, which the U.S. Supreme Court granted.

The Supreme Court held that the company's disability benefits plan did not violate Title VII even though it failed to cover pregnancy-related disabilities. The Court noted that the plan did not exclude anyone because of gender; it merely removed one physical condition—pregnancy—from the list of disabilities that were covered. Even though pregnancy is confined to women, it is significantly different from the typical covered disease or disability. Gender-based discrimination does not result simply because a company's disability benefits plan is less than all-inclusive. Here, the company's plan was just an insurance package that covered some risks while excluding others. Since no pretext for discrimination was shown, the Court reversed the lower courts and upheld the plan. *General Electric Co. v. Gilbert,* 429 U.S. 125, 97 S.Ct. 401, 50 L.Ed.2d 343 (1976). *Newport News Shipbuilding and Dry Dock Co. v. EEOC,* below, overrules this case.

A pregnancy limitation in an employer's health plan that provided fewer pregnancy benefits for spouses of male employees than it did for female employees was held to violate the Pregnancy Discrimination Act. The case overruled *General Electric Co. v. Gilbert,* above, which allowed differential treatment of pregnancy as nongender-based discrimination.

After Title VII was amended in 1978 by the Pregnancy Discrimination Act to prohibit discrimination on the basis of pregnancy, a company amended its health insurance plan to provide its female employees with hospitalization benefits for pregnancy-related conditions to the same extent as for other medical conditions. However, the plan provided less extensive pregnancy benefits for spouses of male employees. The company then filed an action in a Virginia federal district court challenging the Equal Employment Opportunity Commission's guidelines that indicated that its health insurance plan was unlawful. The EEOC also sued, asserting that the plan was discriminatory. The district court ruled for the company, but the U.S. Court of Appeals reversed. The case then came before the U.S. Supreme Court.

The Supreme Court stated that pregnancy limitations for spouses of male employees discriminated against the men who worked for the company. The plan provided less protection to married male employees than it did to married female employees. The Pregnancy Discrimination Act provides that it is discriminatory to exclude pregnancy coverage from an otherwise inclusive benefits plan. The act not only overturned the holding of *General Electric Co. v. Gilbert*, which held that it was lawful to exclude disabilities caused by pregnancy from a disability plan that provided general coverage; it also rejected that Court's reasoning that differential treatment of pregnancy is not gender-based discrimination even though only women can become pregnant. The Court affirmed the court of appeals' decision in favor of the EEOC. *Newport News Shipbuilding and Dry Dock Co. v. EEOC,* 462 U.S. 669, 103 S.Ct. 2622, 77 L.Ed.2d 89 (1983).

In the case below, the Court determined that California's Fair Employment and Housing Act (which prohibits, among other things, discrimination on the basis of pregnancy) was not inconsistent with—and thus not preempted by— Title VII. Accordingly, employers could be required to abide by the state law without violating Title VII.

The California Federal Savings and Loan Association, a federally chartered S&L, was an employer covered by both Title VII and § 12945(b)(2) of the California Government Code. Section 12945(b)(2) prohibits employers from disallowing reasonable pregnancy leaves. The S&L employed a woman as a receptionist for several years. She took a pregnancy disability leave for four months, then notified the S&L that she was able to return to work. However, it informed her that her job had been filled and that no other similar positions were available. It maintained that just because it allowed employees to take unpaid leaves of absence, it was not required to reinstate the employees if similar positions did not exist when they chose to return. The employee filed a complaint with the Department of Fair Employment and Housing which charged the S&L with violating § 12945(b)(2), but before a hearing was conducted, the S&L brought suit in a federal district court, seeking a declaration that § 12945(b)(2) was preempted by Title VII. It argued that compliance with § 12945(b)(2) would open the door for a reverse discrimination suit by disabled males who took unpaid leaves. The district court agreed with the S&L, but the U.S. Court of Appeals, Ninth Circuit, reversed. Appeal was taken to the U.S. Supreme Court.

On appeal, the Court noted that the purpose of both Title VII and § 12945(b)(2) was to achieve equality of employment opportunities. By requiring reinstatement after pregnancy leaves, § 12945(b)(2) ensured that women would not lose their jobs on account of pregnancy. Further, the Court noted that the Pregnancy Discrimination Act, which amended Title VII, did not prohibit employment practices which favored pregnant women. The federal and state laws merely established a minimum standard which employers were required to abide by. Accordingly, the Supreme Court affirmed the court of appeals' decision and held that § 12945(b)(2) was not preempted by Title VII. *California Federal Savings and Loan Ass'n v. Guerra*, 479 U.S. 272, 107 S.Ct. 683, 93 L.Ed.2d 613 (1987).

Discrimination on the basis of sex that is done without malevolent motive or for the protection of employees' health and well-being still violates Title VII. If a class of employees wishes to be exposed to risks that another class is encountering, the employer cannot prevent those employees from exposing themselves.

A company manufactured batteries, the primary ingredient of which was lead. As a result, in 1982, the company began a policy of excluding pregnant women and women capable of bearing children from jobs involving lead exposure. In 1984, a group of affected employees initiated a class action against the company, challenging its fetal protection policy as sex discrimination that violated Title VII. A federal district court granted summary judgment to the company, finding that it had established a business necessity defense. The U.S. Court of Appeals, Seventh Circuit, affirmed, and the employees petitioned the U.S. Supreme Court for review.

The Court noted that there was a clear bias in the company's policy, allowing fertile men but not women the choice of risking their reproductive health. Thus, there was clear sex discrimination involved. Even though there was no malevolent motive involved, the policy could not be termed "neutral." Accordingly, the only way for the company to justify the discrimination was by establishing that gender was a bona fide occupational qualification (BFOQ). The Court then stated that the company could not show a valid BFOQ. Decisions about the welfare of future children must be left to parents rather than their employers. The Court next looked to the issue of tort liability and found that it was unlikely that a person could bring a negligence action against the company at a later date for prenatal injuries. Since the company complied with the lead standard developed by the Occupational Safety and Health Administration and issued warnings to its female employees about the dangers of lead exposure, it was not negligent and it would be difficult for a court to find liability against the company. The Court therefore reversed the lower courts' decisions and struck down the company's fetal protection policy. *International Union, UAW v. Johnson Controls*, 499 U.S. 187, 111 S.Ct. 1196, 113 L.Ed.2d 158 (1991).

III. DISCRIMINATION AGAINST ALIENS

Aliens may permissibly be excluded from "important, nonelective executive positions," but they cannot be discriminated against with respect to competitive class state civil service positions.

A New York law provided that only United States citizens could hold permanent positions in the competitive class of the state civil service. Four resident aliens were then discharged from their positions with the city of New

York. They brought suit against various city officials, alleging that the state law violated the Fourteenth Amendment. A three-judge court was convened. It held that the statute violated the Fourteenth Amendment, and appeal was taken to the U.S. Supreme Court. The Court determined that the New York law violated the guarantee of equal protection provided by the Fourteenth Amendment. The state was unable to show that hiring nonaliens would be more efficient or that aliens would be more likely to leave their work than citizens. Even though the state does have an interest in defining its political community, the broad citizenship requirement established by the New York law could not be justified on the "important, nonelective executive positions" exception for discriminatory treatment. The Court affirmed the district court's decision in favor of the resident aliens. *Sugarman v. Dougall*, 413 U.S. 634, 93 S.Ct. 2842, 37 L.Ed.2d 853 (1973).

Although discrimination against persons because of their national origin is prohibited by Title VII, private employers may discriminate against aliens because of their alienage without violating Title VII.

A citizen of Mexico, who resided lawfully in the United States, sought employment as a seamstress with a manufacturing company. Her application was rejected due to a long-standing policy against the employment of aliens. After exhausting her administrative remedies with the EEOC, the applicant sued in federal court, asserting that the company had discriminated against her on the basis of national origin in violation of Title VII. The court granted summary judgment to the applicant, but the U.S. Court of Appeals reversed. It determined that the phrase "national origin" did not include citizenship. The case then came before the U.S. Supreme Court.

The Court held that the company's refusal to hire the woman because of her citizenship was not discrimination on the basis of national origin in violation of Title VII. Even though Title VII protects aliens against discrimination because of race, color, religion, sex, or national origin, it does not prohibit discrimination against aliens on the basis of alienage. Here, the company had not refused to hire the applicant because of her Mexican ancestry, but because she was not a United States citizen. This was not forbidden by Title VII. The Court affirmed the court of appeals' decision against the applicant. *Espinoza v. Farah Manufacturing Co.*, 414 U.S. 86, 94 S.Ct. 334, 38 L.Ed.2d 287 (1973).

Five years after *Sugarman,* the Court stated that police officers were the type of employees for which discrimination against aliens would be allowed because they are "important, nonelective executive employees."

An alien, lawfully in the United States as a permanent resident, applied for a position as a New York state trooper. Because New York law disqualified noncitizens from being appointed to the state police force, he was not allowed to take the competitive examination. He brought suit in a federal district court, asserting that New York's exclusion of aliens from the police force violated the Equal Protection Clause of the Fourteenth Amendment. A three-judge district court upheld the statute as constitutional, and the case was appealed to the U.S. Supreme Court, which stated that as long as there was a rational basis for the law, it would be upheld. It then noted that police enforcement and execution of the laws was a function where citizenship bore a rational relationship to the special demands of the position. Police actions call for a very high degree of judgment and discretion that can seriously affect individuals. It was permissible, then, for states to pick United States citizens who would be more likely to be familiar with and sympathetic to American traditions. Since police officers are "important non-elective ... officers who participate directly in the ... execution ... of broad public policy," the states can confine such jobs to citizens of the United States. The lower court decision was affirmed. *Foley v. Connelie,* 435 U.S. 291, 98 S.Ct. 1067, 55 L.Ed.2d 287 (1978).

The government interest in ensuring public school teaching standards must be rationally related to the method used to advance the interest under the Fourteenth Amendment's Equal Protection Clause. The Court upheld a New York law that prohibited aliens from obtaining teacher certification, since it bore a rational relationship to the government's interest in inculcating students with civic values.

A New York law prohibited any person who was not a citizen of the United States from gaining certification as a public school teacher unless that person manifested an intention to apply for citizenship. Unless a teacher obtained certification, the teacher could not work in public schools in New York. The state Commissioner of Education was authorized to create exemptions from this prohibition, and had done so on several occasions. A citizen of Great Britain who had resided in the U.S. since 1965 and was married to a U.S. citizen sought certification and was denied. A Finnish citizen also applied and was rejected. Both applicants sued the commissioner in a federal district court, seeking to enjoin enforcement of the statute. They argued that it violated the Equal Protection Clause of the Fourteenth Amendment. A federal district court held that the statute was unconstitutional, and the Supreme Court granted review. The Court held that the law did not violate the Equal Protection Clause. The state needed to show some rational relationship between excluding the aliens and a governmental interest. The Court stated that the New York statute bore a rational relationship to the state's interest in furthering its educational goals, especially with respect to having an obligation to promote civic virtues and understanding. The Court reversed and remanded the district court's decision. *Ambach v. Norwick,* 441 U.S. 68, 99 S.Ct. 1589, 60 L.Ed.2d 49 (1979).

In 1982, the Supreme Court expanded on its decision in *Foley v. Connelie,* by holding that probation officer jobs could be limited to United States citizens.

A California law required peace officers and probation officers (including deputy probation officers) to be United States citizens. A group of legal aliens unsuccessfully applied for positions as deputy probation officers, and sued in federal court to challenge the citizenship requirement under the Equal Protection Clause. The district court held for the resident aliens, and the case came before the U.S. Supreme Court. The Supreme Court reversed the district court's decision. It noted that because California probation officers sufficiently partook of the state's power to exercise coercive force over the individual they could be required to be citizens. The "political function" exception applied here because deputy probation officers held an important nonelective executive position; they had the power to make arrests and received training in the use of firearms. Thus, a citizenship requirement was an appropriate limitation, and the law was constitutional. *Cabell v. Chavez-Salido*, 454 U.S. 432, 102 S.Ct. 735, 70 L.Ed.2d 677 (1982).

Discrimination against aliens who wish to become notary publics is violative of the Equal Protection Clause because of the largely clerical and ministerial duties of notaries; thus, the political function exception cannot be used to justify discriminatory treatment.

A resident alien of the state of Texas applied to the Secretary of State to become a notary public. His application was denied because he was not a United States citizen. He sued in federal court, claiming that the Texas law relied on was violative of the U.S. Constitution. The district court ruled for the applicant, but the U.S. Court of Appeals, Fifth Circuit, reversed. The applicant then petitioned for a writ of certiorari, which the U.S. Supreme Court granted. The Supreme Court looked with strict scrutiny at the Texas law and found it to be unconstitutional. It declined to apply the "political function" exception in this case because notaries do not fall within the category of officials who perform functions that go to the heart of representative government. If the function of the position is such that the officeholder will have to "exercise broad discretionary power over the formulation or execution of public policies importantly affecting the citizen population," then the political function exception can be applied to justify the discrimination against aliens. Here, because the Court found that notaries' duties are largely clerical and ministerial, the law prohibiting aliens from becoming notaries violated the Equal Protection Clause. *Bernal v. Fainter,* 467 U.S. 216, 104 S.Ct. 2312, 81 L.Ed.2d 175 (1984).

IV. AGE DISCRIMINATION

A. Generally

In the *Trans World Airlines, Inc. v. Thurston* case, the Supreme Court held that an airline's retirement and transfer policy violated the Age Discrimination in Employment Act (ADEA). However, it could not be liable for double damages due to wilful misconduct because its actions had not been knowingly in violation of the ADEA.

An airline was concerned that its retirement policy, with respect to flight engineers, violated the ADEA. It thus adopted a plan permitting any employee with "flight engineer status" to continue to work in that capacity. However, captains (pilots) had to obtain that status through bidding procedures outlined in the collective bargaining agreement prior to their 60th birthday and hope that a vacancy opened up prior to that time. Otherwise, the captain would be retired. Even though this was the policy for captains displaced by age, it was not the policy for those who were displaced for any other reason (like medical disability or reduction in manpower). Three pilots sued, claiming that this policy violated the ADEA. The district court held for the airline, but the U.S. Court of Appeals reversed, finding that the discrimination had been wilful and awarding double damages against the airline.

On further appeal, the U.S. Supreme Court held that the airline's transfer policy denied 60-year-old captains a "privilege of employment" on the basis of age, and that this violated the ADEA. The only reason some captains were not allowed to "bump" less senior employees was because of their age. Further, there was no bona fide occupational qualification defense that the airline could establish to justify its actions. However, the Court held that the airline should not have been assessed double damages because it did not "know" that its conduct violated the ADEA. Nor did it adopt its transfer policy in "reckless disregard" of the ADEA's requirements. Accordingly, the Court upheld the finding that the airline had discriminated on the basis of age, but reversed the award of double damages because the airline had acted in good faith in attempting to determine whether its policy would violate the ADEA. *Trans World Airlines, Inc. v. Thurston*, 469 U.S. 111, 105 S.Ct. 613, 83 L.Ed.2d 523 (1985).

In *Betts*, the Court held that an employee benefit plan adopted prior to the ADEA's enactment could not be a subterfuge to evade the purposes of the act. So long as the plan was a bona fide employee benefit plan, it was exempted from the purview of the ADEA, unless the plan was a method of discriminating in other, nonfringe benefit aspects of the employment relationship.

The ADEA prohibits age-based discrimination by public and private employers, subject to some exceptions, and permits employers to maintain bona fide employee benefit plans which are not enacted as a subterfuge to evade the act. The Public Employees Retirement System of Ohio (PERS) administered public retirement and disability benefits. PERS maintained separate retirement benefit rates, one of which awarded disabled employees who retired under the age of 60 substantially higher benefits than disabled persons retiring after age 60. A speech pathologist worked for an Ohio county board of mental retardation for seven years. The board's employees were covered under PERS. The pathologist suffered medical problems, and was forced to retire at age 61. Although she qualified for age and service retirement benefits under PERS, she was denied disability retirement benefits because she was over age 60. The pathologist filed an age discrimination complaint against PERS in a federal district court. The court held that the PERS' retirement system was discriminatory on the basis of age. PERS appealed to the U.S. Court of Appeals, Sixth Circuit, which affirmed the district court's decision. PERS appealed to the U.S. Supreme Court.

The Court noted that plans in existence before the ADEA's enactment could not possibly be characterized as subterfuges to evade the act. The PERS system was established in 1933 and the provision governing disability retirement benefits for employees retiring after age 60 had been unchanged since 1959. Thus, the

PERS statutory scheme was not a subterfuge. The Court rejected the pathologist's reliance on a Department of Labor regulation interpreting the Act, 29 C.F.R. § 1625.10, which stated that age-based reductions in employee benefits must be justified on a cost basis. The statute itself made no such requirement, and no deference was due to the agency's interpretation of the statute. Employees bore the burden of proving that benefit plans constituted a subterfuge under the Act. Because the pathologist had not met her burden of proof, the lower courts had incorrectly ruled in her favor. The Court remanded the case to the district court for further consideration. *Public Employees Retirement System of Ohio v. Betts*, 492 U.S. 158, 109 S.Ct. 2854, 106 L.Ed.2d 134 (1989). Subsequently, Congress passed the Older Workers Benefit Protection Act to prohibit discrimination against older workers in all employee benefits "except when age-based reductions in employee benefit plans are justified by significant cost considerations."

In 1993, the Supreme Court held that in a disparate treatment case under the ADEA, liability depends on whether age actually motivated the employer's decision. An adverse decision was insufficient to support an age discrimination claim where the decision was based on years of service, which could be distinguished from age.

A Massachusetts manufacturing employee was fired when he was 62 years old and a few weeks shy of vesting for his pension benefits. He filed suit in a federal district court alleging violations of the ADEA and ERISA. The jury found for the employee on both violations and further determined that the ADEA violation had been wilful. Thus, the employee was entitled to liquidated damages. The district court granted the employer's motion for judgment notwithstanding the verdict with respect to the finding of wilfulness. Both parties appealed to the U.S. Court of Appeals, First Circuit, which affirmed the jury's finding of a wilful violation of the ADEA. The employer appealed to the U.S. Supreme Court. There were two issues on appeal to the Supreme Court: whether an employer's interference with the vesting of pension benefits was a violation of the ADEA and what standard of wilfulness should be used under the ADEA. The ADEA was enacted to prevent discrimination based on age and also to "prohibit the problem of inaccurate and stigmatizing stereotypes about productivity and competence declining with age." However, when an employer's decision is wholly motivated by factors other than age, the stigmatizing stereotypes disappear. The court noted that this was true even when the motivating factor was correlated with age (such as pension status). Because age and years of service may be analytically distinct, an employer could take account of one while ignoring the other. Thus, the court reasoned that it was incorrect to say that a decision based on years of service was necessarily "age-based." Next, the Court analyzed the standard for wilfulness under the ADEA. The Court ruled that once a wilful violation had been shown, the employee need not additionally demonstrate that the employer's conduct was outrageous, prove direct evidence of the employer's motivation, or prove that age was the predominant factor in the employment decision. The Supreme Court remanded the case to the court of appeals to determine if the jury had sufficient evidence to find a violation of the ADEA. *Hazen Paper Co. v. Biggins,* 507 U.S. 604, 113 S.Ct. 1701, 123 L.Ed.2d 338 (1993).

After-acquired evidence of an employee's wrongdoing that would have led to the employee's discharge is not a complete bar to recovery under the ADEA. Where the employee was discharged in violation of the ADEA, such evidence merely limits the damages award available.

A 62-year-old secretary worked for a Tennessee publishing company for over 30 years. She had access to company financial records and made copies of documents when she became concerned that the company would terminate her employment because of her age. The publishing company dismissed the secretary under a workforce reduction plan. She filed a lawsuit against the publisher in the U.S. District Court for the Middle District of Tennessee under the ADEA, seeking back pay and other relief. During the course of pretrial discovery, the publisher learned that the secretary had copied company financial documents. Based on this information, it filed a motion for summary judgment, which the court granted on the basis of the secretary's misconduct. The U.S. Court of Appeals, Sixth Circuit, affirmed the decision and the secretary appealed to the U.S. Supreme Court.

The Court rejected the reasoning of the lower courts that the secretary's misconduct constituted proper grounds for termination based on the after-acquired evidence revealed in discovery. The important antidiscrimination objectives of the ADEA precluded the blanket denial of relief to the former secretary. Employee wrongdoing remained relevant and would preclude reinstatement or front pay as an appropriate remedy in this case. However, on remand, the district court could not impose an absolute rule barring the secretary's recovery of back pay. The remedy should calculate back pay from the date of the unlawful discharge to the date the publisher discovered the wrongdoing. The case was remanded for further proceedings. *McKennon v. Nashville Banner Publ'g Co.,* 513 U.S. 352, 115 S.Ct. 879, 130 L.Ed.2d 852 (1995).

The Supreme Court, in *Commissioner of Internal Revenue v. Schleier,* viewed an ADEA settlement as taxable. The Court distinguished the liquidated damages from tort damages for personal injury or sickness and analogized the damages to back wages.

An airline employee was fired when he reached the age of 60 pursuant to company policy. He filed an age discrimination lawsuit against the airline in a federal district court under the ADEA. The parties reached a settlement prior to trial under which the airline paid the employee $145,000. The parties designated half of the payment as back pay and the other half as liquidated damages. The airline did not withhold any payroll or income tax from the liquidated damages portion of the settlement award. The former employee failed to pay any income tax on the liquidated damages portion of the settlement award and the Commissioner of the IRS served him with a deficiency notice, stating that liquidated damages were includable in his gross income. The former employee filed a U.S. Tax Court action asserting that he had properly excluded the liquidated damage award and seeking a refund of tax paid on his back pay. The tax court held that the entire settlement award was excludable from income as damages received on account of personal injury or sickness within the meaning of the IRS Code. The U.S. Court of Appeals, Fifth Circuit, affirmed the tax court decision, and the commissioner appealed to the U.S. Supreme Court.

On appeal, the former employee argued that his settlement was attributable to a personal injury or sickness because it was based upon a tort or tort-type right under the ADEA. The court disagreed, finding that liquidated damages under the ADEA were distinguishable from tort damages for personal injury or sickness and were analogous to back wages which were of an economic character and therefore fully taxable. In order to exclude damage awards from taxation, taxpayers were required to demonstrate that the underlying cause of action was based upon a tort or tort-type right and that the damages were received on account of personal injury or sickness. Because the settlement award in this case failed both parts of the test, the lower court decisions were reversed. *Comm'r of Internal Revenue v. Schleier,* 515 U.S. 323, 115 S.Ct. 2159, 132 L.Ed.2d 294 (1995).

In *O'Connor v. Consolidated Coin Caterers Corp.*, the Supreme Court refined the *McDonnell Douglas* test. Specifically, the Court determined that the ADEA prohibits discrimination on the basis of age, not class membership.

A 56-year-old North Carolina employee was fired by his employer after twelve years of work and replaced by a 40-year-old man. The discharged employee filed a lawsuit against his former employer in the U.S. District Court for the Western District of North Carolina, alleging age discrimination in violation of the ADEA. The court held for the employer, and the U.S. Court of Appeals, Fourth Circuit, affirmed. The employee appealed to the U.S. Supreme Court, which agreed to review the questions of whether the employee was barred from proving age discrimination under the ADEA solely because he had been replaced by a worker who was 40 years old and also whether the employee was within the class of persons protected by the ADEA.

The Court observed that federal courts analyze ADEA cases under the framework first established in the case of *McDonnell Douglas v. Green,* 411 U.S. 792, 93 S.Ct. 1817, 36 L.Ed.2d 668 (1973). Complaining parties in such cases must demonstrate that they are in a protected group, are discharged or demoted despite competently performing their jobs and are replaced by someone outside the protected class. The Court stated that the evidence must be adequate to create an inference that an employment decision was based on an illegal discriminatory motive. It was nonsensical to prohibit an inference of discrimination based on the class status of the individual who replaces the complaining party. Under that logic, a 40-year-old worker replaced by a 39-year-old worker would be entitled to ADEA protection while the 56-year-old employee in this case would gain no relief despite being replaced by an individual who was 16 years younger. Because the ADEA prohibits discrimination on the basis of age, and not on the basis of class membership, the replacement of an employee by a substantially younger employee was a far more reliable indicator of age discrimination. The lower court decisions were reversed and remanded. *O'Connor v. Consolidated Coin Caterers Corp.,* 517 U.S. 308, 116 S.Ct. 1307, 134 L.Ed.2d 433 (1996).

Before an employer may obtain a waiver or release of potential ADEA claims, the employer must comply with the specific statutory requirements outlined in the OWBPA amendments. If the employer does not comply with the statutory requirements, then the waiver or release becomes unenforceable despite the employee's failure to tender back the severance pay.

The Older Workers Benefit Protection Act (OWBPA) imposes specific requirements upon employers who discharge employees and seek the waiver or release of potential claims against them under the ADEA. The requirements apply where an employee is offered a severance package in return for the waiver of claims against the employer. Among the requirements of a valid OWBPA waiver are a minimum 20-day notice to the employee to consider the waiver, written advice to consult an attorney prior to executing the waiver, a seven-day period after signature of the waiver in which to revoke consent and specific reference to rights or claims arising under the ADEA. A Louisiana employer presented an employee with a severance agreement and waiver after she received a poor performance rating. The employer did not comply with OWBPA requirements, giving her only 14 days to consider the waiver, failing to allow seven days after signing the release during which to change her mind, and making no reference to ADEA claims. The employee signed the release, waiving all claims against the employer in return for $6,258. She then filed an age discrimination complaint against the employer in a federal district court, alleging constructive discharge in violation of the ADEA and state law. The court granted the employer's summary judgment motion, ruling that she had ratified the defective release by retaining the severance pay. The U.S. Court of Appeals, Fifth Circuit, affirmed. The U.S. Supreme Court agreed to review the case.

The Court found that the lower courts had improperly relied on general contract principles in concluding that the employee's retention of the severance pay effectively waived the ADEA claim. The Court observed that the OWBPA amended the ADEA with specific statutory commands forbidding the waiver of an ADEA claim unless the statutory requirements are met. The Court reversed and remanded the case since the release did not comply with OWBPA standards and was unenforceable. The failure to tender back the severance pay award did not excuse the employer's failure to comply with the OWBPA. *Oubre v. Entergy Operations, Inc.*, 522 U.S. 422, 118 S.Ct. 838, 139 L.Ed.2d 849 (1998).

Congress exceeded its constitutional authority under the Fourteenth Amendment when it included state employees within the coverage of the ADEA. The Supreme Court found that Congress had no reason to believe that the states unconstitutionally discriminated against employees on the basis of age, making the contested amendment to the ADEA improper.

The ADEA prohibits employment discrimination against individuals because of their age. The Fair Labor Standards Amendments of 1974 extended the act's substantive requirements to the states. The U.S. Court of Appeals, Eleventh Circuit, consolidated three Florida cases filed against public employers and found that Congress did not effectively abrogate Eleventh Amendment immunity when it amended the ADEA. Two of the cases consolidated by the Eleventh Circuit involved actions by current and former university employees against public universities. The other case involved the Florida Department of Corrections. Noting a conflict among federal courts on the question of abrogation of Eleventh Amendment immunity, the Supreme Court agreed to hear the consolidated cases.

The court initially explained that the Eleventh Amendment prohibits federal suits against non-consenting states. Congress may abrogate state immunity only by making its intention unmistakably clear in statutory language, and only then as a valid exercise of constitutional authority. In this case, Congress had clearly stated its intent to abrogate Eleventh Amendment immunity by subjecting the states to potential liability for monetary damages in suits filed by individual employees. However, the court held that Congress lacked the power to do so when it amended the ADEA in 1974. Under the standard defined by *Seminole Tribe of Florida v. Florida*, 517 U.S. 44 (1996), Congress has no Article I commerce power to abrogate state immunity. Although Section 5 of the Fourteenth Amendment permits Congress to abrogate state immunity, this affirmative grant of power does not include the power to determine what constitutes a constitutional violation. The court has required a showing of a "congruence and proportionality" between the injury Congress seeks to prevent or remedy and the means adopted to achieve that end. Under the congruence and proportionality test, Congressional action will be struck down if it is out of proportion to a supposed remedial objective that cannot be understood as responsive to, or designed to prevent, unconstitutional behavior. Applying this test, the Supreme Court determined the ADEA as amended was not appropriate legislation under Section 5 of the Fourteenth Amendment, because its substantive requirements were found disproportionate to any perceived unconstitutional conduct by the states.

The Court previously held that age classifications do not violate the Equal Protection Clause. Unlike classifications based on race and gender, age classifications do not reflect prejudice or antipathy, and older persons have not been subjected to a history of purposeful or unequal treatment. Moreover, age classifications are presumptively rational, and states may discriminate on the basis of age without offending the Fourteenth Amendment, if the classification is rationally related to a legitimate state interest. The amended ADEA was out of proportion to its supposed remedial objective because it purported to prevent discrimination that was not protected by the Equal Protection Clause. The court characterized the legislative record of the ADEA as "an unwarranted response to a perhaps inconsequential problem." Congress identified no pattern of age discrimination by the states and had no reason to believe that state and local governments were unconstitutionally discriminating against their employees on the basis of age. Therefore, Congress exceeded its authority under the 14th Amendment when it included state employees within the coverage of the ADEA. *Kimel v. Florida Bd. of Regents*, 528 U.S. 62, 120 S.Ct. 631, 145 L.Ed.2d 522 (2000).

B. Procedural Issues

In a 1989 case, the Court decided that district courts have discretion in ADEA actions to facilitate notice to potential plaintiffs so long as they do not communicate any encouragement to join the suit or any approval of the suit's merits.

A company ordered a reduction in work force and discharged or demoted approximately 1,200 workers. One of the discharged employees filed an age discrimination charge with the Equal Employment Opportunity Commission for himself and all similarly situated employees. A group of affected employees brought suit under the ADEA, and sought discovery of the names and addresses of all similarly situated employees. They also requested that a court-approved consent document be sent out. A federal district court ordered the company to comply with the discovery request, and authorized the sending of consent documents. The U.S. Court of Appeals affirmed, and the U.S. Supreme Court granted review. The Supreme Court held that district courts have discretion in ADEA actions to facilitate notice to potential plaintiffs. As had the court of appeals, the Court declined to examine the terms of the notice used in this case. It noted that the district court was correct to permit discovery of the discharged employees' names and addresses. The Court stated, however, that trial courts have to be careful to maintain neutrality by avoiding even the appearance of endorsement of the merits of an action. The Court affirmed the lower court decisions and remanded the case. *Hoffman-La Roche, Inc. v. Sperling*, 493 U.S. 165, 110 S.Ct. 482, 107 L.Ed.2d 480 (1989).

Federal employees wishing to pursue an age discrimination claim under the ADEA may invoke the EEOC's administrative process or they may file a lawsuit. For a direct suit, employees must give the EEOC notice of their intent to sue at least 30 days before bringing suit, and the notice must be filed within 180 days of the alleged unlawful practice.

A 63-year-old man was accepted into a training program with the Internal Revenue Service (IRS). On April 26, 1987, the man was informed that his performance was not satisfactory. He requested a demotion and transfer so that he could avoid termination. The man felt that he had been a victim of age discrimination, and in September of 1987, attempted to gain relief through the Department of the Treasury. He also notified the IRS of an intent to sue if the matter was not resolved to his satisfaction. The appeal to the Department of the Treasury was dismissed because the man had not acted within 30 days of the employer's action. The man then appealed to the Equal Employment Opportunity Commission (EEOC) which upheld the dismissal. In May 1988, a lawsuit was filed in a federal district court. Again the man's claim was dismissed. The court held that the man could either proceed directly to federal court within 180 days of the employer's action and notify the EEOC within 30 days of bringing suit, or attempt to gain relief through the appropriate agency and bring suit only after an exhaustion of administrative remedies. The suit was brought more than 180 days after the employer's action, so the court determined that it was untimely. The man then appealed to the U.S. Court of Appeals, Fifth Circuit. That court held that the man was not required to bring suit within 180 days of the employer's action, but only needed to serve notice within that time. However, the dismissal was upheld because the man's notice to the EEOC was not within 30 days of his filing suit in a federal court. The case then reached the U.S. Supreme Court.

The Supreme Court ruled that the requirement of notice to the EEOC was incorrectly applied. Section 15(d) of 29 U.S.C. § 633a(d) allows a federal employee to proceed directly to federal court by serving notice of the alleged unlawful practice on the employer within 180 days, and requires only that the employee notify the EEOC of the employee's intent to sue not less than 30 days from when the suit is brought. The man had met this requirement. He had served notice to his employer within 180 days, and had filed suit more than 30 days after notifying the EEOC. The case was reversed and remanded for trial. *Stevens v. Dep't of the Treasury*, 500 U.S. 1, 111 S.Ct. 1562, 114 L.Ed.2d 1 (1991).

The Supreme Court has held that employers may compel arbitration with respect to an age discrimination claim if the procedures are adequate and the arbitration agreement is not the result of unequal bargaining power.

A corporation hired a middle-aged man as its manager of financial services. As required by his employer, he then registered as a securities representative with several stock exchanges, including the New York Stock Exchange (NYSE). In 1987, at the age of 62, the manager was discharged. He filed a claim with the Equal Employment Opportunity Commission, then brought suit in a North Carolina federal district court under the ADEA. His employer filed a motion to compel arbitration because NYSE Rule 347 provided for arbitration of any controversy arising out of employment or termination of employment. The district court denied the motion, holding that "Congress intended to protect ADEA claimants from the waiver of a judicial forum." The U.S. Court of Appeals, Fourth Circuit, reversed. The manager appealed to the U.S. Supreme Court. The Court stated that there was no inconsistency between the public policy behind the ADEA and enforcing agreements to arbitrate age discrimination claims. The ADEA was enacted with the idea of providing a flexible approach to claim resolution. Further, the manager failed to show that the arbitration procedures were inadequate. Since he failed to meet the burden of proving that Congress intended to preclude arbitration of claims under the ADEA, the Court held that the arbitration clause could be enforced. *Gilmer v. Interstate/Johnson Lane Corp.*, 500 U.S. 20, 111 S.Ct. 1647, 114 L.Ed.2d 26 (1991).

State administrative agency findings with respect to the ADEA which have not been judicially reviewed have no preclusive effect on federal proceedings.

A 63-year-old New York man was dismissed from his position as a vice president in the mortgage department of a bank. He filed an age discrimination claim with the Equal Employment Opportunity Commission, which referred the matter to the New York State Division of Human Rights. This agency found no probable cause to believe the employee was discharged due to his age, and the Human Rights Appeal Board affirmed that decision. The employee then brought suit in a federal district court under the ADEA rather than appealing the administrative decision in state court. The district court granted the employer's motion for summary judgment, holding that the agency determination precluded the claim in federal court. The U.S. Court of Appeals, Second Circuit, reversed, and further appeal was taken to the U.S. Supreme Court. The Court held that the state administrative proceedings did not preclude the ADEA suit in this case because they had not been judicially reviewed. Both § 626(d)(2) and § 633(b) of the ADEA assume the possibility of federal consideration after state agencies have finished examining the case. However, if state agency actions were given preclusive effect, federal proceedings would be a mere formality. The Court affirmed the reversal of summary judgment and remanded the case. *Astoria Federal Savings and Loan Ass'n v. Solimino,* 501 U.S. 104, 111 S.Ct. 2166, 115 L.Ed.2d 96 (1991).

Preserving a jury's role in deciding ultimate questions of fact, a unanimous U.S. Supreme Court held that the jury in an ADEA case did not need direct evidence of age discrimination to infer that the former employer intentionally violated the ADEA when it terminated an employee.

Roger Reeves worked for Sanderson Plumbing for 40 years before being terminated. Reeves filed suit under the ADEA, claiming the reason he was terminated was his age, 57. At trial, the company argued that it fired Reeves because he had failed to maintain accurate attendance records, but Reeves countered with evidence establishing that his record keeping was proper and, contrary to the company's assertions, he had never falsified any information. A jury agreed with Reeves, awarding him $98,000 in damages. On appeal, the Fifth Circuit concluded that the evidence was sufficient to show that Sanderson Plumbing's explanation for the termination was pretextual, but was not enough under *St. Mary's Honor Center v Hicks,* 509 U.S. 502 (1993), to prove intentional discrimination. Although Reeves introduced additional evidence that the person who fired him said he "was so old [he] must have come over on the Mayflower," and that he "was too damn old to do [his] job," those comments were not made in the context of termination and could not prove intent, the Fifth Circuit reasoned. For these reasons, the circuit court directed the district court to enter judgment in favor of Sanderson Plumbing.

On appeal, the Supreme Court concluded that once Reeves offered substantial evidence from which a jury could conclude that Sanderson Plumbing's explanation for the termination was not the real reason he was fired, the jury was then free to infer intentional discrimination and hold Sanderson liable. "Such an inference is consistent with the general principle of evidence law that the factfinder is entitled to consider a party's dishonesty about a material fact as 'affirmative evidence of guilt,'" Justice Sandra Day O'Connor wrote for a unanimous court. According to the Supreme Court, the appeals court wrongly confined its review of the verdict to derogatory age-related comments that Powe Chesnut, director of Sanderson's manufacturing operations and husband of owner Sandra Sanderson, made to Reeves and to evidence that Chesnut had singled Reeves out for harsher treatment than younger employees. The Fifth Circuit "believed that only this additional evidence of discrimination was relevant to whether the jury's verdict should stand," O'Connor wrote. "In so reasoning, the Court of Appeals misconceived the evidentiary burden borne by plaintiffs who attempt to prove intentional discrimination through indirect evidence." The Supreme Court disagreed, finding the court of appeals improperly discounted the record as a whole, ignoring critical evidence that Chesnut treated an employee who was substantially younger than Reeves more leniently and that even though two other company officials joined him in the termination recommendation, Chesnut wielded "absolute power" over all company decisions. *Reeves v. Sanderson Plumbing Products*, 530 U.S. 133, 120 S.Ct. 2097, 147 L.Ed.2d 105 (2000).

C. Mandatory Retirement

In 1976, the Supreme Court upheld a mandatory retirement law for state police officers against constitutional attack. The Court noted that age is not a "suspect class." As long as the law was rationally related to a legitimate governmental interest, it would be upheld.

A Massachusetts law required automatic retirement at the age of 50 for its uniformed state police officers. An officer who was automatically retired sued the state board of retirement in a federal district court, asserting that the law denied him equal protection. Four months before his retirement, he had passed a rigorous examination and he stated that he was still capable of performing the duties of a uniformed officer. The district court agreed with the officer that compulsory retirement at age 50 was irrational and violated equal protection. The board then was granted leave to appeal the case to the U.S. Supreme Court.

The Court first determined that the proper standard to use in deciding whether the law violated equal protection was the "rational basis" standard. So long as the law was rationally related to a legitimate state interest, the Court would uphold it as valid because officers over 50 are not a "suspect class" of persons requiring heightened judicial scrutiny. It then noted that the Massachusetts law was rationally related to a legitimate state interest because physical ability generally declines with age. Further, the state's needs in protecting the public outweighed the interests of the few officers who were still capable of performing their duties after age 50. Although the state could have chosen a more individualized means to determine fitness than an arbitrary cut-off at age 50, its law did not violate equal protection merely because it was not perfect. The Court reversed the district court's decision and upheld the mandatory retirement law. *Massachusetts Bd. of Retirement v. Murgia*, 427 U.S. 307, 96 S.Ct. 2562, 49 L.Ed.2d 520 (1976).

Three years later, the Court again upheld a mandatory retirement statute—this time for participants in the foreign service.

The U.S. Congress enacted a mandatory retirement age of 60 for participants in the foreign service retirement system. Employees covered by the civil service retirement system were not required to retire until age 70. A group of past and present foreign service employees sued in a federal district court, challenging the constitutionality of the classification requiring earlier retirement, and a special three-judge court was convened to hear the case. It held that the law was violative of equal protection and that no distinction should be made between civil service and foreign service employees. The government then sought review from the U.S. Supreme Court. The Supreme Court noted that so long as there was a rational basis for the law, it would be upheld, because foreign service personnel over age 60 were not members of a suspect class of people who required strict judicial scrutiny. The Court then determined that an earlier mandatory retirement furthered a legitimate governmental interest in two ways. First, it created incentives to morale and performance by assuring more predictable promotions. Second, it removed from service those who were too old for overseas duty. Even if the decision by Congress may not have been wise, Congress had chosen a rational means to achieve a legitimate end. The Court refused to find the law unconstitutional and reversed the district court's decision. *Vance v. Bradley*, 440 U.S. 93, 99 S.Ct. 939, 59 L.Ed.2d 171 (1979).

The ADEA, 29 U.S.C. § 621 *et seq.*, makes it unlawful for an "employer" to discharge any individual who is at least 40 years old because of such individual's age. In *EEOC v. Wyoming,* the Court held that the ADEA did not violate the U.S. Constitution by including states and political subdivisions of states in the term "employer."

A supervisor with the Wyoming Game and Fish Department was involuntarily retired at the age of 55 pursuant to a state law. He filed a complaint with the Equal Employment Opportunity Commission (EEOC), alleging that the state had violated the ADEA. The EEOC sued the state in federal court, but the suit was dismissed. The district court held that the ADEA violated the Tenth Amendment by regulating the state's employment relationship with its game wardens. The case was directly appealed to the U.S. Supreme Court. The Court held that the ADEA could lawfully be extended to cover state and local governments. Under the Commerce Clause, Congress could legislate to enforce compliance by the states with the ADEA. Here, the ADEA did not directly impair the state's ability to "structure integral operations in areas of traditional governmental functions." The degree of federal intrusion involved in this case was not sufficient to override Congress' choice to extend the ADEA to the states. If the state could show that age was a bona fide occupational qualification, it could still enforce a policy of mandatory retirement on its game wardens. The district court decision was reversed and the case was remanded. *EEOC v. Wyoming,* 460 U.S. 226, 103 S.Ct. 1054, 75 L.Ed.2d 18 (1983).

In the following case, the Court determined that the U.S. Court of Appeals had improperly interpreted the federal civil service statute when it ruled that age 55 was a bona fide occupational qualification for municipal firefighters.

Six Maryland firefighters brought suit in a federal district court to challenge the city of Baltimore's municipal code provisions that established a mandatory retirement age lower than 70 for firefighters and police personnel. They asserted that the provisions violated the ADEA, which prohibited employers from discriminating on the basis of age against employees between the ages of 40 and 70—the upper limit of 70 was removed by a 1986 amendment. The city maintained that age was a bona fide occupational qualification (BFOQ) for firefighters, and that it could thus require a lower retirement age. The district court found for the firefighters, but the U.S. Court of Appeals reversed.

On further appeal, the U.S. Supreme Court reversed. It held that even though the federal civil service statute established age 55 as the retirement age for federal firefighters, this did not mean that age 55 was a BFOQ for nonfederal firefighters. Congress had not determined that age was an employment qualification, but rather that it wished to maintain the image of a youthful work force by making early retirement attractive and financially rewarding. Thus, the court of appeals should not have given any weight to the civil service statute's provisions regarding retirement age. The case was remanded for further proceedings. *Johnson v. Mayor and City Council of Baltimore*, 472 U.S. 353, 105 S.Ct. 2717, 86 L.Ed.2d 286 (1985).

In 1985, the Supreme Court stated that the BFOQ exception to the ADEA's prohibition on age discrimination was intended to be extremely narrow. The age limit must be "reasonably necessary" to the safe performance of the job, not merely reasonable for the employer.

An airline company required all cockpit crew members (pilots, copilots and flight engineers) to retire at the age of 60. A Federal Aviation Administration regulation prohibited persons from serving as pilots or copilots after turning 60, but made no similar provision for flight engineers. A group of flight engineers, and pilots who wished to become flight engineers, sued the airline in federal court, contending that the mandatory retirement provision violated the ADEA. The airline defended by arguing that the age 60 limit was a bona fide occupational qualification (BFOQ) which was reasonably necessary to the safe operation of the airline. A jury held for the employees, and the U.S. Court of Appeals affirmed. The U.S. Supreme Court granted certiorari.

The Court stated that the BFOQ exception to the ADEA's prohibition on age discrimination was intended to be extremely narrow. The BFOQ standard, held the Court, is one of "reasonable necessity," not reasonableness. Thus, even if it was "rational" for the airline to set age 60 as the limit for flight engineers, the airline still had to show that it had reasonable cause to believe that all or substantially all flight engineers over 60 would be unable to safely perform their job duties, or that it would be highly impractical to deal with older employees on an individual basis to determine whether they had the necessary qualifications for the job. Because the airline had not shown this, the Court affirmed the lower courts' decisions in favor of the employees. *Western Air Lines, Inc. v. Criswell,* 472 U.S. 400, 105 S.Ct. 2743, 86 L.Ed.2d 321 (1985).

Appointed state judges can be compelled to retire at a specified age because they are not protected by the ADEA. The ADEA does not cover appointees at the policymaking level, which includes judges.

Four Missouri state judges filed suit in federal court, challenging the mandatory retirement provision of the Missouri Constitution under both the ADEA and the Equal Protection Clause. The court held that the judges were not protected by the ADEA because they were appointees on a policymaking level and thus excluded from the ADEA's definition of "employee." The court also held that the Equal Protection Clause was not violated by the provision. The U.S. Court of Appeals affirmed the district court's decision, and the case came before the U.S. Supreme Court. The Court noted that when Congress extended the ADEA's provisions to include the states as employers, it redefined "employee" to exclude all elected and most high-ranking state officials, including appointees at the policymaking level. Since the Court determined that judges were presumptively appointees at the policymaking level, they were not covered by the ADEA. Further, mandatory retirement did not violate the Equal Protection Clause because there was a rational basis for distinguishing 70-year-old judges from other state employees for whom no mandatory retirement applied. The Court affirmed the lower court decisions and upheld the mandatory retirement provisions. *Gregory v. Ashcroft*, 501 U.S. 452, 111 S.Ct. 2395, 115 L.Ed.2d 410 (1991).

V. DISABILITY DISCRIMINATION

Section 504 of the Rehabilitation Act, 29 U.S.C. § 794, prohibits discrimination against otherwise qualified individuals with disabilities solely because of their disabilities. In comparison, Title VI, 42 U.S.C. § 2000d *et seq.*, provides more limited protection because it only allows employment discrimination actions to be brought when the employer receives federal financial assistance primarily intended to provide employment.

A railroad employee, working as a locomotive engineer, was involved in an accident that required amputation of his left hand and forearm in 1971. After being disabled, the railroad allegedly refused to employ him without justification for finding him unfit to work. In 1979, he sued the railroad's successor in interest (Conrail) for violating § 504 of the Rehabilitation Act of 1973. That section provides that no otherwise qualified individual with a disability can be discriminated against solely because of his or her disability "under any program or activity receiving Federal financial assistance." A 1978 amendment to the act made available to such victims all the remedies set forth in Title VI of the Civil Rights Act. However, Title VI made employment discrimination actionable only when the employer received federal financial assistance "the primary objective of which [was] to provide employment."

A federal district court determined that the aid the government had given to Conrail did not have the primary objective of providing employment. The U.S. Court of Appeals reversed and remanded the case, finding that § 504 was not limited in the same way as was Title VI. On further appeal, the U.S. Supreme Court agreed with the court of appeals that the financial assistance extended to Conrail did not have to have the primary objective of providing employment in order for the employee to continue the suit. Further, the fact that the employee had died after the start of the suit did not make it moot, for his estate was still entitled to back pay if the discrimination was proven. The amendment had not been intended to add the primary objective requirement of Title VI into the Rehabilitation Act. Accordingly, the Court affirmed the court of appeals' decision and held that the lawsuit against Conrail could be maintained. *Consolidated Rail Corp. v. Darrone*, 465 U.S. 624, 104 S.Ct. 1248, 79 L.Ed.2d 568 (1984).

In the *Arline* case, the Supreme Court held that a person with a contagious disease could be considered a "handicapped individual" within the meaning of § 504 of the Rehabilitation Act.

In a Florida case, the U.S. Supreme Court held that a teacher with tuberculosis qualified for protection under the Rehabilitation Act. The case involved an elementary school teacher who was discharged because of the continued recurrence of tuberculosis. She sued the school board under § 504 but a federal district court dismissed her claims. However, the U.S. Court of Appeals, Eleventh Circuit, reversed the district court's decision and held that persons with contagious diseases fall within § 504's coverage. The school board appealed this decision to the U.S. Supreme Court.

The Supreme Court noted that the regulations implementing § 504 define an individual with a disability as "any person who (i) has a physical or mental impairment which substantially limits one or more major life activities, (ii) has a record of such impairment, or (iii) is regarded as having such an impairment." The regulations define "physical impairment" as a disorder affecting, among other things, the respiratory system and further define "major life activities" as "functions such as caring for one's self ... and working." Here, the teacher qualified as a person with a disability because her tuberculosis affected her respiratory system as well as her ability to work. Allowing discrimination based on the contagious effects of a physical impairment would be inconsistent with the underlying purpose of § 504. The Court remanded the case to the district court to determine whether the teacher was otherwise qualified for her job and whether the school board could reasonably accommodate her. *School Bd. of Nassau County v. Arline,* 480 U.S. 273, 107 S.Ct. 1123, 94 L.Ed.2d 307 (1987).

On remand, the district court held that the teacher was otherwise qualified to teach. The teacher posed no threat of transmitting tuberculosis to her students. The court observed that at the time she was on medication, medical tests indicated a limited number of negative cultures. Her family members tested negative and she had limited contact with students. The court ordered her reinstatement or a front-pay award of $768,724, representing her earnings until retirement. *Arline v. School Bd. of Nassau County*, 692 F.Supp. 1286 (M.D.Fla.1988).

In a case involving a student at the Merchant Marine Academy, the Supreme Court determined that the U.S. government has not waived its immunity against monetary damages for § 504(a) Rehabilitation Act violations.

A first-year student at the U.S. Merchant Marine Academy was diagnosed with diabetes. He was separated from the Academy on the grounds that his diabetes was a disqualifying condition. He filed suit in federal district court against the Secretary of the Department of Transportation and others, alleging that they violated § 504(a) of the Rehabilitation Act (Act). He requested reinstatement, compensatory damages, attorney's fees and costs. The district court granted the student summary judgment, finding that his separation from the Academy violated the Act, and ordered him reinstated. The government disputed the compensatory damages award, contending that it was protected by sovereign immunity. The district court found that the student was entitled to damages. Soon after, the U.S. Court of Appeals, District of Columbia Circuit, held in another case that the government had not waived its immunity against monetary damages for violations of § 504(a). The district court then vacated part of its prior decision and denied compensatory damages. The student appealed and the D.C. Circuit Court of Appeals granted the government's motion for summary judgment.

The U.S. Supreme Court granted certiorari to determine whether Congress has waived the government's sovereign immunity against monetary damage awards for violations of § 504(a). The Court found that a waiver of sovereign immunity must be clearly expressed in the statutory text. The Court found no such language in the text of § 504(a). The student argued that § 505(a)(2) of the Act states that the remedies set forth in Title VI of the Civil Rights Act of 1964 are "available to any person aggrieved by any act... by any recipient of Federal assistance or Federal provider of such assistance under [§ 504]." Because Title VI provides for monetary damages, the student claimed that read together, § 505(a)2 and § 504(a) establish a waiver of the government's immunity against monetary damages. The Court, however, found that this was not an unequivocal expression of a waiver of immunity. It also found that the Department of Transportation is not a provider of financial assistance to the Academy because it manages the Academy itself. Because there is no clear expression of the government's intent to waive its sovereign immunity, monetary damage awards are not allowed under § 504(a) of the Act. The court of appeals' decision was affirmed. *Lane v. Pena*, 518 U.S. 187, 116 S.Ct. 2092, 135 L.Ed.2d 486 (1996).

While § 504 of the Rehabilitation Act only applies to programs receiving federal funding, the Americans with Disabilities Act of 1990 (ADA) expands protection of individuals with disabilities to prohibit discrimination by both public and private employers. The ADA includes many of the same concepts as § 504 such as an employer's duty to provide reasonable accommodations to a disabled employee unless the accommodation would result in an undue hardship to the employer.

A Maine dentist examined an HIV-positive patient in his office and discovered that she had a cavity. He advised her that he maintained a policy against filling cavities of HIV-infected persons in his office, and offered to perform the work at a hospital. The patient filed suit in a federal district court against the dentist, alleging violations of the Americans with Disabilities Act (ADA), which prohibits discrimination against individuals with disabilities by a variety of service and public accommodations, including most employers. The court granted summary judgment to the patient, and the dentist appealed to the U.S. Court of Appeals, First Circuit, which affirmed. The court of appeals ruled that the patient's HIV was a disability even though it had not progressed to the symptomatic stage. Because of the patient's present lack of symptoms, the dentist's policy violated the ADA. The U.S. Supreme Court agreed to review the case and held that asymptomatic HIV is a physical impairment that substantially limits the major life activity of reproduction. Accordingly, the patient was disabled within the meaning of the ADA. The Court affirmed that portion of the judgment and remanded the case to the court of appeals for a determination of whether the patient's HIV infection posed a significant threat to the health and safety of others so as to justify the dentist's refusal to treat her in his office. *Bragdon v. Abbott,* 524 U.S. 624, 118 S.Ct. 2196, 141 L.Ed.2d 540 (1998).

The Supreme Court held that applying for and receiving Social Security disability benefits did not necessarily bar a person from suing for disability discrimination under the ADA. However, a benefits recipient cannot simply ignore her contention that she is too disabled to work.

A Texas employee suffered a stroke and applied for Social Security benefits, alleging that she was disabled and unable to work. When her condition improved, she returned to work and notified the Social Security Administration (SSA), which then denied her claim for benefits. However, her employer fired her less than a week later and she asked the SSA to reconsider the denial of benefits. She also sued her former employer in a Texas federal court for violating the Americans with Disabilities Act (ADA) by refusing to provide a reasonable accommodation that would allow her to perform her job.

A week later, the SSA granted her request for benefits. The court then granted pretrial judgment to the employer, reasoning that because she had asserted that she was disabled in her application for and receipt of Social Security benefits, she had conceded that she was totally disabled. As a result, she could not now claim that she could perform the essential functions of her job. The U.S. Court of Appeals, Fifth Circuit, affirmed the lower court's decision, and the case reached the U.S. Supreme Court.

The Supreme Court held that the pursuit and receipt of Social Security Disability Insurance benefits does not automatically bar a person from litigating a claim under the ADA. However, to survive a motion to dismiss, the person must present a sufficient explanation of the seeming contradiction that she is disabled under the Social Security Act while not disabled under the ADA. The Court noted that because the SSA does not take into account a reasonable accommodation when it determines whether a person is disabled for Social Security benefit purposes, qualifying for such benefits might not disqualify a person from suing under the ADA.

A person might qualify for Social Security benefits under SSA administrative rules and yet, due to special individual circumstances, remain capable of performing the essential functions of the job. Here, the employee had explained the discrepancy between her claim for Social Security benefits and her ADA claim that she could perform the essential functions of the position with the accommodation of training and additional time to do the job. As such, her claim should not have been dismissed at the pretrial stage. The Court also noted that American rules allow a person to plead alternatively where she is not sure under which theory she might succeed. It refused to apply a strong presumption against a recipient's ADA success. *Cleveland v. Policy Management Systems Corp.*, 526 U.S. 795, 142 L. Ed. 2d 30, 119 S.Ct. 1597 (1999).

The Supreme Court decided in the two cases below that the question of whether an impairment rises to the level of "substantially limiting" should be made with reference to the mitigating measures employed. This negates EEOC guidelines that assert otherwise.

In the first case, twin sisters with uncorrected vision of 20/200 or worse but corrected vision of 20/20 or better applied to United Air Lines for positions as global airline pilots. United rejected them because they did not meet its minimum requirement of at least 20/100 uncorrected vision. They sued under the ADA, asserting that United had discriminated against them because of their disability, or because it regarded them as disabled. A Colorado federal court dismissed their lawsuit, and the U.S. Court of Appeals, Tenth Circuit, affirmed.

On further appeal, the U.S. Supreme Court held that the sisters had not shown they were disabled under the ADA. First, because the ADA defines a disability as an impairment that "substantially limits" a major life activity, and because the sisters, with glasses or contacts, had 20/20 vision, they were not *presently* substantially limited as the statute required.

Second, the ADA requires disabilities to be evaluated on an individual basis. By following the EEOC guidelines to judge the sisters in their uncorrected state, United would have to generalize as to how an uncorrected impairment usually affects individuals. This would run directly counter to the ADA's mandated individualized inquiry. Also, if courts and employers could not consider mitigating effects, they could not consider the negative side effects of mitigating measures, even when such side effects were very severe. Third, because Congress had made a finding that 43 million people have one or more disabilities, it could not have intended to cover those people with corrected conditions. That number would be more than 160 million people.

The sisters had also failed to show that they were regarded as disabled by United. Even though it regarded them as unable to perform in the particular position of global airline pilot, it did not regard them as substantially limited in the major life activity of working. Other jobs were still available to them, including jobs such as regional pilots or pilot instructors. The Court stated that an employer does not necessarily violate the ADA by creating physical criteria for a job. The ADA allows employers to prefer some physical attributes over others so long as those attributes do not rise to the level of substantially limiting impairments. *Sutton v. United Air Lines, Inc.*, 527 U.S. 471, 119 S.Ct. 2139, 144 L.Ed.2d 450 (1999).

On the same day that it decided *Sutton*, the Court decided *Murphy*, a case involving a mechanic who was able to control his high blood pressure with medication.

The second case involved a mechanic for UPS who was fired after UPS discovered that he had high blood pressure. Even though he was able to control his condition with medication, he was not qualified for Department of Transportation health certification. As a result, he could not drive commercial motor vehicles, an essential job function for a mechanic at UPS. He sued UPS under the ADA, alleging disability discrimination, and also asserting that UPS regarded him as disabled. A Kansas federal court granted pretrial judgment to UPS, and the U.S. Court of Appeals, Tenth Circuit, affirmed. The case then reached the U.S. Supreme Court.

The Supreme Court held that under the ADA, the determination of whether a person's impairment substantially limits one or more major life activities should be made with reference to the mitigating measures he employs. In other words, because the mechanic's high blood pressure was controllable with medication, his condition did not substantially limit him in the major life activity of working. Thus, he was not disabled under the ADA. The Court also held that he was not regarded as disabled by UPS. Rather, he was regarded as unqualified to work in the single position of UPS mechanic because he could not obtain a DOT health certification. UPS did not regard him as substantially limited in a class of jobs or a broad range of jobs in various classes. Accordingly, his claims under the ADA could not succeed. *Murphy v. United Parcel Service, Inc.*, 527 U.S. 516, 119 S.Ct. 2133, 144 L.Ed.2d 484 (1999).

Where an employer rejects an employee who cannot meet federal safety standards, the employer cannot be held liable for disability discrimination.

A truck driver with monocular vision was fired because he did not meet the visual acuity standards of the Federal Motor Carrier Safety Regulations. Even though he received a waiver from the DOT under an experimental program, his employer refused to rehire him because he did not meet the basic DOT vision standards. He sued under the ADA. An Oregon federal court found that the driver was not otherwise qualified for the job with or without reasonable accommodation. The Ninth Circuit Court of Appeals reversed, and the case reached the U.S. Supreme Court.

The Supreme Court first noted that the driver was not necessarily disabled within the meaning of the ADA. Even though he had monocular vision, his brain had developed subconscious mechanisms for coping with his visual impairment. This was a mitigating measure (like glasses or medication) that had to be taken into account when determining whether he was substantially limited in one or more major life activities.

The Court then held that an employer who requires as a job qualification that an employee meet a federal safety regulation does not have to justify enforcing the regulation simply because the government has waived the safety standard experimentally in an individual case. Here, the employer was not enforcing standards that were different than the DOT standards. Rather, it was complying with the motor carrier safety regulations. Also, the waiver program did not modify the basic visual acuity standards so as to prohibit the employer from insisting that the standards be met. The Court reversed the appellate court's decision and ruled in favor of the employer. *Albertsons, Inc. v. Kirkingburg*, 527 U.S. 525, 119 S.Ct. 2162, 144 L.Ed.2d 484 (1999).

Congress exceeded its authority by allowing monetary damage awards against the states in Americans with Disabilities Act cases, according to the U.S. Supreme Court. The Court determined that Congress did not identify a history and pattern of irrational employment discrimination against individuals with disabilities by the states when it enacted the ADA, therefore, states are entitled to 11th Amendment immunity from ADA suits seeking money damages.

Two Alabama state employees alleged that they were discriminated against by their employers in violation of the ADA. One was a state university nursing director who was demoted upon her return from a medical leave to undergo treatment for breast cancer. The other was a youth services department security officer with chronic asthma and sleep apnea who alleged that the department refused to provide him with reasonable accommodations to mitigate the effects of his disabilities. They filed federal district court actions against the state for monetary damages under the ADA. The court consolidated the cases and granted summary judgment to the state.

The employees appealed to the U.S. Court of Appeals for the 11th Circuit, which reversed the district court judgment, and the state appealed to the Supreme Court, arguing that the ADA did not validly abrogate 11th Amendment immunity in lawsuits seeking monetary relief. The court explained that the 11th Amendment ensures that no state may be sued in a federal court without first consenting to be sued. However, Congress may abrogate this immunity where it does so unequivocally and under a valid grant of constitutional authority.

The Court analyzed the enforcement provisions of Section 5 of the 14th Amendment to the U.S. Constitution. It has held previously that legislation enacted under Section 5 must demonstrate "congruence and proportionality between the injury to be prevented or remedied and the means adopted to that end." In this case, there was no such congruence and proportionality. Congress identified negative attitudes and biases against individuals with disabilities as reasons for enacting the ADA, but did not identify a pattern of irrational discrimination by the states.

The information relied on by Congress in finding that, "historically, society has tended to isolate and segregate individuals with disabilities" included only a handful of examples dealing with discrimination by states. The court held that this limited evidence fell far short of showing a pattern of unconstitutional discrimination under Section 5 of the 14th Amendment. Since there was no pattern of unconstitutional behavior by the states, the ADA failed the "congruence and proportionality" test for 11th Amendment analysis. The Court held that Congress exceeded its authority to authorize suits for monetary damages under the ADA against the states, and reversed the 11th Circuit decision. *Board of Trustees of University of Alabama et al. v. Garrett et al.*, 531 U.S. 356, 121 S.Ct. 955, 148 L.Ed.2d 866 (2001).

VI. RELIGIOUS DISCRIMINATION

Employers must make reasonable efforts to accommodate the religious beliefs of their employees. However, they need not go beyond such good faith efforts. If the accommodation will cause an undue hardship, employers will not have to alter their policies for the benefit of such employees.

An employee of an airline belonged to a religion known as the Worldwide Church of God. It proscribed work from sunset Friday to sunset Saturday. Because of the employee's seniority, the airline was able to accommodate his religious beliefs until he transferred to a new position with low seniority. The airline agreed to permit the union to seek a change of work assignments, but it was unwilling to violate the seniority system. The airline then rejected a proposal that the employee work only four days a week, stating that this would impair critical functions in its operations. Eventually, the employee was discharged for refusing to work on Saturdays. He sued both the union and the airline under Title VII, claiming religious discrimination. A federal court ruled in favor of the defendants, and the U.S. Court of Appeals affirmed in part, holding that the airline did not satisfy its duty to accommodate the employee's religious needs. On appeal to the U.S. Supreme Court, it was held that the airline did make reasonable efforts to accommodate the religious beliefs of others. The Court reversed the court of appeals' decision and held in favor of the airline. *Trans World Airlines, Inc. v. Hardison*, 432 U.S. 63, 97 S.Ct. 2264, 53 L.Ed.2d 113 (1977).

States may not impose on employers an absolute duty to conform their business practices to the religious practices of their employees. An absolute duty would advance religion in violation of the Establishment Clause of the First Amendment.

An employee of a chain of New England retail stores managed a clothing department at a location in Connecticut. Although the store was closed by law on Sundays; when state law allowed, it began to keep Sunday hours. After working occasional Sundays for two years, the employee notified his employer that he would no longer work on that day because it was his Sabbath. A Connecticut law stated that employers could not require their employees to work on their Sabbath days, nor was refusal to work on the Sabbath to be deemed grounds for dismissal. The employer demoted the employee to a clerical position. He then resigned and filed a grievance administratively. He was found to have been discharged in violation of the statute, and a state trial court upheld that decision. The Connecticut Supreme Court reversed, and the case came before the U.S. Supreme Court.

The Court held that the Connecticut law violated the Establishment Clause of the First Amendment. Essentially, it imposed on employers an absolute duty to conform their business practices to the particular religious practices of their employees. Under this law, Sabbath religious concerns automatically controlled over all secular interests at the workplace. The primary effect of this law, then, was the advancement of religion, which is forbidden by the Establishment Clause. The Court affirmed the state supreme court's decision in favor of the employer. *Estate of Thornton v. Caldor, Inc.,* 472 U.S. 703, 105 S.Ct. 2914, 86 L.Ed.2d 557 (1985).

When teachers select an exclusive bargaining representative, they impliedly surrender a measure of their personal choice, including religious accommodation. This follows from the premise that the state has a strong interest in hearing only one voice in collective bargaining matters.

A Connecticut high school teacher belonged to a church that required its members to refrain from secular employment during designated holy days. This practice caused the teacher to miss approximately six school days each year for religious purposes. The teacher worked under terms of a bargaining agreement between the school board and his teachers' union that allowed only three days of leave for religious observation. The agreement also allowed leave for "necessary personal business" which could not be used for religious purposes. The teacher took either unauthorized leave for the extra three religious days he required, scheduled hospital visits on church holidays, or worked on those holidays. He repeatedly asked for permission to use three days of his "necessary personal business" leave for religious purposes. He also offered to pay for a substitute teacher if the school board would pay him for the extra days that he missed. These alternatives were rejected by the school board. When all administrative alternatives were exhausted, he filed a lawsuit alleging that the school board's policy regarding "necessary personal business" leave was discriminatory on the basis of religion. A U.S. district court dismissed the teacher's lawsuit and he appealed. The U.S. Court of Appeals, Second Circuit, said that the school board was bound to accept one of the teacher's proposed solutions unless "that accommodation causes undue hardship on the employer's conduct of his business."

The U.S. Supreme Court modified the appellate court's decision. It decided that the school district was not required to accept the teacher's proposals even if acceptance would not result in "undue hardship." The school board was only bound to offer a fair and reasonable accommodation of the teacher's religious needs. The bargaining agreement policy of allowing three days off for religious purposes was found to be reasonable. Because none of the lower courts had decided whether this policy had been administered fairly the case was remanded for a determination of that question. *Ansonia Bd. of Educ. v. Philbrook*, 479 U.S. 60, 107 S.Ct. 367, 93 L.Ed.2d 305 (1986).

Title VII employment restrictions do not apply to religious educational institutions. In a 1987 decision, the Court ruled that religious schools were free from Title VII's scope even when the job involved was nonreligious.

In a decision affecting private religious educational institutions, the U.S. Supreme Court ruled that such institutions may discriminate on the basis of religion in the hiring for nonreligious jobs involving nonprofit activities. The case involved a man who worked at a Mormon church-operated gymnasium for 16 years. After being discharged for failing to meet several church-related requirements for employment, he sued the church in a federal district court, alleging religious discrimination in violation of Title VII. The church moved for dismissal claiming that § 702 of Title VII exempted it from liability. The man claimed that if § 702 allowed religious employers to discriminate on religious grounds in hiring for nonreligious jobs, then Title VII would be in violation of the Establishment Clause of the First Amendment. The district court ruled for the man, and the church appealed directly to the U.S. Supreme Court.

The question before the Court was whether applying § 702 to the secular nonprofit activities of religious organizations violated the Establishment Clause. Section 702 provides that Title VII "shall not apply ... to a religious corporation, association [or] educational institution ... with respect to the employment of individuals of a particular religion to perform work connected with the carrying on by such [an organization] of its activities." In ruling for the church, the Supreme Court applied the three-part test set out in *Lemon v. Kurtzman. Lemon* requires first that a law serve a secular legislative purpose. Section 702 meets this test, said the Court, since it is a permissible legislative purpose to alleviate ... governmental interference with the ability of religious organizations to define and carry out their missions. The second test required that § 702 have a primary effect that neither advances nor inhibits religion. Section 702 meets that requirement since a law is not unconstitutional simply because it *allows* churches to advance religion, stated the Court. Section 702 does not violate the third part of the *Lemon* test because it does not impermissibly entangle church and state. The Supreme Court reversed the district court's decision and upheld the right of nonprofit religious employers to impose religious conditions for employment in nonreligious positions involving nonprofit activities. *Corporation of the Presiding Bishop of the Church of Jesus Christ of Latter-Day Saints v. Amos*, 483 U.S. 327, 107 S.Ct. 2862, 97 L.Ed.2d 273 (1987).

VII. RETALIATION

Title VII prohibits employment discrimination by employers with 15 or more employees during 20 or more calendar weeks in the current or preceding calendar year. An employer "has" an employee if an employment relationship exists between the parties.

Title VII of the Civil Rights Act of 1964, the federal government's primary antidiscrimination statute, prohibits employment discrimination by employers with 15 or more employees during 20 or more calendar weeks in the current or preceding calendar year. An employee of an Illinois educational materials company filed a sex discrimination complaint against her employer with the U.S. Equal Employment Opportunity Commission (EEOC), asserting that she should have received a promotion. The employer then fired her. The EEOC filed a federal district court action on behalf of the employee against the employer for unlawful retaliation under Title VII. The employer moved to dismiss the case, stating that it did not have 15 employees during 20 weeks in the past two years and did not come within the coverage of the act. The court agreed with the employer, and the U.S. Court of Appeals, Seventh Circuit, affirmed. The U.S. Supreme Court agreed to review the case.

On appeal, the employer argued that an employer "has" an employee for Title VII purposes only when it is actually compensating an individual on a particular working day. The EEOC argued that the appropriate test for when an employer has an employee is whether the parties have an employment relationship on the day in question. This test was already used by the EEOC in age discrimination regulations and the U.S. Department of Labor in Family and Medical Leave Act regulations. The Court agreed with the EEOC that an employer has an employee if an employment relationship exists between the parties. Applying this test, the employer had employment relationships with 15 or more employees for 38 weeks of the calendar year in question and was an employer within the meaning of Title VII. The Court reversed and remanded the case. *Walters v. Metropolitan Educational Enterprises, Inc.*, 519 U.S. 202, 117 S.Ct. 660, 136 L.Ed.2d 644 (1997).

In 1997, the Supreme Court held that Title VII protects former employees from retaliatory action by former employers.

Title VII of the Civil Rights Act of 1964 makes it an unlawful employment practice for an employer to discriminate against employees or employment applicants on the basis of several specified grounds. An oil corporation fired an African-American employee, who then filed a complaint against it with the U.S. Equal Employment Opportunity Commission (EEOC), which enforces Title VII employment complaints. While the charge was pending, the former employee applied for work with another company. When the company contacted the oil corporation for an employment reference, the corporation gave him a negative reference, which he believed was in retaliation for having filed the EEOC charge. The former employee sued the corporation in a federal district court for retaliatory discrimination under Title VII. The court dismissed the case, ruling that § 704(a) of Title VII does not protect the rights of former employees. The former employee appealed to the U.S. Court of Appeals, Fourth Circuit, which affirmed the district court decision. The U.S. Supreme Court agreed to review the case.

The Court found that § 704(a) was ambiguous because it made no reference to past or present employment status. However, other sections in Title VII used the term "employee" to describe more than just a current employee. Sections 706(g)(1) and 717(b) of Title VII applied to the reinstatement or hiring of an employee, necessarily including former employees. In order to be consistent with Title VII's broad scope, the Court construed § 704(a) as protecting former employees from retaliatory action by former employers. In doing so, it agreed with the EEOC that to exclude former employees from § 704(a) protection would undermine Title VII by allowing retaliation against victims of discrimination. This might give an incentive to employers to fire employees who brought EEOC complaints. The Court reversed and remanded the court of appeals' decision. *Robinson v. Shell Oil Co.*, 519 U.S. 337, 117 S.Ct. 843, 136 L.Ed.2d 808 (1997).

VIII. PROCEDURAL ISSUES

A. Equal Employment Opportunity Commission

In 1980, the Supreme Court held that the Equal Employment Opportunity Commission did not have to seek certification as the class representative to obtain class-wide relief because it acts in the public interest.

Four female employees of a telephone company filed charges with the Equal Employment Opportunity Commission (EEOC), complaining of sex discrimination in employment in the form of restrictions on maternity leave, access to craft jobs, and promotion to managerial positions. The EEOC found reasonable cause to suspect discrimination against women, and brought suit in a federal district court under Title VII. It sought injunctive relief and back pay for the women affected by the challenged practices. The EEOC did not seek class certification, and the employer then moved to dismiss the class action aspects of the complaint. After the court denied the motion, the U.S. Court of Appeals affirmed.

The U.S. Supreme Court held that the EEOC could seek class-wide relief under Title VII without being certified as the class representative. Even though the EEOC was acting for the benefit of certain, specific individuals here, it was also acting in the public interest by trying to prevent employment discrimination. Further, if the EEOC prevailed, those who claimed under the court's judgment could be required to relinquish their rights to bring a separate private action—thus preventing undue hardship to the employer and double recovery by individuals. The Court affirmed the appellate court's decision in favor of the EEOC. *General Telephone Co. of the Northwest v. EEOC,* 446 U.S. 318, 100 S.Ct. 1698, 64 L.Ed.2d 319 (1980).

The Title VII mandate against public disclosure of anything said or done during informal EEOC settlement endeavors does not include charging parties within the term "public." The EEOC can disclose information it obtains from employers to the persons who have lodged a complaint with the EEOC.

Title VII of the Civil Rights Act requires that employment discrimination charges not be made public by the EEOC, and also bars public disclosure of anything said or done during informal EEOC settlement endeavors. Seven department store employees filed employment discrimination charges with the EEOC, which requested employment records and other information relating to the store's personnel practices. The store refused to provide the information unless the EEOC agreed not to disclose it to the charging parties (whom the store maintained were part of "the public"). The EEOC refused to give this assurance. Eventually, the EEOC subpoenaed the material it needed. A federal district court held that the EEOC's limited disclosure practices were violative of Title VII. The court held that the EEOC could only obtain the material if it did not disclose the information obtained to the charging parties. The U.S. Court of Appeals affirmed.

On further appeal to the U.S. Supreme Court, the Court held that Congress did not mean to include charging parties within the "public" to whom disclosure of confidential information was illegal under Title VII. Limited disclosure could speed up the EEOC's investigation and enhance its ability to carry out its assigned function of resolving charges through informal conciliation and negotiation. Even if such disclosure sometimes encouraged litigation, this result was not inconsistent with Title VII's ultimate purposes of permitting a private right of action as an important part of the enforcement scheme. The Court reversed the lower courts' decisions. *EEOC v. Associated Dry Goods Corp.*, 449 U.S. 590, 101 S.Ct. 817, 66 L.Ed.2d 762 (1981).

A 1984 decision made clear that EEOC charges did not have to be extremely detailed; they merely had to give the employer fair notice of the existence and nature of the allegations against it.

An EEOC commissioner issued a sworn charge against an oil company, alleging that it had violated and continued to violate the Civil Rights Act of 1964 by discriminating against blacks and females in recruitment, hiring, selection, promotion and other terms and conditions of employment. The charge did not specify a date on which these unlawful employment practices began. When the employer was served with a copy of the charge, it refused to disclose records and data requested by the EEOC because it believed that the notice was factually insufficient to show a basis for the alleged violations. A federal district court enforced a subpoena against the company, but the U.S. Court of Appeals reversed.

On appeal to the U.S. Supreme Court, the Court found that the charge complied with regulatory requirements. It was in writing, under oath or affirmation, and contained "a clear and concise statement of the facts, including the pertinent dates, constituting the alleged unlawful employment practices." It gave the company fair notice of the existence and nature of the allegations against it. To require more would impose a substantive constraint on the EEOC's investigative authority. The Court reversed the court of appeals and ordered enforcement of the subpoena. *EEOC v. Shell Oil Co.*, 466 U.S. 54, 104 S.Ct. 1621, 80 L.Ed.2d 41 (1984).

When the EEOC issues a right-to-sue letter to a complainant, he or she is deemed to have received it when his or her attorney gets the letter.

After the Veterans Administration (VA) discharged one of its employees, the employee filed a complaint with the EEOC, alleging that he had been fired on the basis of his race and physical disability. The EEOC dismissed the employee's complaint, and issued a right-to-sue letter. His attorney's office received the letter on March 23, 1987; the employee claimed to have received the letter on April 7. When a lawsuit was brought on May 6, 44 days after the EEOC notice was received by the employee's attorney, the VA moved to dismiss because the complaint was not timely filed. Title VII provides that suits against the federal government must be brought within 30 days of receiving a right-to-sue letter. The federal court granted the motion, and the U.S. Court of Appeals affirmed. The U.S. Supreme Court granted a writ of certiorari.

The Supreme Court agreed with the lower courts that the employee's complaint was untimely. The receipt of the letter by the employee's attorney qualified as notice to the employee. Thus, it did not matter if he did not personally receive notice until April 7. Further, the employee's failure to file suit within 30 days of receipt of notice could not be excused by equitable tolling principles because he had not been misled into allowing the deadline to pass. At best, his failure to timely file was a "garden variety" claim of excusable neglect. The Court affirmed the dismissal of the suit. *Irwin v. Veterans Administration*, 498 U.S. 89, 111 S.Ct. 453, 112 L.Ed.2d 435 (1990).

The Equal Employment Opportunity Commission (EEOC) has the authority to order federal agencies to pay compensatory damages when they discriminate against federal employees.

The plaintiff filed a complaint with the Dept. of Veterans Affairs, claiming that the department had engaged in gender discrimination when it denied him a promotion. Although the department found against the employee, the EEOC subsequently found in his favor and awarded him the promotion and back pay. The district court dismissed the employee's claim on the grounds that he had not exhausted his administrative remedies. The department argued that the dismissal was correct because the employee failed to present his damages claim to the department and to the EEOC. The U.S. Court of Appeals, Seventh Circuit, reversed, finding that because the EEOC lacked the legal power to award compensatory damages, there was no administrative remedy to exhaust.

After reviewing the history and text of Title VII, the 1972 extension and the 1991 Compensatory Damages Amendment (CDA), the U.S. Supreme Court addressed the three arguments made by the department in favor of a more limited interpretation of the statute. First, the use of the word "action" in the statute should not be construed as limiting the recovery of compensatory damages to judicial proceedings. Second, the CDA does not implicitly forbid an EEOC award, in spite of the fact that 42 U.S.C. § 1981a(c) guarantees a jury trial. The court noted that one could interpret the jury trial provision in § 1981a(c) as meaning that either party was guaranteed a jury trial with respect to compensatory damages if a complaining party proceeded to court. Finally, the court stated that the statutory language, taken together with the statutory purposes, history and "absence of any convincing reason for denying the EEOC the relevant power," support a conclusion that the CDA waives the government's sovereign immunity with respect to an award of compensatory damages. *West, Secretary of Veterans Affairs v. Gibson,* 528 U.S. 803, 120 S.Ct. 297, 145 L.Ed.2d 27 (1999).

B. Judicial Action

A federal district court's order refusing to enter a consent decree equates to an order refusing an injunction and is appealable.

A class of present and former black employees and applicants sued an employer and two unions under 42 U.S.C. § 1981 and Title VII, alleging that the defendants had engaged in racially discriminatory employment practices. The parties negotiated a settlement and sought to enter a consent decree with a federal district court. The proposed decree would permanently enjoin the defendants from discriminating against black employees, and would force them to give certain preferences to blacks. The court refused to enter the decree because the defendants denied having discriminated in the past, and because there had been no showing of present or past discrimination. Further, the court stated that the decree could not be entered in any event because it would extend relief to all present and future employees rather than to just actual victims of discrimination. The U.S. Court of Appeals dismissed the appeal for want of jurisdiction on the ground that the district court's order was not appealable.

On further appeal, the U.S. Supreme Court held that the district court's interlocutory order refusing to enter the consent decree was "an order refusing an injunction and was therefore appealable." The order had the practical effect of refusing an injunction; accordingly, 28 U.S.C. § 1292 (a)(1) allowed the order to be appealed—partly because the order might have serious, perhaps irreparable consequences, and partly because the order could only be "effectually challenged" by an immediate appeal. This was because the plaintiffs could lose their opportunity to settle their case on the negotiated terms if the case went to trial and a final judgment was entered. The Court thus reversed the appellate court's decision. *Carson v. American Brands, Inc.*, 450 U.S. 79, 101 S.Ct. 993, 67 L.Ed.2d 59 (1981).

An employee's right to use statutory administrative procedures to adjudicate the lawfulness of a discharge is a property right protected by the Due Process Clause of the U.S. Constitution. That right cannot be defeated by an error on the part of a state administrative agency.

The Illinois Fair Employment Practices Act barred employment discrimination against individuals with disabilities where the disabilities were unrelated to ability to perform job requirements. To obtain relief under the act, a claimant had to file a charge of unlawful conduct within 180 days. The act then gave the state commission 120 days to convene a fact-finding conference. An Illinois company discharged a shipping clerk, purportedly because his short left leg made it impossible for him to perform his duties. He filed a timely charge with the state commission, but it inadvertently scheduled the fact-finding conference for 125 days later. The Illinois Supreme Court held that the failure to comply with the 120-day requirement deprived the commission of jurisdiction to consider the claimant's charge. The claimant appealed to the U.S. Supreme Court.

On appeal, the claimant argued that his due process and equal protection rights would be violated if the commission's error were allowed to extinguish his cause of action. The Court agreed, finding that the claimant's right to use the act's adjudicatory procedures was protected by the Due Process Clause. The claimant had been deprived of a protected property interest in violation of that clause by the failure of the commission to consider his claim. It was not enough for the claimant to be provided with a post-termination tort action. The state system involved here destroyed the claimant's opportunity to be heard by failing to convene a timely fact-finding conference. The Court also concluded that the claimant's equal protection rights had been violated by the state's action. The Court reversed and remanded the case. *Logan v. Zimmerman Brush Co.,* 455 U.S. 422, 102 S.Ct. 1148, 71 L.Ed.2d 265 (1982).

Where a state court has entered a judgment in a discrimination action brought by an employee, the employee will be barred from re-litigating the issues in a Title VII action in federal court. However, if only administrative remedies have been pursued, a Title VII lawsuit will not be barred.

A Polish Jew worked as an engineer for a New York construction company for two years until he was laid off. Several employees were rehired, but the engineer was not. He then filed a discrimination charge with the EEOC asserting that the action taken against him had been because of his national origin and his Jewish faith. The EEOC referred the charge to the New York State Division of Human Rights which rejected the claim as meritless. This decision was upheld on administrative appeal. On further appeal, the New York Supreme Court, Appellate Division, affirmed. Eventually, the engineer received a right-to-sue letter and he brought a Title VII action in federal court. The court dismissed the complaint on *res judicata* grounds. The U.S. Court of Appeals, Second Circuit, affirmed, and the U.S. Supreme Court granted certiorari.

The Supreme Court noted that 28 U.S.C. § 1738 requires federal courts to afford the same full faith and credit to state court judgments as state courts would. The district court had to give preclusive effect to the state court decision in favor of the employer. The Court stated that Title VII did not repeal § 1738. Even though an initial resort to state administrative remedies does not deprive a Title VII claimant of the right to a federal trial *de novo*, a prior state court judgment cannot be disregarded. Because the engineer had received a full and fair opportunity to litigate the merits of his case in state court, he had received sufficient due process to satisfy constitutional requirements. The Court affirmed the lower court decisions. *Kremer v. Chemical Construction Corp.*, 456 U.S. 461, 102 S.Ct. 1883, 72 L.Ed.2d 262 (1982).

In an action based upon a state civil rights enforcement agency's jurisdiction over a private school, the Supreme Court ruled that federal courts should permit the state agency proceedings to run their course.

An Ohio private school refused to renew the contract of a teacher after it discovered that she was pregnant, due to its belief that a mother should stay home with her young children. The teacher contacted an attorney and threatened the school with a lawsuit. The school rescinded its nonrenewal decision, but then terminated her employment because she had circumvented the school's internal grievance procedure. This, the school claimed, violated the "biblical chain of command." After the termination, the teacher filed a sex discrimination complaint with the Ohio Civil Rights Commission (OCRC). When the OCRC began its investigation of the complaint, the school sued in federal district court to prevent any action by the OCRC. The school based its arguments on the First

Amendment's guarantee of freedom of religion. The district court dismissed the complaint, but the U.S. Court of Appeals, Sixth Circuit, reversed the decision. The court of appeals stated that the OCRC investigation would impermissibly interfere with the practice of the school's religious beliefs.

On appeal to the U.S. Supreme Court, the district court's ruling was reinstated. The federal courts should be reluctant to interfere with a state administrative or judicial proceeding until the proceeding is completed. Further, the Supreme Court was unwilling to find that merely because an administrative body had jurisdiction over a religious school, the school's First Amendment rights would be violated. The OCRC was allowed to go forward with its investigation. *Ohio Civil Rights Comm'n v. Dayton Christian Schools*, 477 U.S. 619, 106 S.Ct. 2718, 91 L.Ed.2d 512 (1986).

The Court ruled in 1986 that a state administrative proceeding on a Title VII discrimination claim could be appealed to the federal court system when the state administrative proceeding remained unreviewed by state courts.

The University of Tennessee Agricultural Extension Service discharged a black employee, allegedly for inadequate work and misconduct on the job. The employee requested a hearing under the state Uniform Administrative Procedures Act to contest his termination. Before his administrative hearing took place, the employee also filed a claim in a U.S. district court under federal civil rights laws, alleging that his dismissal had been racially motivated. The district court entered a temporary restraining order halting the state administrative hearing, but it later allowed the hearing to go forward. The results of the hearing were that the dismissal had not been racially motivated. The university moved to dismiss the employee's federal court lawsuit because it had already been resolved in the administrative hearing. The district court agreed and dismissed the case, holding that it would not afford the employee a chance to relitigate the same case in federal court. The U.S. Court of Appeals, Sixth Circuit, reversed the decision and allowed the employee's case to remain in federal court. The university appealed the decision to the U.S. Supreme Court, which held that the employee's case should be heard by the district court. The Court ruled that a state administrative proceeding on a Title VII claim that was not reviewed by a higher state board could be heard in federal court. Since the administrative hearing was not reviewed by the state courts, it had no preclusive effect. The employee had the right to introduce his claim anew. *Univ. of Tennessee v. Elliot*, 478 U.S. 788, 106 S.Ct. 3220, 92 L.Ed.2d 635 (1986).

The Supreme Court held that federal courts have discretion to remand a case which has been removed from state court back to state court if remand would best accommodate the values of economy, convenience, fairness and comity.

A private university employee sued the university in a Pennsylvania trial court, claiming that the school had violated the federal Age Discrimination in Employment Act (ADEA). He also brought state law claims for wrongful discharge, breach of contract and other violations. The case was removed from state court to a U.S. district court because the alleged violation of the ADEA gave federal court jurisdiction over the entire lawsuit. The employee then discovered that the federal claim could not be successful because he had failed to file a timely age discrimination charge with a federal or state agency. He requested that the federal claim be deleted and that the case be remanded to the Pennsylvania trial court in which it was filed. The U.S. district court granted this request. The university then requested that the U.S. Court of Appeals, Third Circuit, order the U.S. district court not to remand the case to the state court. The court of appeals denied that request and the university asked the U.S. Supreme Court to review that decision.

The Supreme Court noted that when a case is removed from state to federal court because it contains a federal claim, the federal court can exercise jurisdiction over the entire case, including claims arising under state law. The federal and state law claims must arise from the same "operative facts." In cases where the federal claim is dropped from the lawsuit after removal, a federal court has discretion to dismiss the case and let the plaintiff start over again in state court. The question in this case, however, was whether the federal court had discretion to remand the case to the state court, thereby preserving state law claims that would otherwise be lost if state statutes of limitation had run before the plaintiff could file the case in state court. The Supreme Court asserted that the legal doctrine concerning cases in which state law claims reach federal court because they are coupled with a federal claim "is designed to enable courts to handle cases involving state-law claims in the way that will best accommodate the values of economy, convenience, fairness and comity." The court concluded that federal courts therefore had discretion to remand a case which had been removed from state court back to state court if such action would best accommodate these values. The Supreme Court ruled that the employee's case could be remanded to the Pennsylvania trial court in which it was originally filed. *Carnegie-Mellon Univ. v. Cohill*, 484 U.S. 343, 108 S.Ct. 614, 98 L.Ed.2d 720 (1988).

The Supreme Court has ordered a private university to allow access to peer review materials for the purpose of determining whether an individual has been discriminated against.

The University of Pennsylvania, a private institution, denied tenure to a female associate professor. The professor filed a charge with the EEOC alleging discrimination based on race, sex and national origin in violation of Title VII of the Civil Rights Act of 1964. During its investigation, the EEOC issued a subpoena seeking disclosure of the professor's tenure review file and the tenure files of five male faculty members identified as having received more favorable treatment. The university refused to produce a number of documents and asked the EEOC to modify the subpoena to exclude "confidential peer review information." The EEOC refused and successfully sought enforcement of its subpoena through a federal district court. The U.S. Court of Appeals, Third Circuit, affirmed and rejected the university's claim that policy considerations and the First Amendment principles of academic freedom required recognition of a qualified privilege or the adoption of a balancing approach that would require the EEOC to demonstrate a need to obtain peer review materials. The U.S. Supreme Court then agreed to hear the case.

The Supreme Court held that a university does not enjoy a special privilege requiring a judicial finding of necessity prior to access of peer review materials. The Court was reluctant to add such a privilege to protect "academic autonomy" when Congress had failed to do so in Title VII. The Court also stated that "academic freedom" could not be used as the basis for such a privilege. The university's assertion that the quality of instruction and scholarship would decline as a result was too speculative. The Court affirmed the lower court decisions. *Univ. of Pennsylvania v. EEOC,* 493 U.S. 182, 110 S.Ct. 577, 107 L.Ed.2d 571 (1990).

C. Statute of Limitations

Generally, a complainant must file a discrimination charge with the EEOC within 180 days of the occurrence of the alleged unlawful employment practice. That time period is extended to 300 days if the complainant initially institutes proceedings with a state or local agency empowered to grant or seek relief from the practice charged. After filing a charge with a state or local agency, a complainant must wait 60 days to file a charge with the EEOC unless the agency's proceedings have been terminated earlier.

A corporation discharged a senior marketing economist. Two-hundred-ninety-one days later, the economist sent the EEOC a letter in which he asserted that he had been discriminated against because of his religion. However, since New York had a law prohibiting such practices, no charge could be filed with the EEOC before the expiration of 60 days after state agency proceedings had been commenced. The EEOC notified the appropriate state agency, then made a determination that there was no probable cause to believe the charge. It issued a right-to-sue letter to the employee. The employee sued, but the case was dismissed as untimely because the unfair employment practice charge had not been "filed" within 300 days as required by law (291 days plus 60 days equals 351 days). The U.S. Court of Appeals, Second Circuit, reversed the dismissal, and the U.S. Supreme Court agreed to hear the case.

The Supreme Court reversed the court of appeals' decision, holding that the charge had not been timely filed. The EEOC could not allow the charge to be filed on the day it received the letter (291 days after the discrimination); it had to wait 60 days to do so. By then, the 300-day limitation period had run, and the lawsuit could not continue. This result was mandated by clear congressional policy that all employment discrimination charges be promptly processed. *Mohasco Corp. v. Silver,* 447 U.S. 807, 100 S.Ct. 2486, 65 L.Ed.2d 532 (1980).

In a 1980 employment case brought under Title VII, the Court concluded that the statute of limitations began to run on the date the teacher was denied tenure, rather than on his final employment date.

A black Liberian teacher taught at a state-supported Delaware college that was attended predominantly by blacks. The faculty committee on tenure recommended that he not be given tenure, and the college faculty senate and board of trustees adhered to this recommendation. The teacher then filed a grievance with the board's grievance committee, which took the case under advisement. The college offered him a one-year "terminal contract" in accordance with state policy. After the teacher had signed the terminal contract without objection, the grievance committee denied his grievance. The teacher then attempted to file a complaint with the EEOC. However, he was notified that he would first have to exhaust state administrative remedies if he wanted to file a claim under Title VII of the 1964 Civil Rights Act. After the appropriate state agency waived its jurisdiction, the EEOC issued a right-to-sue letter. The teacher then filed a lawsuit in a federal district court, alleging that the college had discriminated against him on the basis of his national origin in violation of Title VII and 42 U.S.C. § 1981. The district court dismissed the teacher's claims as untimely because the Title VII complaint was not filed with the EEOC within 180 days and the § 1981 claim had not been filed in federal court within three years. The U.S. Court of Appeals, Third Circuit, reversed, holding that the limitations on Title VII and § 1981 did not begin to run until the teacher's terminal contract expired. It reasoned that a terminated employee should not have to file suit until termination had actually occurred. The U.S. Supreme Court granted certiorari.

The Court reversed the court of appeals' decision and reinstituted the district court's finding that both the Title VII and § 1981 claims were untimely. It held that statutes of limitations exist to ensure that plaintiffs promptly assert their rights and to protect employers from the burden of defending stale actions. The teacher's complaint did not state that the college discriminated against him on the basis of national origin, it concentrated on the college's denial of tenure. The teacher had failed to make out a *prima facie* case of employment discrimination under Title VII, because he had stated no continuing violation of his civil rights. The Court noted that, in fact, the teacher had received essentially the same treatment accorded to other teachers who were denied tenure. The statute of limitations began to run when the teacher was denied tenure, specifically, on the date the college had offered him a terminal contract. As the district court was correct in that holding, the Court upheld its decision. *Delaware State College v. Ricks*, 449 U.S. 250, 101 S.Ct. 498, 66 L.Ed.2d 431 (1980).

Where an employee files a Title VII lawsuit alleging discrimination, but fails to file a timely charge with the EEOC, the courts will still have jurisdiction to decide the case. The requirement of a timely filing is subject to waiver or estoppel, but it is not a jurisdictional prerequisite.

An airline followed a policy of grounding all female flight attendants who became mothers. Males who became fathers were permitted to continue flying. The union representing the flight attendants then brought a class action suit against the airline in federal court, asserting that it violated Title VII. After the union was found to be an inadequate representative, individual class members were appointed. The district court granted summary judgment to the plaintiff class, but the U.S. Court of Appeals held that the claims of most of the members of the class were barred by their failure to timely file charges with the EEOC. Settlement proceedings were then entered into whereby retroactive seniority was granted to the subclass who had not timely filed. The district and appellate courts approved the settlement, and the U.S. Supreme Court granted review.

The challenge to the settlement was that the timely filing of an EEOC charge was a jurisdictional prerequisite to bringing a Title VII lawsuit. The Supreme Court disagreed, finding that the filing of a timely charge was not a jurisdictional prerequisite; it was merely a requirement that was subject to waiver, estoppel and equitable tolling, much like a statute of limitations. Accordingly, the suit had properly been brought before the district court. Next, the Court held that the district court had the authority to award retroactive seniority to the members of the subclass who had not timely filed with the EEOC. Despite the union's objection that awarding retroactive seniority contrary to the collective bargaining agreement was improper where it had not been found guilty of discrimination, the Court held that such relief could be awarded. This was an appropriate remedy. The Court reversed in part and affirmed in part the lower court decisions. *Zipes v. Trans World Airlines, Inc.*, 455 U.S. 385, 102 S.Ct. 1127, 71 L.Ed.2d 234 (1982).

Title VII, at 42 U.S.C. § 2000e-5(f)(1), provides that the recipient of a right-to-sue letter from the EEOC has 90 days in which to file a complaint (commence an action). If the recipient waits more than 90 days to bring suit, the suit will generally be dismissed.

On November 6, 1979, an Alabama woman filed a complaint with the EEOC alleging that she had been treated in a discriminatory manner. The EEOC investigated her complaint, finding no probable cause to proceed, and issued her a right-to-sue letter on January 27, 1981. She was informed that she had 90 days in which to file suit. She mailed the right-to-sue letter to a federal district court and requested the appointment of counsel. The court mailed her an application for court-appointed counsel, which she did not complete and return until the 96th day after receiving the EEOC's letter. The court then ruled that the employee had forfeited her right to pursue her claim under Title VII because of her failure to file a "complaint" within 90 days of receiving the right-to-sue letter. The U.S. Court of Appeals reversed, holding that the filing of the letter with the district court tolled the time period provided for by Title VII. The employer appealed to the U.S. Supreme Court.

On appeal, the Court agreed with the district court that the employee's filing of the right-to-sue letter did not amount to the filing of a "complaint." A complaint must contain "a short and plain statement of the claim showing that the pleader is entitled to relief." To allow the filed letter to serve as a complaint would be to give Title VII actions a special status under the Rules of Civil Procedure. The Court could find no satisfactory basis for doing so. Further, the Court noted that the employee had received adequate notice of her obligation to file a complaint within 90 days. She had been told three times what she had to do to preserve her claim and she had failed to do what was required. The Court reversed the court of appeals' decision. *Baldwin County Welcome Center v. Brown*, 466 U.S. 147, 104 S.Ct. 1723, 80 L.Ed.2d 196 (1984).

A state law that established a procedure for the administrative resolution of employment discrimination complaints was held not to provide the appropriate statute of limitations for actions brought under the Civil Rights Acts. The administrative period provided was too short for all the practical difficulties facing an aggrieved person.

Coppin State College, a predominantly black college in Maryland, employed a white male and a white female in its minority affairs office. Their primary responsibility was to recruit students of diverse ethnic backgrounds to attend the school. In June 1976, the employees were notified that their contracts would not be renewed because the college was not satisfied with their recruitment efforts. They filed complaints of racial discrimination with the EEOC, and eight months after being notified of the nonrenewal of their contracts, they sued the college and various officials, eventually amending their complaint to allege causes of action under 42 U.S.C. §§ 1981, 1983, 1985 and 1986, among other claims. The defendants removed the action to a federal district court, then sought to dismiss the case on statute of limitations grounds. The district court granted the motion to dismiss, borrowing the six-month limitations period contained in a Maryland statute (which established a procedure for the administrative resolution of employment discrimination complaints). The U.S. Court of Appeals reversed, and the case came before the U.S. Supreme Court.

The Supreme Court affirmed the court of appeals' decision, finding that the district court should have applied Maryland's three-year statute of limitations for all civil actions for which a statutory limitation period was not otherwise provided. The six-month administrative period was too short for all the practical difficulties facing an aggrieved person under the Civil Rights Acts. The administrative scheme was set up with different goals (the prompt identification, conciliation and private settlement of employment disputes) than those of the Civil Rights Acts. The Court held that the lawsuit had been timely filed. *Burnet v. Grattan*, 468 U.S. 42, 104 S.Ct. 2924, 82 L.Ed.2d 36 (1984).

In 1987, the Supreme Court held that 42 U.S.C. § 1981 has a much broader focus than contractual rights. Since it does not contain a statute of limitations, and the most appropriate or analogous state statute of limitations should be selected, the state limitations period governing personal injury actions is the one that ought to be used.

In 1973, individual employees of a steel company brought suit against their employer and their collective bargaining agents, asserting racial discrimination claims under Title VII and 42 U.S.C. § 1981. The federal district court held that the six year statute of limitations governing contract claims was the appropriate limitation period to be applied in § 1981 claims. It further held that both the employer and the agents had discriminated in certain respects. On appeal to the U.S. Court of Appeals, Third Circuit, it was held that Pennsylvania's two year statute of limitations governing personal injury actions was the more proper limitations period to apply. The finding of liability against the employer and the agents was affirmed.

The U.S. Supreme Court granted certiorari and affirmed the Third Circuit's ruling. It noted that § 1981 actions related to more than just personal rights to contract; § 1981 also speaks to rights to sue and testify, and acts to secure equal rights under all laws for the security of persons and property. The Court then noted that the lower courts had properly found both the agents and the employer to have violated Title VII and § 1981. There had been more than mere passive acquiescence by the unions in the employer's acts of discrimination. The unions had deliberately chosen not to process grievances by African-Americans. *Goodman v. Lukens Steel Co.*, 482 U.S. 656, 107 S.Ct. 2617, 96 L.Ed.2d 572 (1987).

In 1988, the Court held that a state agency's decision to waive its exclusive 60-day period for the initial processing of a discrimination claim (under a work-sharing agreement with the EEOC) amounts to a termination of agency proceedings so as to allow the EEOC to immediately begin processing the charge.

A Colorado woman filed a charge of discrimination with the EEOC, alleging that, 290 days earlier, a commercial office products company discharged her because of her sex in violation of Title VII. The EEOC sent a copy of the charge to the Colorado Civil Rights Division (CCRD), but pursuant to a work-sharing agreement, undertook the initial charge processing—the CCRD waived its right to initially process the charge; however, it retained jurisdiction to act on the charge after the conclusion of the EEOC proceedings. When the company refused to comply with the EEOC's administrative subpoena, a federal district court ruled that the EEOC lacked jurisdiction because the charge had not been filed within the 300-day period required by Title VII. The U.S. Court of Appeals affirmed, and the case came before the U.S. Supreme Court.

The Supreme Court first noted that if the CCRD's decision to waive its exclusive 60-day period for the initial processing of claims was a "termination" of agency proceedings, then the EEOC could immediately deem the charge filed and begin to process it (the charge would be timely because only 290 days would have elapsed). However, if the waiver was not a "termination," the charge was not timely filed (because the 60-day deferral period plus the 290 days already elapsed equaled well over 300 days). The Court then decided that the waiver was a termination because the CCRD stated that it would not proceed, if at all, before the conclusion of the EEOC proceedings. Next, the Court held that, even though the charge was untimely under state law (which granted only 180 days to file), it was timely under federal law. Accordingly, the Court reversed the lower court decisions and remanded the case. *EEOC v. Commercial Office Products Co.*, 486 U.S. 107, 108 S.Ct. 1666, 100 L.Ed.2d 96 (1988).

The following case has been overturned by the 1991 Civil Rights Act. Now, even if an employer's discriminatory rule was adopted years earlier, there will be no statute of limitations problem if an employee is subjected to it at a later time. The statute will begin to run from the time of the last discriminatory act.

Under a collective bargaining agreement (CBA), seniority at a corporation was determined by years of plant-wide service. However, in 1979, under a new CBA, the manner of computing seniority was changed so that employees promoted to higher positions would have their seniority tested as of the date of promotion. Subsequently, as a result of this new system, three women were selected for demotion during an economic downturn; they would not have been demoted under the old system. They sued after receiving right-to-sue letters from the Equal Employment Opportunity Commission, but a federal district court granted summary judgment to the employer. They appealed unsuccessfully to the U.S. Court of Appeals, and further appealed to the U.S. Supreme Court.

The Supreme Court held that a seniority system having a disparate impact on men and women is not unlawful unless discriminatory intent is proven. Here, the system did not discriminate on its face or as it was applied; thus, it could only be held discriminatory if it was enacted with a discriminatory intent. However, if it had been adopted with a discriminatory intent, the statute of limitations had run in the years since the CBA had been signed. The Court affirmed the decision in favor of the employer. *Lorance v. AT&T Technologies, Inc.,* 490 U.S. 900, 109 S.Ct. 2261, 104 L.Ed.2d 961 (1989). The 1991 Civil Rights Act states that the statute of limitations under Title VII will begin to run not just when the employer's rule is adopted, but also whenever an individual is subjected to it, and whenever a person is aggrieved by the rule's application.

D. Attorneys' Fees and Prejudgment Interest

1. Attorneys' Fees

The Supreme Court has determined that Title VII authorizes the awarding of attorneys' fees to prevailing plaintiffs for work done in state administrative and judicial proceedings.

A woman applied for a position as a waitress at a club, but was informed that no position was available. She filed a charge with the Equal Employment Opportunity Commission (EEOC), alleging that the club and its manager had denied her a position because of her race. After an investigation in which the woman was represented by counsel, an administrative determination was made that the club had discriminated against the applicant; it was ordered to hire her and pay back wages. The EEOC then issued a right-to-sue letter to the woman, and she brought suit seeking, among other things, attorneys' fees. A federal court denied her request for attorney's fees, but the U.S. Court of Appeals reversed. The case reached the U.S. Supreme Court.

The Court held that Title VII authorized a federal court action to recover an award of attorney's fees for work done by the prevailing complainant in state administrative and judicial proceedings to which she was referred by Title VII. The language "any action or proceeding" (in Title VII) indicated an intent to subject the losing party to an award of costs and attorney's fees for administrative proceedings as well as for court cases. Even though the state did not authorize such fees here, federal law overrode any interest the state might have in not authorizing the fees. The Supreme Court affirmed the appellate court's decision.

New York Gaslight Club, Inc. v. Carey, 447 U.S. 54, 100 S.Ct. 2024, 64 L.Ed.2d 723 (1980).

Section 1983 claimants who prevail in federal court proceedings are entitled to attorneys' fees under 42 U.S.C. § 1988. However, § 1983 claimants are not entitled to fees for administrative hearings (as they would be in Title VII lawsuits).

A black elementary school teacher was fired by a Tennessee school board in 1974, following complaints by white parents that he had administered corporal punishment to their children. He retained an attorney to help fight what he felt was a racially motivated dismissal. After four years of administrative proceedings, the board finally decided not to rehire him. He then sued in federal court under § 1983 of the Civil Rights Act, alleging racial discrimination. A U.S. district court in Tennessee ordered the teacher reinstated and awarded him $15,400 in damages. The teacher then filed a motion with the court to collect the cost of his attorney's fees from the board. He sought to collect $21,165, based on an hourly rate of $120. This included the time his attorney spent in representing him before the school board in administrative hearings. The district court awarded the teacher only $9,734 and the U.S. Court of Appeals, Sixth Circuit, affirmed. The case was appealed to the U.S. Supreme Court.

The Supreme Court upheld the lower court decisions and ordered the board to pay the attorney's fees for the teacher's federal court proceedings but not the costs of the administrative proceedings before the board. Because the lawsuit had been filed under § 1983 of the Civil Rights Act, the teacher was entitled to attorneys' fees only for court proceedings. The Court stated that if the teacher had filed suit under Title VII of the Civil Rights Act he would have received attorneys' fees for all stages of the proceedings, including his numerous appearances before the school board. *Webb v. Bd. of Educ. of Dyer County*, 471 U.S. 234, 105 S.Ct. 1923, 85 L.Ed.2d 233 (1985).

In the following case, the Court held that attorneys' fees cannot be awarded against intervenors in Title VII cases (who are not charged with violating Title VII) unless the intervention is frivolous, unreasonable or without foundation.

A group of female flight attendants brought a class action suit against an airline, claiming that its policy of discharging flight attendants who became mothers constituted sex discrimination which violated Title VII. Eventually, a settlement agreement was reached in which class members would be credited with full company and union "competitive" seniority. At this point, the flight attendants' bargaining agent intervened in the lawsuit on behalf of incumbent flight attendants who would be adversely affected by the seniority relief. When this challenge was rejected, the group of female flight attendants sought an award of attorneys' fees under 42 U.S.C. § 2000e–5(k). The federal court awarded fees to the group, and the U.S. Court of Appeals affirmed.

On further appeal, the U.S. Supreme Court held that, with respect to intervenors who are not charged with Title VII violations, attorneys' fees may only be awarded against them where their action is frivolous, unreasonable, or without foundation. Even though the purpose of the attorneys' fees provision of Title VII is to provide victims of wrongful discrimination with an incentive to file suit, assessing such fees against blameless intervenors is not essential to that purpose. Accordingly, the Court reversed the lower courts' decisions and remanded the case for a determination as to whether the intervention had been frivolous. *Independent Federation of Flight Attendants v. Zipes*, 491 U.S. 754, 109 S.Ct. 2732, 105 L.Ed.2d 639 (1989).

2. Prejudgment Interest

The "no-interest rule" essentially provides that the government cannot be compelled to pay interest in a suit brought against it absent an express waiver. Even though § 706(k) of Title VII makes the United States liable for costs the same as a private person sued under Title VII, this does not expressly waive the government's immunity from interest.

A black employee of the Library of Congress filed three complaints with the library's equal employment office. His complaints were rejected. Eventually, his attorney negotiated a settlement wherein the employee was to be promoted retroactively with back pay on the condition that the Comptroller General (CG) make a determination that the library had authority to do so absent a specific finding of discrimination. When the CG ruled that the library lacked such authority, the employee sued under Title VII. A federal district court determined that Title VII authorized such relief. The court then awarded attorneys' fees to the employee and increased the "lodestar" amount (a reasonable number of hours times a reasonable rate) by 30 percent to compensate the attorney for the delay in receiving payment. The U.S. Court of Appeals affirmed, and the case then reached the U.S. Supreme Court.

The Supreme Court noted that the "no-interest rule" provides that interest cannot be recovered in a suit against the government in the absence of an express waiver of sovereign immunity from an award of interest. Here, the no-interest rule applied so as to preclude the award of increased compensation to the employee's attorney. Even though the United States is liable under Title VII "the same as a private person," the immunity from interest is not waived by this provision. The government is merely liable for costs, including a reasonable attorney's fee. The Court reversed the appellate court's decision and remanded the case. *Library of Congress v. Shaw*, 478 U.S. 310, 106 S.Ct. 2957, 92 L.Ed.2d 250 (1986).

Title VII authorizes prejudgment interest awards as part of the back pay remedy in suits against private employers. In the case below, the Court determined that the Postal Service, like any other "private" employer, could be held liable for prejudgment interest because of the Postal Reorganization Act.

The Postal Service discharged a male employee who brought suit against it, contending that his firing was the result of sex discrimination in violation of Title

VII. A federal district court held for the employee, ordering reinstatement and back pay, but it refused to award prejudgment interest. The U.S. Court of Appeals affirmed the denial of prejudgment interest, finding that Congress had not waived the Postal Service's sovereign immunity with respect to Title VII prejudgment interest. The U.S. Supreme Court granted review. The Court held that prejudgment interest may be awarded in a suit brought under Title VII against the Postal Service. By virtue of the 1970 Postal Reorganization Act, which included a "sue and be sued" clause and launched the Postal Service into the commercial world, Congress made the Service like any other business with respect to liability. Since Title VII authorizes interest, and since the Postal Service's immunity had been waived, the Court reversed the lower court decisions and remanded the case. *Loeffler v. Frank,* 486 U.S. 549, 108 S.Ct. 1965, 100 L.Ed.2d 549 (1988).

E. Retroactivity

In a pair of cases on the issue of retroactivity, the Supreme Court held that the Civil Rights Act of 1991 did not apply to Title VII and § 1981 cases pending on appeal when the statute was enacted.

A female employee at a Texas plant operated a machine that produced plastic bags. A fellow employee repeatedly harassed her with inappropriate remarks and physical contact. Her complaints to her immediate supervisor resulted in no relief, but when she reported the incidents to the personnel manager, he conducted an investigation, reprimanded the other employee, and transferred him to another department. Four days later the employee quit her job. She filed a charge with the Equal Employment Opportunity Commission, which determined that she had likely been the victim of sexual harassment creating a hostile work environment in violation of Title VII, but concluded that her employer had adequately remedied the violation. It issued a notice of right to sue. She then sued her employer alleging constructive discharge. A federal district court found that she had been sexually harassed, but held that her employment was not terminated in violation of Title VII; thus, she was not entitled to equitable relief. Also, because Title VII did not then authorize any other form of relief, the court dismissed her complaint. While her appeal was pending, the Civil Rights Act of 1991 became law. Section 102 of that act included provisions that created a right to recover compensatory and punitive damages for intentional discrimination violative of Title VII. The act also allowed for a trial by jury if such damages were sought. The U.S. Court of Appeals affirmed the district court decision and rejected the employee's argument that her case should be remanded for a jury trial on damages under § 102.

On further appeal to the U.S. Supreme Court, it was held that § 102 did not apply to a Title VII case that was pending on appeal when the 1991 act was enacted. The Court reasoned that because the president had vetoed a 1990 version of the act partly because of perceived unfairness in the bill's elaborate retroactivity provision, it was likely that the omission of comparable language in the 1991 act was a compromise that resulted in passage of the act. Here, the Court found that the new statute would impair the rights that employers possessed and increase their liability for past conduct or impose new duties with respect to transactions already completed if it was given retroactive effect. The Court affirmed the decision against the employee. *Landgraf v. U.S.I. Film Products,* 511 U.S. 244, 114 S.Ct. 1483, 128 L.Ed.2d 229 (1994).

In another retroactivity case, the Supreme Court held that § 101 of the Civil Rights Act of 1991, which defines § 1981's "make and enforce contracts" phrase to embrace all phases and incidents of the contractual relationship, also did not apply to a case that arose before it was enacted. In this case, two garage mechanics were discharged and brought suit alleging that the firings had been because of their race in violation of 42 U.S.C. § 1981. Their claims were dismissed because of the decision in *Patterson v. McLean Credit Union,* 491 U.S. 164, 109 S.Ct. 2363, 105 L.Ed.2d 132 (1989), which held that § 1981 did not apply to conduct which occurred after the formation of a contract and which did not interfere with the right to enforce established contract obligations. While their appeal was pending, the Civil Rights Act of 1991 became law. Section 101 of the act provided that § 1981's prohibition against racial discrimination in the making and enforcement of contracts applied to all phases and incidents of the contractual relationship, including discriminatory contract terminations. The U.S. Court of Appeals ruled that § 1981 as interpreted in *Patterson* governed the case. The Supreme Court affirmed this decision for essentially the same reasons as set forth in *Landgraf* and denied retroactive application of the act. *Rivers v. Roadway Express, Inc.,* 511 U.S. 298, 114 S.Ct. 1510, 128 L.Ed.2d 274 (1994).

CHAPTER TWO

Employee Benefits

I. PENSION BENEFITS

A. Generally

The Employee Retirement Income Security Act (ERISA) 29 U.S.C. § 1001 *et seq.*, allows the contracting parties to a pension agreement to determine the content or amount of benefits that, once vested, cannot be forfeited. ERISA is more an administrative and enforcement statute than one which sets substantive standards about the kinds of benefits that must be provided.

Retired employees in New Jersey, who had received workers' compensation benefits after retiring, challenged in state court the validity of provisions in their employers' pension plans that reduced their pension benefits by the amount of workers' compensation they were owed. The plans were subject to ERISA. After the lawsuits were removed to federal court, it was held that the pension offset provisions were invalid under a New Jersey statute and under ERISA. However, the U.S. Court of Appeals, Third Circuit, reversed after consolidating the appeals. The U.S. Supreme Court granted certiorari.

The Supreme Court held that Congress contemplated and approved the kind of pension provisions being challenged here. Despite the fact that vested rights cannot be forfeited, ERISA leaves it to the contracting parties to determine the content or amount of benefits that, once vested, cannot be forfeited. Accordingly, ERISA did not prohibit the offset which the employers had bargained for in this case. Next, the Court held that the New Jersey statute that barred such offsets was preempted by ERISA because it eliminated one method of calculating pension benefits—integration or setoff—that was permitted by federal law. The Court affirmed the court of appeals' decision in favor of the employers. *Alessi v. Raybestos-Manhattan, Inc.*, 451 U.S. 504, 101 S.Ct. 1895, 68 L.Ed.2d 402 (1981).

Section 4044(a) of ERISA provides for the orderly distribution of plan assets. Under § 4044(a), plan administrators must first distribute nonforfeitable benefits guaranteed by the Pension Benefit Guaranty Corporation, then distribute all other nonforfeitable benefits, and finally distribute all other benefits under the plan. Remaining funds may be recouped by the employer. Section 4044(a), however, does not create additional benefit entitlements; thus, it did not require "contingent early retirement benefits" to be distributed prior to recoupment.

A corporation sold a subsidiary and terminated the retirement plan which was funded by the employer and covered by ERISA. As a single-employer plan, all accrued benefits automatically vested. The corporation paid out the benefits that had vested, including unreduced early retirement benefits to those employees who met both the age (62) and years of service (30) requirements. A group of employees who did not meet both requirements sued the corporation because it recouped nearly $11 million; they maintained that it was first required to distribute contingent early retirement benefits, even if unaccrued, before recouping plan assets. A federal district court ruled for the corporation, the U.S. Court of Appeals reversed, and the case came before the U.S. Supreme Court. The Court held that the section of ERISA under which this lawsuit was brought did not create benefit entitlements, but merely provided for the orderly distribution of plan assets. However, since there were two alternative sections of ERISA that could potentially lead to a recovery by the employees, the Court remanded the case. *Mead Corp. v. Tilley,* 490 U.S. 714, 109 S.Ct. 2156, 104 L.Ed.2d 796 (1989).

Section 206(d)(1) of ERISA, 29 U.S.C. § 1001 *et seq.*, states that each ERISA pension plan must require "that benefits provided under the plan may not be assigned or alienated." Although there are certain enumerated exceptions, Congress intended generally to bar the alienation or garnishment of ERISA pension plan benefits.

One of the trustees of a sheet metal workers' pension fund embezzled over $375,000 from the union. Two pension plans contended that the trustee had forfeited his right to receive benefits as a result of his criminal misconduct. They also asserted that even if he had not forfeited his benefits, those benefits should be paid to the union, and not to him. A federal district court held that because there was a judgment against the trustee for $275,000, a constructive trust should be imposed on the trustee's benefits until the judgment was paid off. The U.S. Court of Appeals affirmed, and certiorari was granted by the U.S. Supreme Court.

The Court held that the constructive trust violated the prohibition on assignment or alienation of pension benefits called for by ERISA. Here, although the trustee had stolen money from the union, he had not stolen money from the pension funds. Even if the Labor-Management Reporting and Disclosure Act authorized the imposition of a constructive trust when a union officer breached his fiduciary duties, that did not override ERISA's anti-alienation provision. ERISA reflected a congressional policy choice to safeguard a stream of income for pensioners even if that prevented others from obtaining relief for the wrongs done them. The Court reversed the lower courts' decisions and remanded the case. *Guidry v. Sheet Metal Workers National Pension Fund,* 493 U.S. 365, 110 S.Ct. 680, 107 L.Ed.2d 782 (1990).

In the following case, the Supreme Court held that the language, structure and purpose of ERISA demonstrated a congressional intent to preempt a state common law claim that an employee was unlawfully discharged to prevent his attainment of benefits under an ERISA plan.

A Texas man worked for a company as a salesman and distributor of construction equipment. Four months before his pension would have vested, the employee was fired during a reduction in force. He sued the company in state court for wrongful discharge, alleging that a principal reason for his termination was the company's desire to avoid contributing to his pension fund. The trial court granted summary judgment to the employer, the Texas Court of Appeals affirmed, and the case reached the Texas Supreme Court. That court reversed, finding that ERISA did not preempt the employee's lawsuit, and that the employee could recover against the company if he could show that his employer's principal reason for terminating him was its desire to avoid paying benefits. The company then sought review from the U.S. Supreme Court.

The Supreme Court found that the employee's claim was expressly preempted by ERISA. Here, for the employee to prevail on his claim, the court below would have to find that an ERISA plan existed and that the employer had a pension-defeating motive in terminating the employment. Since this "related" to an ERISA plan, it was preempted. Only federal courts could hear this type of case. The Supreme Court reversed the Texas Supreme Court's decision. *Ingersoll-Rand Co. v. McClendon*, 498 U.S. 133, 111 S.Ct. 478, 112 L.Ed.2d 474 (1990).

ERISA allows plan participants to enforce the substantive provisions of the Act. Participants are defined as employees or former employees of an employer who are or may become eligible to receive a benefit of any type from an employee benefit plan. In the case below, the Court determined that, where the question was whether the complainant was an employee, the courts should use traditional agency law principles to ascertain the answer.

An insurance company agreed to enroll an agent in a company retirement plan. In accordance with the terms of the contract, the agent agreed to sell insurance policies of that company exclusively. Additionally, the contract terms stated that the agent would forfeit his retirement benefits if, within a year of his termination and 25 miles of his prior business location, he sold insurance for competitors of the insurance company. The company exercised its contractual right to terminate its relationship with the agent. Within a month, the agent sold insurance policies for several competitors from his old office. The company reacted with the charge that his new business activities disqualified the agent from receiving his retirement plan benefits. The agent sued under ERISA. A federal district court found for the agent and the U.S. Court of Appeals affirmed. The insurance company appealed to the U.S. Supreme Court.

On appeal, the Court noted that the agent's ERISA claim could succeed only if he was an employee. ERISA's definition of "employee" is "any individual employed by an employer," a definition the Court found circular and unhelpful. Consequently, the Court suggested assessing and weighing all of the elements of an employment relationship, including: the location of the work, the duration of the relationship between the parties, the method of payment, and the provision of employee benefits, among others. The Court reversed and remanded for a determination of whether the agent qualified as an "employee" under traditional agency law principles. *Nationwide Mutual Ins. Co. v. Darden*, 503 U.S. 318, 112 S.Ct. 1344, 117 L.Ed.2d 581 (1992).

An employer may condition the receipt of early retirement benefits upon a waiver of employment claims by plan participants without violating § 406 of ERISA.

An aircraft manufacturer rehired an employee who had left to work for a competitor earlier in his career. He was 61 years old at the time of reemployment and excluded from participation in the employer's retirement plan because of his age. When Congress amended ERISA to disallow age-based exclusions in 1979, the manufacturer amended the plan. Employees previously excluded on the basis of age were allowed to participate in the plan, but without credit for service prior to plan enrollment. The manufacturer then offered two programs encouraging early retirement. Acceptance of early retirement benefits was expressly conditioned on the waiver of any employment-related claims. The employee retired without seeking such benefits. Instead, he filed a claim against the employer and plan in a federal district court, seeking an order that they violated their duty of care under ERISA and engaged in a prohibited transaction by funding the early retirement plan with surplus plan assets. The court determined that the early retirement programs violated ERISA because they offered increased benefits in exchange for the release of employment claims, and held that the 1979 amendments to ERISA applied retroactively. On appeal, the U.S. Court of Appeals, Ninth Circuit, affirmed. The U.S. Supreme Court agreed to review the case.

The Court held that the inducement of early retirement through waivers such as that used by the manufacturer did not violate ERISA. Plan sponsors who amend plans when acting in their capacity as employers are not fiduciaries under ERISA. The Court held that because the plan amendments were enacted in an employer capacity, the manufacturer was under no ERISA fiduciary duty and not liable under the act. The payment of benefits in exchange for a waiver did not constitute a prohibited transaction within the meaning of ERISA. In reversing the lower court judgments, the Court also held that the age discrimination amendments to ERISA could not be retroactively imposed. *Lockheed Corp. v. Spink*, 517 U.S. 882, 116 S.Ct. 1783, 135 L.Ed.2d 153 (1996).

Although ERISA supersedes inconsistent state laws relating to any employee benefit plan, ERISA only protects survivor annuity plan participants and their beneficiaries. Also, ERISA requires that every qualified joint and survivor annuity include an annuity payable to a nonparticipant surviving spouse that is not less than 50 percent of the lifetime annuity.

The Retirement Equity Act of 1984 protects surviving spouses of participants in survivor's annuity plans qualified under ERISA. It allows plan participants to designate a beneficiary other than the participant's spouse only where the spouse agrees. A Louisiana telecommunications employee with a wife and three sons participated in several ERISA-qualified retirement plans. Following the death of his wife, the employee remarried. Upon his death several years later, his sons submitted claims against his estate based upon the first wife's will for his undistributed retirement benefits, including a savings plan, an employee stock ownership plan, and a survivor's annuity. A federal district court held that the sons were entitled to a share of the retirement benefits based upon Louisiana community property law. The U.S. Court of Appeals, Fifth Circuit, affirmed the decision and the U.S. Supreme Court agreed to review the case.

The Court stated that ERISA supersedes inconsistent state laws relating to any employee benefit plan but protects only plan participants and their beneficiaries. The sons were not plan beneficiaries and their claims were based upon the first wife's will and conflicting state law. ERISA requires that every qualified joint and survivor annuity include an annuity payable to a nonparticipant surviving spouse that is not less than 50 percent of the lifetime annuity. The surviving spouse was entitled to receive the survivor's annuity since she had not waived her rights or consented to the designation of the sons as beneficiaries. The surviving spouse was also entitled to the stock shares and the savings plan proceeds since the claims of the sons were based upon community property law and were inconsistent with ERISA's anti-alienation provision. *Boggs v. Boggs*, 520 U.S. 833, 117 S.Ct. 1754, 138 L.Ed.2d 45 (1997).

1. Fiduciary Duties

Section 502(a)(3) of ERISA permits plan participants to bring civil actions to obtain "appropriate equitable relief" for violations of ERISA or of the plan. However, the Supreme Court has held that § 502(a)(3) does not authorize suits for money damages against nonfiduciaries who knowingly participate in a fiduciary's breach of duty.

A class of former employees of the Kaiser Steel Corporation who participated in the company's retirement plan brought suit for the plan's losses against a nonfiduciary that knowingly participated in the plan's fiduciaries' breach of their duties. The plan was qualified under ERISA. The nonfiduciary was the plan's actuary in 1980 when Kaiser began to phase out its steelmaking operations, prompting early retirement by a large number of plan participants. The nonfiduciary did not, however, change the plan's actuarial assumptions to reflect the additional costs imposed by the retirements. As a result, Kaiser did not adequately fund the plan. Eventually the plan's assets became insufficient to satisfy the benefit obligations and the plan was terminated. The former employees then began receiving only the benefits guaranteed by ERISA, which were substantially lower than the fully vested pensions due them under the plan. After a federal district court and the U.S. Court of Appeals, Ninth Circuit, dismissed the complaint, the former employees appealed to the U.S. Supreme Court.

ERISA § 502(a)(3) permits plan participants to bring civil actions to obtain "appropriate equitable relief" to redress violations of the plan. The Court determined that requiring the nonfiduciary to make the plan whole for the losses it sustained would not constitute "appropriate equitable relief." What the employees were seeking here was compensatory damages, not "equitable relief." The Supreme Court determined that the text of ERISA indicated that Congress intended equitable relief to include only those types of relief that were typically available in equity, such as injunction, mandamus, and restitution. Accordingly, the Supreme Court affirmed the lower courts' decisions and dismissed the complaint. *Mertens v. Hewitt Associates,* 508 U.S. 248, 113 S.Ct. 2063, 124 L.Ed.2d 161 (1993).

An insurer was held to be subject to the fiduciary obligations of ERISA with respect to "free funds" in the following 1993 case. The Court held that the free funds were plan assets (for which the insurer had a fiduciary responsibility) until they became guaranteed benefits.

The U.S. Supreme Court ruled that the guaranteed benefit policy exclusion in ERISA does not cover funds administered by an insurer that bear no fixed rate of return and have yet to be converted into guaranteed funds. At issue were part of the funds of a group annuity contract (GAC). The contract was between the insurer and a bank acting as trustee for a corporate retirement plan. Under the contract, the deposits to secure retirement benefits were not immediately applied to the purchase of annuities. Instead, these "free funds" were commingled with the insurer's general corporate assets. In this manner, the deposit account balances reflected the insurer's overall investment experience. During the life of the contract, amounts credited to the deposit account could be converted into a stream of guaranteed benefits for individual employees. The trustee asserted that the insurer was managing "plan assets" and was therefore subject to a fiduciary responsibility as mandated by ERISA. The insurer countered that its actions fell within the statutory exclusion for "guaranteed benefit policies."

The Court began its analysis by determining that ERISA preempted state insurance law in this instance. Though the Court agreed with the insurer that the McCarran-Ferguson Act (M-F Act) reserved to the states primary responsibility for regulation of the insurance industry, it noted that ERISA did not order an unqualified deferral to state law. The M-F Act mandates that only laws specifically relating to the business of insurance may supersede state insurance laws. The Court then noted that ERISA, both in general and in guaranteed benefit policy provisions in particular, specifically relates to the business of insurance. ERISA controlled in this instance and it specifically preempted "all state laws" insofar as they related to any employee benefit plan.

However, the guaranteed benefit policy exception excludes from the scope of ERISA's fiduciary requirements assets held pursuant to "an insurance policy or contract to the extent that such policy or contract provides for benefits the amount of which are guaranteed by the insurer." The Court determined that GAC fit this statutory exclusion only in part. Problematic was the insurer's responsibility for administration of the "free funds." The Court concluded that the insurer's fiduciary responsibility applied to the extent that it engaged in the discretionary management of assets attributable to that phase of the contract which provided no guarantee of benefit payments or fixed rates of return. Congress exempts "an insurance policy or contract to the extent that such policy or contract" provides for guaranteed benefits. In applying this analysis to GAC, the Court determined that the part of GAC which consists of annuities would be exempt but that the "free funds" would not be. Hence, each component of the contract had to be examined to determine its exemption and in this instance the insurer had a fiduciary responsibility with respect to the "free funds" until they became guaranteed benefits. *John Hancock Mutual Life Ins. Co., v. Harris Trust and Savings Bank*, 510 U.S. 86, 114 S.Ct. 517, 126 L.Ed.2d 524 (1993).

The Supreme Court held that ERISA did not allow liability for an existing ERISA judgment to be imposed against a third party. Thus, a federal court lawsuit against an officer/shareholder of a corporation that had breached its fiduciary duties could not stand.

A former employee of a closely-held corporation claimed that the corporation and a corporate officer/shareholder violated ERISA by failing to properly administer the corporation's employee pension plan. The former employee filed a federal action against the corporation and the officer/shareholder, obtaining a judgment of $187,000 against the corporation. The former employee was unable to collect on his judgment, even though the shareholder/officer continued to take cash out of the corporation as a favored creditor. After an unsuccessful appeal to a federal circuit court, the former employee filed a new federal lawsuit against the corporate officer, stating that he had engaged in a civil conspiracy to siphon assets from the corporation to prevent satisfaction of the ERISA judgment. The court agreed, and allowed the employee to collect his judgment from the officer. The U.S. Court of Appeals, Fourth Circuit, affirmed, and the officer appealed to the U.S. Supreme Court.

The Court stated that ERISA contains no authority for imposing liability for an existing ERISA judgment against a third party. The complaint in this case did not allege any ERISA violation and the alleged wrongdoing occurred four to five years after termination of the plan itself. There were no independent grounds for a federal court to exercise jurisdiction in this case under a corporate veil-piercing argument. There was also no merit to the former employee's argument that a federal court could exercise jurisdiction over the matter as factually interdependent with and related to the prior lawsuit. The Court found that the claim in this case had no factual or logical interdependence upon the prior suit and failed to allege substantive ERISA violations. Because the case was based on theories of relief that did not exist, the district court lacked jurisdiction to hear it and the lower court decisions were reversed. *Peacock v. Thomas*, 516 U.S. 349, 116 S.Ct. 862, 133 L.Ed.2d 817 (1996).

The Supreme Court held that an employer could use the surplus from a defined benefit pension plan to provide early retirement benefits for current employees. Such action did not infringe on the rights of retirees whose individual contributions had grown, partially accounting for the surplus.

An aircraft manufacturer doing business in Arizona and California established a "defined benefit" pension plan for its employees in 1951. By 1986, plan assets exceeded the value of accrued plan benefits by almost one billion dollars. Even though the plan was funded by both employer and employee contributions, the employer ceased its contributions to the plan and used part of the surplus to fund a separate early retirement plan for current employees. A group of retired participants in the pension plan filed a California federal district court action against the employer and plan, asserting violations of ERISA. The court dismissed the lawsuit, and the participants appealed to the U.S. Court of Appeals,

Ninth Circuit. The Ninth Circuit reversed the district court's decision, holding that the employer's actions violated ERISA.

The case then came before the U.S. Supreme Court, which noted that the retirees, as members of a defined benefit plan, had no interest in the plan's surplus. This was so despite the fact that the plan surplus was partially attributable to the investment growth of the retirees' contributions. *Defined benefit plan* members have a nonforfeitable right to accrued benefits, and the employer is responsible for any shortages. By the same token, the employer is entitled to any windfall produced by the plan. Had this been a *defined contribution plan*, the retirees would have been entitled to whatever assets were dedicated to their accounts, and the employer could not have used the plan surplus to provide early retirement benefits to current employees. Because no fiduciary duty existed to prohibit the plan's amendment, the Court reversed the court of appeals' decision and held for the employer. *Hughes Aircraft Co. v. Jacobson*, 525 U.S. 432, 119 S.Ct. 755, 142 L.Ed.2d 881 (1999).

2. Discrimination

The Supreme Court upheld a grandfather provision in the Railroad Retirement Act which gave greater retirement benefits to a certain class of employees. Because the discrimination was the result of the phasing out of certain benefits, and because the law was rationally related to the governmental interest of saving money, it was valid.

The 1974 Railroad Retirement Act contained a grandfather provision whereby railroad employees who had qualified for dual benefits (from railroad retirement and social security) by the time of the changeover would be able to get the dual benefits while certain nonqualifying employees were unable to reap such dividends. A class action suit was filed wherein the legislation was challenged as violative of the Due Process Clause of the Fifth Amendment. A federal district court held that the legislation was unconstitutional because the distinction between employees was not rationally related to legitimate governmental interests. The U.S. Supreme Court granted review of the issue.

The Supreme Court held that the legislation was valid. It was permissible for Congress to draw lines between groups of employees for the purpose of phasing out these benefits; Congress could have eliminated windfall benefits for all classes of employees. Also, Congress could legitimately determine that persons who had acquired statutory entitlement to windfall benefits and who were still employed in the railroad industry had a greater equitable claim to those benefits than the nonqualifying plaintiffs who did not have a "current connection" to the railroad industry. Accordingly, the Court reversed the district court's decision and upheld the law. *United States Railroad Retirement Bd. v. Fritz*, 449 U.S. 166, 101 S.Ct. 453, 66 L.Ed.2d 368 (1980).

In 1978, the Supreme Court held that Title VII prohibited an employer from requiring women to make larger pension contributions than men (to receive the same benefits) despite the fact that women generally live longer than men. *City of Los Angeles Dep't of Water v. Manhart*, 435 U.S.

702, 98 S.Ct. 1370, 55 L.Ed.2d 657 (1978), Chapter One, section II.A. Five years later, the Court held that Title VII also prohibited employers from offering retirement benefit packages that paid women lower monthly benefits than men.

Beginning in 1974, the state of Arizona offered its employees the opportunity to enroll in a deferred compensation (or voluntary pension) plan. The state selected several private companies to participate in the plan. However, all the companies used sex-based mortality tables to calculate monthly retirement benefits. As a result, women were paid lower monthly benefits than men who had made the same contributions due to the fact that women generally live longer than men. A group of female employees brought a class action suit to challenge the constitutionality of the plan. A federal district court granted summary judgment to the plaintiffs, and the U.S. Court of Appeals affirmed. Further appeal was taken to the U.S. Supreme Court.

The Supreme Court held that paying female retirees lower monthly annuities on the basis of the sex-based mortality tables was violative of Title VII. The Court then stated, "all retirement benefits derived from contributions made after the decision today must be calculated without regard to the sex of the beneficiary." For benefits derived from contributions made prior to the decision, the Court held that they could be calculated under the existing Arizona plan. The Court affirmed in part and reversed in part the court of appeals' decision, and the case was remanded. *Arizona Governing Committee for Tax Deferred Annuity and Deferred Compensation Plans v. Norris*, 463 U.S. 1073, 103 S.Ct. 3492, 77 L.Ed.2d 1236 (1983).

Despite the fact that women generally live longer than men, pension plans cannot discriminate on the basis of sex with respect to either contributions or benefits.

City of Los Angeles Dep't of Water v. Manhart, 435 U.S. 702, 98 S.Ct. 1370, 55 L.Ed.2d 657 (1978), held that unequal pension plan contributions for male and female employees constituted sex discrimination in violation of Title VII. However, the case did not resolve the issue of whether the invalidation of discriminatory contributions gave notice to employers that plans which were nondiscriminatory as to contributions had to be nondiscriminatory as to benefits in every case. Five years later, *Arizona Governing Committee for Tax Deferred Annuity & Deferred Compensation Plans v. Norris*, 463 U.S. 1073, 103 S.Ct. 3492, 77 L.Ed.2d 1236 (1983), extended this nondiscrimination principle to unequal benefits payments. Until *Norris*, Florida's Retirement System for public employees offered three retirement benefit options computed according to sex-based actuarial tables. This yielded lower monthly benefits for male retirees. After *Norris,* Florida adopted unisex actuarial tables to equalize benefits for similarly situated male and female employees retiring after *Norris'* effective date. Certain male employees who had retired before that date sued to get retroactive benefits at the unisex level from the date of *Manhart*. A federal district court ruled for the retirees, and the U.S. Court of Appeals affirmed.

On appeal, the U.S. Supreme Court held that the later date was the appropriate date for determining liability. The earlier case, *Manhart,* did not place Florida on notice that optional pension plans offering sex-based benefits violated Title VII. It was not until *Norris* that Florida became aware of the need for change in its pension system. To impose retroactive liability on employers who offered sex-based pension plans to their employees would be inequitable because it would impose financial costs that would threaten the security of both the plans and their beneficiaries. The Court thus reversed the lower courts' decisions and held that the retirees could only get higher benefits from the later date. *Florida v. Long,* 487 U.S. 223, 108 S.Ct. 2354, 101 L.Ed.2d 206 (1988).

3. Taxation

In a case involving taxation of retirement benefits, the Supreme Court held that a state law which taxed federal retirees but not state or local government retirees violated principles of intergovernmental tax immunity.

A former federal employee paid state income taxes on his federal retirement benefits in accordance with the Michigan Income Tax Act. The act exempted from taxation all retirement benefits paid by the state or its political subdivisions but taxed retirement benefits paid by other employers, including the federal government. He filed suit for a refund, claiming that the state's inconsistent treatment of retirement benefits violated 4 U.S.C. § 111, which authorizes states to tax "pay or compensation as [a federal] employee" so long as the tax does not discriminate against the employee because of the source of the pay. The Michigan Court of Claims denied relief, and the court of appeals affirmed. After the state supreme court denied leave to appeal, the U.S. Supreme Court granted review.

The Supreme Court held that the retiree was an employee within the meaning of § 111 rather than an annuitant for whom the statute had no application. Accordingly, Michigan's tax scheme violated principles of intergovernmental tax immunity by favoring retired state and local government employees over retired federal employees. The Court reversed and remanded the case, noting that the state could resolve the claim either by extending tax exemption to retired federal employees (or to all retired employees), or by eliminating the exemption for retired state and local employees. However, the retiree was entitled to a refund of taxes paid under the invalid scheme. *Davis v. Michigan Dep't of Treasury,* 489 U.S. 803, 109 S.Ct. 1500, 103 L.Ed.2d 891 (1989).

In a 1993 case, the Supreme Court held that an employer's contribution of unencumbered property to several tax-qualified defined benefit pension plans was a prohibited "sale or exchange" under § 4975(c)(1)(A) of ERISA. Since the transfer of property could injure the plan by, for example, leading to a shortage of funds to pay promised benefits, the Commissioner of Internal Revenue could demand substantial excise taxes from the company.

A Texas corporation maintained several tax-qualified deferred pension benefit plans which were subject to the minimum funding requirements under the

Employee Retirement Income Security Act (ERISA). In 1983 and 1984, the company contributed unencumbered property to the pension trust and credited that value against its minimum funding obligation. The Commissioner of Internal Revenue ruled that the company's transfers were sales or exchanges which were prohibited under § 4975(c)(1)(A) of ERISA. This ruling resulted in a determination that the company owed an excise tax liability. The company appealed to the tax court, which entered summary judgment in its favor. After the U.S. Court of Appeals, Fifth Circuit, upheld the decision of the tax court, the commissioner appealed to the U.S. Supreme Court.

The issue on appeal was whether the contribution of unencumbered property was a prohibited sale or exchange under § 4975(c)(1)(A). The Court noted that for income tax purposes the transfer of property in satisfaction of a monetary obligation is usually a sale or exchange of that property. Section 4975 prohibits any direct or indirect sale or exchange of property in satisfaction of a debt. Since Congress was aware when it enacted § 4975 that the phrase "sale or exchange" had been construed to include the transfer of property in satisfaction of a monetary obligation, it intended to prohibit such transfers by the passage of this section. Further, Congress' goal in enacting ERISA was to bar a transaction that was likely to injure the pension plan. Since a transfer of unencumbered property to satisfy a monetary obligation (like the transfer of encumbered property) has the potential to burden a plan, the Supreme Court upheld the decision of the commissioner to levy taxes on the corporation and reversed the court of appeals' decision. *Comm'r of Internal Revenue v. Keystone Consolidated Industries, Inc.,* 508 U.S. 152, 113 S.Ct. 2006, 124 L.Ed.2d 71 (1993).

Five years after the Supreme Court held that states could not tax federal retirees while exempting state and local government retirees, it determined that a state could not refuse to refund taxes paid under such a scheme because of the existence of predeprivation remedies. Those remedies could not be construed as the exclusive remedies for the recovery of unlawful taxes.

The state of Georgia exempted from taxation retirement benefits paid by the state, but not retirement benefits paid by the federal government. After this practice was declared unconstitutional by the U.S. Supreme Court in *Davis v. Michigan Dep't of Treasury,* 489 U.S. 803, 109 S.Ct. 1500, 103 L.Ed.2d 891 (1989), Georgia repealed its special tax exemption for state retirees. A federal military officer from Georgia sought a refund for the tax years 1980 and after in a state trial court. He alleged that a Georgia statute providing "clear and certain" post-deprivation relief from unconstitutional state taxes entitled him to a refund. The Georgia statute provided: "A taxpayer shall be refunded all taxes or fees ... illegally assessed and collected from him under the laws of this state, whether paid voluntarily or involuntarily." The trial court declined to award the refund, and the Georgia Supreme Court affirmed. On reconsideration, the supreme court again held for the state, ruling that the availability of adequate predeprivation remedies precluded relief under the Due Process Clause. The officer appealed to the U.S. Supreme Court.

The Supreme Court noted that the Georgia court had unfairly sanctioned a "bait and switch" scheme when it held the "clear and certain" post-deprivation remedy guaranteed by the state statute not to exist. Because an average taxpayer would not consider the predeprivation procedures to be the exclusive remedies for unlawful taxes—especially in light of the refund statute—the Georgia Supreme Court had improperly denied the officer a refund based on these measures. Instead, the statute's "sweeping language" indicated that state taxes assessed in violation of federal law were "illegally assessed" taxes. In fact, the Court noted that states ordinarily prefer taxpayers to "pay first, litigate later." The Court refused to penalize the taxpayer for adhering to this preference. The holding of the Georgia Supreme Court was reversed and the case was remanded for the provision of "meaningful backward-looking relief." *Reich v. Collins*, 513 U.S. 106, 115 S.Ct. 547, 130 L.Ed.2d 454 (1994).

4. Plan Termination

In *Nachman,* below, the Supreme Court held that a solvent employer that terminated an underfunded pension plan just prior to the effective date of the Employee Retirement Income Security Act, and which had limited its liability under a collective bargaining agreement, could be held liable to pay the vested benefits due its employees, even though the plan had been lawfully terminated.

An employer, pursuant to a collective bargaining agreement, established a pension plan for employees at one of its plants, which contained a clause limiting benefits, upon the plan's termination, to the assets in the pension fund. The employer then closed the plant and terminated the pension plan the day before much of ERISA became effective. At that time, pension fund assets were sufficient to pay only about 35 percent of the vested benefits. The employer then brought suit, seeking a declaration that it had no liability under ERISA for any failure of the pension plan to pay all of the vested benefits in full. The federal court held for the employer, but the U.S. Court of Appeals reversed. The case came before the U.S. Supreme Court.

The Court determined that the vested benefits should be characterized as "nonforfeitable" and thus insured by the Pension Benefit Guaranty Corporation. Just because the employer had disclaimed liability, this did not mean that employees' vested benefits became forfeitable. One of Congress' concerns was exactly what happened here: a solvent employer terminating an underfunded plan. Accordingly, the Court held that the employer was liable for the vested benefits beyond what had been promised in the agreement, even though the plan had been lawfully terminated. The court of appeals' decision was affirmed. *Nachman Corp. v. Pension Benefit Guaranty Corp.*, 446 U.S. 359, 100 S.Ct. 1723, 64 L.Ed.2d 354 (1980).

In the following case, a corporation attempted to negotiate new pension arrangements after terminating the old plan and placing responsibility for the unfunded liabilities on the PBGC. However, the PBGC deemed the new plan to be substantially the same as the old plan and disallowed the termination of the old plan. The Supreme Court upheld that decision.

A corporation filed a petition for reorganization under Chapter 11 of the Bankruptcy Code. At that time, it was the sponsor of three defined benefit pension plans covered by Title IV of ERISA, which were chronically underfunded. At the corporation's request, the Pension Benefit Guaranty Corporation (PBGC) terminated the plans. The corporation and its employees then negotiated new pension arrangements that provided substantially the same benefits as before. Shortly thereafter, the PBGC issued a notice of restoration to undo the termination because the new "follow-on" plans were abusive of the insurance program in its eyes. When the corporation refused to comply with the restoration, a lawsuit followed. The federal court held for the corporation, and the U.S. Court of Appeals affirmed.

On appeal, the U.S. Supreme Court reversed the lower courts. It found that the PBGC's restoration decision was not arbitrary or capricious. It did not matter that the PBGC had not considered all the potentially relevant areas of the law before making its decision. Section 4047 of ERISA gave the PBGC the power to restore terminated plans in any case where it determined such action to be appropriate under Title IV of ERISA. Further, the PBGC had complied with the requirements of § 555 of the Administrative Procedure Act. As such, the agency decision was valid and the corporation had to restore the plans that had been terminated. *Pension Benefit Guaranty Corp. v. LTV Corp.,* 496 U.S. 633, 110 S.Ct. 2668, 110 L.Ed.2d 579 (1990).

B. Multiemployer Benefit Plans

Employer-selected trustees of a trust fund established under § 302(c)(5) of the Labor Management Relations Act (LMRA) are not collective bargaining representatives of the employer. Thus, union coercion to induce employer contributions to such a trust fund is not a violation of § 8(b)(1)(B) of the National Labor Relations Act.

A coal mining company belonged to a national multiemployer group that negotiated a collective bargaining agreement with a union. The company then opened a new mine in Wyoming, but did not join the multiemployer group with respect to that mine; instead, it negotiated a separate contract requiring it to contribute specified sums to the union's national pension and welfare trust funds. The trust funds were administered by three trustees: one selected by the union, one selected by the members of the multiemployer group, and the last one selected by the first two. When the separately-bargained-for contract expired, the union struck the mine, hoping to induce further contributions to the national trust funds. Eventually, the company filed unfair labor practice charges against the union with the National Labor Relations Board, claiming that the trustee appointed by the members of the multiemployer group was in fact a collective bargaining representative of the company and that the union was illegally coercing the company by its actions. The board held for the union, but the U.S. Court of Appeals reversed.

On further appeal to the U.S. Supreme Court, the Court held that employer-selected trustees of a trust fund created under § 302(c)(5) of the Labor Management Relations Act are not "representatives" of the employer for purposes of the provision against coercion in the National Labor Relations Act (NLRA). Here, the trustee's duties of care and loyalty were to the beneficiaries of the trusts. The trustee did not engage in collective bargaining activities; thus, the union's efforts to make the company contribute to the national trust funds did not amount to illegal coercion under § 8(b)(1)(B) of the NLRA. Accordingly, the Court reversed the court of appeals' decision and held in favor of the union. *NLRB v. Amax Coal Co., a Division of Amax, Inc.*, 453 U.S. 322, 101 S.Ct. 2789, 69 L.Ed.2d 672 (1981).

In the following case, the Supreme Court held that the retroactive application of the withdrawal liability provisions of the MPPAA did not violate the Due Process Clause of the U.S. Constitution.

In 1980, Congress enacted the Multiemployer Pension Plan Amendments Act to require employers withdrawing from a multiemployer pension plan to pay a fixed and certain debt to the plan amounting to the employer's proportionate share of the plan's "unfunded vested benefits." The liability provisions took effect approximately five months before the statute was enacted into law. When an Oregon building and construction firm withdrew from a multiemployer pension plan during this five-month period, the plan notified the employer that it had incurred a withdrawal liability. The plan demanded payment. The employer then sued, claiming that the retroactive application of the MPPAA violated the Due Process Clause of the Fifth Amendment. A federal district court rejected this argument, but the U.S. Court of Appeals found that due process was violated because employers had come to rely on the contingent withdrawal liability provisions in ERISA, which had encouraged employer withdrawals from multi-employer plans.

On further appeal to the U.S. Supreme Court, it was held that the retroactive application of the withdrawal liability provisions of the MPPAA did not violate the Due Process Clause. Here, there was a rational legislative purpose justifying the retroactive application. Making the liability provisions effective prior to the enactment of the statute prevented employers from taking advantage of the lengthy legislative process by withdrawing during that time. Employers had had ample notice of the withdrawal liability imposed by the MPPAA. Because the MPPAA merely required withdrawing employers to compensate pension plans for benefits that had already vested with the employees at the time of the withdrawal, the MPPAA was valid. *Pension Benefit Guaranty Corp. v. R.A. Gray & Co.*, 467 U.S. 717, 104 S.Ct. 2709, 81 L.Ed.2d 601 (1984).

In the case below, the Supreme Court held that employers who participated in multiemployer benefit plans that were governed by ERISA had to allow the plans to conduct audits for the purpose of policing the self-reporting system in place.

Two large, multiemployer benefit plans (with thousands of participating employers), governed by ERISA, operated under trust agreements for the purpose of providing health, welfare and pension benefits to employees performing work which was covered by collective bargaining agreements (CBAs) between a union and various employers. Under the CBAs, each employer was required to make weekly contributions to the plans. Because of their size, the plans relied on employer self-reporting to determine the extent of an employer's contribution liability, and they policed this system by conducting random audits of the participating employers' records. However, when certain new signatories refused to allow the plans to conduct audits, the plans sued in federal court. The district court ruled for the plans, but the U.S. Court of Appeals reversed.

On further appeal, the U.S. Supreme Court held that the employers had to allow the plans to conduct the requested audit. The trustees of the plans had the power under the trust agreements to demand and examine pertinent employer records, and the interpretation of the agreements as authorizing the audit was not inconsistent with ERISA. Under ERISA, trustees had the same power they enjoyed under the common law—"all such powers as are necessary or appropriate for the carrying out of the trust purposes." Since the employers had agreed to be bound by the trust agreements in the CBAs, the Court reversed the appellate court's decision, and held in favor of the plans. *Central States, Southeast and Southwest Areas Pension Fund v. Central Transport, Inc.,* 472 U.S. 559, 105 S.Ct. 2833, 86 L.Ed.2d 447 (1985).

ERISA was enacted in 1974 to provide comprehensive regulation for private pension plans. ERISA also established a system of pension benefit insurance; the Pension Benefit Guaranty Corporation was created to administer the insurance program. Subsequently, Congress enacted the Multiemployer Pension Plan Amendments Act to require employers withdrawing from a multiemployer pension plan to pay a fixed and certain debt to the plan, which amounted to the employers' proportionate share of the plan's "unfunded vested benefits." The Supreme Court held that this imposition of withdrawal liability was constitutional.

After becoming concerned that a significant number of multiemployer pension plans were experiencing extreme financial hardship, and that the future implementation of mandatory guarantees might result in the termination of several large plans, Congress enacted the Multiemployer Pension Plan Amendments Act of 1980. This required employers withdrawing from a multiemployer pension plan to pay a fixed and certain debt to the plan amounting to the employers' proportionate share of the plan's "unfunded vested benefits." The trustees of a multiemployer pension fund brought an action challenging the constitutionality of the withdrawal liability provisions of the MPPAA. After summary judgment was entered in favor of the government, the trustees appealed to the U.S. Supreme Court. The Court determined that the imposition of withdrawal liability on employers did not violate the constitutional prohibition against taking property without just compensation. The Court affirmed the lower court's decision against the trustees. *Connolly v. Pension Benefit Guaranty Corp.,* 475 U.S. 211, 106 S.Ct. 1018, 89 L.Ed.2d 166 (1986).

The Multiemployer Pension Plan Amendments Act assesses withdrawal liability against employers withdrawing from a multiemployer plan. The employer's withdrawal liability is its proportionate share of the plan's unfunded vested benefits. In the following case, the Supreme Court held that the act was constitutional as applied to a withdrawing employer.

The Employee Retirement Income Security Act of 1974, 29 U.S.C. §§ 1301-1461, imposes obligations on employers withdrawing from multiemployer pension plans. Employers who withdraw from multiemployer pension plans incur a "fixed and certain debt to the pension plan," known as "withdrawal liability." Multiemployer pension plans are typically maintained pursuant to the terms of a collective bargaining agreement. Participant employers pool funds for the benefit of plan obligations, and employees may take advantage of "portable" service credits, so that they may receive credit for work done for any participating employer. Multiemployer plans also benefit employers by reducing costs and offering risk-sharing mechanisms. A California concrete manufacturer participated in a defined benefit plan that was a qualified multiemployer plan under ERISA. It made contributions to the plan on behalf of employees at one particular plant under a three-year contract from 1978 through 1981. During the course of the contract, production was stopped at the plant and the manufacturer stopped making contributions to the plan. The manufacturer and collective bargaining unit failed to renegotiate a new contract. However, the manufacturer reopened the plant and rehired employees under similar classifications as those covered by the collective bargaining agreement. It failed to contribute to the plan, which then notified the manufacturer of a $268,168.81 withdrawal liability. The manufacturer contended that it had made a "complete withdrawal" from plan participation in 1979, when it initially ceased operations at the plant. The plan sued the manufacturer in the U.S. District Court for the Central District of California, which ordered the parties to arbitrate whether a "withdrawal" had occurred prior to 1980—when ERISA was added to by the Multiemployer Pension Plan Amendments Act. An arbitrator determined that the manufacturer had not withdrawn from the plan prior to the effective date of the MPPAA. However, it reduced the manufacturer's withdrawal liability to $190,465.57. The federal district court then granted the plan's motion to confirm the award. This result was affirmed by the U.S. Court of Appeals, Ninth Circuit. The manufacturer appealed to the U.S. Supreme Court.

On appeal, the manufacturer claimed that the MPPAA was unconstitutional because it denied the manufacturer its right to have an impartial decision-maker. In this case, the decision-maker was the plan sponsor. The manufacturer argued that pension plan trustees could be biased against employers due to their obligation to maximize trust assets that were designated for unions and employees. The Supreme Court found no merit in this argument, stating that the first adjudication in this case had been the arbitration, not the plan sponsor's determination of withdrawal liability. The manufacturer's argument that the act violated its procedural due process rights was equally without merit. The MPPAA required employment of an actuary to determine withdrawal liability. The actuary was required to employ professional standards and was not under the direction of plan trustees. Because of the need for the actuaries to employ professional assumptions and methods, there was no merit to the manufacturer's argument that there was unfairness to withdrawing employers. The Court rejected the manufacturer's argument that the MPPAA violated substantive due process under the Fifth Amendment, because the act had a rational basis. The MPPAA did not constitute a taking without just compensation based upon the manufacturer's assertion that it would have to pay 46 percent of its shareholder equity as its withdrawal liability payment. According to the Supreme Court, diminution in property value did not constitute a taking. This was true even though ERISA originally imposed a maximum contingent withdrawal liability of 30 percent. The legislation was not unconstitutional simply because it upset "otherwise settled expectations." The Supreme Court affirmed the lower courts' decisions for the pension plan. *Concrete Pipe and Products of California, Inc. v. Construction Laborers Pension Trust for Southern California,* 508 U.S. 602, 113 S.Ct. 2264, 124 L.Ed.2d 539 (1993).

In a later withdrawal liability case, the Supreme Court held that interest begins to accrue on the first day of the plan year following withdrawal. Interest does not accrue before the first withdrawal payment is owed.

The Multiemployer Pension Plan Amendments Act of 1980, 29 U.S.C. §§ 1381-1461, requires employers who withdraw from underfunded multiemployer pension plans to pay a fair share of the plan's unfunded liabilities. The MPPAA gives withdrawing employers the option to pay their withdrawal liability in a lump sum, or to amortize the amount in level annual payments "calculated as if the first payment were made on the first day of the plan year following the plan year in which the withdrawal occurs and as if each subsequent payment were made on the first day of each subsequent plan year." A brewing company withdrew from an underfunded plan with a withdrawal charge of $23.3 million. Prior to withdrawing, it had typically made annual payments of approximately $4 million to the fund, and the relevant annual interest rate was seven percent. Although the plan and the brewery agreed on the amount of withdrawal liability, the parties disagreed on the amount of interest that had accrued during the withdrawal year. The plan claimed that interest began accruing on the last day of the plan year preceding withdrawal, while the brewery argued that accrual began on the first day of the plan year following withdrawal. The difference in sums was in excess of $2.6 million. An arbitrator agreed with the brewery, but the U.S. District Court for the Eastern District of Wisconsin reversed. The U.S. Court of Appeals, Seventh Circuit, reversed the district court's decision, and the plan appealed to the U.S. Supreme Court.

On appeal, the plan argued that the brewery's interpretation undermined a basic congressional policy objective of the MPPAA that required withdrawing employers to pay their fair share of underfunding. The Court disagreed, noting that nothing in the MPPAA required withdrawing employers to pay an actuarially perfect fair share of withdrawal liability. It also stated that the MPPAA provision describing withdrawing employer liability did not cause interest to start accruing during the withdrawal year itself. Rather, it called for calculation as if the first payment were made on the first day of the plan year following the plan year in which withdrawal occurs. Because a withdrawing employer owed nothing to a plan until the plan demanded payment as set forth by the MPPAA, the employer was unable to determine its liability until sometime after the beginning of the withdrawal year. Another reason supporting the brewery's position was MPPAA language concerning amortized withdrawal charges. The amount of annual payment was fixed at a level that equated the withdrawing employer's typical contribution in prior years at an interest rate equal to the plan's normal assumptions. Charging the withdrawing employer a full year of interest would constitute an overcharge and a windfall to employers remaining in the plan. The Court affirmed the court of appeals' decision for the brewery. *Milwaukee Brewery Workers' Pension Plan v. Jos. Schlitz Brewing Co.*, 513 U.S. 414, 115 S.Ct. 981, 130 L.Ed.2d 932 (1995).

The MPPAA's six-year statute of limitation commences after a cause of action has accrued, not upon the employer's first missed scheduled payment. Because the MPPAA does not require a withdrawing employer to pay anything until the plan demands payment, a cause of action does not accrue until the employer has been assessed a liability, notified of the amount and means of payment, and fails to make a required payment.

The Multiemployer Pension Plan Amendments Act requires employers who withdraw from underfunded multiemployer pension plans to pay a withdrawal liability. Employers may contest an assessed liability, but are required to make payments pending appeal. An employer made contributions to a multiemployer pension fund for laundry workers in the San Francisco Bay area for several years, then ceased making contributions. The fund's trustees demanded payment of a withdrawal liability and notified the employer of its payment options. The employer sought administrative review of the determination and refused to make payments. However, the fund did not commence an action against the employer until eight years after it withdrew from the fund and over six years after missing its first scheduled payment. The employer moved to dismiss the case as barred by the MPPAA's six-year statute of limitations. A federal district court granted the employer's summary judgment motion, and the U.S. Court of Appeals, Ninth Circuit, affirmed.

The fund appealed to the U.S. Supreme Court, which stated that, in general, the complaining party in any case must possess a complete and present cause of action in order for a limitations period to commence. The Court rejected the employer's claim that its withdrawal commenced the statute of limitations, because the MPPAA does not require a withdrawing employer to pay anything until the plan demands payment. The cause of action did not accrue until the employer was assessed a liability, notified of the amount and means of payment, and failed to make a required payment. Although over six years had passed from the employer's failure to pay the first installment, the fund was entitled to recover all but the first of the installment payments. The Court reversed and remanded the lower court decisions. *Bay Area Laundry and Dry Cleaning Pension Trust Fund v. Ferbar Corp. of California, Inc.*, 522 U.S. 192, 118 S.Ct. 542, 139 L.Ed.2d 553 (1997).

II. DISABILITY BENEFITS

States cannot regulate ERISA plans by enacting statutes in an area that Congress intended to be exclusively within federal regulation.

Various companies that maintained employee welfare benefit plans (which did not provide benefits to employees disabled by pregnancy prior to the effective date of the Pregnancy Discrimination Act) brought suit in federal district courts alleging that the New York Human Rights Law was preempted by ERISA. They were concerned because the state of New York was attempting to enforce its human rights law through regulation of their employee welfare benefit plans. The federal district courts held that ERISA did preempt the state law. The U.S. Court of Appeals affirmed those decisions, and appeal was taken to the U.S. Supreme Court.

The Court first held that the Human Rights Law was preempted by ERISA only where it prohibited practices that were lawful under federal law. The Court then noted that the preemption power of ERISA would not be construed to impair any law of the United States. Since the Human Rights Law provided a means of enforcing Title VII's commands, preemption would impair federal law. The Court also looked at New York's Disability Benefits Law and held that it was not preempted by ERISA. However, the state could not enforce the law through regulation of ERISA-covered benefit plans. *Shaw v. Delta Air Lines, Inc.*, 463 U.S. 85, 103 S.Ct. 2890, 77 L.Ed.2d 490 (1983).

If federal employees are denied disability benefits at the administrative level, the Civil Service Retirement Act does not bar judicial review of those determinations.

A civilian security guard worked for a naval shipyard until he was retired on disability resulting from acute and chronic bronchitis, allegedly aggravated in part by his exposure over the years to chemical irritants at the workplace. When he applied for a disability retirement annuity, the Office of Personnel Management turned him down because the evidence failed to establish that his disability was severe enough to prevent him from doing his job. The Merit Systems Protection Board sustained the denial of benefits, finding that even though the Navy had found him "not fit to continue satisfactory duty performance," this was not dispositive of whether he was totally disabled so as to be eligible for a disability annuity. The U.S. Court of Appeals dismissed the employee's appeal as barred by § 8347(c) of the Civil Service Retirement Act which stated that administrative decisions about disability would be final and not subject to judicial review.

The U.S. Supreme Court reversed the appellate court's decision and remanded the case. The Court held that § 8347(c) did not bar judicial review altogether. It only barred review of factual determinations. If errors of law or procedure were alleged, the courts could review those determinations. The court of appeals had jurisdiction to review the administrative decision, and it should not have dismissed the appeal. *Lindahl v. Office of Personnel Management*, 470 U.S. 768, 105 S.Ct. 1620, 84 L.Ed.2d 674 (1985).

ERISA does not provide for extracontractual causes of action between plan beneficiaries and plan trustees. The beneficiary of an ERISA plan is limited to suing for the recovery of benefits under the plan.

A claims examiner for a life insurance company was a beneficiary under two employee benefit plans administered by her employer. After becoming disabled with a back ailment, she received plan benefits for five months until an orthopedic surgeon's report caused the benefits committee to terminate her benefits. She requested a review of the decision, and five months later had her benefits reinstated with retroactive benefits paid in full. Even though she was paid all of the benefits to which she was contractually entitled, she sued her employer for improper refusal to pay benefits. After removal to a federal district court, summary judgment was granted to the employer on the ground that ERISA barred any claims for extracontractual damages arising out of the original denial of her claim for benefits. The U.S. Court of Appeals reversed in part, holding that the 132 days the employer took to process the worker's claim violated the fiduciary's obligation to process claims in good faith, and in a fair and diligent manner.

On further appeal, the U.S. Supreme Court held that § 409(a) of ERISA (which provides that fiduciaries who breach their duties or obligations will be personally liable to make good any losses that result from their breach) did not provide a cause of action for extracontractual damages to a beneficiary caused by improper or untimely processing of benefit claims. Congress intended to provide no relief except for the plan itself. The fiduciary's liability was to the employee benefit plan, and the plan's liability was to the beneficiary. There was no extracontractual cause of action available between the beneficiary and the fiduciary. Accordingly, the Court reversed the appellate court's decision, holding that the employee was not entitled to compensatory or punitive damages from her employer. *Massachusetts Mutual Life Ins. Co. v. Russell,* 473 U.S. 134, 105 S.Ct. 3085, 87 L.Ed.2d 96 (1985).

Black lung benefits claimants are entitled to a presumption of eligibility if they can show at least one of the qualifying facts by a preponderance of the evidence. However, the presumption need not be invoked if conflicting evidence is more reliable.

A black lung benefits claimant had 16 years of coal mine employment. At the benefits hearing, one qualifying X-ray interpretation, two qualifying ventilatory studies, and one qualifying physician's opinion were introduced into evidence. However, there were also seven nonqualifying X-ray interpretations, four nonqualifying ventilatory studies, and five nonqualifying physicians' opinions. The administrative law judge held that the claimant was not entitled to the benefits, but the U.S. Court of Appeals reversed. The U.S. Supreme Court granted certiorari.

The Court held that § 203(a) of the interim regulations required the claimant to establish at least one of the qualifying facts by a preponderance of the evidence. Even though a single item of qualifying evidence might be sufficient to invoke the interim presumption of eligibility, such a single item did not necessarily mean that the presumption had to be invoked. Here, small amounts of qualifying evidence were overcome by more reliable conflicting evidence. The Court reversed the court of appeals' decision and remanded the case, holding that the claimant was not entitled to the presumption of eligibility here. *Mullins Coal Co. v. Director, Office of Workers' Compensation Programs,* 484 U.S. 135, 108 S.Ct. 427, 98 L.Ed.2d 450 (1987).

In the following case, the Supreme Court held that the interim regulations created by the Secretary of Labor violated the Black Lung Benefits Reform Act by being more restrictive than the criteria used prior to the new regulations.

The Black Lung Benefits Reform Act (BLBRA) of 1977 provided that until permanent regulations were issued, cases filed or pending were to be assessed under "criteria not more restrictive than the criteria applicable to a claim filed on June 30, 1973." As of that date, under interim Health, Education and Welfare regulations, a miner could establish presumptive entitlement to benefits if he submitted evidence of pneumoconiosis and showed either ten years of mining service or that his or her impairment arose out of coal mine employment. Acting according to the BLBRA, the Secretary of Labor created an interim regulation that accorded a presumptive claim of entitlement only to miners who had ten years of experience. This was more restrictive than the HEW regulations. In various cases where black lung benefits were denied, appeal was taken. Eventually, the cases were consolidated before the U.S. Supreme Court.

The Court held that the interim regulation promulgated by the Secretary of Labor violated § 902(f)(2) of the BLBRA. By making the criteria for proving causation more restrictive for miners seeking a presumptive entitlement, the regulation necessarily applied more restrictive total disability criteria than those in the HEW regulations. However, for the cases where rulings had become final because of failure to pursue administrative remedies or to appeal on time, the denial of benefits was allowable. *Pittston Coal Group v. Sebben,* 488 U.S. 105, 109 S.Ct. 414, 102 L.Ed.2d 408 (1988).

Even if a government employee provides erroneous information to a benefits claimant such that the claimant loses his or her benefits, the claimant cannot prevent the government from denying benefits if the claimant has relied on the information and taken a job to supplement the disability payments.

A U.S. Navy welder applied for disability retirement with the Office of Personnel Management. The OPM determined that the welder's poor eyesight prevented him from performing his job and made him eligible for a disability annuity under 5 U.S.C. § 8337(a). Section 8337(d) provides that benefits for a disabled federal employee will end if the employee is restored to an earning capacity fairly comparable to the current rate of pay of that position. After taking disability retirement, the welder had the opportunity to earn more money by working overtime on a part-time job. The welder contacted an employee relations specialist at the Navy Public Works Center's Civilian Personnel Department, seeking information on how much he could earn without losing his benefits. The specialist gave the government welder erroneous information from an old handbook. The welder relied on the information and took the overtime work. He then lost his disability benefits by going over the statutory limit. The welder sought review of the decision from the Merit Systems Protection Board, which held that the OPM could not be prevented from enforcing a statutory requirement. The welder then appealed to the U.S. Court of Appeals, Federal Circuit. The court of appeals reversed the MSPB's decision, stating that the use of an out-of-date handbook was "affirmative misconduct" and could prevent the government from denying benefits. The OPM appealed to the U.S. Supreme Court.

The Court noted that Congress had not authorized a money remedy for misinformation, and the government therefore could not be prevented from denying benefits. The Court also noted that awarding benefits for misinformation would invite endless litigation over real and imagined claims and impose an unpredictable and substantial drain on the public funds. The Supreme Court reversed the decision of the court of appeals. *Office of Personnel Management v. Richmond*, 496 U.S. 414, 110 S.Ct. 2465, 110 L.Ed.2d 387 (1990).

In 1991, the Supreme Court held that the third and fourth rebuttal provisions in the Department of Labor regulations (which allow a presumption of eligibility to be rebutted if the evidence establishes that the disability did not arise out of coal mine employment or if it is shown that the miner does not have pneumoconiosis) were not more restrictive than the prior HEW regulations.

A Pennsylvania man filed a claim for black lung benefits which was denied under the Department of Labor interim regulations because his employer met its burden of showing that pneumoconiosis was not a contributing factor in his disability, and thus his disability did not "arise in whole or in part out of coal mine employment." Two other claimants from other states were also initially denied benefits; however, the U.S. Court of Appeals determined that the DOL interim regulations violated the Black Lung Benefits Reform Act because they were more restrictive than earlier regulations of the Department of Health, Education, and Welfare. The U.S. Supreme Court agreed to hear the cases to decide the validity of the DOL regulations.

The Court first held that, since the Secretary of Labor had determined that the interim regulations were not more restrictive than HEW's regulations, that decision had to be accorded deference. The Court then noted that the Secretary's determination was reasonable. Accordingly, the regulations were valid and enforceable. The Court affirmed in part and reversed in part the lower courts' decisions, holding that none of the three claimants were entitled to benefits. *Pauley v. Bethenergy Mines, Inc.,* 501 U.S. 680, 111 S.Ct. 2524, 115 L.Ed.2d 604 (1991).

III. OTHER BENEFITS

A. Health Benefits

Section 302(c)(5) of the LMRA (which requires certain pension funds to be maintained for the sole and exclusive benefit of employees, their families, and their dependents) does not authorize federal courts to review the provisions of a collective bargaining agreement for reasonableness. Thus, an agreement that discriminated against a certain class of widows of coal miners with respect to health benefits was held not to be illegal under § 302(c)(5) of the LMRA.

A 1974 collective bargaining agreement between a union and an association of coal mine operators increased health benefits for widows of coal miners who died prior to the effective date of the agreement and who had been receiving pensions when they died. The moneys were to be paid out of a trust fund financed by contributions from the operators. The agreement, however, did not increase health benefits for widows of miners who died prior to the effective date while they were still working (despite the fact that they were eligible for pensions). A group of these widows brought a class action suit against the trustees of the fund, asserting that the "receiving a pension" requirement had no rational relationship to the purposes of the trust fund and thus was illegal under § 302 of the Labor Management Relations Act. A federal district court denied relief, but the U.S. Court of Appeals reversed on the ground that the eligibility rules did not meet a "reasonableness" standard. The U.S. Supreme Court granted review.

The Supreme Court determined that § 302 did not authorize federal courts to review the provisions of collective bargaining agreements to determine their reasonableness. The language of § 302 embodies no reasonableness requirement. It merely requires employer contributions to employee benefit trust funds to accrue to the benefit of employees (and their families and dependents) to the exclusion of all others. Because there was no conflict with federal law, the trustees breached no fiduciary duties in administering the trust fund in accordance with the collective bargaining agreement. The courts could not substantively modify the agreement's terms. Accordingly, the court of appeals' decision was reversed. *United Mine Workers of America Health and Retirement Funds v. Robinson*, 455 U.S. 562, 102 S.Ct. 1226, 71 L.Ed.2d 419 (1982).

In the following case, the Supreme Court held that a state law requiring the provision of certain minimal health care benefits was not preempted by the NLRA or ERISA.

A Massachusetts law required that certain minimum mental health care benefits be provided to residents of the state who were insured under a general health care plan that covered hospital and surgical expenses. Two insurers who provided health insurance to unions or employers contended that they did not have to comply with the law because ERISA or the National Labor Relations Act preempted it. A trial court required the insurers to provide the coverage mandated by the law, and the Supreme Judicial Court of Massachusetts affirmed.

The U.S. Supreme Court heard the case and determined that the Massachusetts law was a law that regulated insurance. Accordingly, it was not preempted by ERISA. Further, the law was not subject to the NLRA because even though it set a minimum employment standard, it was unrelated to the collective bargaining process and had only an indirect effect on the right of self organization established by the NLRA—it did not limit that right. Accordingly, the lower court's decision was affirmed, and the state law was upheld. The insurers had to provide the minimum coverage mandated by the statute. *Metropolitan Life Ins. Co. v. Massachusetts*, 471 U.S. 724, 105 S.Ct. 2380, 85 L.Ed.2d 728 (1985).

The Supreme Court held that self-funded employee benefit plans are not "insurance" for the purpose of interpreting state insurance laws. Such laws are "saved" from preemption by ERISA. In the following case, the Court held that since the plan was not insurance, ERISA preempted state regulation of it.

A corporation operated a self-funded health care plan under which plan members agreed to reimburse it for benefits paid if the member recovered on a claim in a liability action against a third party. The daughter of a plan member was seriously injured in an automobile accident, and the plan paid part of her medical expenses. A negligence action against the driver of the vehicle in which the daughter was injured settled. The plan member refused to reimburse the plan, asserting that Pennsylvania law precluded subrogation by the plan. The member sought and obtained a declaratory judgment that the state statute prohibited the plan from enforcing the subrogation provision. The U.S. Court of Appeals affirmed, and the case came before the U.S. Supreme Court.

The Court stated that ERISA preempted the application of the Pennsylvania law, and that the plan could seek subrogation. Since Congress clearly intended to exempt from state regulation ERISA employee benefit plans, the state statute could not stand here. State laws that directly regulate insurance are "saved" from preemption, but this does not apply to self-funded employee benefit plans because they are not insurance for purposes of such laws. *FMC Corp. v. Holliday*, 498 U.S. 52, 111 S.Ct. 403, 112 L.Ed.2d 356 (1990).

Section 402(b)(3) of ERISA requires every employee benefit plan to provide a procedure for amending the plan, and for identifying the persons who have authority to amend the plan. The Supreme Court held that a plan could state: "the company reserves the right to amend the plan." This satisfied the requirements of § 402(b)(3).

A corporation maintained and administered a single-employer health plan for its employees. In response to rising health care costs, it discontinued coverage for retirees upon the termination of operations at the facility from which they had retired. After closing a New Jersey facility, the corporation's executive vice president notified retirees of the facility by letter that their post-retirement health benefits were being terminated. The retirees filed a lawsuit against the corporation in the U.S. District Court for the District of New Jersey, alleging that the termination of benefits violated § 402(b)(3) of ERISA, 29 U.S.C. § 1102(b)(3).

Section 402(b)(3) required employee benefit plans to have "a procedure for amending such plan, and for identifying the persons who have authority to amend the plan." The retirees claimed that the company's summary plan description lacked a valid amendment procedure and that its action constituted a plan amendment. The district court agreed with the retirees, and ordered the corporation to pay them over $2.6 million in benefits. The U.S. Court of Appeals, Third Circuit, affirmed the district court's decision and the corporation appealed to the U.S. Supreme Court.

The Supreme Court agreed with the corporation that the minimal language in its summary plan description satisfied the amendment procedure requirement of ERISA § 402(b)(3). Under the plan description, the corporation "reserve[d] the right at any time to amend the plan...." ERISA created no substantive entitlement to employer-provided welfare benefits and employers were allowed to freely modify, amend or terminate welfare plans under most circumstances. The Court reasoned that a plan that simply identified the person or persons having authority to amend a plan necessarily indicated the amendment procedure. The reservation clause contained in the corporation's summary plan description identified "the company" as the person having amendment authority. It was then only necessary to apply corporate law principles to identify the particular individual or corporate committee with decision-making authority. It was unnecessary to further specify the names of individuals or committees within a corporation to satisfy ERISA, and for single-employer health plans it was sufficient to identify the employer as the entity having amendment authority. The Court reversed and remanded the court of appeals' decision, directing the court to consider on remand whether the corporation had complied with its valid amendment procedure. Under this fact inquiry, the court was to apply corporate law principles to determine whether the appropriate corporate officials had actually approved the amendments contained in the revised summary plan description. *Curtiss-Wright Corp. v. Schoonejongen*, 514 U.S. 73, 115 S.Ct. 1223, 131 L.Ed.2d 94 (1995).

The Supreme Court found that the COBRA amendments require group health plan sponsors, including employers, to provide continuation coverage to an employee covered under his or her spouse's plan.

The Consolidated Omnibus Budget Reconciliation Act of 1985 amended ERISA by authorizing qualified beneficiaries of employer group health plans to obtain continuation coverage in specified circumstances including employment termination. A Missouri medical corporation discharged an employee with cancer who was covered under its group health plan. It informed the employee that he had COBRA continuation coverage rights under the plan and could remain covered if he elected to do so and made the necessary payments. The former employee participated in the plan for six months, at which time the employer notified him that he was not entitled to COBRA benefits because he was already covered by a group health plan supplied by his wife's employer as of his election date. The former employee commenced a federal district court action against his former employer, health plan and plan administrators for wrongful denial of coverage. The award of summary judgment to the employer was affirmed by the

U.S. Court of Appeals, Eighth Circuit. The employee appealed to the U.S. Supreme Court.

The Court stated that the COBRA amendments to ERISA require group health plan sponsors, including employers, to provide continuation coverage when plan beneficiaries might otherwise lose coverage upon the occurrence of a qualifying event, such as employment termination or divorce. COBRA coverage may cease on the date on which the qualified beneficiary first becomes covered, after the date of election, under any other group health plan which does not limit or exclude a beneficiary's preexisting health conditions. The former employer and plan argued that the employee was "first" covered by his wife's plan after the time of the election. The Court disagreed, finding that the employee had been continuously covered by his wife's group health plan and did not "first become" covered under the wife's plan after the date of election. Because the former employer could not cut off the former employee's COBRA coverage, the Court vacated and remanded the lower court judgments. *Geissal v. Moore Medical Corp.*, 524 U.S. 74, 118 S.Ct. 1869, 141 L.Ed.2d 64 (1998).

The Supreme Court held that the Coal Industry Retiree Health Benefit Act of 1992 (Coal Act) unconstitutionally deprived an employer of property by requiring it to fund healthcare benefits for retired coal miners and their dependents, since it created a severe, disproportionate and retroactive burden on the employer.

The Coal Act, 26 U.S.C. §§ 9701–9722, established a healthcare funding mechanism for coal industry retirees and their dependents, and was intended by Congress to identify the coal producers most responsible for healthcare liabilities, allocate liabilities among them and stabilize plan funding. It assigns liability to coal operators who were signatories to a sequence of industry-wide agreements from 1946 through 1978. The U.S. Social Security Commissioner calculates premiums to levy against coal operators and their successors in interest, and businesses under their common control. One statutory method of calculating premiums assigns liability to the signatory operator which has employed a coal industry retiree in the industry for a longer time than any other signatory operator prior to a specified 1978 wage agreement. Eastern, which had been a signatory to coal industry collective bargaining agreements until 1964, transferred its coal operations to a subsidiary in 1965 and sold its interest in the subsidiary in 1987. However, the Commissioner identified over 1,000 retirees who had worked for the employer longer than any other pre-1978 signatory coal operator and assigned a 12-month premium of over $5 million. Eastern commenced a federal district court action against the Commissioner in which it alleged that the Coal Act amounted to an unconstitutional taking of its property. The court held for the Commissioner, and the judgment was affirmed by the U.S. Court of Appeals, First Circuit.

The U.S. Supreme Court agreed to review the case, and cited three significant factors in identifying an unconstitutional taking of private property by the government: the economic impact of a government regulation, the resulting interference with reasonable investment-backed expectations, and the character of the action. In this case, all three factors were implicated, since the Coal Act imposed severe retroactive liability on a class of employers that could not have anticipated it, and the liability was substantially disproportionate to the experience of the parties. Eastern's cumulative liability under the Act was estimated at $50 to $100 million, even though it had employed no miners since before 1965, when the retirement and healthcare benefits offered were far less extensive. The Act retroactively divested Eastern of property long after it believed its liabilities were settled. The Court reversed and remanded the judgment. *Eastern Enterprises v. Apfel*, 524 U.S. 498, 118 S.Ct. 2131, 141 L.Ed.2d 451 (1998).

B. Welfare Benefits

In the following case, the Court determined that a state statute which differentiated between ERISA and non-ERISA welfare plans under state garnishment procedures was preempted by ERISA. However, the state's general garnishment statute (which did not single out ERISA plans) was not preempted.

A collection agency obtained money judgments against 25 people who were participants in an employee welfare benefit plan that was governed by ERISA. The covered workers drew their vacation benefits from the plan annually. The collection agency sought to garnish the debtors' plan benefits so as to collect on the money judgments. A Georgia trial court allowed the garnishment, but the court of appeals reversed, holding that a Georgia statute barred the garnishment of funds of an employee benefit plan that was subject to ERISA. The Georgia Supreme Court reversed, deciding that ERISA preempted the Georgia statute. The case reached the U.S. Supreme Court.

The Court first noted that ERISA did preempt the state statute. It then stated that Congress did not intend to preempt general state-law garnishment of ERISA welfare benefit plans, even where the purpose was to collect judgments against plan participants. ERISA only placed a ban on alienation or assignment of *pension* benefits. Here, the vacation benefits could be garnished because they were not part of a pension plan, but merely an employee welfare benefit plan. The Court affirmed the Georgia Supreme Court's decision in favor of the collection agency. *Mackey v. Lanier Collections Agency & Service*, 486 U.S. 825, 108 S.Ct. 2182, 100 L.Ed.2d 836 (1988).

In the following case, the Supreme Court held that a policy of paying discharged employees for their unused vacation time did not constitute an "employee welfare benefit plan" under ERISA.

A Massachusetts bank discharged two vice presidents and allegedly failed to compensate them for vacation time they had accrued but not used. The state charged the bank president with criminal violation of the state law that prohibited this. The bank president moved to dismiss the case against him on the ground that ERISA preempted all state laws relating to an "employee welfare benefit plan." The question of whether payments for unused vacation time constitute an employee welfare benefit plan came before the U.S. Supreme Court.

The Court noted that the creation of a separate fund to pay employees vacation benefits would subject an employer to ERISA; however, the employer here had a policy of paying vacation benefits out of its general assets. Because ERISA had been enacted to prevent mismanagement of accumulated plan funds and to prevent failure to pay benefits from such funds, it did not apply to the situation involved here. The vacation pay owed in this case was fixed, payable from general assets, and not dependent on contingencies outside the employees' control. Accordingly, the criminal action against the bank president was not preempted by ERISA. *Massachusetts v. Morash*, 490 U.S. 107, 109 S.Ct. 1668, 104 L.Ed.2d 98 (1989).

The Supreme Court held that an employer was acting as a plan fiduciary when it promised to preserve employee benefits and salaries after transferring employees to a new subsidiary made up of money-losing divisions. The Court also held that § 502(a)(3) authorized lawsuits for individualized equitable relief for breach of fiduciary obligations.

A manufacturer transferred its money-losing divisions to a new subsidiary to improve financial statements and eliminate employee benefits in the money-losing divisions. The manufacturer advised employees in these divisions that their benefits and salaries would remain the same if they transferred to the new subsidiary. Many employees transferred to the subsidiary, which went into receivership within two years. Employees and retirees who participated in the subsidiary's welfare benefit plan asserted that the manufacturer was aware that the subsidiary was insolvent at its creation and that they had been fraudulently induced to accept employment transfers. The plan participants filed a lawsuit against the manufacturer in the U.S. District Court for the Southern District of Iowa, which held that the manufacturer was acting in its fiduciary capacity and violated its obligation under ERISA to administer the plan in the employees' interest. The court awarded damages to the participants and ruled that they had a right to appropriate equitable relief including reinstatement into the manufacturer's plan. The U.S. Court of Appeals, Eighth Circuit, affirmed much of the district court decision but disallowed a $46 million damage award. The U.S. Supreme Court agreed to review the matter.

The manufacturer argued that it was acting in its capacity as an employer when it made the decision to transfer employees to the new subsidiary and had appropriately exercised its business judgment. It also claimed that ERISA does not permit individual claims for relief but only authorizes remedies that benefit the plan as a whole. The Court found that the manufacturer had been acting as both a plan fiduciary and an employer when it promised to preserve employee benefits and salaries after the transfer. Accordingly, its actions were held to the standard of fiduciary care that subjected it to potential ERISA liability. It rejected the manufacturer's argument that ERISA did not allow individual recoveries, as the statute did not expressly disallow individual relief. The Court affirmed the lower court decisions. *Varity Corp. v. Howe*, 516 U.S. 489, 116 S.Ct. 1065, 134 L.Ed.2d 130 (1996).

Although an employer has the right to unilaterally amend or eliminate a welfare benefit plan, the Supreme Court found that § 510 of ERISA requires the employer to follow the plan's formal amendment process. Section 510 draws no distinction between those rights that vest under ERISA and those that do not.

A railway subsidiary employed workers to transfer cargo between rail cars and trucks at a Los Angeles rail yard. The employees were entitled to railroad retirement benefits and pension, health and welfare benefits under collective bargaining agreements that were covered by ERISA. The contract between the railway and the subsidiary was terminated, and the railway hired another service to do the work formerly done by the subsidiary. The new contractor retained some of the subsidiary's employees; however, it was not required to make railroad retirement contributions and its welfare plan was inferior to the subsidiary's plan. Employees who continued to work for the new contractor claimed that they suffered a substantial reduction in their employment benefits and filed a lawsuit against the railroad, the subsidiary and the new contractor in a federal district court, asserting that the manner of the discharge interfered with their ERISA pension and welfare benefits. The court granted a motion to dismiss the ERISA claims, and the employees appealed to the U.S. Court of Appeals, Ninth Circuit. The court reinstated the claim for interference with pension benefits, but agreed with the district court that ERISA did not protect employees from elimination of the welfare benefits, which did not vest. The U.S. Supreme Court agreed to review the case.

The Court found that § 510 of ERISA prevents an employer from discharging a plan participant or beneficiary for the purpose of interfering with the attainment of any right to which the participant might be entitled. Section 510 draws no distinction between those rights that vest under ERISA and those that do not. Further, although an employer has the right to unilaterally amend or eliminate a welfare benefit plan, § 510 requires the employer to follow the plan's formal amendment process. The Court vacated the judgment and remanded the case for further proceedings. *Inter-Modal Rail Employees Ass'n v. Atchison, Topeka and Santa Fe Railway Co.*, 520 U.S. 510, 117 S.Ct. 1513, 137 L.Ed.2d 763 (1997).

In the case below, the Supreme Court held that ERISA did not preempt a New York statute imposing a gross receipts tax on patient services at hospitals. The statute constituted a revenue raising measure and did not refer to or relate to an ERISA plan.

The U.S. Supreme Court considered a claim that a New York statute imposing a gross receipts tax on patient services at hospitals was preempted by ERISA. The case was brought by the trustees of a self-insured, multiemployer welfare benefit plan that owned and operated medical centers in New York. The Court held that the gross receipts tax was a revenue raising measure and not a hospital regulation. It operated in a field traditionally occupied by the states and did not expressly refer to an ERISA plan. The law did not require employers to provide benefits or determine a method of calculating benefits and was one of general applicability that did not relate to an ERISA plan. Accordingly, the court upheld the state gross receipts tax. *DeBuono v. NYSA-ILA Medical and Clinical Services Fund*, 520 U.S. 806, 117 S.Ct. 1747, 138 L.Ed.2d 21 (1997).

C. Termination Benefits

In a 1986 case, the Supreme Court held that a labor organization had standing to sue on behalf of its individual members to challenge guidelines issued by the Secretary of Labor.

The Trade Act of 1974 provides federally funded trade readjustment allowance (TRA) benefits as a supplement to state unemployment benefits for workers who have lost their jobs because of import competition. The Secretary of Labor issued guidelines in 1975 which required a worker to have 26 weeks of employment in the year preceding the layoff; leaves of absence, sick leaves, vacations and military leaves did not count toward the 26-week requirement. A 1981 amendment to the act permitted the periods of nonservice to be counted toward benefit eligibility. A union, some of whose members had been denied TRA benefits because of the guidelines, brought suit in federal court. The court held that the guidelines were inconsistent with the act, but the U.S. Court of Appeals reversed, holding that the union had no standing to bring the action. The case reached the U.S. Supreme Court.

The Supreme Court held that the union did have standing to litigate the action: its members would otherwise have had standing to sue in their own right; the interests it sought to protect were germane to its purpose; and the participation of individual members was not required in the suit. The Court noted that the union had the ability to proceed on behalf of its aggrieved members. Accordingly, it reversed the court of appeals' decision and remanded the case for a determination of whether the Secretary of Labor had properly interpreted the TRA eligibility provisions in the promulgated guidelines. *International Union, UAW v. Brock*, 477 U.S. 274, 106 S.Ct. 2523, 91 L.Ed.2d 228 (1986).

The Supreme Court determined that a state statute requiring severance pay upon a plant closing was not preempted by ERISA or by the NLRA. The statute did not "relate to" an employee benefit plan, but merely to employee benefits. There was no "plan" involved. Also, the state statute did not impermissibly intrude upon the collective bargaining process.

A packaging and processing company discontinued operations at a plant, laying off almost all its employees. Some of them then filed suit against the company seeking severance pay under Maine law. The company asserted that ERISA preempted the plant-closing statute (which required the company to provide severance pay). The Maine Supreme Judicial Court held that the company was liable for severance pay under the statute because ERISA only preempted benefit plans created by employers or employee organizations. The company sought further review from the U.S. Supreme Court.

The Court held that the Maine statute was not subject to preemption by ERISA. Here, the state law merely required a one-time lump-sum payment that was triggered by a single event (the plant closing). There was no ongoing administrative program the employer had to meet. Thus, there was no potential problem with multiple regulation by state and federal statutes. Further, the Maine statute was not preempted by the NLRA because it did not impermissibly intrude upon the collective bargaining process. *Fort Halifax Packing Co. v. Coyne*, 482 U.S. 1, 107 S.Ct. 2211, 96 L.Ed.2d 1 (1987).

A "participant" in an employee benefit plan does not include a person who claims to be, but is not, entitled to a plan benefit. Before it can be determined if employees are entitled to severance pay, it must be determined if they are "participants" in the termination pay plan.

An employer sold its plastics division as a going concern to another corporation. Most of its employees were rehired by the corporation and continued in their same positions. At the time of sale, the employer maintained, and was the plan administrator and fiduciary of, a termination pay plan covered by ERISA. Certain former employees brought suit against the employer after it denied their requests for severance benefits and for information about their benefits. A federal district court granted summary judgment to the employer, and the U.S. Court of Appeals, Third Circuit, affirmed in part and reversed in part. Appeal was taken to the U.S. Supreme Court.

The Court first held that the correct standard of review for the denial of benefits was the *de novo* standard that allowed for greater review and gave less deference to the plan administrator. The Court then defined a "participant entitled to disclosure" as either an employee in (or reasonably expected to be in) currently covered employment, or a former employee who has a reasonable expectation of returning to covered employment (or has a colorable claim to vested benefits). Because the court of appeals did not attempt to determine whether these former employees were participants, the case had to be remanded for such a determination. *Firestone Tire and Rubber Co. v. Bruch*, 489 U.S. 101, 109 S.Ct. 948, 103 L.Ed.2d 80 (1989).

CHAPTER THREE

Freedom of Expression

I.   FREEDOM OF SPEECH

In a 1968 termination lawsuit brought by an Illinois teacher against his school district, the Court ruled that teachers were entitled to constitutional protection to communicate on matters of public concern unless there was proof that the communication was made in reckless disregard for the truth. Speech on matters of public importance could not form the basis for termination.

An Illinois school district fired a high school teacher for sending a letter to the editor of the local newspaper. The letter criticized the board and district superintendent for their handling of school funding methods. Voters in the district voted down a tax rate increase to fund a bond issue for two new schools. The local teachers organization published an article in support of a second tax increase issue, as did the superintendent. District voters then rejected a second tax rate increase proposal. The teacher's letter came as a response to the superintendent and teacher organization articles and the second electoral defeat of the tax rate increase. The letter particularly criticized the board's handling of the bond issue and allocation of funding between school educational and athletic programs. The teacher also charged the superintendent with attempting to stifle opposing views on the subject. The board then held a hearing at which it charged the teacher with publishing a defamatory letter. After deeming the teacher's statements to be false, the board fired the teacher. An Illinois court affirmed the board's action, finding substantial evidence that publication of the letter was detrimental to the district's interest. The Illinois Supreme Court affirmed the dismissal, ruling that the teacher was unprotected by the First Amendment because he had accepted the position, which required him to refrain from statements about school operations.

The U.S. Supreme Court reversed and remanded the case, finding no support for the state supreme court's view that public employment subjected the teacher to deprivation of his constitutional rights. The state interest in regulating employee speech was to be balanced with individual rights. The Court outlined a general analysis for evaluating public employee speech, ruling that employees were entitled to constitutional protection to comment on matters of public concern. The public interest in free speech and debate on matters of public concern was so great that it barred public officials from recovering damages for defamatory statements unless they were made with reckless disregard for their truth. Because there was no evidence presented that the letter damaged any board member's professional reputation, the teacher's comments were not detrimental to the school system, but only constituted a difference of opinion. Since there was no proof of reckless disregard for the truth by the teacher and the matter concerned the public interest, the board could not constitutionally terminate his employment. The Court reversed and remanded the state court decision. *Pickering v. Bd. of Educ.*, 391 U.S. 563, 88 S.Ct. 1731, 20 L.Ed.2d 811 (1968).

In *Mount Healthy City School Dist. v. Doyle*, the Court ruled that the Eleventh Amendment does not bar private claims against local political subdivisions. While teachers enjoy certain First Amendment speech protections, marginal employees were not entitled to blanket protection if there were additional nonspeech grounds for termination.

An untenured teacher was not rehired after a number of incidents that led the school board to conclude that he lacked tactfulness in handling professional matters. Included in these incidents were a shouting match with a school cafeteria employee over the amount of spaghetti served the teacher; an argument with another teacher which resulted in a face-slapping and obscene gestures made by the teacher to two girls when the girls failed to obey his directives; and a telephone call placed by the teacher to a local radio station in which the teacher aired his opinions about a new school dress code. After the board decided not to reemploy the teacher, he asked for and received a list of the reasons for the board's decision. The board stated its reason for not rehiring in a general manner but also specifically cited the obscene gesture and radio station incidents. The teacher sued for reinstatement on the grounds that his discussion with the radio station was protected by the First Amendment and that to refuse reemployment on the basis of his exercise of a constitutionally protected right was a violation of his free speech rights. A U.S. District Court agreed and ordered reinstatement with back pay. This result was affirmed by a federal court of appeals, and the school board appealed to the U.S. Supreme Court.

The Court first rejected the school board's argument that the Eleventh Amendment barred private lawsuits against local political subdivisions such as the school district in federal lawsuits. City and county governments were not "states" within the meaning of the Eleventh Amendment. However, the Court overturned the court of appeals and district court decisions, holding that apart from the actions for which the teacher might claim First Amendment protection, the board could have chosen not to rehire him on the basis of several other incidents. The radio station incident, while clearly implicating a protected right, was not the substantial reason for nonrenewal. The board could have reached the same decision had the teacher not engaged in constitutionally protected conduct. A marginal employee should not have employment questions resolved in his favor simply because he engages in a constitutionally protected activity. But neither should marginal employees be able to prevent dismissal by engaging in constitutionally protected activity and then hiding under a constitutional shield as protection from all other actions that were not constitutionally protected. The lower courts were instructed to determine whether the board's decision could have been reached absent the constitutionally protected activity of phoning the radio station, and, if such a decision could have been reached, whether remedial action to correct the constitutional violation would be necessary. *Mount Healthy City School Dist. v. Doyle*, 429 U.S. 274, 97 S.Ct. 568, 50 L.Ed.2d 471 (1977).

The Supreme Court upheld the right of a Mississippi teacher to voice opposition to the racial policies of her school district. It held that public employees retained First Amendment protection when they made private communications with their employers.

A Mississippi junior high school English teacher was discharged by her school district for allegedly not cooperating with administration officials over school policy. The teacher then intervened in a federal district court action ordering the school district to desegregate. She sought reinstatement, arguing that the school district had violated her First and Fourteenth Amendment rights to free speech by firing her in retaliation for vocally opposing the school district's segregative policies. Before the federal district court, the school district contended that it had dismissed the teacher for justifiable reasons. It pointed to several earlier encounters between the teacher and school officials, in which the teacher had allegedly made petty and unreasonable demands in a rude manner. However, the district court concluded that the teacher had been discharged for exercising her free speech rights. The teacher had legitimately been speaking out against school policies that she thought were racially discriminatory. Thus, the dismissal violated the First Amendment. The U.S. Court of Appeals, Fifth Circuit, reversed. It concluded that because the teacher had privately expressed her concerns with the school principal, the speech was not protected under the First Amendment. It stated that public employees do not have a right to privately express their views to a higher authority. The U.S. Supreme Court granted certiorari.

The Court rejected as clearly erroneous the court of appeals' conclusion that public employee speech in private situations was unprotected by the First Amendment. The Court's previous decisions in *Pickering v. Bd. of Educ.* and *Mount Healthy City School Dist. v. Doyle*, above, did not stand for the proposition that public employee expression in private was without constitutional protection. Those cases had involved public employees making public criticism of school policies. However, protection of speech was not dependent on the public character of the speech. The principal, by opening his door to the teacher, had not been an "unwilling recipient" of the teacher's views. The Court refused to adopt the view that the First Amendment makes a distinction between private and public speech by public employees. The Court vacated the court of appeals' decision and remanded the case. *Givhan v. Western Line Consolidated School Dist.*, 439 U.S. 410, 99 S.Ct. 693, 58 L.Ed.2d 619 (1978).

In cases of prior restraint or censorship by the government, the First Amendment requires a substantial government interest and restriction of speech no more than is reasonably necessary to protect that interest. The case below demonstrates protection of the substantial governmental interest in maintaining the respect for duty and discipline necessary for military effectiveness.

An Air Force reserve officer distributed petitions relating to grooming standards on an Air Force base. The petitions were addressed to members of Congress and to the Secretary of Defense, and were aimed at reducing racial tension, and improving morale. However, the officer did not obtain permission to circulate the petitions even though he knew he needed command approval to do so. He was removed from active duty as a result. Subsequently, he brought suit in federal court, challenging the validity of the regulations as violative of the First Amendment. The court granted summary judgment to the officer, and the

U.S. Court of Appeals affirmed. Further appeal was taken to the U.S. Supreme Court.

The Court held that the regulations requiring prior approval did not violate the First Amendment. They protected a substantial government interest—maintaining the respect for duty and discipline necessary for military effectiveness—and restricted speech no more than was reasonably necessary to protect that interest. Further, the regulations did not impinge on the officer's right to communicate with a member of Congress (guaranteed by federal law). He was free to write to the people addressed in his petitions. Accordingly, the Court reversed the lower courts' decisions and held that the circulation of petitions could be restricted. *Brown v. Glines*, 444 U.S. 348, 100 S.Ct. 594, 62 L.Ed.2d 540 (1980).

The Supreme Court clarified the holding in *Pickering v. Bd. of Educ.*, **in the following case. Public employee speech rights are substantially less protected if the speech does not involve a matter of public concern. General comments about the workplace do not warrant protection as matters of public concern.**

An assistant district attorney in New Orleans had the responsibility of trying criminal cases. When the district attorney proposed to transfer the assistant to prosecute cases in a different section of the criminal court, she opposed the transfer. She then expressed her views on the matter to several of her superiors. Shortly thereafter, she prepared and distributed a questionnaire to other assistant district attorneys in the office concerning the office's transfer policy, morale, the level of confidence in superiors, and whether the employees felt pressured to work for political campaigns, among other things. The district attorney then fired her for refusing the transfer and for the act of insubordination in distributing the questionnaire. The assistant sued in federal court, alleging that she had been discharged in violation of her First Amendment rights. The district court agreed and she was reinstated with backpay and attorney's fees. The U.S. Court of Appeals, Fifth Circuit, affirmed and the U.S. Supreme Court granted review.

The court stated that in order to determine a public employee's rights of free speech, the balancing test of *Pickering v. Bd. of Educ.*, must be utilized. The interests of the employee as a citizen in commenting upon matters of public concern must outweigh the interest of the state, as employer, in promoting efficiency in the workplace. As a threshold matter, the Court stated that when a public employee speaks not as a citizen upon matters of public concern, but instead as an employee upon matters of only personal interest, a federal court is not the appropriate forum in which to review the wisdom of a personnel decision taken by a public agency in reaction to that speech. Here, except for the assistant's question regarding pressure to work in political campaigns, the questions were not matters of public concern. The state also need not prove substantial disruption of the office in order to justify dismissal when the First Amendment right is limited. In this case, the district attorney's action was reasonable if he thought that the speech in question would disrupt the office, undermine his authority and destroy working relationships in the office. *Connick v. Myers,* 461 U.S. 138, 103 S.Ct. 1684, 75 L.Ed.2d 708 (1983).

Whether the protections of the First Amendment apply to individual speech may depend upon the nature of the "forum" for speech. As implied in earlier cases, the workplace is not a "public forum."

The Combined Federal Campaign, a charity drive aimed at federal employees, was conducted in the workplace largely by voluntary efforts of federal employees. Participating organizations confined their fundraising activities to a 30-word statement submitted for inclusion in the campaign literature. Only tax-exempt, nonprofit charitable organizations supported by contributions from the public that provided direct health and welfare services to individuals were eligible to participate. A group of political advocacy and legal defense organizations, specifically excluded from participating, brought suit in federal court alleging that their exclusion was violative of their First Amendment right to solicit charitable contributions. The district court granted summary judgment in their favor, and the U.S. Court of Appeals affirmed. Further appeal was taken to the U.S. Supreme Court.

The Court first noted that solicitation in the context of the campaign was speech protected by the First Amendment. However, the Court then stated that the groups were seeking access to a particular means of communication (the campaign), which was a nonpublic forum. To be valid, the government's decision to restrict access to a nonpublic forum need only be reasonable. The record supported an inference that the groups' participation in the campaign would be detrimental to the campaign and disruptive of the workplace. The Court reversed the lower courts' decisions and remanded the case for a determination of whether the government had impermissibly excluded the organizations because it disagreed with their viewpoints. *Cornelius v. NAACP Legal Defense & Educational Fund*, 473 U.S. 788, 105 S.Ct. 3439, 87 L.Ed.2d 567 (1985).

The Court considered a First Amendment rights case in 1987 that involved an employee's comments following an attempted Presidential assassination. Although the comments were not deemed to be a matter of public concern, the Court reasoned that the employee's free speech rights were still protected due to the government's failure to show that the statements disrupted the workplace.

A data entry employee in a Texas county constable's office was discharged for a remark to a coworker, after hearing of an attempt on President Reagan's life, "If they go for him again, I hope they get him." The statement was overheard by another employee, who reported it to the constable. The constable questioned the employee about the remark and then fired her. The employee brought suit in a federal district court alleging that the constable had violated her First Amendment rights by firing her. The district court held for the constable, ruling that the employee's speech was unprotected. The U.S. Court of Appeals, Fifth Circuit, vacated the holding and remanded on the ground that substantial issues of material fact remained regarding the context in which the statements had been made. On remand, the district court once again held for the constable. The court of appeals reversed, holding that the employee's remark had addressed a matter of public concern. The U.S. Supreme Court granted certiorari and affirmed the court of appeals' decision.

The Court stated that the content, form, and context of the employee's statement supported the conclusion that her speech was on a matter of public concern. Although a statement that amounted to a threat to kill the President would not be protected by the First Amendment, the court stated that the employee's speech, in this instance, could not be characterized as a threat. The Court also stated that the employee's relatively low position in the office and the lack of evidence that her statement interfered with the efficient functioning of the office undermined the argument that the state had an interest outweighing the employee's First Amendment rights. *Rankin v. McPherson,* 483 U.S. 378, 107 S.Ct. 2891, 97 L.Ed.2d 315 (1987).

Connick v. Myers **held that the First Amendment protects a government employee's speech if it is on a matter of public concern and if the employee's interest in expressing herself on the matter is not outweighed by the potential injury to the government's interest. Eleven years later, the Supreme Court held that the** *Connick* **test should be applied to what the government employer reasonably thought was said rather than to what was determined to have been said.**

A nurse at an Illinois public hospital allegedly gave a negative report about the obstetrics department to a cross-trainee. For example, she stated that the department was a bad place to work, that her supervisor was trying to find reasons to fire her, and that she had been wrongly blamed following a patient complaint. She also criticized her supervisors, saying that they were "ruining the hospital." The cross-trainee reported this conversation to the nurse's supervisor. After twice reviewing the record, the hospital discharged the nurse. The nurse filed suit in a U.S. district court alleging that the discharge was in response to her criticism of the hospital's cross-training and staffing policies in violation of her First Amendment rights. The district court held for the supervisor and the hospital. On appeal, the U.S. Court of Appeals, Seventh Circuit, reversed, holding that the employee was discharged for engaging in speech protected by the First Amendment. The supervisor and the hospital appealed to the U.S. Supreme Court.

The issue on appeal was whether the test set out in *Connick v. Myers,* 461 U.S. 138, 103 S.Ct. 1684, 75 L.Ed.2d 708 (1983), should be applied to what the government employer reasonably thought was said, or to what the trier of fact ultimately determines was said. The Court noted that government action based on protected speech may violate the First Amendment even if the public employer honestly believes the speech is not protected. However, the Court expressly declined to adopt a specific test to determine when to adopt procedural safeguards protecting employee speech. Instead, the Court held that it must look to the facts as the employer reasonably found them to be. For example, it may be unreasonable for the employer to take adverse employment actions based on extremely weak evidence. Here, the court determined that the employee had sufficient evidence to create a material issue of disputed fact about the supervisor's actual motivation. The supervisor had previously reacted negatively to the employee's criticisms of the cross-training and staffing policies. On remand, if a jury determined that the employee was discharged for these reasons, the court would then have to determine whether the employee's criticisms were protected speech. The holding of the court of appeals was vacated and the case was remanded for further proceedings. *Waters v. Churchill*, 511 U.S. 661, 114 S.Ct. 1878, 128 L.Ed.2d 686 (1994).

The Supreme Court held that § 501(b) of the Ethics in Government Act violated the First Amendment. That section prohibited federal employees from accepting any compensation for making speeches or writing articles. The Court stated that the ban on honoraria imposed the kind of burden that abridged speech under the First Amendment.

An amendment to the Ethics in Government Act broadly prohibited federal employees from accepting any compensation for making speeches or writing articles. Specifically, the act provided that "an individual may not receive any honorarium while that individual is a member, officer or employee" of the federal government. Officer or employee included nearly all employees. Member included any representative, delegate or resident commissioner to Congress. An honorarium encompassed any compensation paid to a government employee for "an appearance, speech or article." Regulations promulgated pursuant to the act permitted remuneration for performances using "artistic, athletic or other such skills or talent." Two unions and several career civil servants below grade GS-16 filed suit in a U.S. district court, challenging the constitutionality of the act. The district court held for the employees and the U.S. Court of Appeals, District of Columbia Circuit, affirmed. The government appealed to the U.S. Supreme Court.

The Supreme Court noted that a restraint on employees' right to comment on matters of public concern must be balanced against the government's interest in promoting the efficiency of the public services it performs. Although congressional directives are generally deemed valid, the widespread impact of the honorarium ban improperly chilled potential speech before it happened. Consequently, the government's burden was greater with respect to this statutory restriction on expression than with respect to an isolated disciplinary action based on a single employee's protected speech. The government contended that its concern that federal officers not misuse power by accepting compensation for their unofficial and nonpolitical writing and speaking activities justified the ban. The Supreme Court disagreed, ruling that the blanket restriction on remuneration for any type of employee expression—even if the subject matter was not related to the individual's official duties—belied this assertion. Because the act was not reasonably necessary to protect the alleged government interest, it was unconstitutional as applied to executive branch employees below grade GS-16. However, the act reasonably applied to members of Congress, judges and high-ranking officials in the executive branch. *United States v. National Treasury Employees Union*, 513 U.S. 454, 115 S.Ct. 1003, 130 L.Ed.2d 964 (1995).

In the following case, the Supreme Court held that the protections of the First Amendment extended to independent government contractors. As a result, their contracts could not be terminated in retaliation for their criticisms.

A Kansas trash hauler who had an at-will contract with a county to haul trash was an outspoken critic of the board of county commissioners. After the commissioners voted to terminate (or prevent the automatic renewal of) the contract, he sued two of the commissioners in a federal district court under 42 U.S.C. § 1983, alleging that they had terminated his contract in retaliation for his criticisms. The court held that the contract had been terminated in retaliation for the speech, but that the First Amendment did not prohibit the commissioners from considering the criticisms as a factor in deciding to terminate the contract. The U.S. Court of Appeals, Tenth Circuit, reversed, holding that "an independent contractor is protected under the First Amendment from retaliatory government action, just as an employee would be."

On further appeal, the U.S. Supreme Court held that the First Amendment protects independent contractors from the termination or prevention of automatic renewal of their at-will government contracts in retaliation for their exercise of freedom of speech. The Court utilized the *Pickering* balancing test to weigh the government's interests as a contractor against the trash hauler's First Amendment rights. Although the government's and the individual's rights are generally less strong in an independent contractor case than in an employment case, the fact that independent government contractors are similar in most relevant respects to government employees compels the conclusion that the same form of balancing analysis should apply to each. The Court affirmed the court of appeals' decision. *Bd. of County Comm'rs, Wabaunsee County, Kansas v. Umbehr*, 518 U.S.668, 116 S.Ct. 2342, 135 L.Ed.2d 843 (1996).

After Arizona amended its constitution to establish English as the official language of the state, a public employee challenged the amendment based on violation of the First and Fourteenth Amendments to the U.S. Constitution and Title VI. The Supreme Court found that although the employee initially had a viable claim, when she left her state job to take employment in the private sector where her speech was not governed by the amendment, she lacked a vital claim. Thus, her later employment in the private sector rendered the challenge moot.

Arizona amended its constitution to establish English as the official language of the state. An insurance claims manager employed by the Arizona Department of Administration believed the amendment meant she would lose her job or face other sanctions if she did not immediately refrain from speaking Spanish while serving the state. As a result, she filed suit in federal district court under 42 U.S.C. § 1983, alleging that the amendment violated the First and Fourteenth Amendments to the U.S. Constitution and Title VI of the Civil Rights Act of 1964. The district found in favor of the manager and denied post-judgment motions. Appeal was then taken to the U.S. Court of Appeals, Ninth Circuit. Prior to the court of appeals' decision, however, the manager resigned from public sector employment to pursue work in the private sector. Rather than rendering the case moot, the court of appeals found that her constitutional claims could entitle her to nominal damages and construed the amendment as manifestly overbroad. On further appeal, the U.S. Supreme Court held that the case was moot and should not have been retained for adjudication on the merits.

Although the manager had a viable claim at the outset of the litigation, when she left her state job to take employment in the private sector where her speech was not governed by the amendment, she lacked a vital claim. The plea for nominal damages could not revive the case. The Court vacated and remanded with directions to dismiss. *Arizonans for Official English v. Arizona*, 520 U.S. 43, 117 S.Ct. 1055, 137 L.Ed.2d 170 (1997).

II. POLITICAL ACTIVITIES

The Hatch Act, 5 U.S.C. §§ 7321-27, prohibits all employees of the executive branch or any individual employed by the government of the District of Columbia from using the employee's official authority or influence for the purpose of interfering with or affecting the outcome of an election. The employee retains the right to vote as the employee chooses and to express an opinion on political matters. The political prohibitions of the Hatch Act do not apply to educational or research institutions in the District of Columbia, or to any employee paid from the appropriation for the office of the President. It also does not apply to the department head or assistant head of any executive or military department, or to employees appointed by the president with the advice and consent of the Senate or the mayor of the District of Columbia and other District of Columbia officials. Any employee who violates the political activity prohibition may be removed. However, the act allows employees to engage in nonpartisan political activity.

The constitutionality of the Hatch Act has been brought before the Supreme Court twice and upheld on both occasions. In *U.S. Civil Service Comm'n v. National Ass'n of Letter Carriers*, 413 U.S. 548, 93 S.Ct. 2880, 37 L.Ed.2d 796 (1973), the court held that the prohibition against employees assuming an active role in political campaigning or management was neither overbroad nor unconstitutionally vague. In *United Public Workers of America v. Mitchell*, 330 U.S. 75, 67 S.Ct. 556, 91 L.Ed 754 (1947), the Court stated that it was within Congress' power to regulate the political conduct of federal employees. The *National Ass'n of Letter Carriers* case also held that the act forbids such activities as organizing political clubs or parties, participating in political fund-raising, becoming a partisan candidate for elected office, managing the campaign of a partisan candidate, initiating a nominating petition for a partisan candidate or serving at a party convention. The Merit System Protection Board will determine whether an employee's action violates the Hatch Act. The Hatch Act does not apply to most state and local employees, but many states regulate the political activities of their employees by statute, regulation or departmental rules.

In 1993, Congress passed the Hatch Act Reform Amendment to cure perceived deficiencies in the act by broadening the type of political activities in which a federal employee can participate. Under the amendment, federal employees may take part in "political management or in political campaigns" subject to certain express prohibitions, including engaging in partisan political activity while on duty or in government facilities.

A. Loyalty Oaths

In a 1950 case, the Court ruled that restrictions, such as loyalty oaths and affidavits swearing disavowal of Communist Party affiliation, on new public employees were permissible as an exercise of legislative standards on employee competency.

In 1941, the California legislature amended the city of Los Angeles charter to disqualify from public employment any public employee or official who had taught or advocated the violent overthrow of the government during the previous five years. In accordance with the charter, the city then passed an ordinance requiring all city officers and employees to take an oath swearing that they had not and would not become members of the Communist Party, nor advocate the violent overthrow of the government. The ordinance also required that employees execute affidavits swearing that they had never been Communist Party members, or if they had been, certifying the dates during which they were members. After they were discharged for refusing to execute affidavits or refusing to take oaths, a group of civil service employees sued the city board in a California trial court for reinstatement and unpaid salaries. They attacked the ordinance, claiming that it violated Article I, § 10 of the U.S. Constitution, which prohibits states from passing bills of attainder and *ex post facto* laws. In addition, the group alleged that the ordinance deprived them of freedom of speech and assembly, and the right to petition the government for a redress of grievances. After a California appellate court denied the group's claims, the employees appealed to the U.S. Supreme Court.

The Court held first that the affidavit provision of the ordinance was valid because states have a legitimate interest in inquiring into employee backgrounds. This was because past conduct and loyalty may have a reasonable relationship to present and future trust. The Court then upheld the oath provision of the charter, stating that it was valid under the Constitution as a reasonable regulation to protect municipal service. The Court held that the ordinance was not an *ex post facto* law and rejected the group's argument that the ordinance was a bill of attainder. It held that constitutional guarantees against such legislation were not intended to prevent legislative establishment of public employment standards. The statute declared general and prospective standards for public employment eligibility. Finally, the oath did not violate due process of law. The oath would not harm those innocent of belonging to such groups but would punish only those who intended to continue such associations. *Garner v. Los Angeles Bd.*, 341 U.S. 716, 71 S.Ct. 909, 95 L.Ed. 1317 (1950).

In another early loyalty oath case, the Court held that the state interest in protecting public education from the dangers of subversive groups outweighed teacher associational rights, at least where minimal due process rights were respected.

The New York legislature passed a civil service law which prohibited anyone who advocated the violent overthrow of the government, or belonged to any organization doing so, from being a public employee. It also adopted the

"Feinberg Law," which allowed the implementation of the civil service law by giving the state board of regents authority to eliminate "subversive" persons from the public school system. The law also required the discharge of superintendents, teachers and school employees for treasonable or seditious acts or utterances. The Feinberg Law set out the alleged problem of subversive teachers in the classroom. The legislature concluded that because subversive people belonging to the Communist Party have a duty to advocate the party line, infiltration of Communist ideas into the classroom could go undetected, unless teachers were properly screened. The law also allowed the state board of regents to make a list of subversive organizations after first giving them notice and a hearing. After the list was to be made, membership by any school employee in a listed organization would constitute *prima facie* evidence requiring discharge or disqualification. School employees challenged the civil service law, as implemented by the Feinberg law, in a New York trial court. The court held that the laws violated the Fourteenth Amendment's Due Process Clause and enjoined enforcement. The New York Supreme Court, Appellate Division, reversed and the New York Court of Appeals affirmed. The U.S. Supreme Court agreed to hear the case.

The Court held that teachers have a constitutional right to think, speak and believe as they wish. However, teachers do not have a right to work for the public school system on their own terms. School districts have the power to inquire into an employee's background to determine eligibility as a teacher. The state interest in education is strong. Therefore, the state may properly inquire into its teachers' organizational associations. If a person is disqualified from teaching in the public school system because of membership in an organization advocating violent overthrow of the government, he or she is not denied freedom of speech or assembly. The Court rejected the employees' argument that participation in a subversive organization as a *prima facie* cause for dismissal was a violation of due process. Because the teachers had a chance to rebut the presumption of unfitness for teaching at a hearing, they received adequate due process. The Court refused to consider the employees' claim that the statutes were unconstitutionally vague, ruling that it would not pass upon the constitutionality of a state statute until state courts have had an opportunity to do so. The Court upheld the New York courts' decisions, ruling that the statutes were constitutional. *Adler v. Bd. of Educ.*, 342 U.S. 485, 72 S.Ct. 380, 96 L.Ed. 517 (1951).

In a later case, the Court ruled that public employees have constitutional protection from arbitrary laws.

An Oklahoma law required all state officers and employees to take a loyalty oath. The oath certified that the employee did not advocate the violent overthrow of the government, or associate with an organization advocating such activity. In addition, the oath required the employee to swear to uphold U.S. laws and the U.S. Constitution. The act required employees to swear that they would take up arms in defense of the U.S. in times of emergency or war. It allowed employees 30 days to take the oath. A group of faculty and staff members of the Oklahoma Agricultural and Mechanical College failed to take the oath within the permitted 30 days. An Oklahoma taxpayer filed a lawsuit in an Oklahoma trial court to prevent the state from paying the employees until they took the oath. The employees intervened in the lawsuit, attacking the statute as a bill of attainder and an *ex post facto* law. The employees argued that the act impaired their employment contracts with the state and violated the Fourteenth Amendment's Due Process Clause. They sought an injunction to force the state to pay their salaries despite having failed to take the oath. The court ruled for the taxpayer and enjoined state officials from paying the employees. The Supreme Court of Oklahoma affirmed this decision and the U.S. Supreme Court agreed to hear the appeal.

The Court noted that the Oklahoma Supreme Court, in affirming the trial court's decision, concluded that the act required a pledge of nonallegiance to organizations specified on a list compiled by the U.S. Attorney General. The act intended to make loyalty a prerequisite to public employment. The Court stated that as public employees, the employees were already automatically disqualified for association with any organization on the list. The Court reversed the state supreme court's decision and struck down the statute. The Court distinguished its decision in *Adler v. Bd. of Educ.*, above, on the basis that the law there required knowledge of organizational purpose before the regulation applied. Because the employees did not have an opportunity to take the oath after the statute was interpreted, knowledge was not a factor in the Oklahoma statute. Association membership may be innocent and the state could not infer intent by association. The consequences of discharge for an employee who failed to take the oath were great and long lasting. The Court refused to decide whether a right to public employment exists. It held only that public employees affected by an arbitrary or discriminatory statute enjoyed constitutional protection. *Wieman v. Updegraff*, 344 U.S. 183, 73 S.Ct. 215, 97 L.Ed. 216 (1952).

In 1955, as McCarthyism waned, the Court invalidated a New York City charter provision which purported to deprive Communist Party members of their Fifth Amendment right against self-incrimination.

Section 903 of New York City's charter provided that any city employee who used the Fifth Amendment's self-incrimination privilege to avoid answering a question relating to official conduct would lose tenure and be ineligible for future city employment. An associate professor of German at Brooklyn College was called before the U.S. Senate Judiciary Committee's Internal Security Subcommittee to testify about subversive influences within the nation's educational system. The professor testified that he was not a member of the Communist Party and was completely willing to answer questions about his political affiliation from 1941 to the present date. However, he refused to answer questions about his political beliefs during 1940 and 1941 on the grounds that his answers might incriminate him. Allegations had previously been made before another investigative committee that the professor was a Communist Party member in 1941. After the professor testified before the Internal Security Subcommittee, the college suspended him even though he had taught there for 27 years and was entitled to tenure under New York state law. Three days later, his position was vacated in accordance with § 903. If not for § 903, because he was tenured, the professor would have been entitled to notice, hearing and the opportunity to appeal an unfavorable decision, with discharge for just cause being the only appropriate termination.

The New York Court of Appeals had previously held that using the self-incrimination privilege as a defense in tenure cases was tantamount to resignation. Thus, the professor was not entitled to the usual procedural safeguard requirements. The professor filed suit in a New York trial court, challenging the constitutionality of § 903. He argued that the section violated the Privileges and Immunities Clause of the Fourteenth Amendment since it effectively imposed a penalty on the exercise of a federally guaranteed right in a federal proceeding. He also argued that it violated his due process rights under the Fifth and Fourteenth Amendments because the statute did not provide a reasonable basis for his termination.

The Court ruled that the statute violated the Due Process Clause and therefore did not consider the Privileges and Immunities Clause claim. It distinguished *Garner v. Los Angeles Bd.*, above, from this case because in *Garner*, due process in the form of notice and a hearing was provided to the employee. Here, the teacher was dismissed without a hearing. The Court also ruled that taking the self-incrimination privilege could not automatically be interpreted to mean that the teacher had been a Communist Party member. The Court held that such an arbitrary dismissal violated due process. *Slochower v. Bd. of Educ.*, 350 U.S. 551, 76 S.Ct. 637, 100 L.Ed. 692 (1955).

In 1961, the Court struck down a Florida loyalty oath statute because it was impermissibly vague. The statute failed to adequately advise employees of the standard of conduct to which they were to be held.

Florida law required each state employee to submit a written oath, certifying that he or she had never lent counsel, advised, aided or supported the Communist Party. A failure to submit such an oath resulted in the employee's immediate termination. A teacher who had taught in the same Florida school district for nine years was dismissed when he refused to sign the oath. The teacher sought a declaration that the statute was unconstitutional and an injunction to prevent its enforcement. He argued that the statute was an *ex post facto* law and a bill of attainder. A Florida trial court refused to grant an injunction, and the Florida Supreme Court affirmed this decision.

After determining that the case was based on federal law and was properly a matter in which it had jurisdiction, the U.S. Supreme Court struck the statute down as a violation of the Fourteenth Amendment's Due Process Clause. The statute was too vague to pass constitutional standards. It compelled state employees to take the oath or face immediate dismissal. Because the statute lacked objective standards, no employee could truthfully take the oath. Statutes that made persons of average intelligence guess at their possible meanings and applications violated the Due Process Clause because they did not constitute true rules or standards. The Court reversed the Florida court decisions, ruling for the teacher. *Cramp v. Bd. of Public Instruction of Orange County*, 368 U.S. 278, 82 S.Ct. 275, 7 L.Ed.2d 285 (1961).

A Washington statute attempted to prohibit persons identified as subversives from employment as public school teachers. The Court noted the absence of clearly defined standards within the act and struck it down as unconstitutionally vague.

Faculty members at the University of Washington brought a class action suit to declare two state statutes unconstitutional. One statute required all state employees to take loyalty oaths, and the other required all teachers to take an oath as a condition of employment. Both oaths dealt with employee loyalty to the U.S. Constitution and to the government. The public employee statute applied to all public employees and defined a "subversive person" as one who conspired to overthrow the government. The Communist Party was also named as a subversive organization. Persons designated as subversives or Communist Party members were ineligible for public employment. The university board of regents sent a memorandum to all its instructors, requiring them to take the oath. A federal district court held that the public employee act was constitutional. It abstained from ruling on the teachers' act pending consideration by the state courts. The teachers appealed to the U.S. Supreme Court.

Before the Court, the teachers argued that the statutes were vague and overbroad, and violated the Fourteenth Amendment's Due Process Clause. The Court reversed the appeals court decision, holding that both statutes were too unspecific to provide sufficient notice of what conduct was prohibited. This constituted a denial of the teachers' due process rights. The university could not require its teachers to take an oath which applied to some vague behavior in the future, especially since there were First Amendment freedom of speech and association claims at stake. Finally, the court of appeals should have decided the constitutionality of the teachers' act to avoid piecemeal legislation and to avoid possible inhibition of First Amendment rights. *Baggett v. Bullitt*, 377 U.S. 360, 84 S.Ct. 1316, 12 L.Ed.2d 377 (1963).

In accordance with its decision in *Baggett v. Bullitt*, above, the Court invalidated an Arizona statute containing a loyalty oath. The statute attempted to outlaw some political groups. The Court ruled that unless the group showed some specific intent to carry out an illegal purpose, the government could not punish its members.

An Arizona teacher who was a Quaker refused to take an oath required of all public employees under Arizona law. The oath swore that the employee would support both the Arizona and U.S. Constitutions as well as state laws. The legislation also stated that anyone who took the oath and supported the Communist Party or the violent overthrow of government would be discharged from employment and charged with perjury. The teacher sued for declaratory relief in the Arizona courts, having decided she could not take the oath in good conscience because she did not know what it meant. The case eventually reached the Arizona Supreme Court, which upheld the constitutionality of the oath and potential sanctions under the statute. The U.S. Supreme Court vacated the court's decision and remanded the case for reconsideration in light of its decision in *Baggett v. Bullitt*, above. On reconsideration, the Arizona Supreme Court again upheld the oath, distinguishing the case from *Baggett*. The U.S. Supreme Court granted certiorari.

The Court began by noting that political groups may have both legal and illegal aims and that there should not be a blanket prohibition on all groups that might have both legal and illegal goals. Such a prohibition would threaten legitimate political expression and association. The Court held that mere association with a group cannot be prohibited without a showing of "specific intent" to carry out the group's illegal purpose. The Court held that the Arizona statute was constitutionally deficient because it was not confined to those employees with a "specific intent" to do something illegal. The statute infringed upon employee rights to free association by not punishing specific behavior that yielded a clear and present danger to government. The statute was struck down as unconstitutional. *Elfbrandt v. Russell*, 384 U.S. 11, 86 S.Ct. 1238, 16 L.Ed.2d 321 (1965).

In 1967, the Court overruled its *Adler v. Bd. of Educ.* decision, holding that New York statutory prohibitions on treasonable and seditious speech by public employees were unconstitutionally vague. The statute may have allowed dismissal of employees who merely believed in such doctrine, without actually advocating it.

A group of faculty members were employed by the privately owned University of Buffalo in New York. They continued their employment when the university merged into a state operated university. Because they became public employees, the faculty members were required to comply with a state plan that disqualified subversive persons from public employment. Four professors refused to sign a certificate that they were not Communists and that if they ever had been, they had notified the state university's president. One instructor was dismissed immediately for refusing to sign the certificate. Two more continued to teach until their contracts ran out. Another employee who worked in the library refused to answer under oath whether he had ever been a Communist Party member and was dismissed. The group sought injunctive and declaratory relief in a federal district court. The court held that the state requirements were constitutional. The U.S. Supreme Court agreed to hear the case.

The Court first recounted its decision in *Adler v. Bd. of Educ.*, above, in which it upheld the constitutionality of the Feinberg law. The Court then examined the statute, which allowed the removal of public school teachers for "treasonable or seditious" utterances or acts. The Court held that such words were too vague to allow teachers to know the difference between seditious and nonseditious utterances or acts. In addition, another section of the statute allowed dismissal of any person who "by word of mouth or writing willfully and deliberately advocates, advises or teaches the doctrine" of the violent overthrow of government. The Court struck it down as too vague and sweeping, stating that it may allow dismissal of an employee who merely believes in such doctrine, without actually advocating it. Because of such vague provisions, teachers would not know exactly what was prohibited and would stay away from all utterances or acts that might constitute treachery or sedition. Thus, teachers' free speech association rights would be inhibited. Although the state has a legitimate interest in screening teachers, it must do so only in a manner that does not stifle fundamental personal rights. Finally, the Court struck down New York's scheme as unconstitutionally vague. The Court went on to attack the *Adler* premise, that public employment may be conditioned upon the surrender of constitutional rights. In rejecting this premise, the Court struck down the scheme's provision that proscribed mere membership in a communist organization as grounds for dismissal without any showing of specific intent to further an organization's aims. Such a provision is unconstitutionally overbroad and thus infringes on rights. The Court reversed the district court's decision. *Keyishian v. Bd. of Regents*, 385 U.S. 589, 87 S.Ct. 675, 17 L.Ed.2d 629 (1967).

The Court ruled in a 1967 Maryland case involving a loyalty oath that the line between permissible and impermissible conduct must be clearly drawn.

A teacher was offered a position with the University of Maryland. However, he refused to take a required loyalty oath. The oath required the employee to swear that he was not engaged in any attempt to overthrow the government by force or violence. It was authored by the state attorney general and approved by the university board of regents under a state statute that authorized state agencies to establish procedures to determine whether a prospective employee was a subversive person under the act. The act defined a subversive person as someone who attempted or advocated the overthrow, destruction or alteration of the government by revolution, force or violence, or someone who was a member of such an organization. The teacher filed suit in a federal district court, challenging the oath's constitutionality. The board of regents argued that it had the authority to establish the oath under the legislative act. The board also argued that the act should be construed to bar only those who seek to overthrow or destroy the government by force or violence. A severability clause contained in the statute purported to allow the Supreme Court to strike down parts of the statute, while leaving its constitutional parts intact. The district court dismissed the teacher's challenge. The U.S. Supreme Court granted certiorari.

The Court first decided that the oath's constitutionality had to be considered in conjunction with the state statute allowing the university board of regents to establish the oath. In addition, free speech rights were implicated because the First Amendment protects controversial as well as conventional dialogue. The Court held that the authorizing statute was too vague and overbroad. It falsely assumed that someone belonging to a subversive group also supported the violent overthrow of the government. The statute also put continuous surveillance on teachers by imposing a perjury threat. Such a concept was hostile to academic freedom, limiting the free flow of ideas in places of learning. The Court ruled that the line between permissible and impermissible conduct must be clearly drawn. Because the statute failed to clearly define prohibited behavior, the Court reversed the district court's decision. *Whitehill v. Elkins*, 389 U.S. 54, 88 S.Ct. 184, 19 L.Ed.2d 228 (1967).

In 1970, the Supreme Court ruled unconstitutional part of a Florida statute that required public employees to state under oath that they did not believe in the violent overthrow of the government. This violated Due Process Clause rights of the employees.

Florida law required all public employees to swear to a loyalty oath as a condition of employment. Employees were required to swear that they were not members of the Communist Party, nor any other organization that believes in the violent overthrow of the government. Employees were also required to swear that they did not believe in the violent overthrow of the government. A woman who had been hired as a substitute teacher was dismissed for refusing to sign the loyalty oath. A federal district court declared that the portion of the statute requiring the oath disavowing Communist Party affiliation was unconstitutional. However, it upheld the statements pertaining to supporting the U.S. Constitution. The teacher appealed to the U.S. Supreme Court, challenging the constitutionality of the last part of the oath. The Court held that the section of the oath requiring employees to pledge support to the Constitution and the government was no different from that required of all state and federal officers. Therefore, it passed constitutional scrutiny. However, the oath requiring employees to state that they did not believe in the violent overthrow of the government was unconstitutional, since it denied employee due process rights under the Fourteenth Amendment. *Connell v. Higginbotham*, 403 U.S. 207, 91 S.Ct. 1772, 29 L.Ed.2d 418 (1970).

B. Political Patronage

According to the following case, the ability of elected officials to discharge public employees and replace them with their own appointees depends upon the duties of the employees. Broadly speaking, so-called "policymaking" employees are susceptible to political patronage dismissal. However, employees in nonpolicymaking positions are accorded a higher degree of protection by the courts.

Several Illinois noncivil service employees, who had been appointed to their positions by a Republican sheriff, were discharged when the new Democratic sheriff was elected. It had been the practice of newly elected sheriffs to replace noncivil service employees from the opposing party with members of their own party upon assuming office. This time, however, the discharged employees sued in a federal trial court to prevent the terminations. The court ruled against them, and they successfully appealed. The incoming sheriff then appealed to the U.S. Supreme Court.

The Supreme Court noted that patronage dismissals were acceptable if they targeted policymaking employees. However, where nonpolicymaking employees were concerned, it was not acceptable for an incoming party to terminate all those employees who had supported the opposing side. It held that the practice of patronage imposed an unacceptable restraint on freedom of speech in most cases because, to maintain their jobs, employees were required to switch their political affiliations.

The Court further noted that not only would efficiency not be lost by keeping employees from the opposing party, it might actually be promoted by denying wholesale replacement of large numbers of public employees each time political offices changed hands. Finally, the Court determined that the democratic process would not be threatened by the denial of patronage dismissals and hirings. Political parties had existed prior to active patronage and would continue to exist with this diminished patronage power. The Court affirmed the court of appeals' decision, disallowing the patronage dismissals. *Elrod v. Burns,* 427 U.S. 347, 96 S.Ct. 2673, 49 L.Ed.2d 547 (1976).

In the following case, the Supreme Court expanded the protection of public employees in cases of political patronage. While the Court previously held in *Elrod v. Burns*, above, that nonpolicymaking job holders were secure from political patronage, this case ruled that political affiliation for such employees was simply not an appropriate reason for dismissal.

A New York county legislature appointed a Republican public defender who in turn made a number of appointments for positions as assistant public defenders. When control of the legislature shifted to the Democrats, a new public defender was appointed. He then began executing termination notices for six of the assistants in his office. Two assistants brought suit to prevent the discharges. A federal district court held for the employees, and the U.S. Court of Appeals affirmed. The case then came before the U.S. Supreme Court.

The Court noted that the First and Fourteenth Amendments protected the assistants from being discharged solely because of their political beliefs. They did not have to prove that they had been coerced into changing their political allegiance; they merely had to show that they were about to be discharged simply because they were not Democrats. Here, the hiring authority could not demonstrate that party affiliation was an appropriate requirement for the effective performance of the office. Even though a position may be political without being confidential or policymaking in character, the assistants' duties here were to provide representation to individual citizens in controversy with the state. This had no bearing on partisan concerns. Accordingly, the Court affirmed the lower courts' decisions, finding that affiliation to a particular party was not a valid requirement here. *Branti v. Finkel*, 445 U.S. 507, 100 S.Ct. 1287, 63 L.Ed.2d 574 (1980).

The Court continued its disapproval of political patronage in public employment with the following 1990 decision, which restricted the right to protect party-affiliated employees when a state hiring freeze was implemented.

The governor of Illinois instituted a hiring freeze for every agency under his control. Exceptions were granted through the governor's personnel office with a majority going to those employees affiliated with the Republican Party. Five state employees brought suit in a federal district court alleging that they suffered discrimination with respect to promotions, transfers and recalls because they had not been supporters of the state's Republican Party. The district court dismissed the complaint. The employees appealed to the U.S. Court of Appeals, Seventh Circuit, which reversed in part and affirmed in part, noting that only those employment decisions that have the effect of a dismissal violate the First Amendment. The employees further appealed to the U.S. Supreme Court.

On appeal, the Republican Party argued that since the employment decisions were not punitive and did not adversely affect the terms of employment, they did not violate the First Amendment. In a five to four decision, the majority determined that employees who did not compromise their beliefs tended to lose increases in pay and job satisfaction attendant to promotions, transfers and recalls. The court noted that these are significant penalties and are imposed in retaliation for the exercise of rights guaranteed by the First Amendment. The majority, therefore, determined that promotions, transfers and recalls based on political affiliation were an impermissible infringement on the First Amendment rights of public employees. The court established the constitutional principle "that party membership is not a permissible factor in the dispensation of government jobs, except those jobs for the performance of which party affiliation is an appropriate requirement." *Rutan v. Republican Party of Illinois*, 497 U.S. 62, 110 S.Ct. 2729, 111 L.Ed.2d 52 (1990).

In the case below, the Supreme Court found that independent government contractors were entitled to protection from retaliation for their political association.

A private towing service was removed from a city's list of available companies to perform towing services after the towing service's owner refused to contribute to the mayor's reelection campaign, instead supporting the mayor's opponent. Asserting that the removal from the list was in retaliation for the owner's stance on the campaign issue, the towing service sued the city in a federal court under 42 U.S.C. § 1983. The court dismissed the complaint, and the U.S. Court of Appeals, Seventh Circuit, affirmed. The U.S. Supreme Court reversed and remanded the case. It stated that the protections of *Elrod v. Burns* and *Branti v. Finkel* (in which the Court held that government officials may not discharge public employees for refusing to support a political party or its candidates unless political affiliation is an appropriate job requirement) extended to independent contractors who suffered retaliation for protected political association. Those who perform the government's work outside the formal employment relationship do not forfeit their First Amendment rights for that reason. *O'Hare Truck Service, Inc. v. City of Northlake*, 518 U.S. 712, 116 S.Ct. 2353, 135 L.Ed.2d 874 (1996).

III. OTHER EXPRESSIVE ACTIVITIES

42 U.S.C. § 1983 prohibits any person acting under color of state law from depriving any other person of their constitutional rights. In the following case, the Supreme Court refused to grant relief under 42 U.S.C. § 1983 to a police officer's collective bargaining unit which claimed that restrictions on hair length and facial hair violated their constitutional rights.

A New York county police department had a regulation that established hair-grooming standards for male members of the police force. The regulations were directed at the style and length of hair, sideburns, mustaches, beards and goatees. The local patrolmen's benevolent association sued the county in a federal district court under 42 U.S.C. § 1983, claiming that the regulation violated freedom of expression rights under the First Amendment and due process and equal protection rights under the Fourteenth Amendment. The district court and court of appeals held for the association, and the U.S. Supreme Court granted review.

The Supreme Court noted that the association sought the protection of the Fourteenth Amendment, not for members of the citizens at large, but for employees of the police department. The Court stated that this was highly significant because the state has wider latitude in imposing restrictive regulations on its employees than it does in regulating its citizens at large. The association would have to have shown no rational connection between the regulation and the promotion of safety of persons and property. Since the desire to make police officers readily recognizable to the public and to foster the *esprit de corps* that uniforms and appearance may inculcate within the police force is sufficiently related to the department's goals, the regulation was not unconstitutional. *Kelley v. Johnson,* 425 U.S. 238, 96 S.Ct. 1440, 47 L.Ed.2d 708 (1976).

The Religious Freedom Restoration Act of 1993 prohibited the government from substantially burdening a person's exercise of religion even if the burden resulted from a rule of general applicability unless the government could demonstrate that the burden furthered a compelling governmental interest in the least restrictive way. In the case below, the Supreme Court found the RFRA unconstitutional.

A Catholic archbishop in San Antonio applied for a building permit to enlarge a 70-year-old church. City authorities denied the permit on the ground that the church building was part of a historical district. The archbishop brought suit against the city in a federal district court, asserting in part that the denial of the permit violated the Religious Freedom Restoration Act of 1993 (RFRA) which prohibited government from substantially burdening a person's exercise of religion even if the burden resulted from a rule of general applicability unless the government could demonstrate that the burden furthered a compelling governmental interest in the least restrictive way. The district court determined that the RFRA exceeded the scope of Congress' authority under § 5 of the Fourteenth Amendment, but the U.S. Court of Appeals, Fifth Circuit, reversed, finding the RFRA to be constitutional. The U.S. Supreme Court granted certiorari.

The Supreme Court held that the RFRA was unconstitutional. It stated that the RFRA altered the Free Exercise Clause's meaning by granting greater protections than the U.S. Constitution itself provided. The RFRA's sweeping coverage ensured its intrusion at every level of government. The law was not simply remedial or preventive of unconstitutional behavior, but proscribed state conduct that the Fourteenth Amendment did not even prohibit. The Court noted that when the exercise of religion has been burdened by a law of general applicability, it does not follow that the persons affected have been burdened any more than other citizens or that they have been burdened because of their religious beliefs. Since the RFRA contradicted vital principles necessary to maintain separation of powers and the federal-state balance, it was unconstitutional. *City of Boerne, Texas v. Flores*, 521 U.S. 507, 117 S.Ct. 2157, 138 L.Ed.2d 624 (1997).

CHAPTER FOUR

Employer Liability and Immunity

143

I.   42 U.S.C. § 1983

Section 1 of the Civil Rights Act of 1871, which is codified at 42 U.S.C. § 1983, is one of the most frequently used civil rights provisions. Section 1983 provides the basis for a federal court lawsuit to any individual whose constitutional rights, or federal statutory rights, have been violated by the government or its officials. Compensatory damages, punitive damages, injunctions and attorneys' fees may be awarded under § 1983. Two elements are required for a successful § 1983 lawsuit: 1) action by the state or by a person or institution acting "under color of" state law, which 2) deprives an individual of federally guaranteed rights.

42 U.S.C. § 1983. Civil action for deprivation of rights

Every person who, under color of any statute, ordinance, regulation, custom, or usage, of any State or Territory or the District of Columbia, subjects, or causes to be subjected, any citizen of the United States or other person within the jurisdiction thereof to the deprivation of any rights, privileges, or immunities secured by the Constitution and laws, shall be liable to the party injured in an action at law, suit in equity, or other proper proceeding for redress, except that in any action brought against a judicial officer for an act or omission taken in such officer's judicial capacity, injunctive relief shall not be granted unless a declaratory decree was violated or declaratory relief was unavailable. For the purposes of this section, any Act of Congress applicable exclusively to the District of Columbia shall be considered to be a statute of the District of Columbia.

(As amended. Pub. L. 104–317, Title III, § 309(c), Oct. 19, 1996, 110 Stat. 3853.)

A. Constitutional and Statutory Rights

In *Rendell-Baker v. Kohn*, the Court stated the following test for attributing state action to private employers for the purposes of liability under 42 U.S.C. § 1983: Is the alleged civil rights violation "fairly attributable" to the state?

The Fourteenth Amendment prohibits state action which deprives any person within that state's jurisdiction from rights, privileges or immunities secured by the U.S. Constitution. When a privately operated school in Massachusetts fired a teacher for speaking out against school policy, she sued the school under 42 U.S.C. § 1983 on the grounds that the state, acting through the school, had abridged her First Amendment right to free speech. As evidence of the control the state had over the private school she contended that the school issued diplomas approved by the local school districts whose special students the private school contracted to teach, that the private school received 99 percent of its funding from state sources, and that her position on the staff had been created and funded by a state agency. The case was consolidated with that of other teachers and a vocational counselor at the school who were also fired. A federal district court held that the employees were properly dismissed. There was no evidence of government control over school personnel actions. The Supreme Court granted the employees' petition for certiorari.

The Court noted that unlike Title VII claims, and complaints filed under the National Labor Relations Act, § 1983 claims required an affirmative showing by the complaining parties that they had suffered some constitutional infringement at the hands of a state actor, or by one acting under color of state law. According to the Court, state action was present only when the alleged violation of federal rights was fairly attributable to the state, which required a showing of coercion by the state. Even though all of the employees' evidence of state control and funding was true, these factors in themselves were insufficient to show that the state had created an agency with the private school that made the school's actions its own. Absent a showing of actual control by the state, any deprivation of constitutional rights claimed by the employees were matters between them and another private party. Such complaints between private parties are not within the scope of § 1983. The Court affirmed the district court decision for the school. *Rendell-Baker v. Kohn*, 457 U.S. 830, 102 S.Ct. 2764, 73 L.Ed.2d 418 (1982).

Where government officials violate a person's constitutional rights, they will not be held liable unless the right alleged to have been violated is "clearly established" at the time of the violation.

A Florida Highway Patrol employee was discharged in 1977 when he refused to quit his part-time job. He then filed suit against various state officials under 42 U.S.C. § 1983, alleging that the Due Process Clause had been violated because he had been dismissed without a formal pretermination or a prompt post-termination hearing. A federal district court ruled for the employee, and the U.S. Court of Appeals affirmed. The case then came before the U.S. Supreme Court, which noted that at the time of the employee's discharge, there was no clearly established due process right that was violated. Under § 1983, a government official will not be held liable for damages unless the constitutional right he or she is alleged to have violated is "clearly established" at the time of the violation. Here, the employee could not recover because the officials he had sued enjoyed qualified immunity for their actions. The Court reversed the court of appeals' decision and held in favor of the government officials. *Davis v. Scherer*, 468 U.S. 183, 104 S.Ct. 3012, 82 L.Ed.2d 139 (1984).

In 1986, the Court held that § 1983 damages were not permissible for an alleged injury based only on abstract constitutional rights. Rather, damages only compensate for injuries caused by a deprivation of a well-defined constitutional right.

A Michigan public school teacher taught seventh grade courses in life science using a textbook approved by his school board. The course included a six-week section on human growth and sexuality. After instructing his students to obtain signed parental permission slips, the teacher showed two films on human reproduction and sexual development. The films were obtained from the county health department and had been shown in previous school years without incident. The films were shown with boys and girls in separate rooms, the boys viewing "From Boy to Man" and the girls viewing "From Girl to Woman." When rumors spread that the films were explicit, some parents appeared at a school board meeting, demanding that the teacher be fired. Some parents demanded that he be tarred and feathered. The board suspended the teacher without pay. He then filed a § 1983 lawsuit against the school district in a federal district court, claiming that the suspension constituted a violation of his constitutional rights. The court awarded the teacher a final judgment of almost $300,000 in compensatory and punitive damages. The U.S. Court of Appeals, Sixth Circuit, affirmed and the school district appealed to the U.S. Supreme Court.

The Supreme Court held that the trial court had erroneously instructed the jury to attempt to place a dollar value on abstract constitutional rights, rather than to focus on a provable injury. According to the Court, an award of money damages under § 1983 is possible as compensation to a person for actual injuries as the result of a recognized constitutional violation, such as a due process violation. The deprivation of a right without corresponding actual injury was insufficient to justify a § 1983 damage award. The Court reversed the lower court decisions and remanded the case to the district court. *Memphis Community School Dist. v. Stachura*, 477 U.S. 299, 106 S.Ct. 2537, 91 L.Ed.2d 249 (1986).

A state has no duty to provide members of the general public with adequate protective services. Only if a "special relationship" exists can an affirmative duty to protect arise.

County officials in Wisconsin became aware that a young boy was probably being abused. However, they did not feel they had enough evidence to retain the boy in the custody of the juvenile court. Instead, they made recommendations to his divorced father to seek counseling and to enroll the boy in a preschool program. Over the next year, the boy was admitted to the emergency room of a local hospital on two separate occasions. His caseworker also noticed suspicious injuries on the boy's head when she visited the boy at home. Even though all of this information was recorded and presumably made known to the county officials, they continued to take no action. Subsequently, the boy was admitted to the emergency room again, this time in a coma. Emergency brain surgery revealed a series of traumatic injuries inflicted over a long period of time. The boy suffered severe and probably permanent brain damage. His father was convicted of child abuse. His mother then sued the county officials, claiming that they had deprived her son of his liberty interest in bodily integrity in violation of his Fourteenth Amendment rights. The federal district court granted summary judgment to the county officials, and the U.S. Court of Appeals, Seventh Circuit, affirmed.

On further appeal, the U.S. Supreme Court ruled that a state's failure to protect an individual against private violence generally does not constitute a Fourteenth Amendment violation. The Court also held that the county officials' knowledge of the boy's danger and their willingness to protect him did not establish a "special relationship" so as to create an affirmative duty to protect the boy. The county officials did not create the danger to the boy, nor did they do anything to make him more vulnerable to harm. Accordingly, the officials had not committed any constitutional violation, and the grant of summary judgment was affirmed. *DeShaney v. Winnebago County DSS,* 489 U.S. 189, 109 S.Ct. 998, 103 L.Ed.2d 249 (1989).

The Supreme Court has ruled that the U.S. Constitution does not impose an affirmative duty on either the state or its employees (who act in their official capacities) to protect an individual's rights. The Constitution only prohibits the state from depriving an individual of his or her rights.

A Pennsylvania high school student was sexually abused by her band director. The student sued the school district and several school officials alleging that the officials had either known or had recklessly failed to discover that the band director was preying on his female students. The school district asked a federal district court to dismiss the case but the court refused. The school district then appealed to the U.S. Court of Appeals, Third Circuit, which affirmed the district court's ruling. The court of appeals stated that every reasonable school official should know that it was a breach of duty to take no action to protect a student from sexual abuse. The court of appeals held that the Constitution mandated some affirmative action to investigate and protect students from abuse.

The U.S. Supreme Court vacated the judgment and remanded the case to the court of appeals for further consideration in light of *DeShaney v. Winnebago County DSS,* above. In *DeShaney,* the Supreme Court held that the state's failure to protect an individual against private violence does not constitute a civil rights violation. The Court noted that the Constitution does not impose an affirmative duty on the state to protect an individual's rights, but only forbids the state from depriving the individual of these rights. In light of this holding, the Court vacated the judgment and remanded the case for further consideration. *Bradford Area School Dist. v. Stoneking,* 489 U.S. 1062, 109 S.Ct. 1333, 103 L.Ed.2d 804 (1989).

Similarly, the Court vacated the Third Circuit's holding in *Sowers v. Bradford Area School Dist.* The Court noted that since the case was governed by the holding in *Stoneking,* above, the student's 42 U.S.C. § 1983 claim against the school officials was improperly considered. The Court vacated the judgment and remanded the case. *Smith v. Sowers,* 490 U.S. 1002, 109 S.Ct. 1634, 104 L.Ed.2d 150 (1989).

The violation of a federal right implicit in a statute's language and structure constitutes a "direct" violation remediable through a § 1983 lawsuit.

After the Supreme Court held in *Golden State Transit Corp. v. City of Los Angeles,* 475 U.S. 608, 106 S.Ct. 1395, 89 L.Ed.2d 616 (1986), that a city had violated federal law by conditioning the renewal of a taxi cab company's franchise on the settlement of a pending labor dispute between the cab company and its union, a federal district court ordered the city to reinstate the franchise. However, the court concluded that 42 U.S.C. § 1983 did not authorize an award of compensatory damages against the city. The U.S. Court of Appeals affirmed that decision, and appeal was again taken to the U.S. Supreme Court. The Supreme

Court held that the cab company was entitled to maintain a § 1983 cause of action for compensatory damages. The Court stated that the National Labor Relations Act granted the cab company rights that were enforceable under § 1983. Further, the existence of a comprehensive enforcement scheme under the NLRA did not preclude a § 1983 remedy. The Court reversed and remanded the lower court decision. *Golden State Transit Corp. v. City of Los Angeles*, 493 U.S. 103, 110 S.Ct. 444, 107 L.Ed.2d 420 (1989).

Bivens v. Six Unknown Named Agents of the Federal Bureau of Narcotics, 403 U.S. 388, 91 S.Ct. 1999, 29 L.Ed.2d 619 (1971), established that victims of a constitutional violation by a federal official have a right to recover damages against the official in federal court despite the absence of any statute conferring such a right. A *Bivens* action can be defeated if there are "special factors counseling hesitation in the absence of affirmative action by Congress" or if Congress has provided an alternative remedy which it has explicitly declared to be a *substitute* for recovery directly under the U.S. Constitution and which it views to be equally effective. However, if no clearly established constitutional right has been violated, a *Bivens* action must fail.

A clinical psychologist worked for the government until he was notified that his employment was going to be terminated. He then resigned and began working for an army hospital overseas. Because he needed to be "credentialled" to work in the hospital, his prospective supervisor sought information from his previous supervisor. His former supervisor responded with a letter stating that he would not recommend the psychologist because he was inept, unethical and untrustworthy. When the psychologist was denied the necessary credentials and lost his job, he sued his former supervisor in a *Bivens* action, claiming that the supervisor had infringed his liberty interests by maliciously defaming him. A federal court denied the former supervisor's motion to dismiss, but the U.S. Court of Appeals reversed.

On further appeal, the U.S. Supreme Court affirmed the court of appeals' decision. The psychologist had not overcome the former supervisor's qualified immunity defense because he failed to allege the violation of a clearly established constitutional right. The Court noted that injury to reputation by itself, as was alleged here, was not a protected liberty interest. Thus, there was no constitutional right that had been violated. Accordingly, the court of appeals had properly ordered dismissal of the psychologist's *Bivens* claim. *Siegert v. Gilley*, 500 U.S. 226, 111 S.Ct. 1789, 114 L.Ed.2d 277 (1991).

In the case below, the Supreme Court found that a county deputy was not liable for a suspect's death following a high-speed chase because the deputy's behavior did not "shock the conscience."

An 18-year-old motorcyclist and his 16-year-old passenger were speeding down a California road. A deputy sheriff began a high-speed pursuit of the motorcycle and followed it for over a mile until the motorcycle tipped over. The deputy slammed on his brakes, but because of the short distance between his vehicle and the motorcycle, he hit the passenger, causing massive injuries and death. The passenger's estate sued the deputy, the sheriff's department and the county in a federal court under 42 U.S.C. § 1983, alleging a deprivation of the passenger's Fourteenth Amendment substantive due process right to life. The district court granted summary judgment to the deputy, and the U.S. Court of Appeals, Ninth Circuit, reversed. The U.S. Supreme Court granted review and held that high-speed chases with no intent to harm suspects physically or to worsen their legal plight do not give rise to liability under the Fourteenth Amendment. Because the deputy's behavior did not "shock the conscience," there could be no liability under § 1983. The court of appeals' decision was reversed. *County of Sacramento v. Lewis*, 523 U.S. 833, 117 S.Ct. 1708, 140 L.Ed.2d 1043 (1998).

In *Crawford-El v. Britton*, the Supreme Court rejected the imposition of a clear and convincing evidence standard for unconstitutional-motive cases.

A litigious and outspoken prisoner in the District of Columbia's correction system was transferred to Florida because of overcrowding. His belongings were transferred separately and he did not receive them until several months later. He sued a District of Columbia correctional officer in a federal district court under 42 U.S.C. § 1983, alleging that the diversion of his property was in retaliation for exercising his First Amendment rights. The court dismissed the complaint. On appeal, the U.S. Court of Appeals, District of Columbia Circuit, held that in an unconstitutional-motive case against a public official, a plaintiff must establish motive by clear and convincing evidence. The U.S. Supreme Court vacated the court of appeals' decision, holding that the appellate court had erred in fashioning a heightened burden of proof in unconstitutional-motive cases against public officials. Nothing in the text of § 1983, any other federal law or the Federal Rules of Civil Procedure provided support for imposing a clear and convincing burden of proof upon plaintiffs in such cases. *Crawford-El v. Britton*, 523 U.S. 574, 118 S.Ct. 1584, 140 L.Ed.2d 759 (1998).

B. Employer Liability

1. States and State Officials

A private physician under contract with the state was held to be acting "under color of state law" within the meaning of § 1983 when he was treating inmates at a correctional center.

An inmate at a correctional center tore his Achilles tendon while playing volleyball. A physician under contract to provide medical care to the inmates treated the injury, but did not perform surgery on the leg. By state law, the inmate was barred from seeing a doctor of his own choosing. He sued the physician when his leg did not heal to his satisfaction, bringing suit under 42 U.S.C. § 1983. He alleged that the physician had violated his right to be free from cruel and unusual punishment. A federal court dismissed the case because the physician was not acting under color of state law, and the U.S. Court of Appeals affirmed. The U.S. Supreme Court granted certiorari and held that the case should not have been dismissed. Here, the physician, by virtue of his contract with the state, had been acting "under color of state law" when he treated the inmate. The alleged infringement of the inmate's constitutional right was fairly attributable to the state. Thus, a valid claim had been stated, and the case would have to proceed. The Court reversed the lower courts' holdings. *West v. Atkins*, 487 U.S. 42, 108 S.Ct. 2250, 101 L.Ed.2d 40 (1988).

In the case below, the Supreme Court held that neither states nor state officials acting in their official capacities were "persons" within the meaning of § 1983.

A Michigan state police employee sought a promotion. He was denied the promotion and he alleged that the denial was due to a "red squad file" which was maintained by the department concerning his brother, who was a student activist. The employee sued the department in a Michigan trial court under 42 U.S.C. § 1983, which provides that any person who deprives an individual of his or her constitutional rights under color of state law will be liable to that individual. The Court remanded the case to the Michigan Civil Service Commission for a grievance hearing. The commission ruled for the employee, stating that the police department and officials had refused to promote the employee due to partisan considerations. The department and officials appealed to a Michigan trial court, which determined that the employee had established a constitutional violation. The trial court judge ruled that the department and its officers were "persons" under § 1983. However, the court of appeals remanded the case for a determination of the police director's liability for damages. On appeal to the Michigan Supreme Court, the court affirmed the dismissal and reversed the judgment permitting possible liability of the director. The court ruled that state officials acting in their official capacities were not "persons" under § 1983. The employee appealed to the U.S. Supreme Court.

The Supreme Court held that states were not persons under the act. Thus, § 1983 could not be used as the basis of a lawsuit against the department. Section 1983 did not alter the constitutional balance among states and the federal government. The principal purpose of § 1983 was to provide a federal court forum for civil rights claims, not to provide a forum for claims against the states. Finally, § 1983 claims against state officials acting in their official capacities were lawsuits against the offices and not against the officials themselves. The Supreme Court affirmed the Michigan Supreme Court's decision for the police department and officials. *Will v. Michigan Dep't of State Police*, 491 U.S. 58, 109 S.Ct. 2304, 105 L.Ed.2d 45 (1989).

In the following case, the Supreme Court clarified that state officials who act in their official capacities can be liable under § 1983 if sued in their personal capacities rather than their official capacities.

The newly elected Auditor General of Pennsylvania discharged a group of employees in her office, claiming they had "bought" their jobs through payments to a former employee of the office. The employees sued the auditor general, seeking monetary damages under 42 U.S.C. § 1983. A federal district court dismissed the § 1983 claims under *Will v. Michigan Dep't of State Police*, above, in which the Supreme Court held that state officials "acting in their official capacities" are outside the class of "persons" subject to liability under § 1983. The court of appeals reversed, holding that since the employees sought damages from the auditor general in her personal capacity, they could maintain an action under § 1983. The auditor general then appealed to the U.S. Supreme Court.

The Supreme Court held for the employees. The Court stated that the holding in *Will* did not mean that officials who act in their official capacity are immune to suit under § 1983. The phrase "acting in their official capacity" is best understood as a reference to the capacity in which the state officer is sued, not the capacity in which the officer inflicts the injury. State officials sued in their personal capacities are "persons" within the meaning of § 1983. Unlike official-capacity defendants—who are not "persons" because they assume the identity of the government that employs them—officers sued in their personal capacity fit comfortably into the statutory term "person." *Hafer v. Melo*, 502 U.S. 21, 112 S.Ct. 358, 116 L.Ed.2d 301 (1991).

2. Counties and Municipalities

In the following case, the Supreme Court held that municipalities and school districts could be found liable for damages under § 1983. Municipalities were liable in damages to the extent that they denied individual civil rights as a result of an official practice or policy under the statute.

A group of female employees of New York City's Department of Social Services and Board of Education sued the department and its commissioner, the board and its chancellor, and the city and its mayor under 42 U.S.C. § 1983. They complained that the department and board had an official policy of compelling pregnant employees to take unpaid leaves of absence before such leaves were required for medical reasons. A federal district court ruled that the group's petition was moot because the city had since changed its policy. The new policy stated that no pregnant employee would be forced to take a leave unless she was medically unable to perform her job. The district court held that requiring pregnant employees to take a leave of absence was unconstitutional. However, the court denied a back pay award to the complaining parties because any damages would have had to come from the city. This ran afoul of the sovereign immunity principle embodied in the Eleventh Amendment and common law. When the aggrieved employees appealed to the U.S. Supreme Court, it agreed to hear the case.

The Court reversed the district court's decision, reversing a previous case that held that municipalities are immune from liability in lawsuits brought under 42 U.S.C. § 1983. The Court had previously interpreted Congress' rejection of the "Sherman Amendment" to the Civil Rights Act of 1871, which later became § 1983, as a rejection of liability for municipalities. The Court determined that nothing in the legislative history of § 1983 precluded municipal liability. The Court applied § 1983 to the local school district as though it were a municipality.

It held that municipalities cannot be held liable under the theory of *respondeat superior*; in other words, municipalities are not automatically liable for the acts of their employees. Employees asserting claims against school districts must show that district employees acted under some official policy which caused them to violate individual constitutional rights. The Court reversed the district court's decision, finding that the employees' constitutional rights had been violated as a direct result of the department's official policy. *Monell v. Dep't of Social Services*, 436 U.S. 658, 98 S.Ct. 2018, 56 L.Ed.2d 611 (1978).

A city sued under 42 U.S.C. § 1983 does not have available the defense of qualified immunity. After the case below was decided, it was clear that city officials sued in their official capacities also could not use the defense.

Two people were assaulted by an officer of the Memphis Police Department who had a history of violent behavior that was well known in the department. They obtained a judgment against the officer and against the director of the police department "in his official capacity" under 42 U.S.C. § 1983. The U.S. Court of Appeals reversed the judgment against the director because he had acted in good faith and had not had actual knowledge of the officer's disciplinary record. The court granted him immunity. On further appeal, the U.S. Supreme Court held that because the suit against the director was brought against him only in his official capacity and not against him individually, the city was liable if it received notice and an opportunity to respond. This rule was plainly implied in *Monell v. New York City Dep't of Social Services*, above. There was no qualified immunity available to the city here. That was a defense available only to officials sued in their individual capacities. The Court reversed and remanded the case. *Brandon v. Holt*, 469 U.S. 464, 105 S.Ct. 873, 83 L.Ed.2d 878 (1985).

Before § 1983 liability can be assessed against a municipality, it must be shown that the municipality had a policy that caused the injurious incident.

Responding to a robbery in progress at an Oklahoma City bar, a police officer shot and killed a man he believed was carrying a gun. In fact, the man only possessed a toy pistol. His widow sued the city and the officer in federal court under 42 U.S.C. § 1983. The jury found in favor of the officer, but held against the city, deciding that a municipal "policy" had caused the victim to be deprived of his constitutional rights. The U.S. Court of Appeals affirmed, and the case came before the U.S. Supreme Court. The Supreme Court held that the jury had been improperly instructed with respect to the standard for imposing liability on municipalities under § 1983. Under the instructions given, the jury could have found liability without any proof submitted of a single action taken by a municipal policymaker. Here, the instructions allowed the jury to infer a "thoroughly nebulous policy of inadequate training" based on a single incident, and also allowed the inference that the city's "policy" was the cause of the incident. This was an error. The Court reversed the lower courts' decisions. *City of Oklahoma City v. Tuttle*, 471 U.S. 808, 105 S.Ct. 2427, 85 L.Ed.2d 791 (1985).

In the following case, the Supreme Court held that a county could be liable under § 1983 where county employees acted under a county attorney's directions if the attorney had the authority to establish county policy.

A county prosecutor began investigating charges that a doctor had fraudulently accepted payments from Ohio welfare agencies for services not actually provided to patients. Subpoenas were issued to two of the doctor's employees to appear before the grand jury. When they failed to appear, county deputy sheriffs went to the doctor's clinic to bring the employees to court. The doctor refused to let them enter the employees' area. The sheriffs then called the county prosecutor, who told them to go in and get the employees. They broke down the door with an ax and searched the clinic unsuccessfully for the employees. The doctor then brought suit under 42 U.S.C. § 1983 against the county and others. The court dismissed the claim against the county, and the U.S. Court of Appeals affirmed.

On further appeal, the U.S. Supreme Court reversed. It stated that recovery from the county would be limited to acts that were, properly speaking, "acts of the [county]." Acts by county employees were not sufficient to impose liability unless the officials were responsible for establishing final policy with respect to the activity in question—here, conducting an illegal search of the clinic. Since the court of appeals had already concluded that the county prosecutor could establish county policy under appropriate circumstances, and since the prosecutor had ordered the sheriffs to enter the clinic, the prosecutor had acted as the final decision maker for the county. Accordingly, the county could be held liable under § 1983 and the lower courts had erroneously dismissed the case. The Court remanded the case for further proceedings. *Pembaur v. City of Cincinnati*, 475 U.S. 469, 106 S.Ct. 1292, 89 L.Ed.2d 452 (1986).

Where a city employee is found not to have inflicted a constitutional injury on a § 1983 claimant, the city cannot be liable to the claimant under § 1983.

Two Los Angeles police officers stopped a motorist because of a suspicion that he was intoxicated. After conducting field sobriety tests, they took him to the station to administer a breath test. The motorist became belligerent, an altercation ensued, and he fell through a plate glass window. He sued the city and the police officers under 42 U.S.C. § 1983. In the first part of the trial, the jury found for the police officer who remained as a defendant even though they were not instructed on any affirmative defenses that might have been asserted. The district court then dismissed the city from the lawsuit, but the U.S. Court of Appeals reversed, deciding that the city might still be liable. Further appeal was taken to the U.S. Supreme Court.

The Supreme Court reversed the court of appeals' decision. It stated that since the motorist had not suffered any constitutional injury at the hands of the police officer, there could be no recovery against the city, even if departmental regulations might have authorized the use of constitutionally excessive force. Individual injury is a prerequisite for a recovery of damages. The city was dismissed from the lawsuit and found not liable. *City of Los Angeles v. Heller*, 475 U.S. 796, 106 S.Ct. 1571, 89 L.Ed.2d 806 (1986).

To determine municipal liability under § 1983, it must be shown that officials having "final policymaking authority" created a policy that resulted in constitutional injury.

An architect worked for the city of St. Louis, rising to a management-level city planning position in one of its agencies. The agency had a policy of requiring advance approval before taking on private clients. Some time after this policy went into effect, the architect accepted outside employment without prior approval and was suspended. He successfully challenged the suspension. He was then transferred and subsequently laid off. He sued the city under 42 U.S.C. § 1983, alleging that he had been penalized for exercising his First Amendment rights. A federal court found the city liable, and the U.S. Court of Appeals affirmed. The case then came before the U.S. Supreme Court.

The Court held that the court of appeals had applied the wrong legal standard for determining when isolated decisions by municipal supervisors or employees could expose the city to § 1983 liability. The architect would have had to show the existence of an unconstitutional policy promulgated by officials having such authority. There was no such policy permitting retaliatory transfers or layoffs. Further, there was insufficient evidence to show that supervisors were authorized to establish the employment policies of the city with respect to transfers and layoffs. Thus, the Court reversed the appellate court's decision and remanded the case. *City of St. Louis v. Praprotnik*, 485 U.S. 112, 108 S.Ct. 915, 99 L.Ed.2d 107 (1988).

Cities can be held liable under § 1983 for inadequately training their police officers if the failure to properly train is the result of deliberate indifference to the rights of the citizens.

An Ohio woman was arrested by police officers and taken to the station where she fell down several times and was incoherent. No medical attention was provided for her. After about an hour, she was released and her family took her to a nearby hospital where she was diagnosed as suffering from several emotional ailments. She later sued the city under 42 U.S.C. § 1983 for violating her due process right to receive necessary medical treatment while in custody. A jury ruled in her favor, but the U.S. Court of Appeals reversed and remanded the case. Further appeal was taken to the U.S. Supreme Court.

The Supreme Court held that a municipality may be held liable, in certain circumstances, for constitutional violations resulting from its failure to train its employees. Inadequacy of police training may serve as the basis for § 1983 liability only where the failure to train amounts to deliberate indifference to the rights of persons with whom the police come into contact. To resolve a city's liability, courts must look at the adequacy of the training program in relation to the tasks the officers must perform. The Court thus held that the court of appeals' decision had to be vacated and the case remanded for examination of whether there was deliberate indifference on the part of the city. *City of Canton, Ohio v. Harris*, 489 U.S. 378, 109 S.Ct. 1197, 103 L.Ed.2d 412 (1989).

The Supreme Court has stated that a municipality cannot be held liable for its employees' violations of 42 U.S.C. § 1981 under a theory of vicarious liability. A person discriminated against by a state actor must bring an action against the actor under 42 U.S.C. § 1983.

A white male was employed by the Dallas Independent School District (DISD) as a teacher, athletic director and head football coach at a predominantly black high school. After numerous problems with the school's principal over school policies, the principal recommended that the teacher be relieved of his duties as athletic director and coach. The district's superintendent reassigned the teacher to a teaching position in another school where he had no coaching duties. The teacher sued the school district and the principal, claiming that they had discriminated against him on the basis of race in violation of 42 U.S.C. §§ 1981 and 1983. A federal district court held in the teacher's favor.

The U.S. Court of Appeals, Fifth Circuit, reversed in part and remanded, finding that the district court's jury instructions did not make clear that the school district's liability could only be based on the actions of the principal or superintendent if those officials had been delegated policymaking authority or had acted according to a well-settled custom or official policy. Even if the superintendent could be considered a policymaker for purposes of transferring personnel, the jury did not find that the superintendent's decision to transfer the teacher was either improperly motivated or consciously indifferent to the principal's improper motivations. The court of appeals also rejected the district court's conclusion that the district's § 1981 liability for the principal's actions could be predicated on a vicarious liability theory or that municipalities could be liable for its employees' acts. The Court noted that Congress did not intend that municipalities be subject to vicarious liability under § 1983. The teacher then appealed to the U.S. Supreme Court.

The Supreme Court stated that a municipality may not be held liable for its employees' violations of § 1981 under a vicarious liability theory. The express "action at law" provided by § 1983 for the deprivation of rights secured by the Constitution and laws of the United States is the exclusive federal remedy for the violation of rights guaranteed by § 1981 when the claim is pressed against a state actor. The Supreme Court affirmed part of the court of appeals' decision and remanded the case in order to determine if the superintendent possessed policy-making authority in the area of employee transfer, and if so, whether a new trial was required to determine the DISD's responsibility for the principal's actions in light of this determination. *Jett v. Dallas Indep. School Dist.*, 491 U.S. 701, 109 S.Ct. 2702, 105 L.Ed.2d 598 (1989).

If a city fails to train or warn its employees about known hazards in the workplace, the city has not violated the Due Process Clause, and § 1983 does not provide a remedy for employees who are injured or killed as a result of that failure.

An employee in a Texas city's sanitation department died of asphyxia after entering a manhole to unstop a sewer line. His widow sued under 42 U.S.C. § 1983 alleging that her husband had a right under the Fourteenth Amendment's

Due Process Clause to be free from unreasonable risk of harm and to be protected from the city's custom and policy of deliberate indifference toward its employees' safety. She argued that the city violated that right by failing to properly train its employees and by providing inadequate equipment. A federal district court dismissed the complaint, stating that she failed to allege a constitutional violation. The court of appeals affirmed on the theory that there had been no abuse of governmental power, which the Court found to be a necessary element of a § 1983 action. The U.S. Supreme Court then granted review.

The Supreme Court held that a city's failure to train or warn its employees about known hazards in the workplace does not violate the Due Process Clause. As such, § 1983 cannot provide a remedy for a municipal employee based on such a failure. In addition, the Court stated that an abuse of governmental power is not a necessary element of a § 1983 claim. Section 1983 only requires that a plaintiff's harm be caused by a constitutional violation and that the city be responsible for that violation. Since the Due Process Clause cannot be used to guarantee minimum levels of safety and security in the workplace, the Court affirmed the lower courts' rulings. *Collins v. City of Harker Heights*, 503 U.S. 115, 112 S.Ct. 1061, 117 L.Ed.2d 261 (1992).

In the case below, the Supreme Court held that a showing of deliberate indifference was required to hold a municipality liable for inadequate applicant screening.

An Oklahoma woman refused to exit her vehicle following a police vehicle chase despite two orders by a deputy sheriff to exit. The deputy then used an "arm bar" technique, grabbing her arm at the wrist and elbow, pulling her from the vehicle, and spinning her to the ground which caused severe injury to her knees. The woman filed suit in federal district court against the deputy, county sheriff, and county under 42 U.S.C. § 1983 and state law. Among other allegations, she asserted that the county was liable for the deputy's use of excessive force. Her claim was based on the sheriff's decision to hire the deputy without adequately reviewing his background, which contained driving infractions and other misdemeanors such as assault and battery, resisting arrest, and public drunkenness. After a jury trial, the court entered judgment in favor of the woman, and the county appealed. The U.S. Court of Appeals, Fifth Circuit, affirmed and the U.S. Supreme Court granted certiorari.

The Court reversed, finding that only where adequate scrutiny of an applicant's background would lead a reasonable policymaker to conclude that the obvious consequence of hiring the applicant would be the deprivation of a third party's federally protected rights can the official's failure to adequately scrutinize the applicant's background constitute deliberate indifference. The Court noted that rigorous standards of culpability and causation must be applied to ensure that a municipality is not held liable solely for the actions of its employee. Here, insufficient evidence existed to establish that the sheriff's decision to hire the deputy reflected a conscious disregard of an obvious risk that excessive force would follow from the decision to hire the deputy. The court of appeals' decision was vacated and the case was remanded for further proceedings. *Bd. of County Comm'rs of Bryan County, Oklahoma v. Brown*, 520 U.S. 397, 117 S.Ct. 1382, 137 L.Ed.2d 626 (1997).

For purposes of liability under 42 U.S.C. § 1983, the Supreme Court found that Alabama sheriffs are policymakers for the state, not for the county, when they act in a law enforcement capacity. Thus, the county could not be held liable for the sheriff's actions. However, the Court noted that sheriffs could be county officers in other states based upon the role of sheriffs and importance of counties in that particular state.

After spending six years in prison, an Alabama man was released and his capital murder conviction reversed by the Alabama Court of Criminal Appeals. The court found that the state had suppressed statements from an accomplice and withheld other exculpatory evidence. The man filed a 42 U.S.C. § 1983 suit in the U.S. District Court for the Middle District of Alabama against the county where he had been convicted and numerous officials, including the sheriff. The court dismissed the claims, and the man appealed the dismissal of the claim against the sheriff to the U.S. Court of Appeals, Eleventh Circuit, which affirmed. The U.S. Supreme Court granted certiorari.

Generally, a local government, such as a county, becomes subject to liability under § 1983 for policies, set by the government's lawmakers or those whose edicts or acts represent official policy, that cause constitutional torts. A state, on the other hand, is not subject to § 1983 liability. In a split decision, the Court held that Alabama sheriffs are policymakers for the state, not for the county, when they act in a law enforcement capacity. The Alabama constitutional provisions concerning sheriffs, the historical development of those provisions, and the interpretation given them by the Alabama Supreme Court treat and consider sheriffs as executive officers of the state. The Alabama Code also indicates that the governor and state attorney general, as opposed to the county commission, have direct control over how the sheriff fulfills his law enforcement duty. Therefore, the county was not liable for the sheriff's actions. The Court noted that there was no inconsistency created by court decisions that declare sheriffs to be county officers in one state and not in another because the role of sheriffs and the importance of counties varies from state to state. The judgment of the court of appeals was affirmed. *McMillian v. Monroe County, Alabama*, 520 U.S. 781, 117 S.Ct. 1734, 138 L.Ed.2d 1 (1997).

C. Statute of Limitations

Section 1983 contains no statute of limitations. Courts must look to local law for an appropriate limit on actions. In a 1981 case, the Court agreed with a federal district court that a one-year statute of limitations on lawsuits found in local law was to be strictly construed.

Nontenured administrators in the Puerto Rico Department of Education were given termination letters before June 18, 1977. However, the terminations were not to take place until a month or more later. Exactly one year and one day after the termination letters were delivered, one of the administrators filed suit under 42 U.S.C. § 1983, which allows a person to sue in federal court for constitutional rights violations caused by those acting under color of state law. A federal district court dismissed the suit, stating that the suit was barred by a local one-year statute of limitations. The U.S. Supreme Court agreed, interpreting its prior decision in *Delaware State College v. Ricks*, 449 U.S. 250, 101 S.Ct. 498, 66 L.Ed.2d 431 (1980), to mean that the statute of limitations begins to run when the employee has been terminated, rather than the date that his employment actually ends. *Ricks* established that the focus should be on the discriminatory act and not when the consequences occur. In this case, the employees had been provided appropriate notice when they were terminated. This did not extend the statute of limitations and the claim was barred. *Chardon v. Fernandez*, 454 U.S. 6, 102 S.Ct. 28, 70 L.Ed.2d 6 (1981).

In *Wilson v. Garcia*, the Supreme Court held that the statute of limitations for personal injury actions should be applied to § 1983 actions.

A New Mexico police officer allegedly beat up an arrestee and sprayed his face with tear gas. The arrestee brought suit against the officer and his police chief two years and nine months after the claim arose. He brought his suit under 42 U.S.C. § 1983 in a federal district court. The defendants moved to dismiss on the ground that the action was barred by the two-year statute of limitations contained in the New Mexico Tort Claims Act. The district court denied the motion to dismiss, finding that the residuary four-year limitation period for actions not otherwise provided for should be applied. The U.S. Court of Appeals affirmed the denial of the motion, holding that the three-year limitations period for personal injury actions was the correct period to apply. The U.S. Supreme Court affirmed the court of appeals' decision. It noted that federal law rather than state law governs the characterization of § 1983 claims for statute of limitations purposes. The characterization of the § 1983 claim as a personal injury action was supported by the nature of the remedy available under § 1983 and by the federal interest in ensuring that the borrowed state limitations period did not discriminate against the federal civil rights remedy. *Wilson v. Garcia*, 471 U.S. 261, 105 S.Ct. 1938, 85 L.Ed.2d 254 (1985).

Because § 1983 contains no statute of limitations, courts must apply the applicable statute from the jurisdiction in which the alleged civil rights violation occurs. In a 1985 Pennsylvania case, the Court ruled that the limitation period should be based on the state's six-year personal injury statute, rather than a six-month limitation on claims brought against government employees.

A woman sued a Pennsylvania school district for failing to promote her to an administrative position for three consecutive years. She brought the claim in a federal district court under 42 U.S.C. § 1983, alleging that she was being discriminated against on the basis of gender. The last incident of discrimination alleged by her occurred over six months before she began her lawsuit. A state law set a six-month limitations period for lawsuits brought against government officials for alleged acts or omissions resulting from the execution of official duties. The district court dismissed her claim because it was not brought within the six-month limitations period. The U.S. Court of Appeals, Third Circuit, reversed the district court's decision. It ruled that the application of the six-month limitation would undermine the purposes of § 1983 in providing a remedy for constitutional violations. The U.S. Supreme Court granted certiorari. It vacated the court of appeals' decision and held that § 1983 claims should be characterized as personal injury claims for the purpose of determining which state statute of limitations should apply. The Court remanded the case to the district court. *Springfield Township School District v. Knoll*, 471 U.S. 288, 105 S.Ct. 2065, 85 L.Ed.2d 275 (1985).

In another statute of limitations case, the Court determined that the New York residual period for personal injury claims was more proper than the one-year period for intentional torts.

Two State University of New York police officers allegedly unlawfully arrested a man on the Albany campus, charging him with disorderly conduct. He sued them under 42 U.S.C. § 1983, 22 months later, charging that they had beaten him and deprived him of his constitutional rights. The officers asserted that the complaint had not been timely filed because § 1983 actions were governed by New York's one-year statute of limitations for various intentional torts. The district court denied the motion to dismiss, and the U.S. Court of Appeals affirmed. On further appeal, the U.S. Supreme Court held that the three-year residual statute of limitations for personal injury claims not covered by specific limitations periods was the applicable period here. To eliminate uncertainty, it was better to use the general or residual period rather than one of the multiple intentional tort periods which each state had. Accordingly, the claim had been timely filed under the borrowed state statute of limitations, and the motion for dismissal had been properly denied. *Owens v. Okure*, 488 U.S. 235, 109 S.Ct. 573, 102 L.Ed.2d 594 (1989).

D. Attorneys' Fees

In the following § 1983 case, the Supreme Court held that where only limited success is obtained under the statute, the attorneys' fees and costs awarded under § 1988 should also be limited.

A group of involuntarily confined Missouri patients sued state hospital officials in a federal district court, asserting that they had been mistreated and that the conditions at the hospital violated the U.S. Constitution. They also asserted that they had been placed in the hospital without due process. The district court ruled that there were constitutional violations in several areas, but that several other complaints were not violative. After this limited success, the group filed a request for attorneys' fees. The district court granted that request, and the court of appeals affirmed. Appeal was taken to the U.S. Supreme Court.

The Supreme Court noted that when a party is unsuccessful on a claim unrelated to the successful claims, the hours spent on that claim should be excluded from the amount of reasonable attorneys' fees. However, if the unsuccessful and successful claims are related, the attorneys' fees should not be reduced simply because the court did not rule on each contention raised. In this case, the Court found that only limited success had been achieved against the state officials. Accordingly, it ordered that only those fees that were reasonable in relation to the results obtained should be awarded. The Supreme Court reversed the appellate court's decision, and remanded the case for a determination of what the attorneys' fees should be. *Hensley v. Eckerhart,* 461 U.S. 424, 103 S.Ct. 1933, 76 L.Ed.2d 40 (1983).

A successful plaintiff in an action brought under 42 U.S.C. § 1983 will be entitled to attorney's fees and the costs of the suit under 42 U.S.C. § 1988. However, where a § 1983 suit is against individuals, a city cannot be held liable for costs under § 1988.

After a Kentucky state trooper was murdered, suspicion centered around a man whose license and billfold were found near the site. That evening, 30 to 40 police officers converged on the suspect's father's house, and entered without a warrant, arresting all six people inside. The suspect was not among them. They later sued various individual officers under 42 U.S.C. § 1983, alleging that they had been severely beaten, terrorized, illegally searched, and falsely arrested. The lawsuit settled for $60,000, and the plaintiffs then moved for an award of attorneys' fees under 42 U.S.C. § 1988 against the state. The district court ordered the state to pay fees and costs, and the U.S. Court of Appeals, Sixth Circuit, affirmed. On further appeal, the U.S. Supreme Court held that § 1988 does not allow attorneys' fees to be recovered from a governmental entity when a plaintiff sues government employees only in their personal capacities and prevails. Accordingly, since the case had been litigated as a personal-capacity action, it had been an error for the lower courts to award fees against the state. Because liability on the merits and responsibility for fees went hand in hand, the state could not be forced to pay fees and costs where it had not been prevailed against. The Court reversed the lower courts' decisions. *Kentucky v. Graham,* 473 U.S. 159, 105 S.Ct. 3099, 87 L.Ed.2d 114 (1985).

If a party has prevailed on any significant issue in a claim under 42 U.S.C. § 1983, he or she will be entitled to attorneys' fees under 42 U.S.C. § 1988 at least to the extent of the fees expended in litigating that issue.

A Texas school district prohibited teachers from discussing employee organizations during the school day. The district denied employee organizations access to school facilities during school hours and prohibited them from using school mail and internal communications systems. However, the school district's regulations permitted employee organizations to recruit or meet with teachers on school premises before or after the school day "upon request and approval by the school principal." The state and local teachers' associations and several of their members and employees, sued the district in a federal district court under 42 U.S.C. § 1983, alleging that the district's policy violated their First and Fourteenth Amendment rights. The district court dismissed most of the associations' claims. On appeal, the U.S. Court of Appeals, Fifth Circuit, affirmed in part and reversed in part. It granted the associations summary judgment on their claim that the prohibition of teacher-to-teacher discussions during the school day and the use of internal mail and bulletin board facilities was unconstitutional.

After the U.S. Supreme Court summarily affirmed the court of appeals' judgment, the associations filed for an award of attorneys' fees under 42 U.S.C. § 1988. The federal district court held that the associations were not "prevailing parties" within the meaning of § 1988 and thus were ineligible for any fee award. The court of appeals affirmed, ruling that the associations had not prevailed on the central issue in the litigation, and so were not prevailing parties. The associations then appealed to the U.S. Supreme Court. The Supreme Court stated that a party did not need to prevail on the "central issue" in a case in order to be afforded "prevailing party" status for purposes of attorneys' fees. The Court stated that the party need only succeed on "any significant issue" that materially alters the legal relationship between the parties. Since the teachers' associations prevailed on some of the relief they sought, they had established the basis for an award of attorneys' fees. *Texas State Teachers Ass'n v. Garland Indep. School Dist.*, 489 U.S. 782, 109 S.Ct. 1486, 103 L.Ed.2d 866 (1989).

E. Procedural Matters

In a 1982 case involving a Florida university secretary's § 1983 lawsuit, the Court stated that there was no purpose in requiring § 1983 plaintiffs to exhaust their state administrative remedies. This was because § 1983 had been enacted in the Reconstruction Era as a response to Congressional perceptions that individual civil rights would be abused by state officials.

A white female secretary worked for a Florida university. She alleged that during her employment there, she had been passed over for employment promotions, even though she was qualified for the positions. She sued the university in a federal district court under 42 U.S.C. § 1983, alleging gender and race discrimination. The secretary also claimed that the university actively sought to hire minorities and separated applicant files according to race and gender. A panel of the U.S. Court of Appeals, Fifth Circuit, dismissed the secretary's complaint for failure to exhaust her state administrative remedies. The court then agreed to hear the case *en banc* to determine whether the employee should be required to exhaust her state administrative remedies before she was entitled to file a § 1983 claim in the federal court system. Although the U.S. Supreme Court had on several occasions rejected the argument that a § 1983 action should be dismissed where the plaintiff had not exhausted administrative remedies, the court of appeals held that adequate and appropriate state administrative remedies must be exhausted before a plaintiff could bring a § 1983 action in federal court. The U.S. Supreme Court agreed to hear the case.

The Court examined its rationale in prior decisions, where it had considered the policy of exhausting administrative remedies. Administrative remedy exhaustion ensures that the parties attempt a settlement before proceeding to federal court. The Court examined Congress' intent in not specifically requiring exhaustion of state administrative remedies in § 1983 actions. Congress assigned to the federal courts the primary role of securing individual constitutional rights in the years after the Civil War. Section 1983 was passed during the Reconstruction Era in response to state-sanctioned constitutional violations of the rights of blacks after the ratification of the Fourteenth Amendment. To now require plaintiffs to go through state administrative processes contradicted this purpose. Congress had intended that § 1983 plaintiffs be able to choose the federal district courts as the forum for civil rights lawsuits. The Court rejected the policy reasons adopted by the court of appeals for requiring state administrative remedy exhaustion. It stated that reducing federal court case loads and using state agency expertise in these cases did not outweigh the purposes of § 1983. *Patsy v. Bd. of Regents*, 457 U.S. 496, 102 S.Ct. 2557, 73 L.Ed.2d 172 (1982).

In 1984, the Court considered *Migra v. Warren City School Dist.*, another § 1983 case, which differed significantly in its procedural posture from the *Patsy* case, above. In *Migra*, the Court stated that the judicial doctrine of *res judicata*, or claim preclusion, barred the filing of a new § 1983 lawsuit when the complaining party had already filed a lawsuit based on the same facts in state court proceedings.

An Ohio woman worked under successive contracts as a supervisor of elementary schools. The district offered her a new contract for an upcoming school year, but later revoked the offer and decided not to renew the contract. The supervisor sued the school district in an Ohio trial court for breach of contract and wrongful interference with her employment contract with the school board. The trial court held for the supervisor on the basis of these state law complaints, and ordered her reinstated with compensatory damages. The supervisor then filed a new lawsuit in a federal district court under 42 U.S.C. § 1983, alleging that the school district had refused to renew her contract in retaliation for her creation of a desegregation plan and a social studies curriculum which she had proposed. She claimed that the district had violated her rights to free speech, due process and equal protection under the U.S. Constitution. She sought injunctive relief, as well as compensatory and punitive damages. The district court dismissed her claim and the U.S. Court of Appeals affirmed the decision.

The supervisor appealed to the U.S. Supreme Court, which affirmed the lower court decisions, holding that it "is now settled that a federal court must give to a state court judgment the same preclusive effect that would be given that judgment under the law of the state in which the judgment was rendered." Because the supervisor had not raised her § 1983 claim at the same time she brought her state law claims, she could not now bring a lawsuit based upon the same set of acts under a new theory. The underlying purpose of § 1983 was to create a federal forum for constitutional and civil rights violations. This purpose was not undermined by giving deference to a state court decision based upon state laws. The Court dismissed the supervisor's § 1983 lawsuit. *Migra v. Warren City School Dist.*, 465 U.S. 75, 104 S.Ct. 892, 79 L.Ed.2d 56 (1984).

An arbitrator's decision is not binding with respect to the federal statutory and constitutional rights designed to be protected by 42 U.S.C. § 1983. Thus, an employee can sue under this statute despite an adverse arbitrator's decision.

A Michigan city discharged a police officer who filed a grievance pursuant to the collective bargaining agreement in place. He contended that there was "no proper cause" for his discharge. An arbitrator ruled that there was just cause, but the officer did not appeal that decision. Instead, he filed a lawsuit under 42 U.S.C. § 1983 alleging that he had been discharged in violation of his First Amendment rights. A jury found in his favor against the police chief, but ruled in favor of all the other defendants. The U.S. Court of Appeals, Sixth Circuit, reversed the judgment against the police chief, holding that the officer's First Amendment claims were barred by the earlier decision of the arbitrator. The officer then petitioned the U.S. Supreme Court for certiorari.

On appeal, the Court held that arbitration awards in proceedings brought pursuant to collective bargaining agreements would not have a preclusive effect in § 1983 actions. Because arbitration is not a judicial proceeding, an arbitration award does not have to be given the same "full faith and credit" as a judicial decision in a court of law. The federal statutory and constitutional rights designed to be safeguarded by § 1983 cannot adequately be protected by arbitration proceedings. Accordingly, the court of appeals' decision was reversed and the officer was entitled to recover in his suit against the chief of police. *McDonald v. City of West Branch, Michigan*, 466 U.S. 284, 104 S.Ct. 1799, 80 L.Ed.2d 302 (1984).

II. FEDERAL EMPLOYERS' LIABILITY ACT (FELA)

In a wrongful death action under the Federal Employers' Liability Act, the measure of recovery is "the damages ... [that] flow from the deprivation of the pecuniary benefits which the beneficiaries might have reasonably received." In the following case, the Supreme Court held that the effect of income taxes had to be shown to obtain an accurate picture of damages.

A fireman employed by a railroad suffered fatal injuries in a collision that was caused by the railroad's negligence. The accident occurred when a locomotive collided with a loaded hopper car that was being stored on a siding track. His estate brought suit under the Federal Employers' Liability Act to recover the damages suffered by his survivors as a result of his death. The jury award was $775,000. The employer appealed because the trial court excluded evidence of the income taxes payable on the decedent's earnings and because the judge refused to tell the jury that the award would not be subject to income taxation. The Appellate Court of Illinois found no error in the court's actions, and the case reached the U.S. Supreme Court.

The Court first noted that the measure of damages in a FELA action is a question that is federal in character. Only after-tax income can provide a realistic measure of a wage earner's ability to support his or her family. Thus, the decedent's income tax was a relevant factor in calculating the loss suffered by his dependents, and it should have been included in the evidence. Next, the Court noted that, since Congress had provided that damages received on account of personal injuries were not taxable income, an instruction should have been given to the jury to that effect. It could do no harm, and it could help prevent overinflated awards made on the erroneous assumption that the judgment would be taxed. The Court thus reversed the lower court's decision and remanded the case. *Norfolk & Western Railway Co. v. Liepelt,* 444 U.S. 490, 100 S.Ct. 755, 62 L.Ed.2d 689 (1980).

FELA was enacted to provide a federal remedy for railroad workers who suffer personal injuries as a result of the negligence of their employers or their fellow employees. Employers may not limit their FELA liability. In the following case, the Supreme Court held that even though an injury was caused by conduct that might have been subject to arbitration under the Railway Labor Act, the railroad employee was not deprived of his right to bring a FELA action for damages.

A carman, employed by a railroad, brought a lawsuit against his employer under FELA. He claimed that fellow employees had harassed, threatened and intimidated him, and that the railroad condoned these acts. The railroad answered by asserting that the employee's sole remedy was through the National Railroad Adjustment Board, according to the Railway Labor Act (RLA). It claimed that the RLA set forth binding arbitration procedures that the employee was forced to follow. A federal district court granted summary judgment to the railroad, and the U.S. Court of Appeals, Ninth Circuit, reversed and remanded. Further appeal was taken to the U.S. Supreme Court, which first noted that FELA was enacted to provide a federal remedy for railroad workers who were injured as a result of employer or co-employee negligence. Employers may not limit their FELA liability in any way. The RLA, on the other hand, was set up to provide elaborate procedures for the resolution of labor disputes. Here, although the injury at issue might have been subject to arbitration under the RLA (a dispute arising out of workplace conditions which was similar to a "minor" labor dispute), it was also possibly the type of injury that FELA was enacted to address. The court remanded the case for a determination of whether emotional injury was cognizable under FELA. *Atchison, Topeka and Santa Fe Ry. Co. v. Buell,* 480 U.S. 557, 107 S.Ct. 1410, 94 L.Ed.2d 563 (1987).

In the case below, the Supreme Court held that a state court had improperly awarded prejudgment interest in a FELA action.

A brakeman/conductor for a railroad fell while alighting from a railroad car and suffered a permanent injury to his back. He returned to work in a less physically demanding position, then sued the railroad under the Federal Employers' Liability Act, 45 U.S.C. § 51 *et seq.,* asserting that his fall had been attributable to his employer's negligence, and that his future earning power had been impaired. A jury found for the employee, awarding damages, and the judge assessed an additional amount as prejudgment interest pursuant to Pennsylvania law. The state appellate courts affirmed, and the U.S. Supreme Court granted review. The Supreme Court held that state courts may not award prejudgment interest according to local practice in FELA actions. The question of damages under FELA is a question of substance that must be settled according to federal law.

Further, federal law does not authorize awards of prejudgment interest in FELA actions. The Court also noted that the trial court had improperly taken from the jury the issue of the appropriate rate at which to discount the employee's FELA award to present value. Accordingly, the Court reversed the state court decisions and remanded the case for further proceedings. *Monessen Southwestern Railway Co. v. Morgan*, 486 U.S. 330, 108 S.Ct. 1837, 100 L.Ed.2d 349 (1988).

Despite the existence of FELA, if railroad employees are injured during the process of loading or unloading cargo from ships on navigable waters, the Longshore and Harbor Workers' Compensation Act will provide the exclusive remedy.

Three railroad employees were injured while working at their employers' Virginia terminals, where coal was being loaded from railway cars to ships. Two of the employees were injured while they were cleaning spilled coal from loading equipment to prevent the machinery from fouling. The other employee was injured while repairing a mechanical device necessary for the loading of ships. All three employees brought suit in state court under FELA (which provides a negligence cause of action for railroad employees), but the trial courts dismissed on the grounds that the Longshore and Harbor Workers' Compensation Act (LHWCA) provided the exclusive remedy. The Supreme Court of Virginia reversed, and the U.S. Supreme Court granted review. The Supreme Court reversed the lower court's decision, holding that the LHWCA provided the exclusive remedy. Maritime employment includes not only those who physically handle cargo, but also land-based activity which is an integral or essential part of loading or unloading a vessel. In this case, the employees were maintaining or repairing equipment that was essential to the loading process. Even though the work being performed might be considered traditional railroad work that could be done wherever railroad cars are unloaded, it was being done at a relevant situs and it involved integral elements of the loading process. Thus, the LHWCA applied, and the employees could not bring suit under FELA. *Chesapeake and Ohio Railway Co. v. Schwalb,* 493 U.S. 40, 110 S.Ct. 381, 107 L.Ed.2d 278 (1989).

In the following case, the Supreme Court held that FELA creates a cause of action against a state-owned railroad that is enforceable in state court.

The South Carolina Public Railways Commission, a state agency, employed 300 people in its capacity as a common carrier. One of its employees alleged that he was injured in the course and scope of his employment, and that his injury was caused by the commission's negligence. He sued the commission in state court under the FELA. The trial court dismissed his suit on the ground that FELA did not authorize a damages suit against a state agency, even in state court. The Supreme Court of South Carolina affirmed, and a grant of certiorari brought the case before the U.S. Supreme Court. The Supreme Court held that FELA created a cause of action against a state-owned railroad, which was enforceable in state court. Since many states specifically excluded railroad workers from workers' compensation coverage on the assumption that FELA adequately protects them from employer negligence, to disallow the suit here would dislodge the settled rights and expectations of both employers and employees. Accordingly, the employee's suit should not have been dismissed, and the lower courts' decisions were reversed. The case was remanded for trial. *Hilton v. South Carolina Public Railways Comm'n*, 502 U.S. 197, 112 S.Ct. 560, 116 L.Ed.2d 560 (1991).

The Supreme Court has determined that claims for negligent infliction of emotional distress are cognizable under FELA. Using both FELA principles and common law doctrine, the Court adopted the "zone of danger" test, limiting recovery to those plaintiffs who are in a zone of danger or who sustain a physical impact as a result of the defendant's negligence.

Two railroad workers brought separate suits against their former employer for negligent infliction of emotional distress under the FELA. In the first case, the employee witnessed a friend on his work crew having a heart attack and administered CPR. Despite his efforts, the friend died. While the work crew was waiting for the coroner to arrive, the crew's supervisor ordered the men back to work, within sight of the covered body. The Pennsylvania federal district court granted summary judgment to the railroad, and the U.S. Court of Appeals, Third Circuit, reversed. In the second case, a worker brought a stressful working environment claim. The district court held for the worker, and the court of appeals affirmed. The U.S. Supreme Court granted certiorari. The Supreme Court held that claims for negligent infliction of emotional distress are cognizable under FELA. However, an improper standard was applied by the court below in evaluating the claims. The Supreme Court stated that the proper standard had to be derived from both FELA principles and relevant common law doctrine. In so doing, the Court adopted the "zone of danger" test, which limits recovery for emotional injury to "those plaintiffs who sustain a physical impact as a result of a defendant's negligent conduct, or who are placed in immediate risk of physical harm by that conduct." If within the zone of danger, a plaintiff can recover for emotional distress. The Court then remanded the first case for a full determination of whether the employee satisfied the zone of danger test. However, it ruled that the worker in the second case could not recover against the railroad because his work-related-stress claim did not fall within the zone of danger conception. *Consolidated Rail Corp. v. Gottshall*, 512 U.S. 532, 114 S.Ct. 2396, 129 L.Ed. 2d 427 (1994).

The physical impact rule permits emotional distress claims under FELA where the distress accompanies a physical injury. In the case below, the Supreme Court refused to extend the rule to cover simple physical contact with a substance such as asbestos which threatens some future risk of disease.

The Federal Employers' Liability Act establishes a cause of action for railroad workers to recover damages for injuries resulting from employer negligence. A pipefitter employed by a railroad was exposed to asbestos while removing insulation from pipes over a three-year period. He attended an "asbestos awareness" seminar and began to fear that he would develop cancer or another asbestos-related disease. He filed a FELA action against the employer in a federal district court, seeking damages for emotional distress and his expenses for expected future medical checkups. The employer admitted negligence, but denied that the employee had suffered emotional distress or physical harm. The district court agreed with the employer and dismissed the action, but the U.S. Court of Appeals, Second Circuit, reversed and the U.S. Supreme Court agreed to review the case.

The Court discussed the physical impact rule it had previously set forth in FELA decisions, which permits emotional distress claims where the distress accompanies a physical injury. Employees injured as the result of a physical impact due to employer negligence may also recover damages for negligent infliction of emotional distress. However, the Court refused to extend the physical impact rule to cover simple physical contact with a substance such as asbestos, which threatens some future risk of disease. The Court characterized the employee's contact with asbestos as an exposure, not a physical impact, and reversed the court of appeals' decision. The employee had advanced no evidence of an emotional injury and the Court dismissed the claim for the cost of extra medical checkups. *Metro-North Commuter Railroad Co. v. Buckley*, 521 U.S. 424, 117 S.Ct. 2113, 138 L.ed.2d 560 (1997).

III. IMMUNITY

Based on the Eleventh Amendment of the U.S. Constitution, the doctrine of sovereign immunity shields the government from suit unless the government assents to suit. The federal government and many states have assented to suit through Tort Claims Acts, which waive the government's immunity. However, municipalities do not generally receive immunity protection. Governmental employees also may be granted immunity for their actions. Absolute immunity applies primarily to employees of the judicial and executive branches of government. Qualified immunity, on the other hand, applies to most governmental employees.

A. Sovereign Immunity

In *Owen v. City of Independence,* the Supreme Court held that a city's claim of immunity was not sufficient to bar a § 1983 lawsuit. When a city violates a person's constitutional rights, it can be held liable under § 1983.

A handgun, purported to have been destroyed in a Missouri city's police department's property room, turned up in the possession of a felon. This prompted an investigation, and the eventual dismissal of the police chief by the city manager. The police chief was not given any reason for the discharge, and was only given a written notice that the dismissal was made according to the city charter. He then sued the city, the city manager and the city council members in a federal district court under 42 U.S.C. § 1983, alleging that he had been discharged in violation of his due process rights. The district court ruled for the defendants, and the chief appealed unsuccessfully to the U.S. Court of Appeals, Eighth Circuit. He further appealed to the U.S. Supreme Court.

The Supreme Court held that § 1983 actions were not barred by a city's claim of immunity. It also held that the city's officers could not assert that they had acted in good faith as a defense to a § 1983 action. A city has no discretion to violate the U.S. Constitution. When it does violate the Constitution, it cannot claim that it was exercising its own judgment or discretion and in that way avoid liability. Since it was the liability of the city itself that was at issue, there was little, if any, injustice in subjecting the city's officials to liability. Such liability would not deter an official's willingness to execute his office effectively because, so long as he conducted himself in good faith, the damages would be chargeable to the populace as a whole, and not to him. *Owen v. City of Independence,* 445 U.S. 622, 100 S.Ct. 1398, 63 L.Ed.2d 673 (1980).

In 1994, the Supreme Court held that a *Bivens* action could not be brought against a federal agency. Such an action is limited to suits against federal agents who allegedly violate the Constitution.

The Federal Savings and Loan Insurance Corporation (FSLIC) was appointed as receiver for a failed California-chartered thrift institution. The FSLIC discharged a senior thrift officer pursuant to its policy of firing the management of failed thrifts. The officer filed suit against the FSLIC in a federal district court, alleging that he was unconstitutionally denied his right to continued employment without due process of law. The district court held for the officer and awarded damages. The U.S. Court of Appeals, Ninth Circuit, affirmed, and the FSLIC appealed to the U.S. Supreme Court.

The officer argued that a *Bivens* action (a cause of action for damages against federal agents for deprivation of a federal constitutional right) can also be brought against federal agencies. The Supreme Court disagreed, ruling that such an expansion would potentially subject the federal government to enormous financial burdens. Further, permitting *Bivens* actions against federal agencies would circumvent the qualified immunity defense and encourage claimants to bypass actions against federal officers in favor of suits against federal agencies. As a result, the *Bivens* remedy's deterrent effect against individual federal officers would be lost. Thus, although the FSLIC effectively waived sovereign immunity, the officer could not collect damages pursuant to a *Bivens* remedy. The holdings of the lower courts were reversed. *F.D.I.C. v. Meyer,* 510 U.S. 471, 114 S.Ct. 996, 127 L.Ed.2d 308 (1994).

A bi-state entity created under the U.S. Constitution's Interstate Compact Clause was held not to be qualified for Eleventh Amendment immunity from suit in federal court. Since the states were not financially responsible for the entity, immunity was not warranted.

The Port Authority Trans-Hudson Corporation was created through a bi-state compact between New York and New Jersey to better coordinate commercial activities in New York. It was consented to by Congress pursuant to the Interstate

Compact Clause of the U.S. Constitution and created to be a financially independent entity funded by private investors. Neither of the states was liable for the port authority's debts. However, the two states selected the twelve commissioners of the port authority, each state's governor could veto the commissioners' actions, and the states' legislatures acting jointly could augment the powers and responsibilities of the port authority. Also, the states appropriated minimal sums to cover "salaries, office and other administrative expenses." Two workers injured while working for a commuter railroad operated by the port authority sued it under the Federal Employers' Liability Act (FELA) in a federal district court. The district court held that the port authority was immune from suit under the Eleventh Amendment. On appeal, the U.S. Court of Appeals, Third Circuit, affirmed, and the workers appealed to the U.S. Supreme Court.

The Supreme Court noted that the Eleventh Amendment generally shields states from suit in federal court. However, the states involved here did not intend that the port authority receive this special constitutional protection. Specifically, the states were not financially responsible for the port authority and its survival was not contingent on state support. Rather, the port authority had been self-sustaining for many years and was explicitly barred from pledging the credit of either state. Because bi-state entities created by compact were not subject to the unilateral control of a single state, the Court held that the port authority was not an agency of the United States for Eleventh Amendment purposes. Consequently, it was not entitled to immunity. The holdings of the lower courts were reversed and the injured railroad workers' claims were remanded for further proceedings. *Hess v. Port Authority Trans-Hudson Corp.*, 513 U.S. 30, 115 S.Ct. 394, 130 L.Ed.2d 245 (1994).

The Supreme Court held that Eleventh Amendment immunity rests on potential legal liability, not third-party indemnification.

A New York mathematical physicist sought employment at the Lawrence Livermore National Laboratory, which was operated by the University of California pursuant to a contract with the federal government. He filed suit against the regents of the university in federal court claiming a breach of contract because the university agreed to employ him but wrongfully refused to hire him when he could not obtain the required security clearance from the Department of Energy (DOE). The district court concluded that the Eleventh Amendment which provides for state immunity from lawsuits barred him from maintaining his breach of contract action; however, the U.S. Court of Appeals, Ninth Circuit, reversed. The U.S. Supreme Court granted certiorari. On appeal, the physicist contended that the Eleventh Amendment did not apply because any award of damages would be paid by the DOE, and therefore have no impact on the treasury of the state of California. The Supreme Court rejected this argument, finding that an entity's potential legal liability, rather than its ability to require a third party to reimburse it, or to discharge the liability in the first instance, was the relevant inquiry when determining the immunity issue. The Eleventh Amendment protects a state from the risk of adverse judgments even though the state may be indemnified by a third party. The judgment of the court of appeals was reversed. *Regents of the Univ. of California v. John Doe*, 519 U.S. 425, 117 S.Ct. 900, 137 L.Ed.2d 55 (1997).

Congress exceeded its constitutional authority under the Fourteenth Amendment when it included state employees within the coverage of the Age Discrimination in Employment Act. The Court found that Congress had no reason to believe that the states unconstitutionally discriminated against employees on the basis of age, making the contested amendment to the ADEA improper.

The ADEA, originally enacted in 1967, prohibits employment discrimination against individuals because of their age. The Fair Labor Standards Amendments of 1974 extended the act's substantive requirements to the states. The U.S. Court of Appeals, Eleventh Circuit, consolidated three Florida cases filed against public employers and found that Congress did not effectively abrogate Eleventh Amendment immunity when it amended the ADEA. Two of the cases consolidated by the Eleventh Circuit involved actions by current and former university employees against public universities. The other case involved the Florida Department of Corrections. Noting a conflict among federal courts on the question of abrogation of Eleventh Amendment immunity, the Supreme Court agreed to hear the consolidated cases.

The court explained that the Eleventh Amendment prohibits federal suits against non-consenting states. Congress may abrogate state immunity only by making its intention unmistakably clear in statutory language, and only then as a valid exercise of constitutional authority. In this case, Congress had clearly stated its intent to abrogate Eleventh Amendment immunity by subjecting the states to potential liability for monetary damages in suits filed by individual employees. However, the court held that Congress lacked the power to do so when it amended the ADEA in 1974. Under the standard defined by *Seminole Tribe of Florida v. Florida*, 517 U.S. 44 (1996), Congress has no Article I commerce power to abrogate state immunity. Although Section 5 of the Fourteenth Amendment permits Congress to abrogate state immunity, this affirmative grant of power does not include the power to determine what constitutes a constitutional violation. The court has required a showing of a "congruence and proportionality" between the injury Congress seeks to prevent or remedy and the means adopted to achieve that end. Under the congruence and proportionality test, Congressional action will be struck down if it is out of proportion to a supposed remedial objective that cannot be understood as responsive to, or designed to prevent, unconstitutional behavior. Under that test, the ADEA as amended was not appropriate legislation under Section 5 of the Fourteenth Amendment, because its' substantive requirements were found disproportionate to any perceived unconstitutional conduct by the states.

The Court has previously held that age classifications do not violate the Equal Protection Clause. Unlike classifications based on race and gender, age classifications do not reflect prejudice or antipathy, and older persons have not been subjected to a history of purposeful or unequal treatment. Moreover, age classifications are presumptively rational, and states may discriminate on the basis of age without offending the Fourteenth Amendment, if the classification is rationally related to a legitimate state interest. The amended ADEA was out of proportion to its supposed remedial objective because it purported to prevent discrimination that was not protected by the Equal Protection Clause. The court characterized the legislative record of the ADEA as "an unwarranted response to a perhaps inconsequential problem." Congress identified no pattern of age discrimination by the states and had no reason to believe that state and local governments were unconstitutionally discriminating against their employees on the basis of age. Therefore, Congress exceeded its authority under the 14th Amendment when it included state employees within the coverage of the ADEA. *Kimel v. Florida Bd. of Regents*, 528 U.S. 62, 120 S.Ct. 631, 145 L.Ed.2d 522 (2000).

B. Employee Immunity

1. Absolute Immunity

In 1980, the Court held that the decision to parole a man who later tortured and murdered a teenager could not result in liability to the public employees who made the decision to parole him. They were entitled to absolute immunity.

A California man who was convicted of attempted rape, committed to a state mental hospital, and sentenced to "a term of imprisonment of 1 to 20 years," with a recommendation that he not be paroled was nevertheless paroled five years later to the care of his mother. Five months later, he tortured and killed a 15-year-old girl. Her survivors sued the state officials responsible for releasing the parolee. The trial court sustained a demurrer to the complaint (dismissed the case) and the court of appeal affirmed. The case then reached the U.S. Supreme Court, which held that the California law that granted complete immunity to the public employees who decided to release the parolee was constitutional. Thus, the lower courts had properly dismissed the case. Even though the state had acted to release the parolee, his violent actions five months later could not be characterized as state action. The victim's death was too remote from the state officials' actions for liability to attach under 42 U.S.C. § 1983. The Court affirmed the lower court decisions in favor of the government officials. *Martinez v. State of California*, 444 U.S. 277, 100 S.Ct. 553, 62 L.Ed.2d 481 (1980).

In *Harlow*, the Supreme Court held that two White House aides were not entitled to absolute immunity, but rather only to qualified immunity. Accordingly, they would have to show the objective reasonability of their actions.

A management analyst, with the U.S. Department of the Air Force, appeared before a joint congressional committee and testified to cost overruns, which embarrassed his superiors. The department then conducted a reorganization and reduction in force to promote economic efficiency of the armed forces, and the analyst's position was eliminated. He sued two White House aides in a federal district court, asserting that he had been unlawfully discharged in retaliation for his public statements. The White House aides asked the court to dismiss the suit because they were entitled to absolute immunity, but the court refused. They appealed unsuccessfully to the court of appeals, and further appealed to the U.S. Supreme Court.

The Supreme Court stated that absolute immunity existed for the President, legislators and judges in their judicial functions, and also to certain officials in the executive branch. However, for most executive officials, the Court recognized only a qualified immunity. These officials required some protection to shield them from undue interference with their duties, but they could also be held liable for constitutional violations of citizens' rights. The Court held that in order to be entitled to absolute immunity, a presidential aide would first have to show that his job included functions so sensitive that absolute immunity was essential. Because the aides had not shown that their jobs were of such a sensitive nature, the Court determined that they were not entitled to absolute immunity. It did find, however, that they were entitled to qualified immunity provided that their actions did not violate clearly established statutory or constitutional rights of which a reasonable person would have known. The Court vacated the court of appeals' decision, and remanded the case to the district court for a determination as to whether the aides' conduct fell within the immune category. *Harlow v. Fitzgerald,* 457 U.S. 800, 102 S.Ct. 2727, 73 L.Ed.2d 396 (1982).

In 1985, the Supreme Court held that the Attorney General (a cabinet officer) was not entitled to absolute immunity for his actions in wiretapping a private citizen. However, he retained qualified immunity.

In 1970, the Attorney General of the United States authorized a warrantless wiretap for the purpose of gathering intelligence about activities of a radical group that had made tentative plans to threaten the nation's security. After the wiretaps, the U.S. Supreme Court ruled that warrantless wiretaps were not constitutional in cases involving domestic threats. After this ruling, the man who had been wiretapped sued the Attorney General in a federal district court, asserting that the surveillance he had been subjected to violated the Fourth Amendment. The Attorney General sought to dismiss on immunity grounds, and the man who had been wiretapped sought a declaration that the Attorney General was not immune. The district court ruled against the Attorney General, who then appealed to the U.S. Court of Appeals, Third Circuit. The court of appeals held that he was not entitled to absolute immunity and that he could not appeal the qualified immunity ruling until a final order had been made. The Attorney General appealed to the U.S. Supreme Court, which held that even though he was a cabinet officer, the Attorney General was not absolutely immune from a suit for damages. However, the Court held that he was entitled to qualified immunity for his authorization of the wiretap because his action was not a violation of clearly established law. Even though the Court had held warrantless wiretaps to be illegal and unconstitutional, it had not done so until after the Attorney General had authorized the wiretap. *Mitchell v. Forsyth,* 472 U.S. 511, 105 S.Ct. 2806, 86 L.Ed.2d 411 (1985).

In 1988, the Supreme Court stated that a judge did not have absolute immunity from liability under § 1983 for his decisions to demote and dismiss a court employee. Absolute immunity is only available for judicial acts, not for administrative acts.

A judge hired a woman as a probation officer. He later promoted her, then demoted and fired her. She brought suit in a federal court under 42 U.S.C. § 1983, alleging that the demotion and firing had been on account of her sex in violation of the Equal Protection Clause of the Fourteenth Amendment. After the jury found in her favor, the court granted summary judgment to the judge on the ground that he was absolutely immune to a civil damages suit. The U.S. Court of Appeals affirmed, and the case then came before the U.S. Supreme Court. The Court determined that a state court judge does not have absolute immunity from a § 1983 damages suit for his decisions to demote and dismiss a court employee. Those actions were administrative rather than judicial, thus providing only qualified immunity. Judges are only entitled to absolute immunity for their judicial or adjudicatory acts, primarily to protect judicial independence. Accordingly, the Court reversed the court of appeals' decision and remanded the case for further proceedings. *Forrester v. White*, 484 U.S. 219, 108 S.Ct. 538, 98 L.Ed.2d 555 (1988).

A judge who ordered two police officers to use force in bringing a lawyer into his courtroom was held by the Court to be acting in his judicial capacity. Thus, he was immune from liability.

A Los Angeles County public defender failed to appear for the initial call of a judge's morning calendar because he was in another courtroom waiting to appear there. The judge allegedly ordered two police officers "to forcibly and with excessive force" bring the lawyer into the judge's courtroom. A lawsuit was brought by the lawyer, under 42 U.S.C. § 1983, against the judge for approving and ratifying acts of violence by the officers against the lawyer. A federal district court dismissed the lawsuit, but the U.S. Court of Appeals reversed. The case then came before the U.S. Supreme Court. The Supreme Court held that the judge was immune from liability. Only if his actions had not been taken in his judicial capacity could he be held liable. Even though the judge's order was carried out by police officers, his action in making the order was not transformed from "judicial" to "executive." Accordingly, he should have been granted immunity. The court reversed the court of appeals' decision, holding that the suit should have been dismissed. *Mireles v. Waco*, 502 U.S. 9, 112 S.Ct. 286, 116 L.Ed.2d 9 (1991).

In *Antoine*, the Court stated that a court reporter is not absolutely immune from damages liability for failing to produce a transcript of a criminal trial.

A Washington man was convicted of bank robbery. He promptly appealed and ordered a copy of the transcript from the court reporter who had worked his trial. The court reporter failed to provide a transcript, delaying the man's appeal for four years. As a result, he sued the court reporter and her former employer (who had hired her under its contract to provide reporting services to the court) for damages resulting from the delay. A Washington federal district court held that court reporters are entitled to absolute immunity, and the U.S.

Court of Appeals, Ninth Circuit, affirmed. On further appeal to the U.S. Supreme Court, that decision was reversed. The Court held that the court reporter could not establish the justification for absolute immunity she claimed. Since her job required no discretionary judgment, she was not entitled to immunity as part of the judicial function. *Antoine v. Byers & Anderson, Inc.,* 508 U.S. 429, 113 S.Ct. 2167, 124 L.Ed.2d 391 (1993).

The Supreme Court, in the case below, distinguished between absolute prosecutorial immunity which applies when a criminal prosecutor acts as an advocate, and qualified immunity which applies when she functions as a complaining witness. As a complaining witness, a prosecutor may be held liable for making false statements of fact in an affidavit supporting an application for an arrest warrant.

A prosecuting attorney in Washington began a criminal proceeding against an individual based on the alleged theft of computer equipment from a school. The attorney filed three documents in the county superior court, two of which were unsworn pleadings. The third document was a "Certification for Determination of Probable Cause" which satisfied the requirement that an arrest warrant be supported by an affidavit or sworn testimony establishing the grounds for issuing the warrant. She personally vouched for the truth of the facts set forth in the certification under penalty of perjury. Based on the certification, the court found probable cause and ordered an arrest warrant to be issued. However, the certification contained two inaccurate factual statements. About a month after the individual was arrested and spent a day in jail, the charges against him were dismissed on the prosecutor's motion. He then sued her under 42 U.S.C. § 1983, alleging that she had violated his constitutional right to be free from unreasonable seizures. A federal district court denied her motion for summary judgment on the grounds of absolute immunity, and the U.S. Court of Appeals, Ninth Circuit, affirmed.

On further appeal to the U.S. Supreme Court, the lower court holdings were affirmed. The Court stated that § 1983 may create a damages remedy against a prosecutor for making false statements of fact in an affidavit supporting an application for an arrest warrant, because such conduct is not protected by the doctrine of absolute prosecutorial immunity. Absolute immunity applies when a criminal prosecutor is performing the traditional functions of an advocate. However, when she is functioning as a complaining witness by personally attesting to the truth of the facts set forth in an affidavit, she is functioning as a witness and not as an advocate. Accordingly, she is protected only by qualified immunity. The Court noted that although the law requires an arrest warrant to be supported by an affidavit or sworn testimony, neither federal nor state law made it necessary for the prosecutor to make that certification herself. By doing so, the attorney performed an act that any competent witness might have performed. *Kalina v. Fletcher,* 522 U.S. 118, 118 S.Ct. 502, 139 L.Ed.2d 471 (1997).

The Supreme Court held that absolute legislative immunity from civil liability for legislative activities applies to local legislators.

The administrator and sole employee of the department of health for a Massachusetts city tried to fire an employee who served temporarily under her for making racial and ethnic slurs. The employee was politically well-connected and eventually was suspended, but not fired. During this time, the mayor prepared the city budget. Anticipating a reduction in state aid, the mayor proposed a salary freeze for all city employees and the elimination of some city jobs, including the elimination of the administrator's department. The proposal was adopted and an ordinance was passed by the city council. The administrator sued the city, the mayor, and the vice president of the city council in the U.S. District Court for the District of Massachusetts under 42 U.S.C. § 1983 for race discrimination and violation of her First Amendment rights for filing a complaint against the employee. After a trial, the jury returned a verdict in favor of the defendants on the issue of race discrimination but found in favor of the administrator on the First Amendment issue. Citing absolute legislative immunity, the defendants appealed to the U.S. Court of Appeals, Fisrt Circuit, which stated that the mayor and the vice president's actions were not legislative because they relied on facts relating to a particular individual in the decision-making process. The U.S. Supreme Court granted review.

Noting that federal, state and regional legislators have long been absolutely immune from civil liability for their legislative activities, the Supreme Court held that local legislators are also absolutely immune from suit under § 1983 for their legislative activities. Absolute immunity attaches to all actions taken within the sphere of legitimate legislative activity. The Supreme Court rejected the administrator's argument to look beyond the defendants' formal actions and examine whether the ordinance was legislative in substance. Because the ordinance reflected a discretionary, policymaking decision implicating the budgetary priorities of the city and the services it provided, the Supreme Court reversed the court of appeals' decision. *Bogan v. Scott-Harris*, 523 U.S. 44, 118 S.Ct. 966, 140 L.Ed.2d 79 (1998).

2. Qualified Immunity

To obtain qualified immunity for one's actions, the government official (not the person suing the official) must show that the conduct was justified by an objectively reasonable belief that the conduct was lawful.

A Puerto Rico police officer submitted a sworn statement to his supervisor, asserting that two other agents had offered false evidence in a criminal case they were investigating. As a result of the officer's statement, he was transferred to the police academy, where he was given no investigative authority. The departmental supervisor subsequently found that all the officer's allegations were true. When the "false evidence criminal case" came to trial, the officer was called to testify as a defense witness, which he did. As a result of his testimony, the officer was suspended by his supervisor, who then discharged him without a hearing. The officer appealed to an administrative commission, which reinstated him. He then sued his supervisor in a federal district court under 42 U.S.C. § 1983, contending that his due process rights had been violated, and that his reputation in the community had been damaged. The district court dismissed the case because the supervisor was entitled to qualified immunity for acts done in good faith within the scope of his official duties, and because the officer had failed to state in his pleading that the supervisor had acted in bad faith. The officer appealed unsuccessfully to the U.S. Court of Appeals, First Circuit, and further appealed to the U.S. Supreme Court.

The Supreme Court held that the qualified immunity defense depends on facts which are "peculiarly within the knowledge and control" of the public official making the defense. The official must act sincerely and with a belief that he is doing the right thing by his action. Since the officer could not know if his supervisor was so acting, the court determined that the burden was on the supervisor to plead that "his conduct was justified by an objectively reasonable belief that it was lawful." The Court reversed the appellate court's decision. *Gomez v. Toledo*, 446 U.S. 635, 100 S.Ct. 1920, 64 L.Ed.2d 572 (1980).

The act of applying for an arrest warrant is not in itself objectively reasonable. An officer sued for violating an arrestee's constitutional rights must still prove that a reasonably well-trained officer in his or her position would not have known that the affidavit failed to establish probable cause.

Police in Rhode Island conducted a court-authorized wiretap of a house and determined that marijuana had been used there. Accordingly, an officer drew up felony complaints against several persons, charging them with possession of marijuana. He presented the complaints to a state judge who signed the warrants, and the officer then arrested the suspects. However, the charges were dropped when the grand jury did not return an indictment. The arrestees subsequently sued the officer in a federal district court, asserting violations of their constitutional rights. The court ruled for the officer on immunity grounds and they appealed successfully to the U.S. Court of Appeals, First Circuit. The officer petitioned the U.S. Supreme Court for review, which it granted.

On appeal, the Court ruled that the officer was not entitled to absolute immunity just because he submitted the warrants to a neutral magistrate. It found that he could only assert qualified immunity as a defense. This required that he knew probable cause existed or reasonably believed probable cause existed before seeking the warrants. His act in applying for the arrest warrant was not automatically reasonable because he believed certain facts were true and relied on the judge's determination of whether to issue the warrants. If a reasonably well-trained officer would have known probable cause did not exist, the Court held that seeking the warrants would be unreasonable. The Court affirmed the court of appeals' decision and remanded the case for a determination on that issue. *Malley v. Briggs,* 475 U.S. 335, 106 S.Ct. 1092, 89 L.Ed.2d 271 (1986).

In the following case, the Supreme Court held that even though a government official's actions violate a person's constitutional rights, the official will still be entitled to qualified immunity if he or she acted reasonably (believing the actions to be constitutional).

An FBI agent conducted a warrantless search, with other law enforcement officers, of a Minnesota family's home. He believed a suspected bank robber might be found there, but the suspect was not inside. The family then sued the FBI agent in a Minnesota trial court and the agent removed the case to a federal court, seeking summary judgment on qualified immunity grounds. The court granted the summary judgment and, on appeal, the U.S. Court of Appeals, Eighth Circuit, reversed. It then held that unresolved factual questions existed regarding the agent's probable cause, and further held that the right which the agent had violated (to be protected from warrantless searches) had been clearly established. The agent further appealed to the U.S. Supreme Court.

The Supreme Court held that the agent was entitled to summary judgment on qualified immunity grounds if he could establish that a reasonable officer would have believed the search comported with the Fourth Amendment, even though it did not. Further, the Court ruled that the right the agent had violated was not a clearly established right if probable cause and exigent circumstances existed. Moreover, the Court determined that it was not inappropriate to give qualified immunity to government officials who had acted reasonably. Even if the agent violated the Fourth Amendment, the violation was not necessarily unreasonable just because it was unconstitutional. The Court vacated the court of appeals' decision and remanded the case for a determination as to whether the agent's actions had been reasonable. *Anderson v. Creighton*, 483 U.S. 635, 107 S.Ct. 3034, 97 L.Ed.2d 523 (1987).

The Federal Employees Liability Reform and Tort Compensation Act immunizes government employees from lawsuits where the employees are acting within the scope of their employment. This result does not change even if the claimants are unable to recover under the Federal Tort Claims Act.

A doctor working at an army hospital overseas served as the attending physician during the delivery of a child born with massive brain damage. The parents sued the doctor in federal court, which granted the government's motion to substitute itself for the doctor. The court then dismissed the suit because the Federal Tort Claims Act (FTCA) excludes recovery for injuries sustained abroad. The U.S. Court of Appeals reversed, holding that the Federal Employees Liability Reform and Tort Compensation Act (Act) did not require substitution of the government or immunize the doctor. The U.S. Supreme Court granted certiorari.

The Supreme Court noted that the Act immunized government employees from suit even though the FTCA exception precluded recovery by the parents against the government. Sections 5 and 6 of the Act stated that the FTCA would be the exclusive mode of recovery for the tort of a government employee (acting within the scope of his or her employment). Here, the Act did not allow a lawsuit to be brought against the doctor. Further, since the FTCA barred government liability for torts arising in a foreign country, the parents could not recover for their child's brain damage. The Court reversed the court of appeals' decision. *U.S. v. Smith*, 499 U.S. 160, 111 S.Ct. 1180, 113 L.Ed.2d 134 (1991).

As long as government officials act reasonably under the circumstances, they will likely be entitled to immunity even if their acts are violative of a person's rights.

A California man wrote a letter that rambled on about a "Mr. Image" who wanted to murder the President. He also made an oral statement to the effect that the President should have been assassinated in Germany. Two Secret Service agents visited his home and were invited in. The man refused to answer questions about whether he intended to harm the President. Under a federal law, the two agents arrested the man for making threats against the President. Subsequently, the case was dismissed. The man then sued the agents, seeking recovery under the Federal Tort Claims Act for the agents' violations of his Fourth Amendment rights. A federal district court denied the agents' motion for summary judgment, and the U.S. Court of Appeals affirmed. Before the U.S. Supreme Court, it was noted that the agents would be entitled to immunity if reasonable officers could have believed that probable cause existed to arrest the man. The Court then stated that the agents were entitled to qualified immunity. Even if they had erred in concluding that probable cause existed to make the arrest, their decision was reasonable. Officials did not always have to err on the side of caution for fear of being sued, especially where the specter of Presidential assassination loomed. The Court reversed the court of appeals' decision and remanded the case. *Hunter v. Bryant*, 502 U.S. 224, 112 S.Ct. 534, 116 L.Ed.2d 589 (1991).

In the case below, the Supreme Court found that prison guards employed by a private prison management firm were not entitled to immunity. In particular, the Court held that mere performance of a governmental function does not support immunity for a private person, especially one who performs a job without supervision or direction.

A Tennessee prisoner filed suit in federal district court against two prison guards, alleging violation of his constitutional rights under 42 U.S.C. § 1983. The guards asserted qualified immunity and moved to dismiss the case. The district court denied the motion, holding that because they worked for a private company rather than the government the law did not grant them immunity from suit. The U.S. Court of Appeals, Sixth Circuit, affirmed, and the U.S. Supreme Court granted certiorari. The Court affirmed, finding that private prison guards, unlike those who work directly for the government, do not enjoy § 1983 immunity. The immunity doctrine's purposes, which seek to protect the public from unwarranted timidity on the part of public officials and to ensure that talented candidates are not deterred by the threat of damage suits from entering into public service, do not support application of immunity to private entities. Mere performance of a governmental function does not support immunity for a private person, especially one who performs a job without supervision or direction. The Court cautioned, however, that it had focused only on the question of § 1983 immunity; it did not address whether the guards were liable under § 1983 even though they were employed by a private firm. *Richardson v. McKnight*, 521 U.S. 399, 117 S.Ct. 2100, 138 L.Ed.2d 540 (1997).

3. Procedural Matters–Appeals

Although public officials asserting a qualified immunity defense may immediately appeal the denial of a summary judgment motion, they may not appeal a court's decision to deny summary judgment because there exists a triable issue of fact.

Several police officers observed a diabetic resident having an insulin seizure on a city street. Thinking that he was drunk, they arrested him and brought him to the police station. After waking up at a local hospital with several broken ribs, the arrestee filed suit against the officers in federal district court, alleging that they had used excessive force when arresting him and later, in the booking room at the station house. The district court denied the officers' summary judgment motions based on qualified immunity, and the officers appealed to the U.S. Court of Appeals, Seventh Circuit. The court of appeals refused to consider their appeal, ruling that it lacked jurisdiction to hear such pretrial "evidence insufficiency" claims made by public official defendants who assert qualified immunity defenses. The officers appealed to the U.S. Supreme Court. The Supreme Court noted that *Mitchell v. Forsyth*, 472 U.S. 511, 105 S.Ct. 2806, 86 L.Ed.2d 411 (1985), held that denials of summary judgment motions were immediately appealable "collateral orders" only if the defendant was a public official asserting a qualified immunity defense and was challenging whether or not the facts showed a violation of "clearly established law." However, the Court held that such defendants may not appeal a district court's determination that there was sufficient evidence to raise a triable issue of fact. The latter type of appeal would consume inordinate amounts of appellate time and was less likely to bring important error-correcting benefits than where purely legal matters were at issue. The court of appeals' ruling was affirmed. *Johnson v. Jones*, 515 U.S. 304, 115 S.Ct. 2151, 132 L.Ed.2d 238 (1995).

The Supreme Court in *Behrens v. Pelletier* rejected a one-interlocutory-appeal rule that limited defendants to one appeal on the issue of immunity. The availability of other claims or existence of material fact issues for trial did not preclude a second interlocutory appeal.

A California savings and loan (S&L) association named a high level manager of a previously failed S&L as its managing officer, subject to Federal Home Loan Bank Board consent. The board's supervisory agent withheld its approval based on alleged misconduct by the manager. The California S&L asked him to resign, and when he refused, fired him. The manager filed a *Bivens* damages claim against the board's supervisory agent, alleging procedural and substantive due process violations. The manager alleged that the supervisory agent's letter withholding approval coupled with his continuing efforts to harm his reputation, had cost the manager his position at the S&L and his livelihood within the industry. The district court dismissed in part based on statute of limitation grounds but the ruling was reversed and remanded following an interlocutory appeal. The claims were reinstated by the district court. After his motion for summary judgment based on qualified immunity was denied by the district court, the supervisory agent filed a second interlocutory appeal, which was dismissed by the U.S. Court of Appeals, Ninth Circuit. The supervisory agent appealed to the U.S. Supreme Court.

The Supreme Court noted that one appeal on the immunity issue may not be enough. Because the manager's claims for loss of employment at the S&L had initially been dismissed as time-barred, the court of appeals had refused to decide whether one who holds his job subject to regulatory approval can assert a constitutionally cognizable expectation of continued employment. Consequently, the denial of summary judgment based on qualified immunity was an appealable final judgment. Moreover, neither the availability of other claims nor the existence of material fact issues for trial precluded the second interlocutory appeal. The initial appeal on qualified immunity grounds did not divest the court of appeals of jurisdiction to hear a second appeal based on qualified immunity. *Behrens v. Pelletier*, 516 U.S. 299, 116 S.Ct. 834, 133 L.Ed.2d 773 (1996).

The Supreme Court held that no federal right to an interlocutory appeal exists in state court 42 U.S.C. § 1983 actions.

A former Idaho liquor store clerk employed by the state filed an action for damages under 42 U.S.C. § 1983 in an Idaho state court. She alleged that state officials violated her due process rights under the Fourteenth Amendment to the U.S. Constitution when they terminated her employment. The officials moved to dismiss the complaint on the ground that they were entitled to qualified immunity. The court treated the motion as one for summary judgment and denied it. The Supreme Court of Idaho dismissed the appeal, concluding that an order denying a motion for summary judgment was not appealable. The Supreme Court recognized that if the § 1983 action had been brought in a federal court, the officials would have had a right to take an appeal from the court's order denying their motion for summary judgment. However, because the action had been brought in state court, the officials did not have the right to an interlocutory appeal. The judgment of the Idaho Supreme Court was affirmed. *Johnson v. Fankell*, 520 U.S. 911, 117 S.Ct. 1800, 138 L.Ed.2d 108 (1997).

IV. NONGOVERNMENTAL PARTIES

In the following case, the Supreme Court upheld an award of punitive damages against an insurer because of its acts and the acts of its agent.

An Alabama insurance agent solicited Roosevelt City, Alabama, for health and life insurance for its employees. The agent prepared applications for the city and its employees for group health and life policies. The initial premium payments were taken by the agent and submitted to the insurer with the applications. An arrangement was made for the health insurer to send its premium billings to the agent at his office. The premium payments were to then be effected through payroll deductions with the city clerk issuing a check to the agent. The agent did not remit the premium payments but instead misappropriated most of the funds. However, the insurer did not send notices of lapsed coverage to the employees.

Instead, these notices were sent to the agent. One of the employees was hospitalized and upon her discharge was required to make payment on her bill because the hospital could not confirm her health coverage. Her physician, when he was not paid, placed her account with a collection agency. The agency obtained a judgment against the woman and her credit was adversely affected. The city workers then filed suit against the insurer and the agent, asking for damages for fraud. The case was submitted to the jury and the jury returned a verdict against the insurer and the agent for over $1 million, which included a large sum for punitive damages. The Alabama Supreme Court affirmed this decision and the insurer appealed to the U.S. Supreme Court.

The issue, on appeal, was the constitutionality of certain punitive damage awards. The insurer contended that the award violated due process as the product of unbridled jury discretion. The Court noted that the punitive damage award did not violate due process. First, the trial court's instructions placed reasonable constraints on the exercise of the jury's discretion by expressly describing the purposes of punitive damages to be retribution and deterrence, by requiring the jury to consider the character and degree of the particular wrong, and by explaining that the imposition of punitive damages was not compulsory. Second, the trial court conducted a post-verdict hearing that set forth standards to ensure the meaningful and adequate review of the punitive damages award. Third, the petitioner received the benefit of the appropriate review by the state supreme court, which approved the verdict and brought in all relevant factors for ensuring that the punitive damages were reasonable. The Alabama Supreme Court's decision upholding the punitive damage award was affirmed. *Pacific Mut. Life Ins. Co. v. Haslip*, 499 U.S. 1, 111 S.Ct. 1032, 113 L.Ed.2d 1 (1991).

A misaligned drawbar on a railroad car is not a malfunctioning drawbar for purposes of the Safety Appliance Act where the misalignment occurs during the ordinary course of railroad operations.

A railroad employee worked as a member of a switching crew at a yard in Missouri. His duties included coupling and uncoupling railroad cars and aligning drawbars (so that uncoupled cars could be coupled). While attempting to realign an off-center drawbar, the employee injured his back. He sued the railroad in an Illinois state court, alleging that the railroad had violated § 2 of the Safety Appliance Act (SAA), which requires that cars be equipped with "couplers coupling automatically by impact, and capable of being uncoupled, without the necessity of individuals going between the ends of vehicles." The railroad argued that it was not liable because the misaligned drawbar did not result from defective equipment. The trial court granted the employee's motion for a directed verdict, and the Illinois appellate court affirmed. After the Illinois Supreme Court denied review, the U.S. Supreme Court granted certiorari. The Supreme Court held that § 2 of the SAA does not make a railroad liable as a matter of law for injuries incurred by a railroad employee while trying to straighten a misaligned drawbar. The Court noted that failure to couple will not cause a violation of the SAA if the railroad can show that a coupler has not been set to couple on impact. A railroad does not breach its absolute duty to employees where a drawbar becomes misaligned during the ordinary course of railroad operations. Since misalignment happens frequently as a result of lateral movement of a drawbar's knuckled end (which occurs so that moving cars will not be derailed on a curved track), a misaligned drawbar is not a malfunctioning drawbar for purposes of the SAA. The Court reversed the lower court decision. *Norfolk and Western Railway Co. v. Hiles*, 516 U.S. 400, 116 S.Ct. 890, 134 L.Ed.2d 34 (1996).

In a significant decision regarding punitive damages, the Supreme Court ruled that a federal appeals court used the wrong standard of review when evaluating the constitutionality of a jury's $4.5 million punitive damages award. The high court remanded the case and directed the appeals court to conduct a de novo review of the award.

The issue arose in a trademark infringement and unfair competition lawsuit by Leatherman Tool Group against Cooper Industries over a multifunction tool. Leatherman's lawsuit asserted claims of trade dress infringement, unfair competition, and false advertising under the federal Lanham Act and under common law. After a trial, the jury awarded Leatherman $50,000 in damages and $4.5 million in punitive damages. The district court allowed the award, concluding that it was not grossly excessive. On appeal, the Ninth Circuit affirmed the punitive damages award, saying it was proportional and fair and did not violate Cooper's due process rights.

The Supreme Court explained that legislatures, and subsequently courts, have broad discretion in determining the limits of punitive damage awards. If a trial judge determines that a jury award is within those limits, and if no constitutional challenge is raised, then the reviewing appellate court need only review the trial court's determination under an abuse-of-discretion standard. However, in spite of the broad discretion given state legislatures and courts, they must still act within the strictures of the Due Process Clause and the Eighth Amendment of the federal Constitution, which prohibits excessive fines and "grossly excessive" punishments. The Supreme Court said the relevant constitutional line is inherently precise, and in each instance an independent examination of the relevant criteria is required to determine whether a fine is constitutionally excessive.

In *BMW of North America Inc. v. Gore*, 517 U.S. 559 (1996), the Supreme Court had previously identified three criteria that a district court should use to measure the constitutionality of a damages award: 1) the degree or reprehensibility of the defendant's misconduct; 2) the disparity between the harm or potential harm suffered by the plaintiff and the punitive damages award; and 3) the difference between the punitive damages award and the civil penalties authorized or imposed in comparable cases. In the case before it, the Supreme Court said district courts were entitled to deference only with respect to the first criterion, since the district court was in a somewhat better position to assess witness credibility and demeanor. But, it said appellate courts were equally capable of analyzing the second factor, and were probably better suited to review the third criterion, arguing against a deferential abuse-of-discretion standard of appellate review. Because the appeals court used the improper standard of review, the Supreme Court vacated and remanded the circuit court decision for further proceedings. *Cooper Industries, Inc. v. Leatherman Tool Group, Inc.*, ___ U.S. ___, 121 S.Ct. 1678, 149 L.Ed.2d 674 (2001).

CHAPTER FIVE

Labor Relations

I. NATIONAL LABOR RELATIONS ACT (NLRA)

A. Generally

In *National Woodwork Manufacturers Ass'n v. NLRB*, 386 U.S. 612, 87 S.Ct. 1250, 18 L.Ed.2d 357 (1967), the Supreme Court held that agreements negotiated with the objective of preserving work in the face of a threat to union members' jobs were lawful primary activity. Sections 8(b)(4) and 8(e) of the NLRA were intended by Congress to prevent union efforts directed at affecting business relations of neutral employers and calculated to achieve union objectives outside the primary employer-employee relationship. Since "work preservation" agreements are primary (and not secondary) activity, they are not violative of the NLRA. In the following case, the Court ruled that the NLRB should have focused on the work of longshoremen, which was sought to be preserved rather than on the off-pier work of nonlongshoremen to determine whether a negotiated agreement was a "work preservation" agreement.

With the advent of containers in the shipping business there came a profound decrease in the necessity for on-pier work for longshoremen. Since containers could be loaded and unloaded as whole units, the piece by piece transfers done by longshoremen became threatened by obsolescence. A set of "Rules on Containers" was put into a collective bargaining agreement. The rules defined when containers could be "stuffed and stripped" by longshoremen, even if such work was duplicative of work done off-pier. Two proceedings were brought before the National Labor Relations Board to determine if the rules were "illegal secondary activity" in violation of the National Labor Relations Act (NLRA). The board held that the rules violated the NLRA, but the U.S. Court of Appeals disagreed. The case then reached the U.S. Supreme Court.

The Court affirmed the court of appeals' decision. Here, if the agreement containing the rules was a lawful work preservation agreement, then the board would have to consider whether the shipping associations had the right to control the stuffing and stripping of containers. The board's approach had foreclosed any possibility that longshoremen could negotiate an agreement to permit them to play a part in the loading and unloading of containerized cargo. This was an error. Accordingly, the case was remanded to the board for further proceedings. *NLRB v. International Longshoremen's Ass'n*, 447 U.S. 490, 100 S.Ct. 2305, 65 L.Ed.2d 289 (1980).

Although an employer may be required to bargain over the effects of its decision to shut down part of its business for economic reasons, it does not have to bargain over the decision itself. That decision is not part of the "terms and conditions of employment" set forth in § 8(d) of the NLRA.

A company (engaged in the business of providing housekeeping, cleaning, maintenance, and related services for commercial customers in the New York City area) had a dispute with a nursing home over the size of a management fee. The company terminated the contract, and its employees who worked at the nursing home were discharged. The union had requested a delay in the discharges for the purpose of bargaining, but the company refused to bargain. The union then filed an unfair labor practice charge against the company, alleging that it had violated its duty to bargain in good faith "with respect to wages, hours, and other terms and conditions of employment" under §§ 8(d) and 8(a)(5) of the NLRA. The NLRB upheld the charge, ordering either reinstatement for the employees or equivalent jobs for them at the company's other operations. The U.S. Court of Appeals enforced the board's order.

On further appeal to the U.S. Supreme Court, the Court held that the company was required to bargain about the *effects* of its decision to terminate the nursing home contract. However, the company did not have to bargain over the decision itself. With respect to an employer's need for unencumbered decisionmaking in the running of its business, bargaining over economic decisions by management (which have a substantial impact on the continued availability of employment) should only be required if the benefit outweighs the burden placed on the conduct of the business. Here, since the harm outweighed the benefit to be gained by the union's participation, the purely economic decision by the company was not part of § 8(d)'s "terms and conditions of employment" over which Congress had mandated bargaining. The Court reversed the court of appeals' decision and remanded the case. *First National Maintenance Corp. v. NLRB*, 452 U.S. 666, 101 S.Ct. 2573, 69 L.Ed.2d 318 (1981).

Where an employer fails to comply with a collective bargaining agreement, but maintains that the clause at issue is illegal, the employer is entitled to plead and have adjudicated its defense.

As part of a collective bargaining agreement with the United Mine Workers of America, a coal producer agreed to contribute to certain health and retirement funds on the basis of each ton of coal it produced and each hour worked by its covered employees. The producer also agreed to report its purchases of coal from producers not under contract with the union and to make contributions to the funds on the basis of such purchases (so that contributions with respect to that coal could also be made). After the producer failed to report and make contributions as required by the "purchased-coal" clause, the trustees of the funds sued to enforce the collective bargaining agreement. The producer admitted that it had not complied, but maintained that the clause was unenforceable as violative of the Sherman Act and the NLRA. A federal district court held for the trustees, and the U.S. Court of Appeals affirmed.

On further appeal to the U.S. Supreme Court, the Court held that the producer should have been allowed to plead and have adjudicated its defense based on the alleged illegality of the "purchased-coal" clause. Here, the lower courts had rejected the producer's defense without examining the legality of the clause under either the Sherman Act or the NLRA. According to § 8(e) of the NLRA, "hot cargo" clauses (in which an employer agrees to cease doing business with, or to cease handling the products of, another employer) are void and unenforceable. Here, the producer had raised the defense that the "purchased-coal" clause was a "hot cargo" clause and thus unenforceable. The district court should have examined this defense. The Court therefore reversed and remanded the case. *Kaiser Steel Corp. v. Mullins*, 455 U.S. 72, 102 S.Ct. 851, 70 L.Ed.2d 833 (1982).

Under § 8(e) of the NLRA, with respect to work to be performed at a construction jobsite, it is permissible for an agreement to contain a limitation restricting subcontractors to union members or signatories to the agreement.

Section 8(e) of the NLRA prohibits agreements between unions and employers that require an employer to cease doing business with another party. However, § 8(e) also contains a proviso which exempts agreements in the construction industry with respect to work to be performed at a construction jobsite. Two separate labor disputes arose in the Ninth Circuit. The first involved an impasse in the negotiations for a new collective bargaining agreement over a "hot cargo" agreement (limiting jobsite work to union members or signatories to the agreement). As a result of the impasse, construction sites were picketed. The employer then filed unfair labor practice charges. The National Labor Relations Board held that subcontracting clauses which forbid an employer from doing business with non-signatory subcontractors were lawful when they were sought or negotiated in the context of collective bargaining agreements. The board also held that picketing to obtain such a clause was lawful. In the second dispute, charges were filed as a result of a similar clause. The cases were consolidated before the U.S. Court of Appeals, which enforced the board's orders.

On further appeal to the U.S. Supreme Court, the Court held that Congress clearly intended to protect subcontracting clauses like the ones at issue here. They were protected by the § 8(e) proviso. Even though these clauses tend to create "top-down" pressure for unionization, Congress decided to accept whatever pressure such clauses might entail when it included the proviso in the NLRA. The Court went on to say, however, that the court of appeals had been without jurisdiction to decide that picketing to obtain a subcontracting clause sheltered by the § 8(e) proviso was lawful under the NLRA. Since no objection to this ruling of the board had been made, it could not be considered by the court. The Court affirmed in part the court of appeals' decision. *Woelke & Romero Framing, Inc. v. NLRB*, 456 U.S. 645, 102 S.Ct. 2071, 72 L.Ed.2d 398 (1982).

A lawsuit filed in retaliation for the assertion of rights protected under the NLRA can only be enjoined if the lawsuit is baseless. If the lawsuit has merit, then despite the retaliatory motive, it cannot be enjoined. If genuine factual issues exist, they have to be left to a jury to resolve.

An Arizona restaurant fired one of its waitresses. She filed an unfair labor practice charge with the National Labor Relations Board alleging that she had been fired because of her efforts to organize a union. She also gathered a group of co-workers and picketed the restaurant, distributing leaflets. The restaurant then brought suit in state court against the waitress, alleging that she had harassed customers, blocked access to the restaurant and libeled it by false statements in the leaflets. Again, the waitress filed an unfair labor practice charge against the restaurant, claiming that the civil suit had been brought in retaliation for her protected, concerted activities. An administrative law judge (ALJ) found that the civil action was retaliatory, and the board ordered the restaurant to withdraw its state court complaint. The U.S. Court of Appeals enforced the board's order.

On appeal to the U.S. Supreme Court, the Court held that the ALJ should not have evaluated the evidence and determined that the state court suit was without merit. His inquiry should have been into whether there were genuine and material factual issues presented. If the filing and prosecution of a *well-founded* lawsuit is done only in retaliation for rights protected by the NLRA, such lawsuit cannot be enjoined as an unfair labor practice. Only baseless lawsuits filed in retaliation may be enjoined. To determine whether a state court suit lacks a reasonable basis, the board's inquiry must be structured in a manner that will preserve the state plaintiff's right to have a jury resolve genuine material factual or legal disputes pertaining to the lawsuit. If the plaintiff can show that such genuine issues exist, then the board has to wait for the outcome before it can decide if a violation requiring relief has occurred. The Court vacated the court of appeals' decision and remanded the case. *Bill Johnson's Restaurants, Inc. v. NLRB*, 461 U.S. 731, 103 S.Ct. 2161, 76 L.Ed.2d 277 (1983).

Firing an employee for permissible reasons is an affirmative defense to an unfair labor practice charge resulting from the discharge. Accordingly, the burden of proof is on the employer to show (by a preponderance of the evidence) that the employee would have been fired even if he or she had not been engaged in protected activities.

A bus driver, employed by a transportation company, talked to a union's officials about organizing the drivers who worked with him. Subsequently, the company fired him for leaving his keys in the bus and for taking unauthorized breaks. The driver then filed an unfair labor practice charge with the National Labor Relations Board alleging that he had been discharged because of his union activities in violation of the NLRA. The board found that the driver had proven that anti-union animus contributed to the company's decision to fire him. It noted that the company could avoid the conclusion that it had violated the NLRA if it could prove by a preponderance of the evidence that the driver would have been fired for permissible reasons even if he had not been involved in protected union activities. The board held that the company failed to carry its burden of proof. The U.S. Court of Appeals refused to enforce the board's order on the ground that the burden of proof had been improperly imposed on the company. The U.S. Supreme Court granted certiorari.

The Supreme Court reversed the court of appeals' decision. It stated that placing the burden of proof on the company was consistent with the NLRA. A firing for permissible reasons would be an affirmative defense, and the burden of proof could be allocated to the employer by the board. Here, the Court found that the board was justified in concluding that the driver would not have been fired had the company not considered his protected activities. The company had improperly discharged the driver. *NLRB v. Transp. Management Corp.*, 462 U.S. 393, 103 S.Ct. 2469, 76 L.Ed.2d 667 (1983).

A collective bargaining agreement subject to the NLRA is an "executory contract" which may be rejected by a debtor-in-possession under Chapter 11 of the Bankruptcy Code. Also, the debtor does not commit an unfair labor practice by unilaterally modifying or terminating a provision of the agreement before receiving court approval.

A New Jersey general partnership, in the business of distributing building supplies, filed a voluntary petition in bankruptcy under Chapter 11 (for reorganization). The bankruptcy court authorized it to operate the business as the debtor-in-possession. At the time of the filing, about 45 percent of the distributor's workers were union members. There was also a collective bargaining agreement in place. Subsequent to the filing, the distributor failed to meet some of its obligations under the collective bargaining agreement, including the payment of health and pension benefits and the remittance of dues to the union. It also failed to pay wage increases as called for in the agreement. The union then filed unfair labor practice charges with the National Labor Relations Board, alleging that the distributor had violated the NLRA by unilaterally changing the terms of the collective bargaining agreement, and by failing to pay the money owed. The board ordered the distributor to make the payments. The distributor then asked the bankruptcy court for permission to reject the collective bargaining agreement. The court granted the request. Before the U.S. Court of Appeals, the court refused to enforce the board's order, holding that the distributor could reject the collective bargaining agreement.

On further appeal to the U.S. Supreme Court, the Court agreed with the court of appeals that the agreement in place was an executory contract that could be rejected by the distributor as the debtor-in-possession. The bankruptcy court should permit such rejection, held the Court, if the debtor could show that the agreement burdened the bankruptcy estate and that the equities balanced in favor of rejection. Further, it was not an unfair labor practice for a debtor to reject or modify a collective bargaining agreement before formal rejection was approved by the bankruptcy court. The agreement was not an enforceable contract between the time of filing and formal acceptance of the petition for bankruptcy. Accordingly, the debtor-in-possession did not need to comply with the NLRA's obligation to bargain collectively prior to seeking permission to reject the agreement. The Court affirmed the court of appeals' decision. *NLRB v. Bildisco and Bildisco*, 465 U.S. 513, 104 S.Ct. 1188, 79 L.Ed.2d 482 (1984).

An individual worker's reasonable and honest assertion of a right contained in a collective bargaining agreement is an extension of the concerted action that produced the agreement. Such concerted activity may be protected by § 7 of the NLRA.

A garbage company employee refused to drive a truck that he honestly and reasonably believed to be unsafe because of faulty brakes. The company fired him. When the union decided not to process his grievance under the collective bargaining agreement in place, he filed an unfair labor practice charge with the National Labor Relations Board, challenging his discharge. An administrative law judge (ALJ) determined that even though the employee had acted alone in refusing to drive the truck, he had been asserting a contractual right to refuse to drive an unsafe vehicle. Accordingly, his refusal to operate the truck constituted "concerted activity" which was protected by § 7 of the NLRA (which gives employees the right to bargain collectively and to engage in other concerted activities for the purpose of collective bargaining or other mutual aid or protection). The board adopted the ALJ's findings and conclusions. The U.S. Court of Appeals denied enforcement of the board's order because the employee had taken action solely on his own behalf.

On appeal to the U.S. Supreme Court, the court of appeals' decision was reversed and the case was remanded. The Court found that the employee had been invoking a right which was rooted in the collective bargaining agreement. This was part of the process that gave rise to the agreement. By honestly and reasonably asserting his right to be free from driving unsafe trucks, the employee was actually engaging in the process of enforcing the agreement. Thus, his actions were "concerted activity" under the NLRA. However, on remand, it had to be determined whether the employee's conduct was also protected. Not all concerted activity is protected. If concerted activity is overly abusive or violative of the collective bargaining agreement in place, then it is not protected. This question had to be resolved on remand. *NLRB v. City Disposal Systems, Inc.*, 465 U.S. 822, 104 S.Ct. 1505, 79 L.Ed.2d 839 (1984).

Five years after *NLRB v. International Longshoremen's Ass'n*, above, the Supreme Court encountered the case again. This time, the Court determined that the Rules on Containers, which had been negotiated for the longshoremen were valid as a "work preservation" agreement.

The Rules on Containers (collectively bargained-for guidelines requiring marine shipping companies to allow some of the large cargo containers they owned or leased to be loaded or unloaded by longshoremen at the pier) required containers which would otherwise be loaded or unloaded within the local port area to be loaded or unloaded by longshoremen at the pier. The rules came into place as a result of "containerization" which drastically reduced the amount of on-pier cargo-handling work of the longshoremen. When an objection was filed to the rules, the National Labor Relations Board held that, with two exceptions (shortstopping truckers and traditional warehousers), the rules were valid and enforceable. On cross appeals to the U.S. Court of Appeals, the appellate court held that the rules were lawful in their entirety. The U.S. Supreme Court granted limited review.

The Supreme Court noted that Congress had not intended to prohibit agreements directed to work preservation. The central inquiry in these claims of work preservation was whether the union's objective in making the agreements was to preserve work or whether the agreements were tactically calculated to satisfy union objectives elsewhere. So long as the union had no forbidden secondary purpose to disrupt the business relations of a neutral employer, such effects were "incidental to primary activity." Here, the clear primary objective of the rules was the preservation of work in the face of a threat to jobs. Even if the Rules were economically inefficient it was not the Court's place to outlaw such collective bargaining. That decision had to be left to Congress. The Court affirmed the court of appeals' decision upholding the rules as lawful. *NLRB v. International Longshoremen's Ass'n,* 473 U.S. 61, 105 S.Ct. 3045, 87 L.Ed.2d 47 (1985).

Section 8(b)(1)(B) of the NLRA makes it an unfair labor practice for a union "to restrain or coerce ... an employer in the selection of his representatives for the purposes of collective bargaining or the adjustment of grievances." In the case below, the Supreme Court held that a union's disciplining of two members who were not involved in collective bargaining or grievance adjustment did not amount to an unfair labor practice.

A union fined two of its members, who worked as supervisors, for violating its constitution by working for employers who did not have collective bargaining agreements with the union. The employers then filed unfair labor practice charges with the National Labor Relations Board, alleging that the union had violated § 8(b)(1)(B) of the NLRA by restraining or coercing an employer in the selection of its representatives for the purposes of collective bargaining or the adjustment of grievances. An administrative law judge agreed with the employers, and the board entered an order against the union. However, the U.S. Court of Appeals reversed. The case then came before the U.S. Supreme Court.

The Court held that discipline of a supervisor union member is prohibited under § 8(b)(1)(B) only when that member is engaged in § 8(b)(1)(B) activities, like collective bargaining and grievance adjustment, or some other closely related activity. Since neither supervisor had such responsibilities, the union discipline was not an unfair labor practice. Further, the Court noted that the absence of a collective bargaining relationship between the union and the employer made the possibility of employer coercion too attenuated to form the basis of an unfair labor practice charge. Finally, the Court noted that the employers were not coerced by dint of the supervisors being fined by the union. Accordingly, the Court affirmed the appellate court's decision in favor of the union. *NLRB v. International Brotherhood of Electrical Workers, Local 340,* 481 U.S. 573, 107 S.Ct. 2002, 95 L.Ed.2d 557 (1987).

After bargaining to an impasse, employers bargaining together may implement the terms of their last best good faith wage offer without violating antitrust laws.

After the expiration of the collective bargaining agreement between the National Football League (NFL) and the NFL Players Association, negotiations on a new contract began. The NFL presented a plan that would permit each club to establish a "developmental squad" of substitute players, each of whom would be paid a $1,000 weekly salary. The union asserted that the individual players ought to be free to negotiate their own salaries. When negotiations reached an impasse, the NFL unilaterally implemented the plan. A number of squad players brought an antitrust suit against the NFL, claiming that the employers' agreement to pay them $1,000 per week restrained trade in violation of the Sherman Act. A federal district court ruled for the players, but the U.S. Court of Appeals,

District of Columbia Circuit, reversed. Further appeal was taken to the U.S. Supreme Court. The Supreme Court has created a "nonstatutory" labor exemption from the antitrust laws. It has implied this exemption from federal labor statutes, which set forth a national labor policy favoring free and private collective bargaining. The implicit exemption limits an antitrust court's authority to determine, in the area of industrial conflict, what is or is not a reasonable practice. Accordingly, the Court held that federal labor laws shielded from antitrust attack an agreement among several employers bargaining together to implement after impasse the terms of their last best good faith wage offer. The Court rejected the players' argument that the implied exemption applied only to labor-management agreements. It affirmed the appellate court's decision. *Brown v. Pro Football, Inc.*, 518 U.S. 231, 116 S.Ct. 2116, 135 L.Ed.2d 521 (1996).

B. Preemption

In 1984, the Court held that states could impose more stringent regulations on the qualifications of union officials than did the NLRA.

The New Jersey Casino Control Act required annual registration of unions representing persons employed in casinos or casino hotels. It provided that unions could be prohibited from receiving dues and from administering pension or welfare funds if any union officer was disqualified under certain criteria contained in the act. After state administrative proceedings were initiated to determine if certain union officers were disqualified, the union filed suit in federal court seeking a preliminary injunction to halt the state proceedings. The court refused to grant the injunction, but the U.S. Court of Appeals reversed. The U.S. Supreme Court granted certiorari.

The Court held that New Jersey's regulation of the qualifications of casino industry union officials did not actually conflict with § 7 of the NLRA (which guarantees to employees the right to bargain collectively through representatives of their own choosing). Accordingly, the NLRA did not preempt the state law. Congress apparently decided, held the Court, that states could impose more stringent regulations on the qualifications of union officials in order to fight crime, corruption and racketeering. This was not incompatible with the national labor policy as embodied in § 7 of the NLRA. The Court vacated the court of appeals' decision and remanded the case. *Brown v. Hotel & Restaurant Employees and Bartenders*, 468 U.S. 491, 104 S.Ct. 3179, 82 L.Ed.2d 373 (1984).

In 1986, the Court held that a Wisconsin law that disallowed violators of the NLRA from doing business with the state was preempted by the NLRA because it conflicted with the comprehensive regulatory scheme intended by Congress.

A Wisconsin statute debarred persons or firms who had violated the NLRA three times within a five-year period from doing business with the state. A corporation was subsequently placed on the state's list of labor law violators and debarred. It filed suit in federal court, claiming that the NLRA preempted the

Wisconsin statute. A federal district court granted summary judgment to the corporation, the U.S. Court of Appeals affirmed, and the case reached the U.S. Supreme Court.

The Court held that Wisconsin's statute conflicted with the National Labor Relations Board's comprehensive regulation of industrial relations because it worked as a supplemental sanction for violations of the NLRA. Accordingly, the statute was preempted by the NLRA. The court rejected Wisconsin's "market participant" argument because the state was not acting as a private purchaser by debarring the corporation. Rather, it was essentially regulating by attempting to enforce the NLRA. The Court affirmed the lower courts' decisions, and held that Wisconsin could not refuse to do business with the corporation or refuse to purchase products with components manufactured by the corporation because of the violation of Wisconsin law. *Wisconsin Dep't of Industry, Labor and Human Relations v. Gould,* 475 U.S. 282, 106 S.Ct. 1057, 89 L.Ed.2d 223 (1986).

Where the state is acting within the market, and not regulating the market, the NLRA does not preempt its enforcement of an otherwise lawful collective bargaining agreement.

The Massachusetts Water Resources Authority (MWRA), a state agency, provided sewage services for eastern Massachusetts and was ordered to clean up Boston Harbor after a lawsuit over its failure to prevent the harbor's pollution. Under state law, the MWRA was to own and manage the sewage treatment facilities that were to be built for the cleanup. The MWRA selected a corporation to be primarily in charge of managing and supervising construction activity. The corporation suggested that it be allowed to negotiate an agreement with the Building and Construction Trades Council to assure labor stability over the life of the project. After the MWRA consented, the corporation obtained an agreement that required union membership. The MWRA, in its solicitation for project bids, required successful bidders to abide by the agreement's terms. An organization representing nonunion construction industry employers sued to enjoin the bid specification, claiming that it was preempted by the National Labor Relations Act. The district court denied injunctive relief, the U.S. Court of Appeals, First Circuit, reversed, and appeal reached the U.S. Supreme Court.

The Court held that the NLRA did not preempt enforcement by a state agency (acting as the owner of the project) of an otherwise lawful prehire collective bargaining agreement negotiated by private parties. It stated that *San Diego Building Trades Council v. Garmon,* 359 U.S. 236, 79 S.Ct. 773, 3 L.Ed.2d 775 (1959), required preemption of state and local regulation of activities that are "protected by § 7 of the [NLRA], or constitute an unfair labor practice under § 8." It also noted that *Machinists v. Wisconsin Employment Relations Comm'n,* 427 U.S. 132, 96 S.Ct. 2548, 49 L.Ed.2d 396 (1976), required preemption of state and local regulation of areas that have been left "to be controlled by the free play of economic forces." However, the state agency in this case was not regulating labor, it was acting as a proprietor. Thus, it was not regulating or making policy by its actions. The Court reversed the decision of the court of appeals and remanded the case. *Building & Construction Trades Council v. Associated Builders & Contractors,* 507 U.S. 218, 113 S.Ct. 1190, 122 L.Ed.2d 565 (1993).

In *Livadas*, the Supreme Court held that a state labor commissioner's policy of refusing to enforce the state's labor code (where an employee's terms and conditions of employment were governed by a collective bargaining agreement containing an arbitration clause) was preempted by federal law.

A California grocery clerk was employed under a collective bargaining agreement between her employer and her labor union. The agreement called for binding arbitration to resolve disputes arising from employment termination or suspension. After the employer fired the grocery clerk, it refused to comply with her demand for the immediate payment of the wages owed her. Full payment was made by mail three days later. The clerk filed a claim for a penalty in an amount equal to three days wages under a California statute allowing such claims where an employer wilfully fails to pay wages owed to a discharged employee. The California Division of Labor Standards Enforcement (DLSE) refused to take action to enforce the claim, advising her by letter that it did not resolve disputes arising from collective bargaining agreements that contained arbitration clauses. The clerk filed a lawsuit in the U.S. District Court for the Northern District of California under 42 U.S.C. § 1983, claiming that the DLSE's policy violated her rights under the NLRA. The court granted the clerk's summary judgment motion. The U.S. Court of Appeals, Ninth Circuit, reversed the district court's decision and the U.S. Supreme Court granted review.

On appeal, the DLSE argued that its policy was compelled by federal labor law, which required the application of contractual grievance procedures and preempted nonnegotiable matters of state law. The Court disagreed, finding that the issue of whether the employer had wilfully failed to pay the clerk's wages was independent of the collective bargaining agreement and was a matter of state law. It was unnecessary to look to the collective bargaining agreement except to compute damages. Therefore, there was no basis for federal preemption of the employee's state law claim. The employee was entitled to relief under 42 U.S.C. § 1983 for violation of her rights under the NLRA. The NLRA did not automatically preempt all state law. The Court reversed the court of appeals' judgment. *Livadas v. Bradshaw*, 512 U.S. 107, 114 S.Ct. 2068, 129 L.Ed.2d 93 (1994).

C. Majority Status

If an employer assumes monetary obligations under a prehire contract which is authorized by the NLRA, the union may recover those funds in a § 301 action even though the union has not yet obtained majority support in the relevant unit.

A California construction company began work on a jobsite as a subcontractor. At the time, it was not a signatory to a labor agreement with the local union, and none of its employees were union members. However, the general contractor had signed a Master Labor Agreement (prehire contract) providing that all work at the jobsite would be performed by subcontractors who had signed a labor agreement. Eventually, the president of the construction company signed the

Master Labor Agreement in order to remain on the project. His employees also signed union cards. The agreement required the company to make monthly contributions to fringe benefit trust funds on behalf of each covered employee. For the next six months, the company submitted required monthly reports to the trust funds, but it made no contributions. Instead, it falsely claimed that none of its "covered employees" were employed during this period. The trustees of the funds then asked to audit the company's records to verify the reports. After agreeing to be audited, the company postponed the audit several times, causing the trustees to bring suit against it under § 301 of the Labor Management Relations Act to compel an accounting and to recover payment of any contributions which were due. A federal district court ruled for the trustees and the U.S. Court of Appeals affirmed.

On further appeal to the U.S. Supreme Court, the Court affirmed the lower court decisions. Here, the subcontractor (by signing the Master Labor Relations Agreement) had assumed monetary obligations under a prehire contract authorized for construction industry employees and unions by the NLRA. Thus, the union trustees could recover the contributions due in a § 301 action so long as the contract had not yet been repudiated, even if the union had not obtained majority support in the relevant unit. In this case, the prehire contract was voidable until the union attained majority support. However, the union could still enforce the monetary obligations incurred by the subcontractor even though it was not the employees' bargaining agent. This would not impair the employees' right to select their own bargaining agent or encroach upon the voluntary and voidable aspects of the prehire contract. *Jim McNeff, Inc. v. Todd*, 461 U.S. 260, 103 S.Ct. 1753, 75 L.Ed.2d 830 (1983).

In *NLRB v. Burns International Security Services, Inc.*, 406 U.S. 272, 92 S.Ct. 1571, 32 L.Ed.2d 61 (1972), the Supreme Court ruled that a new employer (succeeding to the business of another) had an obligation to bargain with the union representing the predecessor's employees. In *Burns*, the union was certified as the employees' collective bargaining representative shortly before the transition in employers. In the case below, the union had been certified for more than one year and thus enjoyed the rebuttable presumption of majority status. The Court held that this status continued despite the change in employers.

A corporation that operated a textile dyeing and finishing plant laid off all its employees and went out of business. One of its officers then teamed up with a former customer, acquired the plant, and began to operate a similar business. The new company hired many ex-employees of the old corporation. The union that had represented those employees requested the new company to recognize it as the collective bargaining agent for the new company's employees. The company refused. The union then filed an unfair labor practice charge with the National Labor Relations Board. An administrative law judge found that the new company was a "successor" to the old corporation and that its refusal to bargain was an unfair labor practice. The U.S. Court of Appeals enforced the order, and the case was appealed to the U.S. Supreme Court.

The Court held that there was "substantial continuity" between the two enterprises since the employees' jobs remained essentially unaltered. Further, at the time one full shift of workers had been hired, a majority were ex-employees of the old corporation. Accordingly, even though the union's demand for bargaining had been premature, the new company was under an obligation to bargain once it had a "substantial and representative complement" of its work force in place. The Court affirmed the lower court's ruling. *Fall River Dyeing & Finishing Corp. v. NLRB*, 482 U.S. 27, 107 S.Ct. 2225, 96 L.Ed.2d 22 (1987).

The Supreme Court held that an employer could not rebut the presumption of majority status of a union after acceptance of a contract offer when the employer's good faith doubt about the union's majority status arose from facts known to the employer before the offer was accepted.

A Massachusetts employer recognized a labor organization as the collective bargaining representative of its employees and negotiated a series of collective bargaining agreements with it over an 11-year period. Contract negotiations for a new agreement were unsuccessful, and employees went on strike for over one month. The employer then made an acceptable contract offer. The union accepted by telegraph, but the following day, the employer disavowed the agreement and denied any duty to continue bargaining with the union, claiming that 13 of the 23 bargaining unit employees had resigned from the union and that nine of them had crossed the picket line during the strike. The union filed a complaint with the general counsel of the National Labor Relations Board (NLRB) for violations of the National Labor Relations Act (NLRA). An administrative law judge determined that a contract existed between the parties and that the employer's action violated the NLRA. The NLRB affirmed the decision and ordered the employer to reduce the agreement to writing. The U.S. Court of Appeals, First Circuit, enforced the NLRB order, and the employer appealed to the U.S. Supreme Court.

The Court determined that under prior NLRB decisions, collective bargaining organizations were entitled to a presumption of majority status for one year following certification and for up to three years during the term of any collective bargaining agreement. These presumptions encouraged stability in collective bargaining relationships and furthered a primary NLRA goal of achieving industrial peace. The employer could not raise the issue of majority support after the acceptance of a collective bargaining agreement because to do so would give the employer an unfair advantage in contract negotiations. The strategic challenge to union majority support after contract acceptance protected it from the risk of difficult negotiations. The NLRB presumption of majority support following the entry of a collective bargaining agreement gave employers sufficient options to legitimately advance their interests. The employer was required to bargain under these circumstances. The Court affirmed the NLRB order. *Auciello Iron Works, Inc. v. NLRB*, 517 U.S. 781, 116 S.Ct. 1754, 135 L.Ed.2d 64 (1996).

The Supreme Court upheld the NLRB's standard for reviewing employer polling which requires that the employer have a reasonable, good faith ground to doubt continuing majority support for the union.

The managers of a Pennsylvania truck parts and service factory branch purchased the branch and began operating it as an independent dealership. They hired 32 of the 45 branch employees and learned that eight of them had expressed doubt about support for their existing union. The new employer rejected the union's request for recognition as the employees' collective bargaining representative, then conducted a poll which resulted in a 19-13 loss by the union. An administrative law judge considered an unfair labor practice charge filed by the union against the employer and determined that it had inherited the factory branch's bargaining obligation under the presumption of continuing majority support recognized by the National Labor Relations Board (NLRB). The poll was unlawful because the employer had no objective reasonable doubt about continuing majority support for the union. The NLRB agreed and ordered the employer to recognize and bargain with the union. The U.S. Court of Appeals, District of Columbia Circuit, enforced the order.

The employer appealed to the U.S. Supreme Court, which upheld the NLRB's standard for reviewing employer polling, even though it resembled the high standard required for evaluating an employer's withdrawal of recognition. However, the NLRB's decision in this case was contrary to the standard since at least 20 percent of the employees had expressed doubt about continuing support for the union. The NLRB had disregarded important statements by two employees who had stated that the union would not win an election, supporting the inference of reasonable uncertainty by the employer. Because the employer had a reasonable, good faith ground to doubt the union's majority support, the Court reversed the judgment and remanded the case with instructions to deny enforcement of the NLRB's order. *Allentown Mack Sales and Service, Inc. v. NLRB*, 522 U.S. 359, 118 S.Ct. 818, 139 L.Ed.2d 797 (1998).

D. Covered Individuals

1. "Supervisors"

The National Labor Relations Act, 29 U.S.C. § 141 *et seq.*, defines a "supervisor" as "any individual having authority ... to hire, transfer, suspend, lay off, recall, promote, discharge, assign, reward, or discipline other employees ... or effectively to recommend such action, if ... the exercise of such authority ... requires the use of independent judgment." Supervisors are not considered to be employees (in other words, protected) under the act.

A grocery store chain discharged the managers of its meat departments because they had joined a local union. The union then filed unfair labor practice charges with the National Labor Relations Board. However, the charges were dismissed on the ground that the NLRA did not extend its protection to "supervisors" like the managers. The managers subsequently brought suit in state court under a right-to-work law. Summary judgment was granted to the grocery store chain. The North Carolina Supreme Court upheld that ruling, and appeal was taken to the U.S. Supreme Court. It was conceded before the Court that the second clause of § 14(a) of the NLRA excluded the managers from the protection of the federal statute. The Court went on to hold, moreover, that the second clause of § 14(a) also applied to state laws like the right-to-work law at issue here. The national policy against compulsion upon employers from either federal or state authorities to treat supervisors as employees would be flouted if the state statute were enforced. Accordingly, the lower courts' decisions were affirmed, and the managers' lawsuit for damages could not stand. *Beasley v. Food Fair of North Carolina, Inc.,* 416 U.S. 653, 94 S.Ct. 2023, 40 L.Ed.2d 443 (1974).

The NLRA preempts state law where the conduct at issue is arguably protected or prohibited by the NLRA. In the following case, a ship superintendent's lawsuit against a union was held not to be preempted by the NLRA because the superintendent was a "supervisor" and not an "employee." The NLRA only applies to "employees."

An Alabama man worked for a stevedoring company as a ship superintendent, an immediate superior of the longshoremen working for the company. However, the ship superintendents generally made less money than the longshoremen. As a result, there was an attempt at unionization. A union official allegedly assured the superintendents that the union would get them their jobs back if they were discharged for participating in union-related activities. After being fired, the ship superintendent sued the union, alleging fraud and misrepresentation under state law. A jury entered a verdict in his favor for $75,000. The union then sought to overturn the verdict on the grounds that the NLRA preempted state law, but the court denied the motion. The Alabama Supreme Court affirmed, and the case came before the U.S. Supreme Court.

Before the Court, the union maintained that the National Labor Relations Board had not clearly determined the superintendent to be a "supervisor." Thus, it charged that he was an "employee" covered by the NLRA. However, the Court noted that the union had not pointed to any evidence to support its assertion that the superintendent was an "employee." Because the NLRA does not apply to "supervisors," and because the union had failed to demonstrate that the superintendent was not a "supervisor," the Court held that the NLRA did not apply to preempt the state law. The Court affirmed the verdict in favor of the superintendent. *International Longshoremen's Ass'n AFL-CIO v. Davis,* 476 U.S. 380, 106 S.Ct. 1904, 90 L.Ed.2d 389 (1986).

After the NLRB stated that a nurse's supervisory activity incidental to the treatment of patients was not authority exercised in the interest of the employer (such that four nurses were not supervisors exempted from the coverage of the NLRA), the Supreme Court held that the NLRB's test for determining supervisory status was inconsistent with the NLRA.

The National Labor Relations Act grants employees the right to organize and engage in collective bargaining free from employer interference. Employees are considered "supervisors" and thus are not covered under the NLRA if they have the authority to use independent judgment to "hire, transfer, suspend, lay off, recall, promote, discharge, assign, reward, or discipline other employees, or responsibly to direct them, or to adjust their grievances, or effectively to recommend such action," and they hold that authority "in the interest of the employer." The National Labor Relations Board's general counsel issued a complaint against the owner and operator of an Ohio nursing home, alleging that unfair labor practices had been committed in the disciplining of four licensed practical nurses. An administrative law judge found that the nurses were not supervisors and the NLRB agreed with that decision. The U.S. Court of Appeals, Sixth Circuit, reversed, and the case came before the U.S. Supreme Court.

The Supreme Court held that the NLRB's test for determining whether nurses were supervisors was inconsistent with the NLRA. Here, the NLRB had erroneously concluded that the nurses were not supervisors because their focus was on the well-being of the nursing home residents, not on the interests of the employer. The Supreme Court noted that because patient care is a nursing home's business, attending to the needs of the residents is in the employer's interests. The Court rejected the argument that granting organizational rights to nurses whose supervisory authority concerns patient care would not threaten the conflicting loyalties that the supervisor exception was designed to avoid. The NLRA had to be enforced according to its own terms. The Court affirmed the court of appeals' decision that the nurses were outside the protection of the NLRA. *NLRB v. Health Care & Retirement Corp.*, 511 U.S. 571, 114 S.Ct. 1778, 128 L.Ed.2d 586 (1994).

The Supreme Court ruled that registered nurses in charge of other employees and operations at a residential facility for the mentally retarded and mentally ill were "supervisors" under the National Labor Relations Act, and therefore were not eligible to be members of the bargaining unit that represented facility employees.

At a representation hearing, the NLRB determined a residential care facility's RNs were not supervisors, and therefore were appropriately included in a bargaining unit consisting of all eligible facility employees. Shortly thereafter, the employees voted in favor of union representation. The NLRB ordered the facility to bargain, but the facility refused. The refusal lead to unfair labor practice charges being brought against the facility. The NLRB ruled against the facility, stating that challenges to the composition of a bargaining unit cannot be heard as part of unfair labor practice hearings. The facility appealed to the U.S. Court of Appeals, Sixth Circuit, challenging the placement of the burden of proof on the facility to demonstrate that the nurses were supervisors properly excluded from the bargaining unit and the determination that the nurses were not supervisors. The Sixth Circuit concluded that the burden of proof should have been placed on the NLRB and that the RNs were "supervisors" because they exercised independent judgment in carrying out duties the National Labor Relations Act describes as "supervisory" in nature.

On appeal, the Supreme Court first accepted the NLRB's rule that the burden of proof regarding whether an employee or class of employees are considered supervisors rests with the party challenging the determination. In this case, the party challenging the classification of the nurses was the facility; therefore, the Sixth Circuit erred in placing the burden of proof on the NLRB. The Supreme Court then concluded that part of the NLRB's three-part test for determining supervisory status was inconsistent with the National Labor Relations Act under the circumstances of this case. Employees are considered supervisors if: they have the authority to perform any one of the 12 stated supervisory functions; the "exercise of such authority is not of a merely routine or clerical nature, but requires the use of independent judgment"; and their authority is used "in the interest of the employer." Regarding the nurses, the only part of the test in dispute was whether they used independent judgment when supervising other employees. The Court noted that the term "independent judgment" was ambiguous under the statute, and rejected the NLRB's assertion that a nurse supervising a nurse's aide in administering patient care does not involve independent judgment. By defining independent judgment, the NLRB inserted a categorical exclusion into the act that was not intended, according to the Supreme Court. Based on this conclusion, the Court determined that because the nurses were in charge of other employees and facility operations on a regular basis, they were supervisors under the NLRA. *National Labor Relations Board v. Kentucky River Community Care, Inc.*, 532 U.S. ___, 121 S.Ct. 1861, 149 L.Ed.2d 939 (2001).

2.   Other Individuals

Not all confidential employees are excluded from collective bargaining units by the NLRA. Only those confidential employees with a "labor nexus" are to be excluded (*i.e.*, those employees who assist employers and supervisors in making labor relations policy).

The personal secretary to the general manager and CEO of a rural electric membership cooperative signed a petition seeking reinstatement of a close friend and fellow employee who had lost his arm in the course of his employment, and who had been dismissed. The secretary was then discharged. She filed an unfair labor practice charge with the National Labor Relations Board, asserting that the firing violated the NLRA. Applying the "labor nexus" test (which excludes from bargaining units confidential employees who assist policymakers in the field of labor relations), the board found that the secretary was not such a "confidential employee" and that she had been discharged for engaging in protected concerted activity—a violation of the NLRA. It ordered her reinstatement, but the U.S. Court of Appeals denied enforcement of the order.

In a separate proceeding, a union attempted to become the collective bargaining agent of various employees of a company. At a representation hearing, the employer challenged the inclusion of 18 employees on the ground that they had access to confidential business information. The board rejected the employer's contention, holding that none of the challenged 18 employees was a confidential employee under the "labor nexus" test. After the union was certified as the bargaining agent, the employer refused to bargain with it. The board determined this to be in violation of the NLRA, but the U.S. Court of Appeals denied enforcement. The U.S. Supreme Court granted certiorari in both cases.

The Supreme Court held that it was reasonable for the board to exclude from collective bargaining units only those confidential employees with a "labor nexus." Further, it was acceptable for the board to reject claims that *all* employees with access to confidential information were beyond the scope of the term "employee" as defined by the NLRA. Here, the record supported the board's determination that the personal secretary was not a confidential employee with a labor nexus. However, in the second proceeding, the case had to be remanded because the employer had contended that the 18 employees should be excluded from the bargaining unit for other reasons as well. This had to be examined. The Court reversed the court of appeals' decisions. *NLRB v. Hendricks County Rural Electric Membership Corp.*, 454 U.S. 170, 102 S.Ct. 216, 70 L.Ed.2d 323 (1981).

According to the Supreme Court, the NLRA applies to undocumented (illegal) aliens. Employers can be held liable for committing unfair labor practices against them just as they would be held liable for such actions against U.S. citizens. However, the relief ordered may be different.

A certain union was elected as the collective bargaining representative of the employees of two small leather processing firms which made up a single integrated employer for purposes of the NLRA. The firms then challenged the election with the National Labor Relations Board on the ground that six of the seven eligible voters were illegal aliens. After the board denied the challenge, the firms sent a letter to the Immigration and Naturalization Service (INS), asking it to check into the status of a number of employees. Subsequently, the board determined that the firms had committed an unfair labor practice by reporting their employees (known to be undocumented aliens) to the INS in retaliation for the employees' union activities. The board ordered "the conventional remedy of reinstatement with back pay." The U.S. Court of Appeals modified the board's order, keeping the reinstatement offers open for four years, requiring the offers to be written in Spanish and delivered to allow for verification of receipt, and deciding that even though the employees were not entitled to back pay for the period when they were not legally entitled to be present in the United States, an award of six months' back pay as a minimum mandatory award would be appropriate.

On further appeal, the U.S. Supreme Court held that the NLRA did apply to undocumented aliens with respect to unfair labor practices committed against them. Accordingly, the court of appeals had properly determined that the firms had committed an unfair labor practice against the illegal aliens by constructively discharging them (through reporting them to the INS). However, it had not been proper to award a minimum back pay amount without regard to the employees' actual economic losses. Back pay can only reimburse for actual, not speculative, consequences of an unfair labor practice. The appellate court also exceeded its authority by keeping the offers open for four years, and by requiring them to be written in Spanish and delivered. The Court affirmed in part the court of appeals' decision, holding that a remand to the board was necessary so that appropriate relief could be determined. *Sure-Tan, Inc. v. NLRB,* 467 U.S. 883, 104 S.Ct. 2803, 81 L.Ed.2d 732 (1984).

In the following case, the Supreme Court held that employees with a close family relationship to the owners of the company could be excluded from the collective bargaining unit, and their votes in the representation election could also be excluded.

A retail automobile parts and gasoline dealership was owned by three brothers. One brother's wife worked at the same location as her husband and occasionally took her coffee breaks in his office. The owners' mother worked at another location and worked with one of her sons. In 1981, a union filed a petition with the National Labor Relations Board, requesting that a representation election be held among the employees of the dealership. In the election, the union received a plurality of votes, but enough ballots were challenged by both sides so that the outcome of the election was in doubt. The board's hearing officer found that the wife's interests were different from other clerical employees, and that the mother's interests were more closely aligned with management than with the employees. He thus recommended that the union's challenge be upheld, that those two votes not be counted, and that the union be recognized as the exclusive bargaining representative of the employees.

The U.S. Court of Appeals denied enforcement of the order on the ground that the board had no authority to exclude the wife's and mother's votes based solely on their close family relationship with the owners. On further appeal, the U.S. Supreme Court held that the board did not have to first make a finding that the relatives enjoyed special job-related privileges before excluding them from collective bargaining units. The board had properly considered a variety of factors in deciding whether the employees' familial ties were sufficient to align their interests with management, thereby excluding them from the bargaining unit. Since the board's policy was reasonable, the Court reversed the appellate court and upheld the board's decision. *NLRB v. Action Automotive, Inc.,* 469 U.S. 490, 105 S.Ct. 984, 83 L.Ed.2d 986 (1985).

The Supreme Court held that a worker can be a company's "employee," within the terms of the NLRA, and at the same time be paid by a union to help organize the company.

A Minnesota electrical contractor refused to grant employment interviews to ten job applicants who were union members. The only union applicant accepted for employment was fired after a few days on the job. The union members filed a complaint against the contractor with the National Labor Relations Board (NLRB), asserting that the contractor had failed to hire or retain them because of their union affiliation in violation of the National Labor Relations Act (NLRA). An administrative law judge held for the union members and a panel of the NLRB affirmed the decision. The U.S. Court of Appeals, Eighth Circuit, reversed the NLRB's decision, finding that the job applicants were not "employees" for purposes of the NLRA because they were being paid by the union to organize the company. They were therefore not protected from antiunion discrimination. The U.S. Supreme Court agreed to review the case.

The Court stated that the NLRB's broad, literal interpretation of the statutory term "employee" was consistent with NLRA purposes, one of which was to protect the right of workers to organize for mutual aid without employer interference. The contractor argued that common law agency principles prohibited this interpretation, and that the applicants were paid union organizers who could only serve the union's interest. The Court noted that common law agency principles did not prohibit workers from accepting employment from more than one employer. Union organizing was equivalent to performing work for another employer during non-work hours, which no employer had a legal right to prevent. The Court held that the NLRB's interpretation of the term "employee" was correct, and it vacated and remanded the decision of the court of appeals. *NLRB v. Town & Country Electric, Inc.*, 516 U.S. 85, 116 S.Ct. 450, 133 L.Ed.2d 371 (1995).

The Supreme Court decided the narrow question of whether workers who collected for slaughter chickens raised by independent farmers were exempt agricultural laborers. The court held that they were not exempt from the NLRA.

A poultry processing corporation purchased a company which operated a production plant in North Carolina. The plant employed crews of workers who collected live chickens for slaughter from independent contractor farmers. Before the sale was completed, a labor organization filed a petition to represent crew workers who worked out of the plant. The National Labor Relations Board (NLRB) approved the crew workers as a bargaining unit that was protected by the National Labor Relations Act (NLRA) and determined that they were not excluded from coverage as agricultural laborers. It ordered the corporation to recognize the union and bargain with it. The corporation appealed the NLRB's order to the U.S. Court of Appeals, Fourth Circuit, which enforced the order. The court held that a change in corporate ownership during the union certification process did not alter the corporation's obligation to bargain with the union. It rejected the corporation's argument that the employees were excluded from NLRA coverage as agricultural laborers. The U.S. Supreme Court agreed to review the matter.

The Court observed that for over 20 years, the NLRB has considered poultry production employees who handle and transport chickens from independent growers to be protected by the NLRA, and not excluded as agricultural employees. It rejected the corporation's argument that the work of the employees was incident to or in conjunction with farming operations. The NLRB had properly focused on the status of the corporate employer, which was not a farmer, and noted that despite doing their work at farm locations, the employees began and ended each workday at the production plant. Finding the NLRB's determination consistent with its findings and prior decisions, the Court affirmed the order. *Holly Farms Corp. v. NLRB*, 517 U.S. 392, 116 S.Ct. 1396, 134 L.Ed.2d 593 (1996).

E. National Labor Relations Board

In the case below, the Supreme Court held that even though the NLRA had been violated by a collective bargaining agreement, the National Labor Relations Board did not have to order "complete relief." The board could reserve remedies like reimbursement for especially egregious situations.

To settle a long-standing dispute over the availability of hauling jobs for nonunion dump truck operators, a union entered into a collective bargaining agreement with three contractors' associations prohibiting dealings by the contractors with nonunion dump truck operators. A dump truck owner-operator (previously a nonunion member) joined the union under protest, paying an initiation fee, dues, and a contribution to a fringe benefit plan. Subsequently, he and one of the contractors' associations filed charges with the National Labor Relations Board asserting that the agreement violated § 8(e) of the NLRA which prohibits "hot cargo" contracts (contracts in which an employer agrees not to do business with another person). An administrative law judge held that § 8(e) had been violated. He recommended to the board that it issue a cease-and-desist order and that it order reimbursement for owner-operators who had been forced to join the union. The board adopted the recommended order except for the reimbursement provision. It stated that an order for reimbursement would not effectuate the remedial policies of the NLRA. The U.S. Court of Appeals enforced the board's order in all respects.

On further appeal to the U.S. Supreme Court, the Court held that the board had acted within its authority in deciding that a reimbursement order would not effectuate the policies of the NLRA. The board was not required to order a make-whole remedy. Such relief could be saved for cases where there was "actual coercion" (meaning threats, picketing, a strike, or some other form of coercion that violates § 8(b)(4) of the NLRA). The denial of "complete relief" here was not violative of the NLRA. The Court affirmed the court of appeals' decision in favor of the board. *Shepard v. NLRB*, 459 U.S. 344, 103 S.Ct. 665, 74 L.Ed.2d 523 (1983).

The NLRA preempts state court lawsuits where the issues involved arise under the NLRA. The National Labor Relations Board is given exclusive jurisdiction in cases like the one below so that issues can be decided uniformly by an agency with expertise in the area.

A Georgia power company discharged a supervisor shortly after he was offered the position. He believed the company had been persuaded to fire him by the union because of his decision to work for a nonunion employer some years before. He filed a charge with the Regional Director of the National Labor Relations Board, but the director refused to issue a complaint, finding that there was insufficient evidence to establish that the union had caused the supervisor's discharge. Rather than appealing administratively, the supervisor filed suit in a state trial court, alleging that the union had interfered with his employment contract by coercing the company into breaching the contract. The court dismissed the complaint because the lawsuit was preempted; the subject matter of the complaint was arguably within the board's exclusive jurisdiction. The Georgia Court of Appeals reversed the dismissal and the case came before the U.S. Supreme Court.

The Supreme Court held that the supervisor's state court action against the union was preempted by the NLRA. Where the conduct at issue is of only peripheral concern to the NLRA, the lawsuit will not be preempted. However, in this case the union may have violated § 8(b)(1)(A) of the NLRA—which prohibits unions from coercing employees in the exercise of their right to engage in protected concerted activity. Also, because the employee's supervisory position was so low, it was not unlikely that he would from time to time serve as a non-supervisor and thus again become a statutory employee. (Supervisors are not "employees" under the NLRA.) Further, the union may also have violated § 8(b)(1)(B) of the NLRA—which prohibits unions from coercing employers in the selection of their representatives for the purposes of collective bargaining. Accordingly, it was for the board to decide these issues, not the state courts. *Local 926, International Union of Operating Engineers, AFL-CIO v. Jones*, 460 U.S. 669, 103 S.Ct. 1453, 75 L.Ed.2d 368 (1983).

Where the National Labor Relations Board delays action which results in an impairment of the rights of employees who have been wronged by an employer, the board's delay cannot be used as a defense by the employer to impair the employees' rights.

A union operated a hiring hall for construction workers in New Jersey. Subsequently, the National Labor Relations Board found that the union had violated the NLRA by discriminating against nonmembers in its hiring hall referral practices. The board ordered the union to compensate the five parties who had charged discrimination and "other similarly situated employees" for earnings lost as a result. The board then began to prepare a back pay specification to determine the amount of lost earnings. Because the back pay specification calculations were complex and laborious, the board did not promptly specify the amounts of the lost earnings award. This took several years. Several times the unions sought partial relief, contending that no similarly situated workers had come forward and that implementing the board's order would be impossible. In 1983, the U.S. Court of Appeals modified the board's order by requiring back pay only to the five charging parties and by prohibiting the board from amending its back pay specification.

On further appeal to the U.S. Supreme Court, the case was reversed and remanded because it appeared that the court of appeals might have rested its judgment simply on the failure of the board to act promptly. By doing this, the court would have been punishing wronged employees for the board's nonfeasance. The case had to be remanded so that if the court of appeals wanted to modify the board's order, it would do so for permissible reasons. *NLRB v. International Ass'n of Bridge, Structural & Ornamental Ironworkers, Local 480, AFL-CIO*, 466 U.S. 720, 104 S.Ct. 2081, 80 L.Ed.2d 715 (1984).

If the organizational changes accompanying the affiliation of a local union with an international are substantial enough to create a different entity, then the affiliation will be deemed to raise a "question concerning representation" which can only be resolved through the NLRB's election procedure. However, if continuity of representation and due process are satisfied, then the union's status as the employees' bargaining representative will be unaffected.

In 1970, the National Labor Relations Board certified a local union as the collective bargaining representative of a bank's employees. Eight years later, in an election in which only union members were allowed to vote, the local voted to affiliate with an international and changed its name. The bank refused to recognize the amended certification or to bargain with the new entity. The union petitioned the board to amend its certification to reflect the change it had incurred. The board initially granted the petition, finding that the bank had committed an unfair labor practice by refusing to bargain with the new entity, but eventually decided that, because nonunion employees had not been allowed to vote in the affiliation election, the election did not meet minimal due process standards. It found the affiliation invalid. On appeal to the U.S. Court of Appeals, the court remanded the case because it deemed the board's requirement that nonunion employees be allowed to vote on affiliation questions to be irrational and inconsistent with the NLRA. The case then reached the U.S. Supreme Court.

The Supreme Court held that the board had exceeded its authority under the NLRA in requiring that nonunion employees be allowed to vote for affiliation before it would order the employer to bargain with the affiliated union. Here, even though there was not a "question of representation" (which would allow for decertification) the board effectively circumvented the decertification procedures, and exceeded its statutory authority. This was exactly the type of outside interference in union decision-making that Congress intended to abolish by enactment of the NLRA. Accordingly, the Court affirmed the appellate court's decision to remand the case. *NLRB v. Financial Institution Employees of America Local 1182,* 475 U.S. 192, 106 S.Ct. 1007, 89 L.Ed.2d 151 (1986).

In the case below, the Supreme Court held that a challenge to a decision by the National Labor Relations Board's general counsel had to be brought administratively and not in the courts.

A union filed unfair labor practice charges with the Pittsburgh regional office of the National Labor Relations Board, alleging that an employer and another union had committed an unfair labor practice. The regional director filed the complaints and, before the scheduled hearing, entered into an informal settlement in which the charging union refused to join. It challenged the action before the board's general counsel (unsuccessfully) and then sought review in the U.S. Court of Appeals. The court maintained that it had jurisdiction to review the informal settlement, but the case was brought before the U.S. Supreme Court by the board.

The Court decided that a post-complaint, pre-hearing, informal settlement decision by the general counsel was not subject to judicial review under the NLRA. The NLRA sets out the stages through which unfair labor practice charges must pass and expressly provides for judicial review only for board orders. Since the general counsel's determination was not a board order, it was not subject to judicial review. Accordingly, any challenge would have to be made at the administrative level. The Court reversed the appellate court's decision, holding that the case should have been dismissed. *NLRB v. United Food & Commercial Workers Union*, 484 U.S. 112, 108 S.Ct. 413, 98 L.Ed.2d 429 (1987).

In another jurisdictional case, the Supreme Court held that an employer who unilaterally refused to make employee benefit plan contributions (after the expiration of a collective bargaining agreement) could not be sued in court. The proper forum was the NLRB.

An employer was a party to two multi-employer collective bargaining agreements that required monthly contributions to eight employee benefit plans. It then notified both unions that it had terminated the association's authority to bargain on its behalf, stating that it was prepared to negotiate with the unions independently. After the agreements expired, the employer stopped making contributions. The plans' trustees sued to collect post-contract contributions, alleging a violation of the NLRA by breaching the duty to bargain in good faith. They asserted that the courts had jurisdiction under the Employee Retirement Income Security Act (ERISA) to hear the case. The federal court granted summary judgment to the employer on the ground that § 515 of ERISA did not apply to an employer's obligation under the NLRA. The U.S. Court of Appeals affirmed, and the U.S. Supreme Court granted review. The Court first stated that § 515 of ERISA requires employers to pay to a multi-employer plan the contributions that are required "under the terms of the plan or under the terms of a collectively bargained agreement." The Court then noted that the liability created by § 515 was limited to contractual, "promised contributions." Once the collective bargaining agreement expired, the duty to make contributions would arise under the NLRA; thus, the National Labor Relations Board had exclusive jurisdiction with respect to the employer's duties under the NLRA. The Court affirmed the lower courts' decisions. *Laborers Health & Welfare Trust Fund v. Advanced Lightweight Concrete Co.*, 484 U.S. 539, 108 S.Ct. 830, 98 L.Ed.2d 936 (1988).

The NLRA's mandate that the National Labor Relations Board decide the appropriate bargaining unit "in each case" does not limit the board's broad rule-making powers.

The National Labor Relations Board promulgated a substantive rule applicable to acute care hospitals that provided that eight and only eight employee units would be appropriate in any such hospital. A hospital association brought suit in federal court, challenging the facial validity of the rule on the grounds that the

NLRA required the board to make a separate bargaining unit determination "in each case." Thus, a general rule could not be used to define bargaining units. The federal district court found that the rule violated a congressional admonition to the board to avoid the undue proliferation of bargaining units in the health care industry. It enjoined the rule's enforcement, but the U.S. Court of Appeals reversed. The U.S. Supreme Court granted certiorari, consenting to hear the case.

The Supreme Court held that the board's rule was valid. The NLRA did not require the board to limit its rulemaking powers. It merely indicated that whenever there was a disagreement about the appropriateness of a bargaining unit, the board was to resolve the dispute. The Court also noted that the board had given careful consideration to the potential proliferation of bargaining units in acute care hospitals. Thus, if Congress believed that the board had not complied with its admonition, it could fashion a remedy of its own. The Court affirmed the court of appeals' holding which upheld the board's rule. *American Hospital Ass'n v. NLRB*, 499 U.S. 606, 111 S.Ct. 1539, 113 L.Ed.2d 675 (1991).

The Supreme Court held that a discharged employee's false testimony under oath before an administrative law judge did not preclude the National Labor Relations Board from granting him reinstatement with back pay. The NLRB has primary responsibility for making remedial decisions.

A New Mexico trucking company employed a casual dockworker under a contract that required him to be available prior to a shift in case he was needed. The company fired the employee in a dispute over the contract provision, but he was reinstated after filing a grievance and an unfair labor practice charge. He was fired a second time for allegedly failing to respond to a call under a more stringent verification procedure imposed by the company. The employee was again reinstated pursuant to a successful grievance. The company then instituted a new policy calling for discharge of employees who were late for work twice without good cause. The employee was late for work twice within six days, and on the second occasion called to explain that his car had broken down. The company investigated the incident and determined that he had been lying. He was then fired on the grounds of tardiness under the new policy. The employee filed a second unfair labor practice charge against the company, and repeated his false story about car trouble at a hearing. An administrative law judge determined that the company had illegally discharged the employee on the second occasion. However, he determined that the third discharge had been based upon good cause. The NLRB affirmed the ALJ's finding in the second discharge matter, but reversed the third discharge ruling. Even though the employee had lied about his reason for being late, the company had not actually discharged him for lying. The company had instituted a retroactive policy to include the employee's first late incident and had used it as a pretext to discharge him. Accordingly, the discharge was unlawful and the board reinstated the employee with back pay. The U.S. Court of Appeals, Tenth Circuit, affirmed the board's order and the company appealed to the U.S. Supreme Court.

The Supreme Court addressed the narrow issue of whether the board was required to decide the case by imposing a rule that automatically disqualified employees from benefiting from any proceeding in which they lied. Although false testimony in any formal proceeding was intolerable, the Congressional delegation of powers to the NLRB expressly authorized it to take affirmative action to effectuate federal law. Because the statute did not restrict the NLRB's authority to order reinstatement, it was not required to adopt a strict rule barring reinstatement with back pay for an employee who falsely testified. Because the NLRB had acted within its discretion, its decision was affirmed. *ABF Freight Systems, Inc. v. NLRB*, 510 U.S. 317, 114 S.Ct. 835, 127 L.Ed.2d 152 (1994).

II. FAIR LABOR STANDARDS ACT (FLSA)

A. Scope

In 1968, the Supreme Court held that the application of the Fair Labor Standards Act to all employees of businesses engaged or involved in interstate commerce was constitutional.

In 1961, Congress amended the Fair Labor Standards Act, extending protection to employees of businesses involved in interstate commerce regardless of whether the individual employees were themselves engaged in commerce or production for commerce. This amendment also applied to hospitals and schools. Subsequently, the state of Maryland and 27 other states sued the Secretary of Labor to prohibit enforcement of the amended act. They contended that the expansion of coverage was beyond Congress' power under the Commerce Clause, and that schools and hospitals should be exempt because they were not related to interstate commerce. A three-judge district court determined that the amended law was valid, and the states appealed directly to the U.S. Supreme Court. On appeal, the Court first noted that the extension of coverage to all employees of businesses engaged or involved in interstate commerce was constitutional. Since substandard labor conditions tended to lead to labor disputes and strikes, the whole country's flow of goods could be affected by low wages and nonpayment of overtime. The Court further held that the extension of the act to schools and hospitals was valid as well because regardless of whether they were engaged in interstate commerce they purchased a vast range of out-of-state goods and thereby affected interstate commerce a great deal. The Court thus affirmed the lower court's decision and upheld the act as valid. *Maryland v. Wirtz*, 392 U.S. 192, 88 S.Ct. 2017, 20 L.Ed.2d 1020 (1968).

In *National League of Cities v. Usery*, a case that has since been overruled, the Supreme Court held that the FLSA's 1974 amendments (which made the FLSA applicable to almost all public employees) were invalid with respect to employees working in traditional governmental function jobs. The Court stated that the law impaired the states' abilities to structure their employer-employee relations.

In 1974, Congress amended the FLSA and broadened its coverage to include almost all public employees. Various cities and states and the National League of Cities brought an action in a federal district court to challenge the validity of the amendments, asserting that intergovernmental immunity prevented Congress from so amending the act. A three-judge district court was convened, which dismissed the complaint. Further appeal was taken to the U.S. Supreme Court. On appeal, the Supreme Court held that the 1974 amendments operated to obstruct the states' abilities to structure their employer-employee relationships with respect to areas of traditional government functions. The amendments were invalid because they impaired the states' abilities to function effectively in a federal system. Essentially, the Court determined that Congress could not directly force the states to utilize only Congress' means of conducting integral governmental functions. The Court thus reversed the three-judge court's decision and held the amendments invalid. *National League of Cities v. Usery,* 426 U.S. 833, 96 S.Ct. 2465, 49 L.Ed.2d 245 (1976).

The following case overturned *National League of Cities v. Usery,* above, by holding that it was permissible to require state and local government employers to comply with the FLSA despite the fact that many of the jobs were in areas that were traditionally governmental. Forcing compliance did not destroy states' sovereignty.

The San Antonio Metropolitan Transit Authority (SAMTA), a public mass-transit authority, provided transportation to the San Antonio area with the help of substantial financial assistance under the Urban Mass Transportation Act. In 1979, the Wage and Hour Administration of the Department of Labor issued an opinion that SAMTA's operations were not immune from the minimum wage and overtime requirements of the Fair Labor Standards Act. SAMTA filed a suit in federal district court, asserting under *National League of Cities v. Usery* that it was exempt from the requirements of the FLSA. The district court agreed, and appeal was taken directly to the U.S. Supreme Court.

The Supreme Court noted that drawing boundaries between areas of traditional governmental functions and those areas which were not traditionally run by the government was not only unworkable, but inconsistent with established principles of federalism. Forcing local governments to comply with the FLSA in areas not traditionally governmental, and allowing state immunity for functions which were deemed traditionally governmental would lead to inconsistent results. Further, the Court noted that the FLSA requirements were not destructive of state sovereignty nor violative of the Constitution. Accordingly, the Court overruled *National League of Cities* and reversed the decision of the district court. *Garcia v. San Antonio Metropolitan Transit Authority,* 469 U.S. 528, 105 S.Ct. 1005, 83 L.Ed.2d 1016 (1985).

In 1985, the Supreme Court held that the FLSA applied to a nonprofit religious organization. The "associates" involved with the organization were really employees and thus had to be paid at least minimum wage (either in the form of cash or benefits). If they chose to, they could return any payments made to them, but the decision had to be theirs.

A nonprofit religious organization derived most of its income from the operation of commercial businesses staffed by its "associates." These people, former drug addicts and criminals, received no cash salaries, but were provided with food, clothing, shelter and other benefits. The Secretary of Labor filed an action in federal court against the organization and its officers, alleging violations of the FLSA. The district court held that the organization was an "enterprise" within the meaning of the FLSA. Further, under the economic reality test of employment, the associates were employees of the organization protected by the FLSA. The U.S. Court of Appeals affirmed the finding of liability by the district court, and the case reached the U.S. Supreme Court.

The Court noted that the FLSA contained no express or implied exception for commercial activities conducted by religious or other nonprofit organizations. Further, even though the associates here involved claimed that they were not employees, they did expect compensation of a sort for their work; thus, the economic reality was that they were employees under the FLSA. Finally, the Court held that application of the FLSA did not violate the Free Exercise Clause or the Establishment Clause. The FLSA did not require the payment of cash wages, so the employees could still be paid in the form of benefits. Also, they could return any payments made to them if they so wished, and provided it was voluntary, this would not violate the FLSA. Nor did the FLSA's recordkeeping requirements inhibit religious activities undertaken with a business purpose. The Court therefore determined that the FLSA applied to the organization, and affirmed the lower court's decision. *Tony & Susan Alamo Foundation v. Secretary of Labor,* 471 U.S. 290, 105 S.Ct. 1953, 85 L.Ed.2d 278 (1985).

B. Procedures

The Supreme Court upheld the civil penalty provisions of the FLSA against constitutional attack because, even though the agency that assessed the fines received the fines, no government official stood to gain from their imposition.

A corporation that managed about 40 restaurants was found to have committed over 150 violations of the Fair Labor Standards Act's child labor provisions. The administrator who assessed the fine against the corporation added an amount for wilful violation of the FLSA. However, an administrative law judge reviewed the evidence and determined that the violations were not wilful. He reduced the total assessment. The corporation then brought suit in federal court, challenging the civil penalty provisions of the FLSA as violative of due process because the fines went to the agency that assessed them (as reimbursement for enforcement expenses) and this created an impermissible risk of bias. The district court granted summary judgment to the employer, and the U.S. Supreme Court consented to review the case.

The Court held that the section of the FLSA that provided for civil penalties did not violate the Due Process Clause. No government official stood to profit economically from the vigorous enforcement of the FLSA's child labor provisions. Thus, there was little chance that the administrator's judgment would be distorted by the prospect of gain. Further, the agency's administration of the

FLSA minimized any potential for bias. Accordingly, the Court reversed the district court's decision and remanded the case. *Marshall v. Jerrico, Inc.*, 446 U.S. 238, 100 S.Ct. 1610, 64 L.Ed.2d 182 (1980).

Rights arising out of the Fair Labor Standards Act are individual rights. They cannot be waived by the existence of a collective bargaining system. If an employee believes that his or her employer is violating the FLSA, the question can be litigated in court despite a collective bargaining agreement to the contrary.

Truck drivers, employed by a freight company, were required to conduct safety inspections of their trucks, and transport them to a repair facility if they failed the inspections. They were not paid for their time doing this. Their union filed a grievance on their behalf, but a joint committee rejected the grievance. The truck drivers then filed suit in federal district court, asserting that their time was compensable under the FLSA. They also claimed that the union had breached its duty of fair representation. The court addressed only the fair representation claim, holding against the truck drivers. The U.S. Court of Appeals affirmed, and the case came before the U.S. Supreme Court.

The Court held that the drivers' claims under the FLSA were not barred by the submission of their grievance to the joint committee. Here, the rights at issue arose out of a federal statute, not out of the collective bargaining agreement. The district court should have addressed their claims under the FLSA. The collective bargaining process applies to members of a collective organization, but the rights asserted here were individual rights protected by Congress. They could not be waived. FLSA rights are best protected in a judicial forum, not by an arbitrator. The Court reversed the court of appeals' decision. *Barrentine v. Arkansas-Best Freight System*, 450 U.S. 728, 101 S.Ct. 1437, 67 L.Ed.2d 641 (1981).

In *McLaughlin*, below, the Court held that in order to apply the three-year statute of limitations for wilful violations of the FLSA, the employer had to know or show reckless disregard for the matter of whether its conduct was prohibited by the FLSA. This was the same standard as enunciated earlier in *Trans World Airlines, Inc. v. Thurston*, 469 U.S. 111, 105 S.Ct. 613, 83 L.Ed.2d 523 (1985).

A shoe manufacturer employed seven mechanics to maintain and repair its equipment. In 1984, the Secretary of Labor filed a complaint against the company, alleging that it had failed to pay those employees overtime compensation as required by the FLSA. The company asserted that the two-year statute of limitations precluded the action, but the secretary maintained that the three-year statute (for wilful violations of the FLSA) applied. A federal district court agreed with the secretary, but the U.S. Court of Appeals, Third Circuit, vacated its decision, holding that only where the employer knew or showed reckless disregard for the matter of whether its conduct was prohibited by the FLSA would the three-year statute of limitations apply. On further appeal to the U.S. Supreme Court, this standard was upheld. *McLaughlin v. Richland Shoe Co.*, 486 U.S. 128, 108 S.Ct. 1677, 100 L.Ed.2d 115 (1988).

C. Overtime

In the following case, the Supreme Court ruled that marine engineers and members of an engineering department aboard a seafood processing vessel were "seamen" and thus exempted from the overtime provisions of the FLSA.

A group of employees who worked in the engineering department of a seafood company on a barge that processed fish sued their employer to recover overtime benefits under the FLSA. The employees did not perform any hands-on processing or packing of fish. As members of the engineering department, they were responsible for maintaining all systems for support and continuous operation of the vessel while at moorage or underway. They were on call 24 hours a day to perform work at a moment's notice if necessary to keep the vessel operating. Also, they each performed tasks which conformed to those expected of Coast Guard licensed personnel. However, they maintained that they were not seamen because their duties did not "primarily aid navigation of the vessel." A federal district court held that they were not entitled to protection under the FLSA because they were "seamen" and thus exempted from the provisions of the act. The U.S. Court of Appeals, Ninth Circuit, reversed, holding that the employees were not seamen, but instead were industrial maintenance employees. Accordingly, the court found that the FLSA applied to them. Appeal was taken to the U.S. Supreme Court. The Court held that the court of appeals had improperly arrived at its judgment. The appellate court should only have overturned the district court's findings of fact if they were clearly erroneous. Here, each of the employees was a crewmember who performed maritime work in navigable waters. Thus, they had been properly deemed seamen by the district court. *Icicle Seafoods, Inc. v. Worthington*, 475 U.S. 709, 106 S.Ct. 1527, 89 L.Ed.2d 739 (1986).

Section 15(a)(1) of the Fair Labor Standards Act prohibits "any person" from introducing into interstate commerce goods produced in violation of the minimum wage or overtime pay provisions of the act. In the case below, the Supreme Court held that "any person" included secured creditors of violators who acquired "hot goods" under a security agreement.

A corporation acquired a security interest in a manufacturer's inventory. When the manufacturer began to fail financially, the corporation took possession. However, because some of the inventory had been manufactured during a period in which employees were not paid, the Department of Labor sought to prohibit the sale or transportation of the "hot goods" in interstate commerce. The case came before the U.S. Supreme Court which held that § 15(a)(1) of the FLSA, which prohibits "any person" from introducing into interstate commerce goods produced in violation of the minimum wage or overtime provisions of the act, applied to the corporation here. Even though the corporation was just a secured creditor, it was still subject to the restrictions set forth by the act. *Citicorp Industrial Credit, Inc. v. Brock*, 483 U.S. 27, 107 S.Ct. 2694, 97 L.Ed.2d 23 (1987).

The FLSA allows public employers to compensate their employees with extra time off in lieu of overtime pay—either under collective bargaining agreements or under individual agreements between employers and employees. The Court held that a Texas public employer could provide compensatory time off pursuant to individual agreements even though the employees had designated a union representative (because the state prohibited public sector collective bargaining).

The Fair Labor Standards Act requires employers to pay employees at least time-and-one-half for all overtime hours. However, a congressionally enacted exception allows public employers to compensate their employees with extra time off (comp time) instead of overtime pay. The relevant subsection of the congressional amendment allows comp time "in lieu of" overtime pay when the public agency and representatives of the employees reach such an agreement. In the case of employees not covered by the above provision, an employer and an employee may individually agree to such an arrangement. A Texas sheriff's union represented more than 400 deputy sheriffs. However, the union was prohibited by Texas law from entering into collective bargaining agreements with the county. Each employee was bound by form agreements individually entered into with the county. These form agreements provided, in part, that employees working overtime would be compensated with extra time off. The union filed suit in a U.S. district court alleging that the workers' representation by the union precluded the individual agreements providing for comp time rather than overtime pay. The district court entered summary judgment for the county and the U.S. Court of Appeals, Fifth Circuit, affirmed, albeit on different reasoning. The union appealed to the U.S. Supreme Court.

The issue on appeal was "whether a public employer in a state that prohibits public sector collective bargaining may take advantage of that exception when its employees have designated a union representative." First, the Court rejected the narrow reading of the statute espoused by the county. The county had argued that individual agreements were precluded only when the employees were bound by applicable provisions of a collective bargaining agreement. The Court deemed such an interpretation contrary to the statute's overall structure. Congress had attempted to restrict use of individual agreements "to a limited class of employee." The Court also rejected the union's argument that the mere selection of a representative, regardless of his or her ability to enter into an agreement, precluded individual agreements between the employee and the county. Instead, it determined that individual agreements were precluded only when an elected representative had the authority to negotiate the use of comp time via a collective bargaining agreement. Since the union did not have authority under local law to enter into a collective bargaining agreement, individual agreements authorizing comp time were permitted. The holding of the court of appeals was affirmed. *Moreau v. Klevenhagen*, 508 U.S. 22, 113 S.Ct. 1905, 123 L.Ed.2d 584 (1993).

Under the FLSA, the employer must engage in an actual practice of making pay deductions or maintain an employment policy that creates a significant likelihood of such deductions in order to remove the employee from the exemption for salaried employees. An inadvertent deduction or deduction for reasons other than lack of work will not remove the exemption if the employer reimburses the employee for the deductions and promises to comply in the future.

Several Missouri police officers employed by the St. Louis Police Department filed suit against the Board of Police Commissioners in federal district court, seeking payment of overtime wages under the Fair Labor Standards Act (FLSA). The officers contended that they did not meet the exemption for salaried employees because under the terms of the department manual their compensation could be reduced for disciplinary infractions related to the "quality or quantity" of work performed. They also claimed that they did not meet the other requirement for exempt status: that their duties be of an executive, administrative or professional nature. The district court found that the officers were paid on a salary basis, although not all of the officers satisfied the duties criteria. The U.S. Court of Appeals, Eighth Circuit, affirmed in part and reversed in part, holding that both the salary basis and duties tests were satisfied as to all the officers. The U.S. Supreme Court granted certiorari.

The Court found that the "no disciplinary deductions" element of the salary basis test applied to public sector employees. Moreover, the Secretary of Labor had reasonably interpreted the salary basis test to deny exempt status when either an actual practice of making pay deductions exists or an employment policy creates a "significant likelihood" of such deductions. An inadvertent deduction or deduction for reasons other than lack of work will not remove the exemption if the employer reimburses the employee for such deductions and promises to comply in the future. Furthermore, the regulations do not require immediate payment of the reimbursement. The Court affirmed the decision of the court of appeals. *Auer v. Robbins*, 519 U.S. 452, 117 S.Ct. 905, 137 L.Ed.2d 79 (1997).

In a decision affecting all state and local government employers, the U.S. Supreme Court rejected the appeal of a group of Texas county deputy sheriffs who asserted that their employer could not force them to use accumulated compensatory time under the Fair Labor Standards Act Amendments of 1985. The court held that the FLSA does not prevent public employers from specifying when employees may use their comp time.

Congress amended the FLSA in 1985 to permit states and their political subdivisions to compensate their employees for working overtime at one and one-half their rate of pay for every hour in excess of 40 per week. Employers may agree with their employees either orally or in writing to provide compensatory time off work instead of cash compensation. The act requires employers to honor requests to use compensatory time within a reasonable time period, so long as it does not disrupt the employer's operations. FLSA regulations limit the compensatory time that an employee may accrue. After the maximum is reached, the employer must pay the employee for additional hours worked. A group of Texas county deputy sheriffs agreed individually to accept compensatory time off in lieu of cash compensation for working overtime. The county implemented a budgetary protection policy under which supervisors set a maximum number of hours that could be accumulated by an employee. Employees were advised of the maximum and asked to take voluntary steps to reduce comp time accumulations. Supervisors could specify that employees take their compensatory time at scheduled times. The deputies sued the county in a federal district court, alleging that the compelled use of comp time violated the FLSA. The court awarded summary judgment in their favor, but the county obtained reversal of the order on appeal to the U.S. Court of Appeals, Fifth Circuit.

The deputies, with the support of the U.S. Department of Labor, appealed to the U.S. Supreme Court, contending that the FLSA implicitly prohibits public employers from compelling their employees to take accrued comp time. The court found that the FLSA establishes "a minimum guarantee that an employee will be able to make some use of compensatory time when he requests to use it." However, the law does not expressly or impliedly limit a public employer from scheduling employees to take time off work with full pay. Because the FLSA was silent on the matter of employer-compelled comp time usage, the Court refused to find that the county policy violated the statute, holding that "under the FLSA an employer is free to require an employee to take time off work and an employer is also free to use the money it would have paid in wages to cash out accrued compensatory time." The court affirmed the Fifth Circuit's judgment. *Christensen v. Harris County*, 529 U.S. 576, 120 S.Ct. 1655, 146 L.Ed.2d 621 (2000).

III. LABOR MANAGEMENT RELATIONS ACT (LMRA)

A. Scope

Section 301(a) of the Labor Management Relations Act of 1947, 29 U.S.C. § 185, provides that "suits for violation of contracts between an employer and a labor organization" may be brought in any federal district court regardless of the amount in controversy. Under § 301, it is unlawful for a union to support an unauthorized strike that is in violation of a collective bargaining agreement.

Some local labor unions engaged in a number of unauthorized, "wildcat" strikes at a company's coal mines in violation of the collective bargaining agreements in place between the employer and the international union. The regional subdivision of the international was unsuccessful in attempting in persuade the miners not to strike and to return to work. The employer then sued the international, the regional subdivision, and the local unions under § 301 of the Labor Management Relations Act. The district court granted injunctive relief and damages against all the defendants, but the U.S. Court of Appeals reversed as to the international and the regional subdivision because they did not instigate, support, ratify, or encourage the strikes.

On further appeal, the U.S. Supreme Court held that neither the international nor the regional subdivision could be held liable for the unauthorized strikes. There was no obligation implied in law on their part to use all reasonable means to prevent and end unauthorized strikes. If the strike had been authorized (and in violation of the collective bargaining agreements), then the international would have been liable under § 301, but such was not the case here. Further, it was clear from the agreements that the parties decided not to impose on the international an obligation to take disciplinary action against unauthorized strikers to get them back to work. Accordingly, the Court affirmed the appellate court's decision in favor of the international and the regional subdivision. *Carbon Fuel Co. v. United Mine Workers of America,* 444 U.S. 212, 100 S.Ct. 410, 62 L.Ed.2d 394 (1979).

In the case below, the Supreme Court clarified that the LMRA applies to violations of labor contracts, not claims asserting that a contract is invalid.

Section 301(a) of the Labor Management Relations Act (LMRA), 29 U.S.C. § 185(a), establishes a federal court cause of action to address violations of collective bargaining agreements in industries affecting commerce. A labor organization representing employees who worked at a Pennsylvania manufacturing plant claimed that their employer fraudulently induced them to enter into a collective bargaining agreement that prohibited strikes for any reason. According to the union, absent the employer's fraud, it would not have entered into the collective bargaining agreement and a separate memorandum agreement requiring the employer to give the union a seven-day notice prior to subcontracting out work. The union made the assertion after the employer announced its intention to contract out work that would cause many union members to lose their jobs. A federal district court dismissed the complaint as not arising under the LMRA since it alleged no violation of a labor contract. The U.S. Court of Appeals, Third Circuit, reversed.

The U.S. Supreme Court agreed to review the case, and noted that the LMRA limits federal court jurisdiction to lawsuits for violations of labor contracts, not claims asserting that a contract is invalid. The case had no purpose or object of demonstrating a violation of any contract, as the union argued. The collective bargaining agreement of the parties had already expired, defeating any claim for federal question jurisdiction under the Declaratory Judgment Act. Because the complaint alleged no violation of a collective bargaining agreement, the district court had properly held that it had no jurisdiction over the case, and the Court reversed the judgment of the court of appeals. *Textron Lycoming Reciprocating Engine Div., AVCO Corp. v. United Automobile, Aerospace and Agricultural Implement Workers of America, Int'l Union, Local 787,* 523 U.S. 653, 118 S.Ct. 1626, 140 L.Ed.2d 863 (1998).

B. Preemption

In *Allis-Chalmers Corp. v. Lueck,* below, the Supreme Court held that when the resolution of a state law claim is substantially dependent upon analysis of the terms of an agreement made between the parties in a labor contract, then the state law claim will either be subject to § 301 of the LMRA or it will be preempted by the NLRA.

An employee of a corporation was also a union member; the union and the employer were parties to a collective bargaining agreement. The agreement incorporated by reference a separately negotiated group health and disability plan. While carrying a pig to a friend's house for a pig roast, the employee injured his back. He sought benefits under the plan. However, because of disputes over the manner in which the employer and its insurer handled his claim, he filed suit in state court, seeking to recover for their bad faith in handling his claim. He chose not to follow the grievance procedure set forth in the CBA. The court ruled for the employer because the employee's suit fell under § 301 of the LMRA and the employee had not exhausted the arbitration procedures established in the collective bargaining agreement. Alternatively, the court held that even if the claim did arise under state law, it was preempted by the NLRA. The court of appeals affirmed, but the Wisconsin Supreme Court reversed.

On further appeal, the U.S. Supreme Court held that when resolution of a state-law claim is substantially dependent on analysis of the terms of a collective bargaining agreement, the claim must either be treated as a § 301 claim or dismissed as preempted by the NLRA. Here, the right asserted by the employee was rooted in contract and could have been pleaded as a contract claim under § 301. Also, any attempt at assessing liability would inevitably involve contract interpretation. Thus, the congressional goal of a unified body of labor-contract law required preemption. Accordingly, the Court reversed the state supreme court's decision, finding that the claim should have been dismissed. *Allis-Chalmers Corp. v. Lueck*, 471 U.S. 202, 105 S.Ct. 1904, 85 L.Ed.2d 206 (1985).

Two years later, the Court stated that an injured worker's claim against her union (for breach of the duty to provide her with a safe work place) was not sufficiently independent of the collective bargaining agreement to withstand the preemptive force of § 301 of the LMRA.

An electrical apprentice, and member of a union, worked for a Florida power company. She was assigned to a job in an electrical substation, and was injured when she came into contact with some highly energized components. Two years later, she sued her union, alleging that it had a duty to ensure that she was provided safety in her work place, and that she not be required to take undue risks while performing her duties—risks which were beyond her training and experience. She claimed that the tasks she had been performing at the time of her injury were beyond the scope of her training and experience. The union removed the case to a federal court, which dismissed the suit as untimely, but the U.S. Court of Appeals reversed. The U.S. Supreme Court granted review.

The Supreme Court noted that for the union to have breached a duty to the apprentice, such a duty would have to arise by contract. Thus, § 301 of the LMRA preempted any state-law action she might have had because interpretation of the collective bargaining agreement would be necessary. Under federal law, the court of appeals would be required to determine whether the apprentice's claim was time-barred by the six-month limitations period of the NLRA, or whether some other period should be used. The Court vacated the court of appeals' decision and remanded the case. *International Brotherhood of Electrical Workers, AFL-CIO v. Hechler*, 481 U.S. 851, 107 S.Ct. 2161, 95 L.Ed.2d 791 (1987).

Where a lawsuit is brought on an individual employment contract, the lawsuit will not be dismissed as preempted by § 301 even if a collective bargaining agreement exists unless the individual employment contract is subsumed into the collective bargaining agreement.

Caterpillar Tractor Company hired a group of employees to work at a California facility. Each position hired for was covered by the collective bargaining agreement (CBA). These employees all reached managerial or weekly salaried positions, outside the coverage of the CBA. They held their positions for a number of years, and alleged that Caterpillar made oral and written representations that "they could look forward to indefinite and lasting employment." The company then downgraded them to unionized positions that were supposedly only temporary. Thereafter, the company notified them that it was closing the California facility and that they would be laid off. They sued in state court, contending that Caterpillar had breached the individual employment contracts between them. Caterpillar removed the case to a federal district court, and the case was dismissed for failure of the employees to state a claim under § 301 of the LMRA. The U.S. Court of Appeals, Ninth Circuit, reversed, holding that the case must be heard in state court, and the case came before the U.S. Supreme Court.

The Supreme Court agreed with the court of appeals that the state law contract claims were not preempted by § 301. Here, even though the employees could have brought suit under § 301, they chose to sue under state law on their individual contracts. No interpretation or application of the CBA was necessary to decide their claims. Further, even though the employees were covered by the CBA, their individual contracts were not necessarily subsumed into the CBA. The Court thus affirmed the judgment of the court of appeals, and held that the state law claims should be heard in state court. *Caterpillar Inc. v. Williams*, 482 U.S. 386, 107 S.Ct. 2425, 96 L.Ed.2d 318 (1987).

Where an employee sues an employer asserting a state law cause of action, his or her claim will not be preempted by § 301 if application of the state law will not require the interpretation of a collective bargaining agreement. If the claim is independent of the agreement, it may proceed.

An Illinois woman was apparently injured in the course of her employment. She notified her employer, and requested compensation for her medical expenses under the Illinois Workers' Compensation Act. Shortly thereafter, her employer discharged her for filing a "false" workers' compensation claim. Her union filed a grievance under the collective bargaining agreement (CBA); an arbitrator eventually found in the employee's favor and ordered her reinstated with full back pay. Meanwhile, she brought a retaliatory discharge claim against her employer in a state trial court. The employer removed the case to federal court, then sought dismissal, which the court granted. The U.S. Court of Appeals, Seventh Circuit, affirmed. The employee petitioned the U.S. Supreme Court for review. At issue was whether the employee's claim was preempted by § 301 of the LMRA. The Supreme Court held that it was not. Therefore, if the employee could show that she had been discharged, and that the employer's motive was to deter her from exercising her rights under the workers' compensation act, she could win her suit. No interpretation of the CBA would have to be made. Since the inquiries were purely factual, the claim was independent of the CBA and § 301 did not preempt it. The court reversed the court of appeals' decision and held that the employee could continue her claim. *Lingle v. Norge Division of Magic Chef, Inc.*, 486 U.S. 399, 108 S.Ct. 1877, 100 L.Ed.2d 410 (1988).

In the following case, the Supreme Court held that a wrongful death lawsuit against a union was preempted by § 301 of the LMRA. Also, the plaintiffs could not maintain a § 301 claim against the union because they had only alleged negligence. Mere negligence does not state a claim for breach of the duty of fair representation.

After an underground fire at an Idaho mine, the survivors of four miners filed a state-law wrongful death action against the miners' union, alleging that, based on a collective bargaining agreement, it had negligently conducted safety inspections. The Idaho Supreme Court eventually determined that the survivors had stated a valid claim under state law that was not preempted by § 301 of the LMRA. The U.S. Supreme Court agreed to review the case.

The Supreme Court first held that the survivors' claims that the union had been negligent in its safety inspections were not independent of the collective bargaining agreement. Here, the union's representatives were participating in the inspection process according to the provisions of the agreement. Thus, any duty owed the miners arose out of the agreement, and the state-law tort claim was preempted by § 301. Next, the Court held that the § 301 claim could not succeed against the union because only negligence had been alleged by the survivors. Also, there was no more far-reaching duty owed by the union to the miners by virtue of the agreement. That contract was merely between the union and the employer. Accordingly, the Court reversed the state supreme court's decision, finding that the state-law tort action could not be maintained. *United Steelworkers of America v. Rawson*, 495 U.S. 362, 110 S.Ct. 1904, 109 L.Ed.2d 362 (1990).

C. Procedures

Where an internal union appeals procedure will be unable to reactivate an employee's grievance or grant the employee the complete relief sought under § 301 of the LMRA, the employee will not be required to exhaust such procedures prior to bringing suit.

A union employee was dismissed for violating a plant rule prohibiting defined misbehavior. He sought a grievance on the ground that his dismissal was not for just cause. The union pursued the grievance through the third step of the procedure, but decided not to seek arbitration of his grievance. Even though the union constitution required exhaustion of internal union appeals procedures before going to court, the employee sued in federal court under § 301(a) of the LMRA, alleging that the union had breached its duty of fair representation and that his employer had breached the collective bargaining agreement (CBA) by discharging him without just cause. He sought money damages from both defendants as well as reinstatement from his employer. The court dismissed his suit, and the U.S. Court of Appeals affirmed in part, reversing the dismissal against the employer. Further appeal was taken to the U.S. Supreme Court.

The Supreme Court held that the employee should not have been required to exhaust the internal union appeals procedures because they could not reactivate his grievance or grant him the complete relief he sought under § 301(a). Here, because of the inadequacy of the internal procedures, the employee should have been excused from the exhaustion requirement. Further, because the employee was suing both the union and his employer, the exhaustion defense was not available. The union's procedures could not have gotten the employee his job back, nor could they even have reactivated his grievance (because of certain time restrictions in the CBA for obtaining arbitration of a grievance). Accordingly, the Court determined that exhaustion was not required against either defendant. *Clayton v. International Union, United Automobile Workers of America*, 451 U.S. 679, 101 S.Ct. 2088, 68 L.Ed.2d 538 (1981).

The Supreme Court applied the six-month limitations period in § 10(b) of the NLRA (for unfair labor practice charges) to suits brought against an employer and a union for breach of the collective bargaining agreement (by the employer) and breach of the duty of fair representation (by the union).

Several employees brought two different lawsuits against their employers and their unions, alleging that the employers had breached the collective bargaining agreement in place, and that the unions had breached their duty of fair representation by mishandling the ensuing grievance or arbitration proceedings. The suits were brought under § 301 of the LMRA. In the first case, an employee grieved a discharge after refusing to drive a tractor-trailer that he contended was unsafe. In the second case, two employees challenged work assignments as being violative of the collective bargaining agreement. After rulings for the employers, the employees brought their lawsuits. In seeking dismissals, the employers and the unions contended that the statute of limitations had run. Eventually, the cases were consolidated before the U.S. Supreme Court.

The Supreme Court held that in suits of this type, the six-month limitations period in § 10(b) of the National Labor Relations Act would govern claims against both the employers and the unions. The LMRA contained no express statute of limitations. Usually in such a case the most closely analogous state limitations period would be applied. However, in a suit by an employee against both employer and union, there was no close analogy in state law. Further, the six-month period in § 10(b) was designed to accommodate a balance of interests similar to those at stake here. The union's breach of duty and the employer's breach of the bargaining agreement are often also unfair labor practices (covered by the NLRA). Accordingly, the NLRA limitations period was the correct one to apply. One of the cases had to be dismissed because it was not timely filed. The other case was remanded for a finding of whether certain events had tolled the running of the limitations period. *Del Costello v. International Brotherhood of Teamsters*, 462 U.S. 151, 103 S.Ct. 2281, 76 L.Ed.2d 476 (1983).

Where a collective bargaining agreement reserves the parties' rights to resort to economic weapons upon the failure of various procedures to resolve a dispute, this does not foreclose the seeking of a judicial remedy under § 301 of the LMRA.

A company discharged two employees for "just cause," and the employees disputed this. They believed there had been no just cause, which was required by the collective bargaining agreement (CBA). They invoked the grievance procedures of the CBA without success, and then filed suit against the company under § 301 of the LMRA. A federal district court granted summary judgment to the company; and the U.S. Court of Appeals, Sixth Circuit, affirmed, holding that a strike or other job action is the proper remedy for failure to successfully resolve a grievance where arbitration is not required. The employees sought review from the U.S. Supreme Court. The Court reversed the appellate court's ruling. It noted that § 301 provides a federal remedy for breach of a CBA, and that there was a strong presumption that the federal courts would provide access for the peaceful resolution of disputes under a CBA. Here, since the parties had not agreed to a different method of resolving disputes (*e.g.,* arbitration), a neutral forum would be provided. Even though the CBA allowed strikes or lockouts upon exhaustion of the grievance process, this did not mean that the employees had to resort to such economic weapons as strikes. The Court remanded the case for further proceedings. *Groves v. Ring Screw Works*, 498 U.S. 168, 111 S.Ct. 498, 112 L.Ed.2d 508 (1990).

D. Relief

Section 303(b) of the LMRA, 29 U.S.C. § 187(b), allows parties injured by a union's unfair labor practices to sue for the damages sustained as a result. However, the injured party may not recover the attorneys' fees incurred during NLRB proceedings as an element of "damages" under § 303(b).

A manufacturer of prefabricated modular homes opened a plant in Montana where it utilized unskilled union workers rather than skilled union carpenters. A local carpenters union ordered its members not to work on the installation of the company's homes and then began picketing the plant. The company filed an unfair labor practice charge against the union, alleging that the work stoppage and the picketing violated the National Labor Relations Act. The NLRB found against the union, and its order was judicially enforced. The company then sued the union under § 303 of the LMRA, seeking damages for the union's illegal activity. It asked for both business losses and attorneys' fees incurred in the NLRB proceedings. The court awarded the company its business losses, but refused to award attorneys' fees. The U.S. Court of Appeals affirmed, and the company petitioned the U.S. Supreme Court for review. On review, the Court upheld the denial of attorneys' fees, finding that they were not a proper element of damages under § 303. Generally, attorneys' fees are not recoverable unless a statute or enforceable contract provides for them. Here, § 303 did not expressly authorize the recovery of attorneys' fees incurred during NLRB proceedings. The term "damages" as used by the statute, was not intended by Congress to be expanded so as to include attorneys' fees. Accordingly, the Court affirmed the court of appeals' decision. *Summit Valley Industries, Inc. v. Local 112, United Brotherhood of Carpenters*, 456 U.S. 717, 102 S.Ct. 2112, 72 L.Ed.2d 511 (1982).

To recover money damages in an action for breach of the duty of fair representation, an employee must prove both that the employer's action violated the terms of the collective bargaining agreement, and that the union breached its duty of fair representation in handling the grievance. Also, if a lawsuit seeks money damages, the employees are entitled to a jury trial.

A group of truck drivers was alternatively laid off and recalled several times. This resulted in a loss of seniority rights. A grievance proceeding reinstated those rights. However, further layoffs and recalls occurred, and a second grievance hearing was conducted. When the layoffs and recalls continued, the truck drivers filed a third grievance, but the union declined to refer the charges, finding that the prior proceedings had determined the relevant issues. The drivers then sued in federal court, alleging that the company had breached the collective bargaining agreement in violation of § 301 of the LMRA, and that the union had breached its duty of fair representation. They sought injunctive relief and compensatory damages, requesting a jury trial for the nonequitable issues. The company then filed for bankruptcy, so the union sought to strike the jury demand. The district court denied the union's motion to strike, and the U.S. Court of Appeals affirmed.

The U.S. Supreme Court held that because the claim against the union (for breach of the duty of fair representation) was seeking only compensatory damages, the drivers were entitled to a jury trial. Here, the drivers were not attempting to recover back pay (which is equitable), but were seeking a monetary award for the union's breach of duty. As a result, the Seventh Amendment required that they be allowed the right of trial by jury. The Court affirmed the lower courts' decisions. *Local No. 391 v. Terry*, 494 U.S. 558, 110 S.Ct. 1339, 108 L.Ed.2d 519 (1990).

Section 302 of the LMRA prohibits payments from employers to union representatives, but provides an exception under § 302(c)(5) for payments to an employee trust fund if certain conditions are met, including that the trust fund be "established ... for the sole and exclusive benefit of the employees," and that the payments be "held in trust for the purpose of paying" employee benefits. The Supreme Court held that § 302(e) does not give federal courts authority to issue injunctions against a trust fund or its trustees requiring trust funds to be administered in the manner described in § 302(c)(5).

The Labor Management Relations Act (LMRA) prohibits employers from making payments to labor organization representatives and prohibits the representatives from accepting money from affected employers (§§ 302(a) and (b)). An exception to this rule, found at subsection 302(c)(5) of the LMRA, governs payments to employee trust funds and allows contributions for the sole and exclusive benefit of employees so that payments may be held in trust for the purpose of paying employee benefits. A group of employers that participated in a multiemployer bargaining association made contributions to employee trust funds pursuant to a collective bargaining agreement. The employers broke away from the employers' association and negotiated new collective bargaining agreements. They ended their participation in the trust funds and established a new set of trusts for their employees. Because many employees were vested in benefits under the prior employee funds, the employers sought relief from the formerly used funds and brought a federal district court action to require them to transfer an appropriate share of trust assets to the newly created trusts. They sought relief under the Employee Retirement Income Security Act of 1974, 29 U.S.C. § 1001 *et seq.* The employers also sought relief under LMRA § 302. The district court granted the motion for summary judgment brought by the trust funds, ruling that federal court relief was not required because the funds were not "structurally deficient" (in other words, they were still maintained for the sole and exclusive benefit of the employees). This was because there was no allegation of corruption in the trust funds and because transferring the assets would not further any collective bargaining policy. The U.S. Court of Appeals, Second Circuit, reversed and remanded the district court decision, ruling that the trust funds would suffer a structural defect unless a portion of the funds was transferred to the new trusts. The U.S. Supreme Court granted review.

The Supreme Court held that a federal court does not have authority under § 302(e) of the LMRA to issue injunctions against a trust fund or its trustees requiring the trust funds to be administered in the manner described in § 302(c)(5). The exception to prohibited payments found in § 302(c)(5) describes the character of the trust to which payments are allowed, leaving it to federal trust law under ERISA to determine when breaches of that trust have occurred and how they may be remedied. The case was reversed and remanded to the court of appeals for a ruling on the ERISA portion of the employers' complaint. The district court had ruled against the employers on ERISA issues, but the court of appeals had not reached those issues because of its ruling on § 302. *Local 144 Nursing Home Pension Fund v. Demisay,* 508 U.S. 581, 113 S.Ct. 2252, 124 L.Ed.2d 522 (1993).

IV. LABOR-MANAGEMENT REPORTING AND DISCLOSURE ACT

The Labor-Management Reporting and Disclosure Act was enacted with the idea of protecting the rights of union members as union members. Thus, it was permissible in the following case for the new union president to discharge the business agents who had been appointed by the old union president. The business agents' rights as union members were unaffected.

In a union election in Ohio, the challenger for the presidency of the union defeated the incumbent. He then discharged all of the union's business agents (who had been appointed by the incumbent and who had openly supported the incumbent) as he was authorized to do by the union's bylaws. He believed the agents would be unable to follow and implement his policies and programs because of their loyalty to the incumbent. Their discharges did not prevent them from continuing as union members. However, they filed suit against the new president and the union, alleging that the defendants had violated §§ 101(a)(1) and (2) of the LMRDA, which guarantee free speech rights to union members, and which make it unlawful for a union to discipline members for exercising their rights under the act. A federal district court granted summary judgment to the defendants, and the U.S. Court of Appeals affirmed. On further appeal to the U.S. Supreme Court, the Court agreed with the lower courts that the act does not protect a union employee from discharge by the union president if the employee's rights as a union member are not affected. Congress had sought to protect rank-and-file union members by passage of the act, not the job security or tenure of union officers or employees. The act only disallowed retaliatory actions that affected a union member's rights or status as a member of the union. Since those rights had not been impinged, and since the new union president had the right to choose staff members whose views would be compatible with his own, the Court affirmed the judgment for the defendants. *Finnegan v. Leu*, 456 U.S. 431, 102 S.Ct. 1867, 72 L.Ed.2d 239 (1982).

In the following case, the Supreme Court held that a union rule that prohibited outsider contributions to candidates for union office was not violative of the Labor-Management Reporting and Disclosure Act of 1959.

A union amended its constitution to include an "outsider rule" which prohibited candidates for union office from accepting campaign contributions from nonmembers. It also created a committee to enforce the rule. Certain individuals, including an unsuccessful candidate for union office who had received a lot of financial support for his campaign from sources outside the union, filed suit against the union in a federal district court, claiming that the rule violated the LMRDA. The district court agreed that the rule violated the LMRDA, and the U.S. Court of Appeals affirmed. It not only agreed that the rule violated that part of the LMRDA which prohibited unions from limiting the rights of its members to institute an action in a court or an agency, but also found that the rule violated the "freedom of speech and assembly" provision of the LMRDA. The U.S. Supreme Court granted certiorari.

The Supreme Court held that the rule did not violate the LMRDA. The purpose of the rule was to ensure 1) that nonmembers would not unduly influence union affairs, and 2) that union leaders would remain responsive to the membership. This was a legitimate purpose. The freedom of speech and assembly provision was also not to be afforded all the protections of the First Amendment. Further, the rule did not violate the right-to-sue provision of the LMRDA. Where a union member used funds from outsiders to finance litigation that was campaign-related, the rule simply did not apply. Accordingly, the Court reversed the lower courts' decisions and remanded the case. *United Steelworkers of America v. Sadlowski*, 457 U.S. 102, 102 S.Ct. 2339, 72 L.Ed.2d 707 (1982).

The LMRDA provides union members with certain rights that are enforceable in federal court. The supervising of new elections, however, is a responsibility that belongs exclusively to the Secretary of Labor.

A union held a meeting to nominate candidates for its executive board. Admission to the meeting was restricted to those union members who had receipts indicating that they had paid their union dues. Several union members were prohibited from entering the meeting because they did not bring their receipts. During the meeting, there was a disagreement as to one of the offices up for election. Protests were filed with the union, but they were denied. After the election ballots were distributed (to be mailed back a month later), several union members filed suit against the union seeking a preliminary injunction to stop the election. They claimed that union officers had violated Title I of the LMRDA, which provides union members with an exhaustive "Bill of Rights" enforceable in court. A federal court found that the interrupted election was invalid and set forth detailed procedures to be followed in a new election. The U.S. Court of Appeals affirmed, and appeal was taken to the U.S. Supreme Court.

On appeal, the Court noted that Title I only authorized "appropriate relief" for violations. The Court then stated that the district court had overstepped the bounds of "appropriate relief" under Title I when it halted the ongoing election and ordered a new one conducted pursuant to procedures that it imposed. Only if the remedy needed to eliminate the claimed violation is appropriate will a Title I suit be allowed during the course of an election. Here, the district court's order had directly interfered with responsibilities that belonged exclusively to the Secretary of Labor (the supervising of new elections). Further, the order was inconsistent with the basic objectives of the LMRDA enforcement scheme. Accordingly, the Court reversed the lower court decisions and remanded the case. *Local No. 82, Furniture & Piano Moving, Furniture Store Drivers, Helpers, Warehousemen and Packers v. Crowley*, 467 U.S. 526, 104 S.Ct. 2557, 81 L.Ed.2d 457 (1984).

Section 101 of the LMRDA, 29 U.S.C. § 401 *et seq.*, **grants free speech and assembly rights to union members, but allows unions to make reasonable rules regarding conduct that would interfere with the performance of their contractual obligations. Because § 101 has no express statute of limitations for actions brought under it, the Supreme Court determined that the applicable statute of limitations should be state general or residual personal injury statutes of limitations.**

A union officer received reimbursement from the local union for "time lost" carrying out his union duties. After an audit, the union's president disallowed the payments, ruling that, because he had failed to obtain prior approval for them and because his salary as an officer was intended to cover all his official duties, he was not entitled to them. However, other officials received similar payments. Threatening to sue, the union official alleged that more strict standards had been applied to his reimbursement claim because he had been critical of the local's president. He did not bring the suit, though, until two years later, alleging at that time that he had been harassed for expressing his views on union matters in violation of § 101 of the LMRDA. The union and its officers moved to dismiss the suit as untimely, but the district court denied the motion. The U.S. Court of Appeals reversed, and the U.S. Supreme Court granted certiorari.

The Court held that because § 101 did not have a specific statute of limitations, claims brought under it would be governed by state general or residual personal injury statutes of limitations. Since to use the state statutes would not frustrate or interfere with federal policy, the state statutes would be used. Further, since the North Carolina statute of limitations for personal injury actions was three years, the suit had been timely filed. The Court reversed the court of appeals' decision. *Reed v. United Transp. Union*, 488 U.S. 319, 109 S.Ct. 621, 102 L.Ed.2d 665 (1989).

In the following case, the Supreme Court held that the removal of a local union official, in retaliation for statements made at a union meeting, violated the LMRDA.

A local union in the midst of a financial crisis asked the international union for help. A trustee was sent to put the local back on sound economic ground. At a special meeting set up to vote on a dues increase, one of the local's officials voiced opposition to the increase because the trustee would not commit to lowering expenditures. After the vote for a dues increase failed, the trustee removed the elected official because of his outspoken opposition to the increase in union dues. In a federal court, the official challenged his removal as violative of his free speech rights under the LMRDA. The court ruled for the international, but the U.S. Court of Appeals reversed.

On further appeal, the U.S. Supreme Court held that the removal of the elected union official, in retaliation for the statements he made at the dues meeting, violated the LMRDA. It not only interfered with his Title I rights— which protected him if he spoke out against the union leadership—but it also denied the members who voted for him the representative of their choice, chilling their Title I free speech rights as well. The Court affirmed the court of appeals' decision, holding that the official's statements were entitled to protection, and that the removal was invalid even though it was carried out during a trusteeship that was lawfully imposed. *Sheet Metal Workers' International Ass'n v. Lynn*, 488 U.S. 347, 109 S.Ct. 639, 102 L.Ed.2d 700 (1989).

In the following case, a union member who alleged that he was the victim of personal vendettas of two union officers (who failed to refer him for employment because he supported one of their political rivals) did not state a valid claim against the union under the LMRDA. The actions of the officers could not be attributed to the union. However, the Court held that the union member had stated a valid claim for breach of the duty of fair representation. Such a claim is not equal to an unfair labor practice claim.

A local union operated a hiring hall through which it referred both members and nonmembers for construction work. A union member brought suit against the union for violating its duty of fair representation by passing him over in making job referrals and in refusing to honor the employer requests for his services—all because he supported a rival business manager candidate. He also alleged that the union violated the LMRDA by its actions. A federal district court dismissed the suit as outside its jurisdiction, and the U.S. Court of Appeals affirmed. The U.S. Supreme Court granted review. The Court first held that the district court did not lack jurisdiction over the suit. Further, the union member stated a valid claim of breach of the duty of fair representation. However, the failure of the business manager and business agent to refer him for employment could not be attributed to the union for the purpose of maintaining a claim under §§ 101(a)(5) and 609 of the LMRDA. Here, it was not the union that was attempting to discipline the member for his political convictions; it was only individual officers who allegedly did so. Also, the Court noted that the fair representation claim did not require a concomitant claim against an employer for breach of contract; whatever an employer's liability, the union member would still have a legal claim against the union. The Court reversed in part the lower courts and remanded the case. *Breininger v. Sheet Metal Workers International Ass'n Local Union No. 6,* 493 U.S. 67, 110 S.Ct. 424, 107 L.Ed.2d 388 (1989).

Section 401(c) of the LMRDA places every union under a duty to comply with all reasonable requests of any candidate for union office "to distribute by mail or otherwise at the candidate's expense campaign literature." The Supreme Court held that § 401(c) did not require a court to evaluate the reasonableness of a union rule prohibiting pre-convention mailings before deciding whether a candidate's request was reasonable.

An unsuccessful candidate for a union office in prior years notified the union that he would be a candidate again in the upcoming election. He requested that he be provided with mailing labels so that he could mail out election literature before the union's nominating convention. The union denied his request. It stated that a union rule prohibited such pre-convention mailings. Thereafter, the candidate filed suit under § 401(c) of the LMRDA, asserting that the union had breached its duty to comply with his reasonable request. A federal district court granted a preliminary injunction in favor of the candidate, and the U.S. Court of Appeals affirmed. On further appeal, the U.S. Supreme Court held that § 401(c) did not require a court to evaluate the reasonableness of a union rule before deciding whether a candidate's request was reasonable. So long as the request was reasonable, it had to be complied with. Here, the candidate intended to mail the election literature at his own expense. Therefore, his request was reasonable even though it conflicted with a union rule. Accordingly, the union should have distributed the mailing labels per the candidate's request. The Court affirmed the lower courts' decisions. *International Organization of Masters, Mates & Pilots v. Brown,* 498 U.S. 466, 111 S.Ct. 880, 112 L.Ed.2d 991 (1991).

In *Wooddell*, the Court held that a union member who brought suit under the LMRDA was entitled to a jury trial even though he was seeking injunctive relief as well as money damages. The injunctive relief was incidental to the damages. The Court also found that § 301 of the LMRA was not limited to suits brought by a party to an inter-union contract, and that an individual union member could sue on such a contract.

A member of a local electrical union sued both it and its officers in a federal district court. He asserted that, because of his opposition to proposed union actions, they had discriminated against him with respect to certain job referrals. This would be a violation of the LMRDA. He also alleged that their conduct breached the LMRA by violating the union's constitution and bylaws, which amounted to breaches of contract redressable under § 301. The district court dismissed all the claims, and the U.S. Court of Appeals affirmed in part, reversing the dismissal of the LMRDA claim. The U.S. Supreme Court then agreed to hear the case. The Court first held that the union member was entitled to a jury trial on the LMRDA action. Even though he sought injunctive relief as well as damages, the court compared a LMRDA action to a personal injury action for which a jury trial right existed. Further, the federal courts had jurisdiction to hear suits brought under the LMRA against unions by individual members. Here, even though the union member's suit under the LMRA was a third-party suit seeking to enforce a contract between the local and international union, § 301 of the LMRA did not limit itself to suits by the contracting parties. His suit was governed by federal law. The Court reversed the court of appeals' decision and remanded the case. *Wooddell v. International Brotherhood of Electrical Workers, Local 71,* 502 U.S. 93, 112 S.Ct. 494, 116 L.Ed.2d 419 (1991).

V. OCCUPATIONAL SAFETY AND HEALTH ACT (OSH ACT)

The Occupational Safety and Health Act of 1970, 29 U.S.C. 651 *et seq.*, authorizes the Secretary of Labor to promulgate federal occupational safety and health standards. Under the OSH Act, employers must provide a place of employment that is "free from recognized hazards that are causing or are likely to cause death or serious physical harm." Employers' duties are of two kinds: first is the general duty to provide a safe work environment, and second is the specific duty to conform to particular health and safety standards which are set forth by the Secretary of Labor. In the following case, the Court found that it was permissible to use an agency to adjudicate violations of the OSH Act.

Several companies were cited by the Secretary of Labor for violations of the OSH Act. The companies contested the citations and were granted hearings before an administrative law judge (ALJ). After the hearings, the companies' violations were upheld, and immediate abatement of the hazards was ordered. The companies sought review before different circuits of the U.S. Court of Appeals, challenging the factual findings of the ALJ as well as the constitutionality of the OSH Act's enforcement procedures. The appellate courts affirmed the Occupational Safety and Health Review Commission's orders, and the cases came before the U.S. Supreme Court. The Court held that using an agency to adjudicate violations of the OSH Act did not violate the Seventh Amendment right to a trial by jury. Here, Congress had created new statutory "public rights," which could be enforced and adjudicated by an ALJ. This did not interfere with the command of the Seventh Amendment, which preserved jury trials for "suits at common law." Accordingly, the appellate courts' decisions upholding the commission's orders were affirmed. The companies had to abate their hazards and pay their fines. *Atlas Roofing Co., Inc. v. Occupational Safety and Health Review Comm'n,* 430 U.S. 442, 97 S.Ct. 1261, 51 L.Ed.2d 464 (1977).

Under the OSH Act, employees cannot be required to perform certain tasks if they have a reasonable apprehension of death or serious injury and a reasonable belief that no less drastic alternatives are available. Nor can they be discriminated against for refusing to perform such tasks.

Two employees of a corporation refused to perform their usual maintenance duties on a suspended wire-mesh screen that hung about 20 feet above the plant floor. They believed the screen was unsafe (and, in fact, one fatality had already resulted from an employee's fall through an old part of the screen). The corporation suspended the employees, and placed written reprimands in their files. The Secretary of Labor then brought suit against the corporation for discriminating against its employees in violation of the OSH Act. The district court held for the corporation, but the U.S. Court of Appeals reversed. The case reached the U.S. Supreme Court.

The Court held that the regulation that allowed an employee to choose not to perform an assigned task because of a reasonable apprehension of death or serious injury (coupled with a reasonable belief that no less drastic alternative was available) was valid. Here, the employees had exercised their rights under the OSH Act, and the corporation had taken adverse actions against them. The regulation involved here helped effectuate the general duty clause of the OSH Act, which requires employers to provide a place of employment free from recognized hazards that are likely to cause serious injury or death. The Court affirmed the court of appeals' decision, thus requiring the corporation to pay the employees for the period of time they were suspended, and to pull the reprimands from their files. *Whirlpool Corp. v. Marshall,* 445 U.S. 1, 100 S.Ct. 883, 63 L.Ed.2d 154 (1980).

Before the Secretary of Labor can set specific standards (for example, with respect to exposure limits to various substances) appropriate findings must be made to support those standards. The secretary cannot simply create a standard arbitrarily.

The Occupational Safety and Health Act gives the Secretary of Labor broad authority to promulgate standards to ensure safe and healthful working conditions. With respect to carcinogens, the position was taken that no safe exposure level could be determined, and that the OSH Act required the exposure limit to be set at the lowest technologically feasible level that would not impair the viability of the industries regulated. The secretary then lowered the benzene exposure limit to one part per million, causing benzene producers to challenge the standard. The U.S. Court of Appeals held the standard to be invalid, and the U.S. Supreme Court granted certiorari.

The Court determined that the court of appeals had correctly refused to enforce the one ppm exposure limit because it was not supported by appropriate findings. Here, the secretary had not made a finding that the workplace was "unsafe" before creating the standard. The Court noted that "safe" is not the equivalent of "risk-free." There must be a significant risk of harm before a workplace can be termed "unsafe." Even though certain assumptions indicated that the number of leukemia cases might be reduced by lowering the exposure level from ten ppm to one ppm, there had never been a finding that leukemia was caused by exposure to ten ppm of benzene. The Court affirmed the court of appeals' decision, holding that the secretary had exceeded his power in setting the new standard. *Industrial Union Dep't v. American Petroleum Institute,* 448 U.S. 607, 100 S.Ct. 2844, 65 L.Ed.2d 1010 (1980).

Section 6(b)(5) of the Occupational Safety and Health Act, 29 U.S.C. § 655(b)(5), requires the setting of safety and health standards "to the extent feasible" to assure that employees will not suffer a material impairment to their health. When standards are being set, no cost-benefit analysis needs to be made to determine the reasonableness of the standards. Health concerns take precedence over economic concerns.

The Occupational Safety and Health Act requires the promulgation of safety and health standards with respect to exposure to toxic materials or harmful physical agents. Under the Act, the Secretary of Labor must set the standard "which most adequately assures, to the extent feasible, on the basis of the best available evidence," that no employee will suffer a material impairment of his or her health. After the secretary promulgated a cotton dust standard—to limit occupational exposure to cotton dust—representatives of the cotton industry sued to challenge the standard. They claimed that the OSH Act required a standard that reflected a reasonable relationship between the costs and benefits associated with the standard (the estimated cost of compliance with the standard was $656 million). The U.S. Court of Appeals upheld the standard, and appeal was taken to the U.S. Supreme Court.

The Supreme Court held that the OSH Act did not require a cost-benefit analysis in the promulgation of a standard because a feasibility analysis was required. Congress placed the "benefit" of workers' health above all other considerations except those that made attainment of this "benefit" unachievable. The Court also applied the substantial evidence test wherein the secretary's determinations would be conclusive if supported by substantial evidence in the record considered as a whole. Finally, the Court noted that when the secretary required, as part of the regulations, the transfer of employees unable to wear respirators to other available positions with safe exposure limits and with no loss of earnings or other employment rights and benefits, the Occupational Safety and Health Administration had failed to make the necessary determination or statement of reasons that this requirement was related to the achievement of health and safety goals. The Court affirmed in part the appellate court's decision. *American Textile Manufacturers Institute, Inc. v. Donovan,* 452 U.S. 490, 101 S.Ct. 2478, 69 L.Ed.2d 185 (1981).

Procedurally, an employer has 15 days after issuance of an OSHA citation in which to contest it. (Employees also have 15 days to challenge "the period of time fixed in the citation for the abatement of the violation" as unreasonable.) If an employer contests a citation and the Secretary of Labor wishes to enforce it, the secretary must file a complaint with the Occupational Safety and Health Review Commission within 20 days. The employer then has 15 days to file an answer. In the following case, after all this was accomplished, the secretary sought to vacate the citation, and the Supreme Court held that he had unreviewable discretion to do so.

In the Supreme Court case of *Cuyahoga Valley Railway Co. v. United Transp. Union*, 474 U.S. 3, 106 S.Ct. 286, 88 L.Ed.2d 2 (1985), a railway company was cited for a violation of the OSH Act. However, when it contested the citation, the Secretary of Labor moved to vacate the citation as not within his jurisdiction. The railway employees' union objected to the withdrawal. When the issue reached the U.S. Supreme Court, the Court stated that the secretary has unreviewable discretion to withdraw a citation against an employer.

Section 210(a) of the Energy Reorganization Act of 1974 makes it unlawful for a nuclear industry employer to retaliate against an employee for reporting safety violations. In the following case, an employee was discharged after reporting safety violations. The Supreme Court held that her lawsuit against the employer for intentional infliction of emotional distress was not preempted by § 210(a).

A laboratory technician at a nuclear-fuels production facility complained to management and to the Nuclear Regulatory Commission about perceived violations of nuclear safety standards. When the company did not adequately address her concerns, she deliberately failed to clean some contamination left by a previous work shift. She outlined the contaminated areas with red tape, then pointed them out to her supervisor a few days later (when they still had not been cleaned). Her employer then discharged her for her knowing failure to clean up radioactive contamination. After unsuccessfully pursuing an administrative remedy, the technician sued her employer in federal district court for intentional infliction of emotional distress. The court dismissed her claim as conflicting with § 210(a) of the Energy Reorganization Act. The U.S. Court of Appeals, Fourth Circuit, affirmed, and the case reached the U.S. Supreme Court.

The Supreme Court held that the technician's claim was not preempted by § 210(a). This section was primarily intended to protect employees even though it did bear some relation to the field of nuclear safety. Accordingly, not all state law claims arising from the section were included in the field (nuclear safety), which Congress intended to preempt. The Court reversed the court of appeals' decision and remanded the case for a trial on the merits. *English v. General Electric Co.*, 496 U.S. 72, 110 S.Ct. 2270, 110 L.Ed.2d 65 (1990).

In *Martin v. OSHRC*, the Supreme Court determined that where the Secretary of Labor and the Occupational Safety and Health Review Commission each have reasonable but conflicting interpretations of an ambiguous regulation promulgated by the secretary under the OSH Act, reviewing courts should defer to the secretary's interpretation.

A steel corporation equipped 28 of its employees with respirators that failed an "atmospheric test." The test was designed to ascertain whether such respirators were sufficiently tight so as to protect the wearers from carcinogenic emissions. As a result, some employees were exposed to coke-oven emissions exceeding the regulatory limit. A compliance officer, under the direction of the Secretary of Labor, issued a citation to the steel company for violating an OSH Act regulation. The company contested the citation, and the Occupational Safety and Health Review Commission vacated the citation because the officer had cited the wrong regulation. The secretary appealed to the U.S. Court of Appeals, Tenth Circuit, which affirmed the commission's order. The secretary then sought review from the U.S. Supreme Court.

The question before the Court was to whom should a reviewing court defer when the secretary and the commission have reasonable but conflicting interpretations of an ambiguous regulation promulgated by the secretary. The Court decided that it would defer to the secretary, who is more likely to develop the expertise relevant to assessing the effect of a particular regulatory interpretation. The Court thus reversed the court of appeals' decision and remanded the case for a determination of whether the secretary's interpretation was reasonable. *Martin v. OSHRC*, 499 U.S. 144, 111 S.Ct. 1171, 113 L.Ed.2d 117 (1991).

The Supreme Court held that a state law which "directly, substantially, and specifically" regulates occupational safety and health makes it an "occupational standard" for purposes of preemption analysis even if it also has a non-occupational impact. Accordingly, such a law is preempted by the OSH Act, unless the state has obtained approval of its law from the Secretary of Labor.

The Occupational Safety and Health Administration created regulations that set standards for the initial and routine training of workers who handle hazardous wastes. Subsequently, the state of Illinois enacted two laws requiring the licensing of workers at certain hazardous waste facilities. The state laws had specific training and examination requirements that were at odds with the federal requirements. An association of businesses involved in hazardous waste management then brought suit in a federal district court, seeking to enjoin the Illinois Environmental Protection Agency from enforcing the state laws. The court held that the state laws were not preempted by federal law, but the U.S. Court of Appeals only affirmed in part, holding that the OSH Act preempts all state law that "constitutes, in a direct, clear and substantial way, regulation of worker health and safety" unless the Secretary of Labor explicitly approves the law. Before the U.S. Supreme Court, that decision was affirmed. The Court stated that Illinois' licensing acts were preempted by the OSH Act to the extent that they established occupational safety and health standards for training those who worked with hazardous wastes. The fact that the state laws had other non-occupational purposes, such as public safety, was not enough to save them from preemption by the Act. Accordingly, the Illinois EPA could not enforce the state laws against the association. *Gade v. National Solid Wastes Management Ass'n*, 505 U.S. 88, 112 S.Ct. 2374, 120 L.Ed.2d 73 (1992).

Where a mining company sought to prevent enforcement of regulations under the Mine Safety Health Amendments Act, 30 U.S.C. § 801 et seq., the Supreme Court held that a federal district court could not exercise jurisdiction over the challenge. The statutory review procedures did not deprive the mining company of due process.

The federal Mine Safety Health Amendments Act of 1977, 30 U.S.C. § 801 et seq., was enacted to protect the health and safety of coal miners. Under the act, the Secretary of Labor may designate an agent to conduct unannounced health and safety inspections of mines. Mine operators are authorized to accompany the secretary's agent during inspections. Miners may designate their own representatives under the act. A Wyoming surface coalmine that was subject to the act employed about 500 nonunion miners. The miners selected two non-employees as their representatives for the walk around inspection. The representatives worked for the United Mine Workers of America (UMWA). The mining company refused to post information concerning the representatives as required by federal regulations under the mine act. The company complained to the Mine Safety Health Administration (MSHA) that posting notice compromised its rights to exclude union organizers from its property under the National Labor Relations Act and violated principles of collective bargaining. The U.S. District Court for the District of Wyoming granted the company's request for a preliminary injunction preventing the MSHA from enforcing the regulation. The U.S. Court of Appeals, Tenth Circuit, reversed the district court decision, finding that the district court had no jurisdiction over the dispute because of the mine act's comprehensive enforcement and administrative review scheme. The mine company appealed to the U.S. Supreme Court.

The Supreme Court determined that the mine act empowered the labor secretary to control violations of health and safety standards by proposing civil penalties. The act imposed a detailed structure for reviewing violations and specified a 30-day period during which citations could be challenged. Appeals could be brought before an administrative law judge with the possibility of review by the federal Mine Safety and Health Review Commission, which had the actual authority to impose the civil penalties proposed by the secretary. Only then could mine operators resort to the federal court system by bringing an appeal to the court of appeals with the possibility of Supreme Court review. Accordingly, the court of appeals had correctly ruled that the district court was without jurisdiction to review the matter. The mine company's argument that the presence of UMWA designees at the mine presented a risk of irreparable harm was speculative. *Thunder Basin Coal Co. v. Reich*, 510 U.S. 200, 114 S.Ct. 771, 127 L.Ed.2d 29 (1994).

VI. RAILWAY LABOR ACT (RLA)

In the following case, the Supreme Court held that employees of a state-owned railroad (which was engaged in interstate commerce) could strike under the RLA even though a state law prohibited public employees from striking.

The state of New York acquired the Long Island Rail Road in 1966, after 132 years of private ownership. The railroad was engaged in interstate commerce. Subsequently, 13 years later, the union and the railroad failed to reach an agreement after conducting collective bargaining negotiations under the Railway Labor Act (RLA). After mediation efforts also failed, a 30-day cooling-off period was triggered by the RLA, after which time the union could strike, unless the Taylor Law covered the dispute (in which case the public employees would be prohibited from striking). The union sued for a declaratory judgment in federal court, asserting that the RLA applied here. The court agreed with the union, rejecting the railroad's argument that applying the RLA would be inconsistent with *National League of Cities v. Usery*, 426 U.S. 833, 96 S.Ct. 2465, 49 L.Ed.2d 245 (1976)—where it was held that Congress could not impose the requirements of the Fair Labor Standards Act on state and local governments. The U.S. Court of Appeals reversed.

On further appeal to the U.S. Supreme Court, the Court held that the RLA applied to the state-owned railroad. This did not impair the state's "ability to carry out its constitutionally preserved sovereign function" under the Tenth Amendment. The Court noted that operation of a railroad engaged in interstate commerce was not an integral part of traditional state activities generally immune from federal regulation. Here, the state knew that the railroad was subject to such regulation, and in fact had accepted it for 13 years without claiming that its traditional sovereignty had been impaired. Accordingly, it was the RLA, and not the Taylor Law, which applied here; the union could strike. *United Transp. Union v. Long Island Rail Road Co.*, 455 U.S. 678, 102 S.Ct. 1349, 71 L.Ed.2d 547 (1982).

The Railway Labor Act, 45 U.S.C. § 151 *et seq.*, does not expressly address what role a minority union is entitled to play in company-level grievance and discipline proceedings. However, the Supreme Court has held that a railroad employee is not entitled, under the RLA, to be represented at company-level grievance or disciplinary proceedings by a union other than his or her collective bargaining representative.

An engineer employed by a railroad belonged to the United Transportation Union (UTU). However, the collective bargaining agent for railroad engineers was another union. When the engineer was charged with a violation of company work rules, he requested that the UTU be allowed to represent him at the internal disciplinary hearing. The request was denied. He then represented himself and received a 30-day suspension. Following that, he sued the railroad and the majority union, contending that his rights under the RLA had been violated because the UTU was not allowed to represent him. The district court and the U.S. Court of Appeals ruled against him, and the case then reached the U.S. Supreme Court. The Court held that the engineer was not entitled to have the UTU represent him at company-level proceedings. The other union could adequately represent him. Further, if the dispute was not resolved at that level, the UTU could represent the engineer in an appeal to the National Railroad Adjustment Board. The Court affirmed the lower courts' decisions. *Landers v. National Railroad Passengers Corp.*, 485 U.S. 652, 108 S.Ct. 1440, 99 L.Ed.2d 745 (1988).

In 1989, the Supreme Court decided that the Railway Labor Act did not require an employer to lay off junior crossover employees in order to reinstate more senior striking employees at the conclusion of an economic strike. The RLA (like the NLRA) protects an employee's right to choose not to strike. Also, an employer's crossover policy (which creates incentives to avoid joining or to abandon strikes) does not constitute impermis-

sible coercion to induce union members not to remain members of the union in violation of the RLA.

After unsuccessful bargaining over wages and working conditions, and after pursuing the required dispute resolution mechanisms of the RLA, a flight attendants union went out on strike. The airline continued its operations by hiring permanent replacements along with those who had not gone out on strike or who had abandoned the strike. After the strike ended, an agreement was entered into whereby strikers who returned to work would be reinstated with their same seniority, but only as vacancies arose. The union then filed suit, contending that even if the strike was economic, the full-term strikers were entitled to displace junior crossover attendants. A federal district court denied relief to the union, but the U.S. Court of Appeals held that the less senior crossovers could be displaced. Further appeal was taken to the U.S. Supreme Court, which held that the airline was not required by the RLA to lay off the junior crossovers. Since new hires could not be displaced after an economic strike, it would be unfair to differentiate between them and junior crossovers. The airline had simply lawfully exercised its economic power during the strike. *Trans World Airlines v. Independent Federation of Flight Attendants*, 489 U.S. 426, 109 S.Ct. 1225, 103 L.Ed.2d 456 (1989).

In the event of a "major" dispute (relating to disputes over the formation of collective agreements or efforts to secure them) the RLA requires the parties to undergo a lengthy process of bargaining and mediation—maintaining the status quo until those procedures have been exhausted. A "minor" dispute (where the claim is to rights which allegedly have vested in the past, not to the acquisition of future rights) is subject to compulsory and binding arbitration. In the following case, the Supreme Court held that an employer's proposed drug screening policy gave rise to a "minor" dispute that was subject to the exclusive jurisdiction of the National Railroad Adjustment Board (or an adjustment board established by the employer and the unions).

A railroad corporation had in place a policy that required its employees to undergo periodic physical examinations and examinations upon return from leave. Occasionally, drug screening was a part of the exams. The railroad then announced a policy of including drug screening in all exams. The union challenged this policy in a federal district court, which held that the case involved a "minor dispute" under the RLA. The U.S. Court of Appeals reversed, holding that the dispute was major, and an appeal was taken to the U.S. Supreme Court. The Court noted that "major disputes seek to create contractual rights," while minor disputes seek to enforce them. Here, the employer was asserting a contractual right to take a contested action that was arguably justified by the terms of the parties' collective bargaining agreement. Thus, it was a minor dispute under the RLA. Since the railroad's arguments were not obviously insubstantial, the minor dispute came within the exclusive jurisdiction of an adjustment board. The Court reversed the court of appeals' decision, and allowed the case to go before the board. *Consolidated Rail Corp. v. Railway Labor Executives' Ass'n* 491 U.S. 299, 109 S.Ct. 2477, 105 L.Ed.2d 250 (1989).

In *Pittsburgh & Lake Erie Railroad Co. v. RLEA*, the Supreme Court remanded the case for a determination of whether the RLA creates a duty not to strike while its dispute resolution mechanisms are underway. The Court also noted that the Norris-LaGuardia Act's prohibition against issuing injunctions in labor disputes had to give way when necessary to enforce a duty specifically imposed by another statute.

A railroad agreed to sell its assets to a newly formed subsidiary of another railroad (buyer). The buyer did not intend to assume the seller's collective bargaining contracts, needing only 250 of the 750 employees then working for the seller. The Railway Labor Executives' Association then sued to determine the seller's obligations under the RLA, and to enjoin the sale until those obligations could be met. The unions filed § 156 notices proposing extensive changes in existing agreements, and went on strike. Subsequently, the buyer obtained an exemption from the Interstate Commerce Commission (ICC), which essentially amounted to an approval of the sale, and a federal district court enjoined the work stoppage. The federal court also issued an injunction against the sale, and the U.S. Court of Appeals affirmed; however, it set aside the injunction against the strike. The U.S. Supreme Court granted review.

The Court held that the RLA did not require or authorize an injunction against the sale of the seller's assets to the buyer. Also, the § 156 notices did not obligate the seller to postpone the sale beyond the approval date set by the ICC. However, the seller did have a limited duty to bargain regarding the effects of the sale. This obligation ceased on the date for closing the sale. Next, the Court decided that the case had to be remanded for a determination as to whether the RLA created a duty not to strike while its dispute resolution mechanisms were underway. The court reversed the injunction against the sale, and vacated the judgment setting aside the injunction against the strike, remanding the case for further proceedings. *Pittsburgh & Lake Erie Railroad Co. v. RLEA,* 491 U.S. 490, 109 S.Ct. 2584, 105 L.Ed.2d 415 (1989).

In 1991, the Supreme Court held that the exemption in the Interstate Commerce Act for rail carrier consolidations worked to exempt a carrier from its legal obligations under a collective bargaining agreement made binding by the RLA.

The Interstate Commerce Commission approved applications for two railway mergers under the conditions set forth in the Interstate Commerce Act. Under that act, a carrier in such a consolidation "is exempt from the antitrust laws and from all other law, including State and municipal law, as necessary to let it carry out the transaction." The ICC exempted the railways from the provisions of collective bargaining agreements then in effect, but the U.S. Court of Appeals reversed, finding that the act did not authorize the ICC to relieve the railways from collectively bargained obligations that impeded the implementation of the mergers. The U.S. Supreme Court granted certiorari.

The Court held that the act's exemption "from all other law" included a carrier's legal obligations under a collective bargaining agreement where necessary to carry out an ICC-approved merger or transaction. Here, the RLA, which made the collective bargaining agreement binding, was superseded by the act's exemption provision. Thus, if it was necessary to breach the collective bargaining agreements in order to effectuate the mergers, then the agreements could be breached. The Court reversed the court of appeals' decision and remanded the case for further proceedings. *Norfolk and Western Railway Co. v. American Train Dispatchers Ass'n*, 499 U.S. 117, 111 S.Ct. 1156, 113 L.Ed.2d 95 (1991).

Although the RLA preempts "minor disputes" that are grounded in collective bargaining agreements, the Supreme Court held that the act did not preempt an ex-employee's state-law causes of action against an airline because they involved rights and obligations that existed independent of the CBA in effect.

A Hawaii aircraft mechanic had a Federal Aviation Administration license that authorized him to service and approve aircraft for flight. The FAA could revoke or suspend the license if he failed to perform required repairs. The mechanic recommended replacement of a part during an inspection of an aircraft. His supervisor refused to replace the part, and at the end of the shift, the mechanic refused to sign a maintenance record approving the plane for flight. The supervisor suspended the mechanic pending a termination hearing and the mechanic reported the incident to the FAA. The mechanic filed a grievance under the collective bargaining agreement between his employer and his labor union. The agreement prohibited discharge without just cause and prohibited discipline for refusing to perform work in violation of safety laws. The hearing officer recommended termination for insubordination and the employee filed a lawsuit in a Hawaii circuit court for violation of the Hawaii Whistleblower Protection Act. He also claimed that the airline had breached the collective bargaining agreement. The airline removed the action to the U.S. District Court for the District of Hawaii, which dismissed the breach of contract claim as preempted by the RLA (which covers the airline industry as well as railways). The federal court also remanded the state claims to the state trial court. The trial court dismissed the mechanic's claimed public policy violation as preempted by the RLA. The mechanic filed a second lawsuit in state court, which held that his state law claims were preempted by the RLA.

The Supreme Court of Hawaii held that the state tort actions were not preempted by the RLA. The U.S. Supreme Court granted the airline's petition for review. The Supreme Court reviewed the history of the RLA and other federal labor statutes that applied preemption analyses. It held that such statutes promoted stability in labor-management relations by offering comprehensive frameworks for resolving labor disputes. Although the RLA preempted minor disputes under collective bargaining agreements, it did not preempt substantive protections under state laws. In this case, the mechanic alleged that the airline had a state law obligation not to fire him in violation of public policy or in retaliation for whistleblowing. The RLA and other similar federal labor statutes did not preempt such state law claims. The Supreme Court affirmed the decision of the Supreme Court of Hawaii. *Hawaiian Airlines, Inc. v. Norris*, 512 U.S. 246, 114 S.Ct. 2239, 129 L.Ed.2d 203 (1994).

The Supreme Court held that time spent waiting for "deadhead transportation" to a duty site was to be classified as on-duty time, while time spent waiting for transportation from a duty site would be classified as limbo time under the Hours of Service Act.

The federal Hours of Service Act (HSA) states that railroad employees can work shifts of up to 12 consecutive hours. The employer must then allow the employee at least 10 consecutive hours off or face considerable penalties. The HSA states, at 49 U.S.C. § 21103(b)(4), that time spent in transportation to a duty assignment is on-duty time, but time spent in transportation from a duty assignment at the end of a shift is neither time on duty nor off duty. Because many railroad workers spend considerable time periods being transported from worksites, the HSA recognizes a category, known as limbo time, which applies to employees who are not working but are being transported from a worksite. This time is not assessed against the 12-hour limitation. The Federal Railroad Administration (FRA) changed a long-standing interpretation of the act pursuant to a 1992 decision by the U.S. Court of Appeals, Ninth Circuit, that declared time spent waiting to travel to be on-duty time which counted against the 12-hour prohibition. Nine major railroads filed a lawsuit in the U.S. Court of Appeals, Seventh Circuit, for review of the FRA's changed interpretation. The court agreed with the railroads and held that time spent waiting for transportation is limbo time.

The U.S. Supreme Court noted the inconsistent decisions by the Ninth and Seventh Circuits and agreed to review the matter. It stated that the HSA limits the hours a railroad employee may work to support an important policy of reducing injuries and accidents caused by employee fatigue. It treated time spent in transit to a worksite as on-duty time because this time contributed to worker fatigue. However, the HSA did not treat time spent traveling from a worksite at the end of a shift as on-duty time because there was no similar safety concern in transporting an employee to an eventual point of release from work. For the same reason, time spent waiting to be transported to a worksite should be regarded as on-duty time, which was assessed against the 12-hour limitation, while time spent waiting for transportation at the end of a shift should be treated as limbo time, which did not count against the 12-hour limit. Because this interpretation supported HSA safety goals and granted the railroads a necessary measure of flexibility, the Court affirmed the Seventh Circuit decision. *Brotherhood of Locomotive Engineers v. Atchison, Topeka & Santa Fe Railroad Co.*, 516 U.S. 152, 116 S.Ct. 595, 133 L.Ed.2d 535 (1996).

VII. OTHER IMPORTANT STATUTES

A. WARN Act

The Supreme Court rejected the notion that the six-month limitations period of the NLRA should be applied in WARN Act cases. Instead, the appropriate limitations period was to be drawn from the state in which the case was venued.

The Worker Adjustment and Retraining Notification Act, 29 U.S.C. § 2101 *et seq.*, requires covered employers to serve written notice upon employees or their representatives 60 days in advance of a plant closing or mass layoff. Violation of the notice requirement may result in civil liability and employees may collect back pay for each day of the violation. The statute does not contain a limitation on actions. A manufacturing company laid off 85 employees at a plant without giving the required 60-day notice. The employees sued the company in a federal district court in Pennsylvania, which denied the employer's summary judgment motion on the basis of a state statute of limitations. The court decided that the case was not barred because the limitations period from the most appropriate analogous state law did not bar the lawsuit. Another Pennsylvania federal district court determined that the sixth-month limitations period from the National Labor Relations Act was more analogous to WARN than any state statute of limitations. Accordingly, it applied the federal statute in barring another WARN claim. The U.S. Court of Appeals, Third Circuit, consolidated the cases and determined that the applicable statute of limitations was that found in Pennsylvania law. Because this decision conflicted with the decisions of federal appeals courts in the Second, Fifth and Sixth Circuits, the U.S. Supreme Court agreed to consider the cases.

The Court observed the general rule that where Congress fails to specify a limitations period in a federal law, the appropriate statute of limitations is drawn from the state in which the case is venued. Since 1830, state laws have supplied the appropriate limitations period for such claims under federal law, except where to do so would frustrate an important congressional purpose. In this case, it was entirely appropriate to apply Pennsylvania law as the limitations period for WARN actions. The employers had set forth no reason to deviate from the general rule, and the court of appeals' decision was affirmed. *North Star Steel Co. v. Thomas*, 515 U.S. 29, 115 S.Ct. 1927, 132 L.Ed.2d. 27 (1995).

In a later case brought under the WARN Act, the Court held that a union had the authority to sue for monetary damages on behalf of its members.

A manufacturing company advised the labor union representing employees working at a Missouri plant that a permanent layoff of 277 employees would occur 60 days later. The union charged that the manufacturer had already begun the layoff in violation of the federal WARN Act, which requires covered employers to give employees or their representatives at least 60 days notice prior to a plant closing or mass layoff. An employer violating the notice requirement must pay each employee wages for each day of the violation, and unions are specifically authorized to file suit on behalf of injured employees. The union filed a WARN lawsuit for employee wages against the manufacturer in the U.S. District Court for the Eastern District of Missouri. The court dismissed the lawsuit, finding that the union could not recover monetary damages on behalf of individual union members without their participation in the lawsuit. The U.S. Court of Appeals, Eighth Circuit, affirmed the district court decision, stating that individual union members must be joined in the lawsuit in order to determine their individual claims for damages. The union appealed to the U.S. Supreme Court, which granted its petition for review.

The manufacturer argued that even though the WARN Act explicitly allows unions to recover damages on behalf of individual union members, the unions were not similarly situated to individual employees and were barred from asserting a claim by the Constitution. The Supreme Court determined that the Constitution did not prohibit Congress from conferring legal standing upon labor organizations to sue for damages on behalf of their individual members. Earlier decisions of the Court restricting monetary damage claims by representative organizations prohibited such claims as a matter of judicial convenience, and not as a constitutional prohibition. The Court reversed and remanded the decision of the court of appeals. *United Food and Commercial Workers Union Local 751 v. Brown Group, Inc.*, 517 U.S. 544, 116 S.Ct. 1529, 134 L.Ed.2d 758 (1996).

B. Civil Service Reform Act

Even though federal employees must be granted "official time" if they are involved in collective bargaining during on-duty hours, they are not entitled to a *per diem* allowance or travel expenses incurred in connection with collective bargaining.

Under the Civil Service Reform Act, federal agencies must grant "official time" to employees representing their union in collective bargaining—if they bargain during hours when they would otherwise be on duty. This allows employee negotiators to be paid for bargaining they do during working hours. The Federal Labor Relations Authority, in interpreting the act, decided that the act also authorized a *per diem* allowance and reimbursement for travel expenses incurred in connection with collective bargaining. It ordered a federal agency to pay an employee union representative *per diem* and travel expenses. The U.S. Court of Appeals, Ninth Circuit, enforced the FLRA's order, and appeal was taken to the U.S. Supreme Court.

On appeal, the Court held that the FLRA's interpretation of the act was incorrect. Even though federal law provided for a *per diem* allowance for a federal employee "traveling on official business away from his designated post of duty," employee negotiators are not on "official business" of the government when they are engaged in bargaining. The FLRA's position was not "reasonably defensible." Accordingly, the Court reversed the court of appeals' decision, holding that the employee was not entitled to *per diem* and travel expenses incurred in connection with bargaining. *Bureau of Alcohol, Tobacco and Firearms v. FLRA*, 464 U.S. 89, 104 S.Ct. 439, 78 L.Ed.2d 195 (1983).

Before the Federal Labor Relations Authority can determine whether there exists a compelling need for certain labor regulations, the specific procedures outlined in § 7117(b) of the Federal Service Labor-Management Relations Statute, 5 U.S.C. § 7117 *et seq.*, must be followed.

The Aberdeen Proving Ground notified its employees' union representatives that it intended to curtail operations for the three days following Thanksgiving; employees would thus be placed on forced annual leave. The representatives requested that the employees be granted administrative leave instead, but management maintained that the regulations did not permit this. The union then filed an unfair labor practice charge with the FLRA. An administrative law judge held for the employer because the union's proposal was inconsistent with agency regulations, and because the FLRA had not previously found that there was "no compelling need for the regulations." The FLRA held that the charge had been properly filed because the employer had undertaken a unilateral change in the conditions of employment, but the U.S. Court of Appeals reversed.

On further appeal, the U.S. Supreme Court stated that where a matter is covered by a regulation, there is no duty on the employer to bargain until the FLRA "has first determined that no compelling need justifies adherence to the regulation." Here, since there had been no such determination, the duty to bargain had not arisen. Accordingly, the FLRA could not make the "compelling need" determination in connection with the unfair labor practice proceeding. The Court affirmed the court of appeals' decision in favor of the employer. *FLRA v. Aberdeen Proving Ground, Dep't of the Army*, 485 U.S. 409, 108 S.Ct. 1261, 99 L.Ed.2d 470 (1988).

In *Karahalios*, below, the Supreme Court determined that Title VII of the Civil Service Reform Act does not create a private cause of action against a union for breach of the duty of fair representation. The FLRA and its general counsel have exclusive enforcement authority in this matter.

The Defense Language Institute (DLI) is a federal agency. A course developer for the DLI was demoted to instructor when his position was abolished. Five years later, the DLI reopened and advertised the position. The former course developer did not reapply and another instructor was awarded the job. The developer filed a grievance against the DLI, asserting that he should have been assigned the position and that there should have been no competitive application process. The developer's labor organization accepted his claim and successfully arbitrated the matter. The developer was reassigned to the job. The previously selected instructor was demoted. The employees' labor organization then refused to handle the instructor's grievance, claiming that it had a conflict of interest because it had previously represented the developer.

The instructor filed an unfair labor practice charge with the FLRA, claiming that the DLI had violated its collective bargaining agreement and that the labor organization had breached its duty of fair representation. The FLRA's general council upheld only the fair representation claim. The FLRA and labor organization reached an agreement in which the labor organization posted notice that it would represent all employees. The instructor contended that this settlement gave him no relief and sued the DLI and labor organization in a federal district court. The court dismissed the charge against the DLI but permitted the unfair labor practice charge against the labor organization as a private action for breach of the duty of fair representation. The labor organization appealed to the U.S. Court of Appeals, Ninth Circuit, which reversed the district court's decision. The court ruled that the federal Civil Service Reform Act (CSRA) created no private cause of action against the labor organization. The U.S. Supreme Court granted the instructor's petition for certiorari.

The Supreme Court ruled that although the CSRA was patterned after the NLRA, it did not imply a private right of action. Because Congress expressed no intention to provide a private legal remedy to enforce the duty of fair representation, the instructor had no recourse. Because the FLRA had final authority to issue unfair labor practice complaints, the appeals court had correctly denied the instructor's private action against the labor organization. *Karahalios v. National Federation of Federal Employees, Local 1263*, 489 U.S. 527, 109 S.Ct. 1282, 103 L.Ed.2d 539 (1989).

The Civil Service Reform Act requires management officials to bargain over certain proposals that affect conditions of employment. However, "determinations with respect to contracting out" work to the private sector are reserved to management.

The National Treasury Employees Union (NTEU) proposed that contractual grievance and arbitration provisions be designated as the internal appeals procedure required for employee complaints relating to contracting-out of work during collective bargaining negotiations. The Internal Revenue Service refused to bargain over the proposal, claiming that its subject matter was nonnegotiable under Title VII of the Civil Service Reform Act of 1978, because it limited management's rights. Only if the proposal dealt with employment conditions would the IRS be required to bargain over it. The Federal Labor Relations Authority, which is charged with administrating the act, held that the IRS was required to negotiate over the NTEU proposal because the act specifies that agreements must contain grievance settlement procedures. The IRS appealed to the U.S. Court of Appeals, D.C. Circuit. The court of appeals enforced the order in part and set it aside in part. The IRS further appealed to the U.S. Supreme Court.

The Court noted that another section of the act provided that "nothing in this act shall affect the authority of agency management officials in accordance with applicable laws to make contracting-out determinations." Since the arguments presented by the FLRA to overcome this section's plain meaning lacked merit, the Court held that the act did not require the IRS to bargain over the NTEU's proposal. Essentially, it stated that this was a "management's rights" problem which was outside the NTEU's authority to negotiate. The Court reversed the appellate court's decision. *Dep't of Treasury, I.R.S. v. FLRA*, 494 U.S. 922, 110 S.Ct. 1623, 108 L.Ed.2d 914 (1990).

Federally owned and operated schools are not allowed to refuse to negotiate matters with employees if the matters fall within "conditions of employment."

A union's collective bargaining agent who represented the employees of two schools owned and operated by the U.S. Army submitted proposals asking for mileage reimbursement, paid leave, and salary increases on behalf of the schools' employees. The schools refused to negotiate, stating that under Title VII of the Civil Service Reform Act of 1978 they were not required to negotiate these matters. The union filed a complaint with the FLRA, which held that the union's proposals were negotiable. The schools appealed to the U.S. Court of Appeals, Eleventh Circuit, which upheld the FLRA's decision. The schools then appealed to the U.S. Supreme Court.

Title VII of the Civil Service Reform Act defines conditions of employment as matters "affecting working conditions" but excludes matters relating to prohibited political activities, classification of positions, and those specifically provided for by federal statute. The Court determined that the union's proposals were "conditions of employment." The Supreme Court, affirming the appellate court's decision, held that the schools were required to negotiate salary increases and fringe benefits. *Fort Stewart Schools v. FLRA*, 495 U.S. 641, 110 S.Ct. 2043, 109 L.Ed.2d 659 (1990).

C. Federal Service Labor-Management Relations Act

The question of disclosure of federal employee names and addresses to their unions came before the Supreme Court in the case below.

Two federal employee labor organizations requested the names and addresses of all their bargaining unit employees from their respective federal agencies. After the agencies refused to divulge the requested information, the labor associations brought separate unfair labor practice complaints against them with the Federal Labor Relations Authority. In both cases the authority reversed its own initial decisions and ruled that the agencies must disclose names and home addresses to the labor organizations. The authority agreed with the labor organizations' argument that the information was necessary for collective bargaining purposes under the Federal Service Labor-Management Relations Act (FSLMRA). The agencies petitioned the U.S. Court of Appeals, Eighth Circuit, for review of the decisions, and the authority cross-petitioned for enforcement.

The court of appeals considered the cases together. It examined the FSLMRA's requirement for agency disclosure of data reasonably necessary for the collective bargaining process. It also examined the conflict between the Privacy Act, which prohibits disclosure of federal employee personnel files without consent, and the Freedom of Information Act, which generally requires disclosure of government records. The court ruled that employees had cognizable privacy interests in their home addresses, which must be weighed against the public interest in disclosure. The competing interests of privacy and disclosure could best be served by requiring disclosure of the names and addresses of those employees who did not request confidentiality. The court affirmed the authority's cross-petition in part, limiting the disclosure to those employees who consented to disclosure. The FLRA petitioned the U.S. Supreme Court for review. The Supreme Court vacated and remanded the appeals court decision because both agencies had meanwhile issued new regulations requiring disclosure of employee names and addresses where necessary for union representation. *FLRA v. U.S. Dep't of Agriculture*, 488 U.S. 1025, 109 S.Ct. 831, 102 L.Ed.2d 964 (1989).

The Privacy Act of 1974 forbids the disclosure of employee addresses to collective bargaining representatives pursuant to requests made under the Federal Service Labor-Management Relations Statute. The Privacy Act bars disclosure of records such as home addresses unless disclosure is required under the Freedom of Information Act, 5 U.S.C. § 552.

Two local unions requested various federal agencies to provide them with the names and home addresses of employees whom the unions sought to represent. The agencies refused to disclose the home addresses and the unions filed unfair labor practice charges with the Federal Labor Relations Authority. The authority required the agencies to disclose the home addresses and the agencies appealed to the U.S. Court of Appeals, Fifth Circuit. The court of appeals affirmed, holding that the Freedom of Information Act required disclosure of the home addresses. The agencies appealed to the U.S. Supreme Court. The Supreme Court noted that the Federal Service Labor-Management Relations Statute requires federal agencies to provide unions with collective bargaining data "to the extent not prohibited by law." However, the Privacy Act of 1974 prohibits agency disclosure of "records" unless disclosure is required by the FOIA. The FOIA generally requires full disclosure unless an express statutory exemption applies. Exemption six of the FOIA provides that these broad disclosure requirements do not apply to "personnel and medical files and similar files the disclosure of which would constitute a clearly unwarranted invasion of personal privacy." First, the Supreme Court determined that employee addresses were records and therefore protected by the Privacy Act. Second, the Court balanced the public interest supporting disclosure against the privacy interest of the bargaining unit employees to determine whether the disclosure of employee names and home addresses would be "unwarranted invasions of personal privacy." Here, the disclosure of employee addresses would not enhance the citizens' right "to be informed about what the government is up to." Further, the employees had substantial privacy interests in avoiding unwanted union mailings and telephone calls. The employees' privacy interest in nondisclosure outweighed the "negligible public interest in disclosure." Thus, the Privacy Act prohibited the release of employee addresses to the unions. The holding of the court of appeals was reversed. U.S. Dep't of Defense v. FLRA, 510 U.S. 487, 114 S.Ct. 1006, 127 L.Ed.2d 325 (1994).

The Supreme Court determined that the Federal Service Labor-Management Relations Statute did not automatically bar midterm bargaining in the federal sector. Nor did it automatically compel such bargaining.

The Federal Service Labor-Management Relations Statute requires federal agencies and their employees' unions to bargain in good faith and grants the FLRA certain powers to enforce such bargaining. The FLRA initially held that the statute's good-faith bargaining requirement did not extend to union-initiated proposals during the term of the basic collective bargaining agreement. After it reversed its position, a federal employees' union sought to require the Department of the Interior to negotiate, at its request, midterm matters not in the original contract. The FLRA ordered the Department to bargain over the issue, but the U.S. Court of Appeals, Fourth Circuit, set aside that order.

The Supreme Court reviewed the case and found that the statute was ambiguous about the matter. It did not absolutely prohibit the parties from engaging in midterm bargaining. Nor did it absolutely compel such bargaining. Given the fact that the law was ambiguous, the Court sent the case back to the FLRA to resolve the question of bargaining during the term of a contract. *Nat'l Federation of Federal Employees, Local 1309 v. Dep't of Interior*, 526 U.S. 86, 119 S.Ct. 1003, 143 L.Ed.2d 171 (1999).

VIII. UNION ACTIVITIES

A. Agency Fees

In 1977, the Court ruled that the First Amendment prohibited states from compelling teachers to pay union dues or agency fees where their labor unions used the fees for purposes unrelated to collective bargaining.

Michigan authorized local government employees to select collective bargaining representatives. When labor unions and government employees agreed, "agency shops" were instituted so that, as a condition of employment, all bargaining unit employees were required to pay either union dues or an equivalent agency fee. Detroit teachers elected a labor association to become its exclusive collective bargaining representative, and instituted an agency shop agreement. All bargaining unit employees were to pay either union dues or the agency fee within 60 days of employment. Failure to pay this amount resulted in termination. Teachers were not otherwise required to participate in union activities. A group of teachers filed a class action lawsuit in a Michigan trial court, stating that they would not pay dues for agency fees because of their opposition to collective bargaining in the public sector. They specifically disapproved of the union's political and social activities, which they claimed were unrelated to the collective bargaining process.

The teachers argued that the agency's shop agreement violated state law and the First and Fourteenth Amendments to the U.S. Constitution. The court dismissed the lawsuit for failure to state a claim upon which relief could be granted. While the matter was pending before the Michigan Court of Appeals, the case was consolidated with the complaint of another group of teachers. At about the same time the Michigan legislature expressly authorized the agency shops by amending the state Public Employment Relations Act. The court of appeals then held that the amendment applied retroactively to the teachers, who argued that retroactive application violated the U.S. Constitution. When the Michigan Supreme Court refused to review the case the U.S. Supreme Court accepted jurisdiction on the federal constitutional complaints.

The Supreme Court drew on its earlier private sector decisions concerning labor relations and noted that compelled support of collective bargaining representatives implicated teacher First Amendment rights to free speech and association and religious freedom where individual teachers objected to union policies. However, some constitutional infringement on free speech, association and religious exercise was justified in the interest of peaceful labor relations. The interest in preserving peaceful labor relations was just as strong in the public sector as in the private sector, and the Court upheld the Michigan act. Public employees had no greater rights than private sector employees in avoiding compelled union contributions. The Court agreed with the teachers that compelled agency fees should not be used to support political views and candidates that were unrelated to collective bargaining issues. Because the state court had dismissed the case without a trial, the teachers had not had the opportunity to make specific allegations that their contributions were being used to support activities with which they disagreed. There was no evidentiary record and the Court remanded the case, vacating the court of appeal's decision. If the teachers could prove a First Amendment violation, they were entitled to relief in the form of an injunction from expending their contributions for ideological causes which the teachers opposed, or a *pro rata* refund of fees being used for such purposes. *Abood v. Detroit Bd. of Educ.*, 431 U.S. 209, 97 S.Ct. 1782, 52 L.Ed.2d 261 (1977).

Nonunion employees who pay agency fees under a compelled contribution program need not pay more than their *pro rata* share of the expenses of negotiating agreements and settling grievances. They do not have to help pay for union political or ideological activities.

An airline and a union implemented an agreement in 1971 that required all of the airline's clerical employees join the union within 60 days of commencing employment. This was permitted by the Railway Labor Act. Under the agreement, the employees did not have to become formal members of the union, but they did have to pay agency fees equal to members' dues. A group of employees subsequently brought a lawsuit against the union, challenging the use of their compelled dues for specified union activities, namely: a convention, litigation not involving the negotiation of agreements or settlement of grievances, union publications, social activities, death benefits for employees, and general organizing efforts. A federal district court found that the union could not spend the objecting employees' money on these activities, but it held that the union could collect the money in advance, use it, and then refund the portion attributable to these activities. The U.S. Court of Appeals affirmed in part, but decided that the six challenged activities ultimately benefited the union's collective bargaining efforts. Thus, the activities could be financed by dues collected from objecting employees.

On further appeal to the U.S. Supreme Court, the Court determined that the rebate approach used by the union (refunding that part of the dues expended for improper purposes) was inadequate. There were other acceptable alternatives that could be used, such as the advance reduction of dues. The court then looked to the challenged expenditures to ascertain whether they were necessarily or reasonably incurred for the purpose of performing the duties of an exclusive representative of the employees in dealing with the employer on labor-management issues. The Court found that convention expenses were necessary as they were central to collective bargaining. Also, the costs of union social activities and union publications (insofar as they reported on appropriate activities) could be charged to the objecting employees. The other activities could not be charged to the objecting employees. The Court thus affirmed in part and reversed in part the court of appeals' decision. *Ellis v. Brotherhood of Railway, Airline and Steamship Clerks*, 466 U.S. 435, 104 S.Ct. 1883, 80 L.Ed.2d 428 (1984).

When a school board and a teachers' union make an agency shop agreement which allows union dues to be deducted from the paychecks of nonunion teachers, the union must provide for a reasonably prompt decision by an impartial decision-maker as to whether the deductions are being used properly. This requirement was imposed by the U.S. Supreme Court in instances where a school board compels nonmember employees to support their collective bargaining representative.

Although the Supreme Court held in *Abood v. Detroit Bd. of Educ.*, above, that nonunion teachers could be compelled to pay a "service fee" to the union to help defray the cost of contract administration and grievance handling, the court prohibited the use of such funds by the union for political or ideological activities not germane to the union's duties as collective bargaining agent. This prohibition was designed to prevent any infringement of nonmember teachers' free speech rights in being forced to fund political causes with which they might disagree. The Supreme Court found that the Chicago Teachers Union had not adequately protected the free speech rights of nonunion teachers. In 1982, the Chicago school board and the teachers' union agreed to deduct "proportionate share payments" from the paychecks of any nonunion employee. The deduction was fixed at 95 percent of the dues for union members, and no explanation was given as to how that figure was reached. This method of deduction was held to violate First Amendment freedom of speech protections. To guard against the possibility of nonunion teachers' service fee payments being used for political purposes disagreeable to the nonmember, the Supreme Court ruled that there must be an adequate accounting and explanation of the basis for the deduction. In case of challenge there must be an opportunity for a reasonably prompt decision by an impartial decision-maker as to whether any part of the service fee deduction has gone to fund political causes. Any amount reasonably in dispute must be held in an escrow account during the challenge. *Chicago Teachers Union v. Hudson*, 475 U.S. 292, 106 S.Ct. 1066, 89 L.Ed.2d 232 (1986).

Section 8(a)(3) of the NLRA permits an employer and a union to enter into an agreement requiring all employees in the bargaining unit to pay union dues as a condition of continued employment, whether or not the employees become union members. However, § 8(a)(3) does not permit a union, over the objections of dues-paying nonmember employees, to spend money collected from them on noncollective bargaining activities.

Under a collective bargaining agreement, employees of a company who chose not to become union members were required to pay the union "agency fees" to be represented by it in collective bargaining. A group of these employees initiated a lawsuit against the union, challenging its use of agency fees for purposes other than collective bargaining. A federal district court found that such expenditures violated the First Amendment rights of nonmembers, and enjoined the collection of fees for purposes other than collective bargaining. The U.S. Court of Appeals agreed that the excess fees could not be collected, but based its ruling on § 8(a)(3) of the National Labor Relations Act. The case reached the U.S. Supreme Court. The Court affirmed the court of appeals' decision, finding that § 8(a)(3) did not permit a union to expend funds collected from nonmember employees, over objection, on activities unrelated to collective bargaining. *Communications Workers of America v. Beck*, 487 U.S. 735, 108 S.Ct. 2641, 101 L.Ed.2d 634 (1988).

In *Lehnert*, **below, the Court noted that chargeable activities must be: 1) germane to collective bargaining activity, 2) justified by the government's interest in labor peace and the avoidance of free riders, and 3) only insignificantly adding to the burdening of free speech that is inherent in the allowance of an agency or union shop.**

A local teachers union, the exclusive bargaining representative of the faculty at a state college in Michigan, entered into an agency-shop arrangement with the college, requiring nonunion bargaining unit employees to pay a service fee equivalent to a union member's dues. Employees who objected to particular uses by the unions of their service fee brought suit under 42 U.S.C. § 1983, claiming that using the fees for purposes other than negotiating and administering the collective bargaining agreement violated their First and Fourteenth Amendment rights. A federal court held that certain expenses were chargeable to the dissenting employees, the U.S. Court of Appeals affirmed, and the U.S. Supreme Court granted certiorari. The Court first noted that chargeable activities must be "germane" to collective bargaining activity and be justified by the policy interest of avoiding "free riders" who benefit from union efforts without paying for union services. It then stated that the local union could charge the objecting employees for their *pro rata* share of costs associated with chargeable activities of its state and national affiliates, even if those activities did not directly benefit the local bargaining unit. The local could even charge the dissenters for expenses incident to preparation for a strike that would be illegal under Michigan law. However, lobbying activities and public relations efforts were not chargeable to the objecting employees. The Court affirmed in part and reversed in part the lower courts' decisions and remanded the case. *Lehnert v. Ferris Faculty Ass'n*, 500 U.S. 507, 111 S.Ct. 1950, 114 L.Ed.2d 572 (1991).

In the case below, the Supreme Court held that employees can not be compelled to arbitrate agency fee assessments in absence of an arbitration agreement.

The collective bargaining agreement between a commercial airline and the union representing its pilots included an agency shop clause under which each pilot who was not a union member was required to pay the union a monthly agency fee. The fee was based only on expenditures attributable to collective bargaining and was equal to 81 percent of the amount of full union dues. A number of nonunion pilots filed a federal district court action against the union, asserting that the agency shop clause was unlawful. The court denied their motion for a preliminary order and the union began collecting fees. The dissenting pilots claimed that the agency fee overstated collective bargaining expenses and amended their complaint to contest the method of calculating the fee. Union policies and procedures provided for the arbitration of fee calculations, but the collective bargaining agreement did not specify arbitration. The union treated objections to the fee calculation as requests for arbitration and referred them to an arbitrator, who consolidated the cases and recalculated the agency fee. The union moved the court for summary judgment, asserting that the pilots were required to exhaust their arbitral remedies before filing suit. The court agreed with the union, finding that 62 pilots who had not joined the arbitration were bound by the decision. The U.S. Court of Appeals, District of Columbia Circuit, reversed the decision, and the union appealed to the U.S. Supreme Court.

The Court observed that the parties had not appealed the lower court's decision applying the procedural requirements of *Chicago Teachers Union v. Hudson*, 475 U.S. 292, 106 S.Ct. 1066, 89 L.Ed.2d 232 (1986), a public employment case requiring public employee unions to provide objecting employees a reasonably prompt opportunity to challenge the amount of an agency fee by appeal to an impartial decision-maker. This rule did not require a party to accept arbitration where no arbitration agreement between the parties existed, since arbitration is a matter of contract. The requirement of an impartial decision-maker did not bar the dissenting pilots' immediate resort to federal district court. The Court rejected the union's assertion that arbitration was necessary to assure a prompt decision by an impartial decision-maker. The Court affirmed the judgment. *Air Line Pilots Ass'n v. Miller*, 523 U.S. 866, 118 S.Ct. 1761, 140 L.Ed.2d 1070 (1998).

B. Striking

1.   Secondary Picketing

The NLRA § 8(b)(4) makes it an unfair labor practice for a labor organization to "threaten, coerce, or restrain any person" where an object thereof is to force the person to cease doing business with another. Essentially, secondary picketing which amounts to coercion of neutral parties is prohibited; primary picketing is lawful. In the following case, the Supreme Court held that the secondary picketing at issue amounted to prohibited coercive activity.

After contract negotiations between a title insurance company and its employees' union reached an impasse, the employees went on strike. They not only picketed their employer, but also five local title companies who derived over 90 percent of their gross incomes from the sale of the insurer's policies. The employer and one of the local title companies filed a complaint with the National Labor Relations Board, charging the union with an unfair labor practice by picketing to promote a secondary boycott against the local title companies. The board ordered the union to cease picketing, but the U.S. Court of Appeals set aside the board's order. The case reached the U.S. Supreme Court.

The Supreme Court reversed the appellate court's decision and remanded the case. The Court noted that the secondary picketing amounted to coercion of neutral parties with the object of forcing them to cease dealing in the primary party's product. Successful secondary picketing would force the local title companies to choose between survival and cutting their ties with the insurer. Section 8(b)(4)(ii)(B) of the NLRA barred such coercive activity. Further, application of this section of the NLRA to the picketing involved here did not violate the First Amendment. The board's order to stop the picketing had to be enforced, held the Court. *NLRB v. Retail Store Employees Union, Local 1001,* 447 U.S. 607, 100 S.Ct. 2372, 65 L.Ed.2d 377 (1980).

A union may not engage in a "political" secondary boycott against a neutral employer as a means of pressuring a foreign nation to cease its "wrongful" actions. The effect of such a boycott is to impose a heavy burden on neutral employers, and this is prohibited by the NLRA.

An American importer of Russian wood products contracted with an American shipper for delivery of the products. The shipper hired a stevedoring company to unload its ships. The stevedore's employees were members of a Longshoremen's union. After the Soviet Union invaded Afghanistan, the union refused to handle cargo arriving from or going to the Soviet Union. This boycott completely disrupted the importer's shipments as well as its business generally. The importer then sued the union under § 303 of the Labor Management Relations Act, claiming that the union's refusal to unload the importer's shipments amounted to an illegal secondary boycott under § 8(b)(4)(B) of the NLRA. A federal district court dismissed the complaint on the grounds that the union's boycott was a purely political, primary boycott of Russian goods and thus not within the scope of § 8(b)(4)(B). However, the U.S. Court of Appeals reversed.

On further appeal to the U.S. Supreme Court, the Court held that the union's boycott was an illegal secondary boycott under § 8(b)(4)(B). First, the union's activity was "in commerce" and thus within the scope of the NLRA. Second, the prohibition against secondary boycotts in § 8(b)(4)(B) applied to the facts of this case. The effect of the union's action—however commendable its objectives might have been—was to impose a heavy burden on neutral employers like the importer. This, the NLRA was designed to prevent. Further, § 8(b)(4)(B) contained no exception for political secondary boycotts. Accordingly, the boycott was in violation of the NLRA, and the Court affirmed the court of appeals' decision in favor of the importer. *International Longshoremen's Ass'n, AFL-CIO v. Allied International, Inc.,* 456 U.S. 212, 102 S.Ct. 1656, 72 L.Ed.2d 21 (1982).

2. Disciplinary Sanctions

In the following case, the Supreme Court held that union member supervisors who crossed a picket line to perform rank-and-file work could be disciplined by the union for their actions.

Certain supervisory personnel for a telephone company belonged to the same union as the rank-and-file employee members. Subsequently, the union engaged in a lawful economic strike against the company. The company asked its supervisors to cross the picket line, but left the decision to each employee, promising that it would not penalize those who chose not to work. The union, however, warned its supervisor members that it would discipline them if they crossed the picket line to perform rank-and-file work during the strike. When some supervisors crossed the line in violation of the union's warning, they were fined by the union. They brought unfair labor practice charges before the National Labor Relations Board, which found that the union's disciplining of the supervisors violated § 8(b)(1)(B) of the NLRA. The U.S. Court of Appeals denied enforcement of the board's orders, and the case reached the U.S. Supreme Court.

The Court held that the union did not commit an unfair labor practice under § 8(b)(1)(B) by disciplining its supervisor members who had crossed the picket line and performed rank-and-file work. Since the supervisors were not performing the duties of grievance adjusters or collective bargainers during the lawful economic strike, the union's action against them was not coercion of an employer's selection of its collective bargaining representatives. The Court affirmed the court of appeals' decision. *Florida Power & Light Co. v. International Brotherhood of Electrical Workers, Local 641*, 417 U.S. 790, 94 S.Ct. 2737, 41 L.Ed.2d 477 (1974).

Employers may not impose more severe sanctions on union officials than on other employees for participating in an unlawful work stoppage unless the officials have a duty (set forth in a contract) to enforce a no-strike clause by complying with the employers' directions.

Despite a no-strike clause in a collective bargaining agreement, a company's union member employees participated in four unlawful work stoppages between 1970 and 1974. On each occasion, the employer disciplined the local union officials more severely than the other participants. Twice the union filed a grievance because of the disparate treatment, but each time the arbitrator upheld the employer's actions, finding that union officials have an affirmative duty to uphold the agreement, and that the breach of that duty justified the higher sanctions. Subsequently, another union set up an informational picket line, which the local union members refused to cross. After this settled, the employer again disciplined the local union officials more severely because they failed to attempt to end the strike by crossing the picket line. An unfair labor practice charge was filed, and the National Labor Relations Board held that the selective discipline against the union officials violated the NLRA. The U.S. Court of Appeals enforced the board's order.

On further review before the U.S. Supreme Court, the Court found that, absent an explicit contractual duty to attempt to enforce a no-strike clause by complying with the employer's directions, the imposition of more severe sanctions on union officials than on other employees for participating in an unlawful work stoppage violates the NLRA. Holding a union office is a protected concerted activity. Imposing more severe sanctions against such officials inhibits qualified employees from holding office. This is a violation of the NLRA. Further, even though a union may waive the protection afforded its officials, no waiver occurred here. The two prior arbitration decisions in favor of the employer (and the union's silence after those decisions) did not amount to a binding waiver. Accordingly, the Court affirmed the court of appeals' decision against the employer. *Metropolitan Edison Co. v. NLRB*, 460 U.S. 693, 103 S.Ct. 1467, 75 L.Ed.2d 387 (1983).

When employee union members refuse to support a strike, they are refraining from "concerted activity," a right that is granted to them by § 7 of the NLRA, 29 U.S.C. § 157. In the following case, employees resigned from a union during a strike (even though the union constitution prohibited this) so that they could return to work, and the Supreme Court held that the union could not levy fines against them because of § 8(b)(1)'s anti-coercion provision.

A national union amended its constitution to provide that resignations or withdrawals from the national or its locals would not be permitted during a strike or lockout, or at a time when either appeared imminent. Ten union members violated this provision by resigning during a strike and returning to work. After the strike ended and a new collective bargaining agreement was signed, the union fined the ten employees. The employers' representative then filed charges with the National Labor Relations Board against the union, claiming that the imposition of fines was an unfair labor practice. The board agreed that it was unfair—in violation of § 8(b)(1)(A) of the NLRA—and the U.S. Court of Appeals affirmed. On further appeal, the U.S. Supreme Court held that the levying of fines against the employees here violated their § 7 rights because it coerced or restrained them from choosing not to engage in "concerted activities." Further, the Court stated that the board had justifiably concluded that by restricting the right of employees to resign from the union, the provision in question impaired the policy of voluntary unionism implicit in § 8(a)(3) of the NLRA. Finally, the Court noted that Congress' intent to preserve for unions the control over their own "internal affairs" did not suggest an intent to authorize restrictions on the right to resign. The Court affirmed the board's decision against the union. *Pattern Makers' League of North America v. NLRB*, 473 U.S. 95, 105 S.Ct. 3064, 87 L.Ed.2d 68 (1985).

3. Replacement Workers

The Supreme Court held that a bargaining impasse was not sufficient justification for a company to withdraw from a multi-employer bargaining unit. Only if unusual circumstances existed could an employer unilaterally withdraw. In the case below, the company hired permanent replacement workers and withdrew from the association.

A linen supply company was a member of an association formed to negotiate collective bargaining agreements with a truck drivers' union as a multi-employer unit. During negotiations for a proposed agreement, an impasse was reached, and the union began a selective strike against the company. The company hired permanent replacements and notified both the union and the association that it was withdrawing from the association. When a collective bargaining agreement was later executed, the company refused to sign it. The union filed an unfair labor practice charge against the company with the National Labor Relations Board. The board held for the union, and the U.S. Court of Appeals agreed with it.

Before the U.S. Supreme Court, it was held that the bargaining impasse did not justify the company's withdrawal from the multiemployer bargaining unit. Here, there was no unusual circumstance to justify the unilateral withdrawal by the employer. To permit withdrawal at an impasse would undermine the utility of multiemployer bargaining as a practical matter. Even if this rule adopted by the board denied employers a particular economic weapon, it did so to maintain the stability of the multiemployer bargaining unit. The Court affirmed the appellate court's decision and required the company to implement the new collective bargaining agreement. *Charles D. Bonanno Linen Service v. NLRB*, 454 U.S. 404, 102 S.Ct. 720, 70 L.Ed.2d 656 (1982).

The rights of replacement workers to keep their jobs after striking workers return to work can be litigated in state court. Here, the lawsuits were not preempted by the NLRA because they did not concern conduct that was arguably prohibited or protected by the NLRA.

A corporation that sold hardware products and building materials entered into a collective bargaining agreement with a union which eventually expired. Due to an impasse in negotiations, approximately 400 employees went out on strike. The corporation then unilaterally granted a wage increase for employees who stayed on the job. It also advertised for and hired "permanent" replacements to take over for the strikers. The NLRA allows employers to hire permanent replacements where employees engage in an economic strike (but not where they strike over unfair labor practices). After the unilateral wage increase, the union filed unfair labor practice charges with the National Labor Relations Board. The parties then settled their disputes, and the corporation laid off the permanent replacements to make room for the returning strikers. The laid off replacement workers sued the corporation for misrepresentation and breach of contract. A Kentucky trial court granted summary judgment to the corporation on the ground that the lawsuit was preempted by the NLRA. The Kentucky Court of Appeals reversed, and appeal was taken to the U.S. Supreme Court.

The Supreme Court affirmed the court of appeals' decision, finding that the causes of action for breach of contract and misrepresentation were not preempted. Under *San Diego Building Trades Council v. Garmon*, 359 U.S. 236, 79 S.Ct. 773, 3 L.Ed.2d 775 (1959), state regulations and causes of action are presumptively preempted if they concern conduct that is actually or arguably either prohibited or protected by the NLRA. However, in this case, the board's focus would be on the strikers' rights under the NLRA, while the state court claims would concern the replacement employees' rights under state law. These were only peripherally connected to the controversy before the board. Further, the state interests were strong. Accordingly, the NLRA did not preempt the replacement workers' lawsuit. *Belknap, Inc. v. Hale*, 463 U.S. 491, 103 S.Ct. 3172, 77 L.Ed.2d 798 (1983).

The National Labor Relations Board does not have to presume that striker replacements oppose the union. Such a replacement may support the union and desire representation but be forced to work by his or her economic circumstances.

After the expiration of a collective bargaining agreement, an economic strike ensued. The employer hired permanent replacement employees. When the union attempted to accept the employer's previous offer, the employer informed it that the offer was no longer available and it then withdrew recognition from the union, refusing to further bargain with it. The employer felt that the union was no longer supported by a majority of the employees in the unit. The union then filed an unfair labor practice charge with the NLRB, asserting that the employer had violated the National Labor Relations Act.

Using a case-by-case approach, the NLRB found that the employer's evidence of its replacements' union sentiments was not sufficient to rebut the presumption of the union's majority support. The U.S. Court of Appeals held that the NLRB had to presume that striker replacements oppose the union. The case then came before the U.S. Supreme Court, which held that the NLRB did not have to presume opposition to the union by the replacements. A replacement who otherwise supports the union may be forced by economic concerns to work for a struck employer. The Court thus reversed the court of appeals' ruling and remanded the case. *NLRB v. Curtin Matheson Scientific, Inc.*, 494 U.S. 775, 110 S.Ct. 1542, 108 L.Ed.2d 801 (1990).

In 1991, the Court stated that the tripartite standard (relating to a union's duty of fair representation) announced in *Vaca v. Sipes*, see cite below, applied to all union activity, not just to contract administration and enforcement. However, a union's actions will be deemed arbitrary only where the union's behavior is so far outside a wide range of reasonableness as to be irrational.

Continental Airlines filed a petition for reorganization under Chapter 11 of the Bankruptcy Code. It then repudiated its collective bargaining agreement with the pilots' union and cut pilots' salaries and benefits by more than half. This resulted in a strike that lasted for more than two years. During the strike, Continental set up a system of bidding for vacancies, and assigned all the positions to working pilots. This effectively ended the strike. The union then entered into an agreement with Continental whereby striking pilots were allowed to participate in the bidding allocation. Thereafter, a group of pilots sued their union, alleging that it had breached its duty of fair representation by negotiating an agreement that arbitrarily discriminated against striking pilots. A federal district court ruled for the union; the U.S. Court of Appeals, Fifth Circuit, reversed; and the case then came before the U.S. Supreme Court.

The court held that the rule announced in *Vaca v. Sipes*, 386 U.S. 171, 87 S.Ct. 903, 17 L.Ed.2d 842 (1967)—that a union breaches its duty of fair representation if its actions are either "arbitrary, discriminatory, or in bad faith"—applies to *all* union activity, including contract negotiation. The court then stated that a union's actions would be arbitrary only if the union's behavior was so far outside a "wide range of reasonableness" as to be irrational. This had to be determined in light of the factual and legal landscape at the time of the union's actions. Here, even if the union had made a bad settlement, its actions at the time of the settlement were not irrational. Thus, it did not breach its duty to the pilots. The Court reversed the court of appeals' decision. *Air Line Pilots Ass'n International v. O'Neill*, 499 U.S. 65, 111 S.Ct. 1127, 113 L.Ed.2d 51 (1991).

4.   Norris-LaGuardia Act

The Norris-LaGuardia Act prohibits injunctions in "any" labor dispute, and defines a labor dispute as including "any controversy concerning terms or conditions of employment." It does not make an exception for labor disputes that arise out of political protests. Accordingly, the strike in the following case could not be enjoined even though it was not economically motivated.

In January 1980, President Carter announced that certain trade with the Soviet Union would be restricted due to that country's intervention in Afghanistan. The International Longshoremen's Association then announced that its members would not handle any cargo bound to, or coming from, the Soviet Union. Subsequently, one of its affiliated local unions refused to load an agricultural fertilizer that was not included in the Presidential embargo. In response to this work stoppage, the employer sued the union and its officials in federal district court under the Labor Management Relations Act, alleging that the work stoppage violated the collective bargaining agreement (CBA) in place (which contained a no-strike clause and a provision requiring arbitration of disputes). The district court ordered the union to arbitrate the question of whether the work stoppage violated the CBA. The court also enjoined the work stoppage, holding that § 4 of the Norris-LaGuardia Act did not apply in this case because the work stoppage was politically motivated. The U.S. Court of Appeals affirmed in part, but held that the Norris-LaGuardia Act did apply to the case, and that the work stoppage could not be enjoined. The case was further appealed to the U.S. Supreme Court.

The Supreme Court noted that the Norris-LaGuardia Act prohibits injunctions in *any* labor dispute, and does not make an exception for labor disputes that are politically motivated. Even though noneconomic motives were involved here, the Act continued to apply because "the employer-employee relationship [was] the matrix of the controversy." Further, the Court stated that even though the work stoppage could be enjoined if the dispute underlying it was arbitrable, the underlying dispute in this case was either an expression of moral outrage or an expression of sympathy for the people of Afghanistan. However, it was plainly not arbitrable under the CBA. The Court affirmed the court of appeals' decision. The work stoppage could not be enjoined, and the question of whether the work stoppage violated the CBA had to be submitted to arbitration. *Jacksonville Bulk Terminals, Inc. v. International Longshoremen's Ass'n*, 457 U.S. 702, 102 S.Ct. 2672, 73 L.Ed.2d 327 (1982).

The Norris-LaGuardia Act, 29 U.S.C. § 101 *et seq.*, prohibits federal courts from issuing injunctions against activities "growing out of" a labor dispute. In the following case, the Supreme Court held that a federal court could not enjoin secondary picketing in a railroad dispute.

A union had a dispute with a railroad over the renewal of a collective bargaining agreement. The union struck the railroad, then extended its picketing to other railroads which interchanged traffic with the struck railroad. These railroads filed suit to enjoin the picketing, and a federal district court issued an injunction against the picketing. In finding that the case did not "grow out of a labor dispute" as defined by the Norris-LaGuardia Act, and that none of the picketed railroads were "substantially aligned" with the struck railroad, the court determined that the injunction could issue. The U.S. Court of Appeals reversed, and the U.S. Supreme Court granted review. The Court held that the district court did not have jurisdiction to enjoin the secondary picketing in the railway labor dispute. The Norris-LaGuardia Act was enacted to preclude courts from enjoining secondary as well as primary activity—railroads were to be treated no differently than other industries in this regard. Because the definition of "labor dispute" is supposed to be broad, the adoption of the "substantial alignment" test (which would narrow that definition) would defeat Congress' intent by requiring courts to second-guess which activities are truly in the union's interest. Further, there was nothing in the Railway Labor Act to indicate that Congress intended to permit federal courts to enjoin secondary activity as a means of settling strikes and avoiding interruptions to commerce. The Court affirmed the appellate court's decision. *Burlington Northern Railroad Co. v. Brotherhood of Maintenance of Way Employees,* 481 U.S. 429, 107 S.Ct. 1841, 95 L.Ed.2d 381 (1987).

5.   Other Important Cases

When a no-strike provision in a collective bargaining agreement is violated by a wildcat strike, the employers who have been struck may not bring an action for damages against individual union members. The LMRA authorizes such lawsuits only against unions that have participated in or authorized the illegal strike.

Three trucking companies were parties to a collective bargaining agreement (CBA) with the Teamsters Union; the CBA contained a no-strike clause. Subsequently, some of the companies' employees began a wildcat (illegal) strike because they believed that the union was not properly representing them in negotiations to amend the CBA. Shortly thereafter, the companies sued the employees in their individual capacities under § 301(a) of the Labor Management Relations Act, which gives federal courts jurisdiction to decide suits alleging violations of CBAs. Among other things, the companies sought money damages against the employees for all losses arising out of the wildcat strike. The district court dismissed this claim, and the U.S. Court of Appeals affirmed, holding that Congress did not intend to create a cause of action for damages through § 301 against individual union members for breach of a no-strike agreement.

On further appeal to the U.S. Supreme Court, the Court agreed with the lower courts that § 301(a) did not sanction damages actions by employers against individual employees for violating the no-strike provision of a CBA, regardless of whether the union participated in or authorized the strike. Congress intended to shield individual employees from liability for such damages by enacting § 301. Employers could only seek a damages remedy against unions under § 301, not against individuals—and then they could do so only when the unions participated in or authorized the illegal strike. The Court affirmed the lower courts' decisions on this issue. *Complete Auto Transit, Inc. v. Reis*, 451 U.S. 401, 101 S.Ct. 1836, 68 L.Ed.2d 248 (1981).

While the NLRA structures the labor-management relationship, Congress has left certain areas "to be controlled by the free play of economic forces." Accordingly, states are prohibited from imposing additional restrictions on economic weapons of self-help (like strikes and lockouts).

A taxicab company applied for a franchise renewal with the city of Los Angeles. While the application was pending, the company's drivers went on strike. The city council then conditioned renewal of the franchise on a settlement of the labor dispute. When the settlement did not occur by the renewal date, the franchise expired. The company brought suit in federal court, alleging that the city's action was preempted by the NLRA. The district court granted summary judgment to the city and the U.S. Court of Appeals affirmed. The U.S. Supreme Court granted certiorari.

The Supreme Court held that the city's action in conditioning the franchise renewal on the settlement of the labor dispute was preempted by the NLRA. Here, the city had attempted to regulate conduct that Congress had intended to be unregulated, and had impermissibly imposed additional restrictions on economic weapons of self-help that the company was justified in using to withstand the strike. Because the NLRA creates a balance of power between employer and employee, and because the city had destroyed that balance of power, Congress' intent had been contravened. The Court reversed the lower courts' decisions and remanded the case. *Golden State Transit Corp. v. City of Los Angeles*, 475 U.S. 608, 106 S.Ct. 1395, 89 L.Ed.2d 616 (1986).

In 1988, the Court held that an amendment to the Food Stamp Act (which disallowed eligibility in the food stamp program while household members were on strike) was constitutional.

In 1981, Congress amended the Food Stamp Act to provide that no household could become eligible to participate in the food stamp program while any of its members was on strike. Further, there could be no increase in the allotment of food stamps already being received due to a drop in income to a striking member. Certain unions and union members challenged the constitution-ality of this amendment (§ 109) in a federal district court. The court granted them summary judgment, finding § 109 to be unconstitutional because it interfered with strikers' associational and expressive rights and because it violated their equal protection rights. Direct appeal was taken to the U.S. Supreme Court.

The Court held that the § 109 did not infringe the associational rights of the unions or their members, nor did it abridge their right to express themselves about union matters free of coercion by the government. The constitution did not "confer an entitlement to such funds, as may be necessary to realize all the advantages of that freedom." Further, the Court noted that § 109 did not violate the equal protection rights of the unions and their members because it was rationally related to the legitimate governmental objective of avoiding undue favoritism in private labor disputes. The Court reversed the district court's decision and upheld the constitutionality of the amendment. *Lyng v. International Union, UAW,* 485 U.S. 360, 108 S.Ct. 1184, 99 L.Ed.2d 380 (1988).

C. Handbilling

In the following case, the Supreme Court held that § 8(b)(4) of the NLRA was not intended to proscribe peaceful handbilling, unaccompanied by picketing, of a neutral employer. Handbilling, if it is not accompanied by violence, picketing, patrolling or other intimidating conduct, need not be held "coercive" within the meaning of the NLRA.

A company hired a contractor to build a department store for it in a mall. A union believed that the contractor was paying substandard wages and fringe benefits. It thus engaged in peaceful handbilling of the businesses in the mall, asking customers not to shop there until the mall's owner publicly promised that all construction at the mall would be done using contractors who paid fair wages. The mall owner, after failing to convince the union to alter the handbills to state that the dispute was not with the owner, filed a complaint with the National Labor Relations Board, charging the union with engaging in unfair labor practices under § 8(b)(4) of the NLRA. The board dismissed the complaint, concluding that the handbilling was protected by § 8(b)(4)'s provision exempting nonpicketing publicity which is intended to truthfully advise the public that products are produced by an employer with whom the union is involved in a labor dispute. The U.S. Court of Appeals affirmed, but the U.S. Supreme Court reversed on the ground that the mall owner and its other tenants did not distribute the contractor's products. The Court then remanded for a determination of whether § 8(b)(4) had been violated. *Edward J. DeBartolo Corp. v. NLRB,* 463 U.S. 147, 103 S.Ct. 2926, 77 L.Ed.2d 535 (1983).

On remand, the board ordered the union to stop distributing the handbills because the handbilling was an attempt to inflict economic harm on secondary employers. This constituted economic retaliation and was therefore a form of coercion prohibited by § 8(b)(4)(ii)(B). The U.S. Court of Appeals denied enforcement of the board's order, holding that there was no clear congressional intent to proscribe such handbilling in the NLRA. The U.S. Supreme Court again granted certiorari.

The Supreme Court held that § 8(b)(4) did not contain any clear expression of congressional intent to prohibit this kind of handbilling. Further, since there were serious constitutional problems, including First Amendment free speech concerns, with the board's construction, a clear expression that that was

Congress' purpose would be required before such an interpretation would be adopted. Accordingly, the peaceful handbilling, which was unaccompanied by picketing, did not have to be considered coercive even though it was outside the protection of § 8(b)(4)'s publicity proviso. The Court affirmed the court of appeals' decision denying enforcement of the Board's order. *Edward J. DeBartolo Corp. v. Florida Gulf Coast Building & Construction Trades Council,* 485 U.S. 568, 108 S.Ct. 1392, 99 L.Ed.2d 645 (1988).

Where a union does not have reasonable access to employees, it is appropriate to balance an employer's privacy rights against NLRA § 7 rights. However, if reasonable access to employees exists, a union cannot compel an employer to allow nonemployee organizers onto the employer's property.

A food and commercial workers union attempted to organize employees at a Connecticut retail store. The employer refused to allow the union onto store property to distribute handbills. The union then filed a complaint with the National Labor Relations Board alleging that the employer had violated the NLRA by barring the union organizers from its property. The board ordered the employer to cease and desist from barring the union from the parking lot. The employer then sought review in the U.S. Court of Appeals, Fifth Circuit, which affirmed the board's decision. The employer appealed to the U.S. Supreme Court. The Court noted that § 7 of the NLRA provides that "employees shall have the right to self-organization, to form, join, or assist labor organizations." Further, the NLRA also makes it an unfair labor practice for an employer "to interfere with, restrain, or coerce employees in the exercise of [these] rights." The court determined that these sections gave *employees* rights, not unions or their organizers (nonemployees). Thus, the Court reasoned, "the right to distribute is not absolute, but must be accommodated to the circumstances." If it is unreasonable for a union to distribute literature to employees entirely off the employer's premises, distribution in parking lots or other common areas may be warranted. The Court concluded that there were no "unique obstacles" for the union to reach the employees, because it had access to the list of names and addresses. Therefore, the Supreme Court reversed the appellate court's decision and determined that the employer did not violate the NLRA by preventing union organizers from distributing handbills in the parking lot. *Lechmere, Inc. v. NLRB,* 502 U.S. 527, 112 S.Ct. 841, 117 L.Ed.2d 79 (1992).

D. First Amendment Concerns

In a 1976 case, the Supreme Court rejected a decision by the Wisconsin Supreme Court that would have severely curtailed the rights of teachers to speak publicly about collective bargaining issues. However, union representatives did not have a monopoly on speaking about such issues.

The Madison Board of Education and an employee labor union conducted collective bargaining negotiations. One of the proposals submitted by the union called for the approval of a "fair share" clause, which would require all teachers to pay a fee which was equivalent to union dues for collective bargaining expenses, regardless of whether the teachers were union members. The school board resisted this provision and another that required binding arbitration for teacher dismissals. The negotiations came to a standstill. Two Wisconsin teachers, who were bargaining unit members but not union members, mailed letters of opposition to the "fair share" proposal to other teachers. Almost 200 teachers responded, most expressing opposition to the proposal. The two teachers created a petition calling for a one-year delay in the fair share implementation. At the next public school board meeting, the union president spoke and presented a petition signed by 1,300 teachers requesting the expedient resolution of the negotiations. One of the teachers who supported the fair share petition also spoke and presented the petition. He stated that because teachers were confused about the fair share proposal, it should be delayed. The board acquiesced to all union demands, except for the fair share proposal. The union then approved the agreement. A month later, the union filed a complaint with the Wisconsin Employment Relations Committee (WERC), claiming that the board had engaged in unfair labor practices by allowing the teacher opposed to the fair share arrangement to speak at the board meeting. The union alleged that allowing the teacher to speak constituted negotiations with someone other than the union's exclusive collective-bargaining representative, in violation of Wisconsin labor law. WERC concluded that the board was in violation of state law and ordered it not to allow nonunion representatives to speak at future board meetings on collective bargaining issues. A Wisconsin trial court affirmed, granting an injunction against future board appearances by the nonunion teacher. The Wisconsin Supreme Court also affirmed the decision. The U.S. Supreme Court agreed to hear the case.

The Court reversed the Wisconsin Supreme Court's decision, ruling that the teacher's speech did not present a "clear and present danger" which justified infringement of individual First Amendment speech rights. The Court re-examined the trial court's conclusion that the teacher's statement constituted negotiation. It held that the teacher was only making a position statement, and was not seeking to negotiate or enter into an agreement with the board. The speech did not change the fact that union representatives were the exclusive bargaining entities. The meeting was open to the public and the teacher had made his presentation as a concerned citizen. He was not required to relinquish his free speech rights because he was a teacher. To allow only union representatives to exercise their speech rights would amount to a monopoly. The ban on future appearances by teachers before the board would effectively ban all citizens' rights to petition their government. The Court struck down the injunction. *Madison School Dist. v. Wisconsin Employment Relations Comm'n*, 429 U.S. 167, 97 S.Ct. 421, 50 L.Ed.2d 376 (1976).

In a 1979 case, the Court held that the National Labor Relations Board had no jurisdiction over religiously-affiliated schools because of potential infringement of school rights under the religion clauses of the U.S. Constitution.

The NLRA, 29 U.S.C. § 141 *et seq.*, established the National Labor Relations Board, which governs unionization and collective bargaining matters in all aspects of the private sector. The courts have ruled that "pervasively religious" schools may be able to avoid any obligation under the NLRA to bargain with employees. This exception to the NLRA's coverage is based upon First Amendment religious freedom considerations. When the NLRB authorized labor associations to serve as certified collective bargaining representatives for Catholic high schools in Chicago, the Catholic Bishop refused to recognize the associations. The Bishop claimed that any intervention by the NLRB violated the church's right to freely exercise religion under the U.S. Constitution's religion clauses. The NLRB argued that the parochial school curriculum included secular instruction and accused the Bishop of unfair labor practices in violation of the NLRA. The case reached the U.S. Supreme Court.

The Court said that the religion clauses of the U.S. Constitution, which require religious organizations to finance their educational systems without governmental aid, also free the religious organizations of the obviously inhibiting effect and impact of unionization of their teachers. This followed the line of reasoning employed in cases such as *Lemon v. Kurtzman,* 403 U.S. 602, 91 S.Ct. 2105, 29 L.Ed.2d 745 (1971). The Court agreed with the Bishop's contention that the very threshold act of certification of the union by the NLRB would necessarily alter and infringe upon the religious character of parochial schools. This would mean that the Bishop would no longer be the sole repository of authority as required by church law. Instead, he would have to share some decision-making with the union. This, said the Court, violated the religion clauses of the U.S. Constitution. *NLRB v. Catholic Bishop of Chicago,* 440 U.S. 490, 99 S.Ct. 1313, 59 L.Ed.2d 533 (1979).

In another private education case, the Court found a different ground for holding the NLRA inapplicable to a private university. Unlike *NLRB v. Catholic Bishop of Chicago*, above, in which the Court based its opinion on constitutional grounds, the Court used language from the NLRA itself. Because the university's faculty members had considerable managerial responsibilities, the Court deemed them to be outside the scope of the NLRA.

In *NLRB v. Yeshiva Univ.,* the U.S. Supreme Court held that in certain circumstances, faculty members at private educational institutions could be considered managerial employees. Yeshiva's faculty association had petitioned the NLRB seeking certification as bargaining agent for all faculty members. The NLRB granted certification but the university refused to bargain. After the U.S. Court of Appeals declined to enforce the NLRB's order that the university bargain with the labor union, the NLRB appealed to the U.S. Supreme Court, which upheld the appeals court decision. The Supreme Court's ruling was based on its conclusion that Yeshiva's faculty were managerial employees. It stated:

The controlling consideration in this case is that the faculty of Yeshiva University exercise authority which in any other context unquestionably would be managerial. Their authority in academic matters is absolute. They decide what courses will be offered, when they will be scheduled, and to whom they will be taught. They debate and determine teaching methods, grading policies, and matriculation standards. They effectively decide which students will be admitted, retained, and graduated. On occasion their views have determined the size of the student body, the tuition to be charged, and the location of a school. When one considers the function of a university, it is difficult to imagine decisions more managerial than these. To the extent the industrial analogy applies, the faculty determines within each school the product to be produced, the terms upon which it will be offered, and the customers who will be served.

The Court noted that its decision applied only to schools that were "like Yeshiva" and not to schools where the faculty exercised less control. Schools where faculty do not exercise binding managerial discretion do not fall within the scope of the managerial employee exclusion. *NLRB v. Yeshiva Univ.*, 444 U.S. 672, 100 S.Ct. 856, 63 L.Ed.2d 115 (1980).

In a 1983 case, the Court ruled that a school district's exclusive collective bargaining representative was entitled to use the school district's internal mail system and teacher mailboxes. A rival union that had lost the certification election had no right to use the mail system because the system was not a "public forum" for First Amendment purposes. The policy was also upheld on Equal Protection Clause grounds because the district could legitimately draw distinctions relating to the special use of its property.

The Supreme Court of the United States upheld a collective bargaining agreement between an Indiana school board and the local teacher union which provided that the teacher union, to the exclusion of a rival union, which was not certified by election, had access to the school district's internal mail and delivery system. The rival union challenged the denial of access to the mail system on grounds that the restriction violated its free speech rights under the First Amendment and the Equal Protection Clause under the Fourteenth Amendment. The Supreme Court, reversing a U.S. Court of Appeals decision, held that since the interschool mail system was not a public forum generally available for use by the public, access to it could be reasonably restricted without violating either free speech or equal protection rights. The Court noted the special responsibilities of the exclusive bargaining representative and the fact that other channels of communication remained available to the rival union. The school district had a legitimate interest in preserving the school mail facilities for their intended purpose, which was to enable the teachers' exclusive bargaining representative to perform its obligations. The non-certified union had no official responsibilities with the district and was not entitled to similar rights. The different treatment of labor organizations was constitutionally permissible because the school district had a strong interest in peaceful labor relations. As the district policy satisfied the Equal Protection Clause, the Court ruled for the school board and the certified union. *Perry Educ. Ass'n v. Perry Local Educators' Ass'n*, 460 U.S. 37, 103 S.Ct. 948, 74 L.Ed.2d 794 (1983).

In 1984, the Court reaffirmed the view that an exclusive bargaining representative that is duly elected by school employees should have the sole voice in discussing employment-related matters with the employer.

The Minnesota Public Employment Labor Relations Act authorized state employees to use collective bargaining to determine employment terms and conditions with their employers. Under the statute, public employers were required to bargain only with the exclusive bargaining representative of public employees. The statute granted professional employees, such as college faculty members, the right to "meet and confer" with their employers on matters outside the scope of the collective bargaining agreement but required the employer to meet only the elected bargaining representative. Faculty members who were not union members objected to the "meet and confer" provision, saying that rights of professional employees within the bargaining unit who are not members of the exclusive representative and who may disagree with its views, were violated by their inability under the statute to express their views. Nonunion Minnesota community college faculty members brought suit against the Minnesota State Board for Community Colleges alleging that the statute violated their First Amendment and equal protection rights. They claimed that they were denied an opportunity to participate in employer policymaking. A federal district court agreed with the faculty members, granting an injunction against enforcement of the statute. The board appealed to the U.S. Supreme Court.

The Supreme Court held that the "meet and confer" provision did not violate the faculty members' constitutional rights. There was no constitutional right, either as members of the public, as state employees, or as college instructors, to force public employers to listen to the nonunion members' views. The fact that an academic setting was involved did not give them any special constitutional right to a voice in the employer's policymaking decisions. Further, the state had a legitimate interest in ensuring that its public employer heard one, and only one, voice presenting the majority view of its professional employees on employment related policy questions. The statute did not restrain nonunion employees from free speech. Although the presence of a collective bargaining representative in the meet and confer process amplified the union's voice in the policymaking process, the union presence did not impair any employee constitutional rights. It was rational for the state to give the exclusive bargaining representative a unique role in employment policy matters as it helped ensure the state's legitimate interest in hearing a majority-view voice. The Supreme Court reversed the district court's decision. *Minnesota State Bd. for Community Colleges v. Knight*, 465 U.S. 271, 104 S.Ct. 1058, 79 L.Ed.2d 299 (1984).

IX. ARBITRATION

After an arbitration hearing upholding a discharge, the Supreme Court held that an ex-employee had only 90 days in which to bring a § 301(a) lawsuit (the effect of which would be to vacate the arbitrator's decision if the suit were successful).

An employee of a delivery service company who worked as a car washer was discharged for dishonest acts, including falsifying his timecards and claiming payment for hours he had not worked. The employee denied the charges and was represented by his union at an arbitration hearing, where his discharge was upheld. Seventeen months later, the employee sued the union and his ex-employer under § 301(a) of the Labor Management Relations Act, alleging that the union had breached its duty of fair representation and that the company had discharged him in its effort to replace fulltime employees with part-time workers. A federal district court dismissed the action as time-barred by New York's 90-day limitations period for actions to vacate arbitration awards. The U.S. Court of Appeals reversed, and the U.S. Supreme Court granted a writ of certiorari. The Supreme Court held that the district court had properly dismissed the case. By reference to the appropriate state statute of limitations, the 90-day period was better than the alternative of New York's six-year limitations period for breach of contract actions. In this case, the effect of the employee's suit, if it was successful, would be to vacate the arbitration award upholding the discharge. It was more closely related to an action to vacate an arbitration award than it was to a breach of contract action. Further, the system would become unworkable if arbitration awards and decisions which gave meaning and content to the terms of an agreement could be called into question as much as six years later. The Court reversed the appellate court's decision. *United Parcel Service, Inc. v. Mitchell*, 451 U.S. 56, 101 S.Ct. 1559, 67 L.Ed.2d 732 (1981).

In the following case, the Court held that a federal district court could not overrule an arbitrator's decision simply because the court believed that its interpretation of the collective bargaining agreement was better than the arbitrator's.

An employer, faced with the prospect of liability for violations of Title VII of the Civil Rights Act (in certain of its hiring practices), signed a conciliation agreement with the Equal Employment Opportunity Commission (EEOC). This agreement conflicted with the seniority provisions of the existing collective bargaining agreement (CBA). After giving certain work assignments to women ahead of men with greater seniority, and after laying off two male employees under the conciliation agreement but in violation of the CBA, grievances were filed. The employer sought an injunction to prohibit arbitration. However, the U.S. Court of Appeals compelled arbitration. The arbitrator awarded back pay damages against the employer under the CBA. The employer then brought an action to overturn the award, and a district court ruled in its favor. However, the U.S. Court of Appeals reversed.

On further appeal to the U.S. Supreme Court, the Court held that the award was properly to be enforced. Even though the arbitrator had awarded damages under the CBA, the employer's liability stemmed from its own breach of the seniority provisions of the CBA. Thus, the arbitrator's decision did not violate public policy. It merely held the employer to its obligations under the CBA. Further, even though the employer and the EEOC had agreed to nullify the CBA's seniority provisions, this conciliation process had not included the union. And the CBA could not be altered without the union's consent, absent a judicial determination. The Court affirmed the court of appeals' decision upholding the arbitrator's award. *W.R. Grace and Co. v. Local Union 759*, 461 U.S. 757, 103 S.Ct. 2177, 76 L.Ed.2d 298 (1983).

In the case below, the Court held that where neither the trust agreements creating employee benefit trust funds nor the collective bargaining agreement involved evidenced any intent by the parties to condition judicial enforcement on exhaustion of arbitration procedures, the trustees of the funds could seek judicial enforcement of the contract terms without first seeking arbitration.

Two employers entered into collective bargaining agreements (CBAs) with a union that required them to participate in two multiemployer employee benefit trust funds. The trust agreements required them to contribute to the funds pursuant to the terms stated in the CBAs. The terms of the trust agreements were incorporated by reference into the CBAs and authorized the trustees to initiate any legal proceedings they deemed to be in the best interest of the funds "to effectuate the collection or preservation of contributions." Subsequently, the trustees of the funds filed suit against the employers in federal district court alleging that the employers had failed to meet their contribution requirements and had refused to allow an audit. They asked for an accounting and for the immediate payment of all sums that were due. The employers asserted in defense that the complaints raised conflicting interpretations of the CBAs that had to be submitted to arbitration. The court dismissed the suit, but the U.S. Court of Appeals reversed.

On further appeal to the U.S. Supreme Court, the Court noted that the trustees could seek judicial enforcement of the trust terms against the employers without first submitting to arbitration an underlying dispute over the meaning of a term in the CBAs. Even though the CBAs provided for arbitration of differences between the employers and the union (or employees) as to the meaning or application of the agreements' provisions, the parties did not intend to force the trustees to exhaust arbitration procedures prior to seeking judicial enforcement of the trust agreements. Accordingly, the Court affirmed the court of appeals' decision and remanded the case. *Schneider Moving & Storage Co. v. Robbins*, 466 U.S. 364, 104 S.Ct. 1844, 80 L.Ed.2d 366 (1984).

The Civil Service Reform Act provides that an arbitrator may not sustain an agency's disciplinary action against an employee if the employee shows "harmful error" in the application of the agency's procedures in arriving at its decision. However, where the error is prejudicial only to the union, and not to the employee, the arbitrator cannot overturn the agency's action on this ground.

Two employees of the General Services Administration, who were union members, were discharged for falsification of records, among other reasons. The discharges stemmed from an incident in which a supervisor had been drinking while on duty—the employees had been involved in a cover-up of the incident. As was their right, they challenged their removal under the grievance and arbitration procedures established by the collective bargaining agreement rather than appeal to the Merit Systems Protection Board. The arbitrator found that the GSA had committed procedural errors by failing to inform the employees that they could have a union representative present during questioning, and by unreasonably delaying the issuance of notices of removal. The arbitrator then found that these errors, while they did not prejudice the employees, were "harmful error" to the union, justifying a reduction in the penalty to two weeks' suspension. The U.S. Court of Appeals affirmed. On further appeal, the U.S. Supreme Court held that § 7701(c)(2)(A) of the Civil Service Reform Act prohibited an arbitrator from sustaining an agency's disciplinary decision if the employee could show an error that caused substantial prejudice to his or her individual rights. It was not sufficient that the error was harmful to the union. Since the MSPB had interpreted the act in this way, the arbitrator also had to do so in the interests of consistent interpretation. The union had its own adequate remedies for enforcing agency compliance with the procedural requirements of the collective bargaining agreements. Thus, the employees' discharges had been wrongfully reduced to suspensions. The Court reversed the court of appeals' decision. *Cornelius v. Nutt*, 472 U.S. 648, 105 S.Ct. 2882, 86 L.Ed.2d 515 (1985).

In the following case, the Court held that it was the responsibility of federal courts to determine whether parties to a collective bargaining agreement intended to arbitrate grievances concerning layoffs for lack of work.

After a collective bargaining agreement was entered into to cover telephone equipment installation workers, the union filed a grievance challenging the employer's decision to lay off 79 installers from its Chicago location for lack of work. The agreement contained a standard arbitration clause, but also provided that the employer would be free to exercise certain management functions, like hiring, placing and terminating employees, and that subject to certain limitations, this would not be subject to the arbitration clause. Layoffs were governed by a separate provision of the agreement. When the employer refused to arbitrate, the union sued in a federal district court to compel arbitration. The court held that the arbitrator should determine whether the grievance should be arbitrated, and the U.S. Court of Appeals affirmed.

On further appeal, the U.S. Supreme Court held that the district court should have determined the arbitrability of the dispute over the layoffs. It was the lower court's duty to interpret the collective bargaining agreement to find out if the parties had intended grievances concerning layoffs to be arbitrated. In Justice Brennan's concurring opinion, he noted that due to the presence of the standard arbitration clause, the dispute would be arbitrable unless the agreement contained explicit language exempting such disputes from arbitration, or unless the employer showed that such disputes were not meant to be arbitrated—by examining the bargaining history. The Court vacated the appellate court's decision and remanded the case for further proceedings. *AT&T Technologies, Inc. v. Communications Workers of America*, 475 U.S. 643, 106 S.Ct. 1415, 89 L.Ed.2d 648 (1986).

The Federal Arbitration Act provides that contractual arbitration provisions are valid, irrevocable and enforceable if the contract itself is validly entered into. The act also mandates judicial enforcement where a party has failed, neglected or refused to arbitrate. Also, being federal law, the act preempts state law to the contrary.

A California man brought an action against his former employer and two of its employees for breach of contract and conversion, centered around a dispute over commissions on the sale of securities. He refused to submit the dispute to arbitration, and the defendants then sought to stay further proceedings and compel arbitration under §§ 2 and 4 of the Federal Arbitration Act (Act). The demands for arbitration were based on a form that the former employee had signed in connection with his application for employment (agreeing to arbitrate any dispute with his employer). The state trial court denied the petition to compel arbitration on the basis of a state law which provided that wage collection actions could be maintained without regard to the existence of any private agreement to arbitrate. The state court of appeal affirmed, and eventually the case reached the U.S. Supreme Court, which stated that § 2 of the Act (mandating enforcement of arbitration agreements) preempted the state law. Congress intended that arbitration be favored where it had been agreed to previously, and this overrode the state law at issue here. Accordingly, the Court reversed the lower courts' decisions, and held that arbitration was required. *Perry v. Thomas*, 482 U.S. 483, 107 S.Ct. 2520, 96 L.Ed.2d 426 (1987).

Absent fraud by the parties or the arbitrator's dishonesty, reviewing courts are not authorized to reconsider the merits of an arbitrator's award, since this would undermine the federal policy of privately settling labor disputes by arbitration without governmental intervention. Courts cannot overturn arbitrators' decisions simply because they disagree with those decisions, or with the factual findings, the contract interpretations, or the choice of remedies.

A Louisiana man worked for a company as a machine operator on a hazardous machine. Company rules provided that the use or bringing of controlled substances onto the premises would result in discharge. Subsequently, police officers found the employee in another person's vehicle on company premises where marijuana was present. They also found marijuana gleanings in the employee's car. The company learned of the first incident and fired the employee. He contested his discharge and filed a grievance seeking arbitration under the collective bargaining agreement. Shortly before the arbitration hearing, the company learned of the marijuana found in the employee's car. However, the arbitrator then held for the employee because there was insufficient proof that the employee had used marijuana on the premises. The company appealed to a federal district court, which overturned the arbitrator's decision. The U.S. Court of Appeals, Fifth Circuit, affirmed, and the case reached the U.S. Supreme Court.

The Supreme Court noted that the lower courts had erred in overturning the arbitrator's decision because of public policy concerns. Here, the arbitrator's refusal to consider the later evidence was not bad faith or affirmative misconduct. Further, arbitrators have wide discretion in formulating remedies, and it was error for the courts to overturn this arbitrator's decision because they viewed discharge as the proper remedy. The Court reversed the lower courts' holdings and upheld the arbitrator's decision. *United Paperworkers International Union v. Misco, Inc.*, 484 U.S. 29, 108 S.Ct. 364, 98 L.Ed.2d 286 (1987).

NLRB v. Katz, **369 U.S. 736, 82 S.Ct. 1107, 8 L.Ed.2d 230 (1962), announced the unilateral change doctrine which provides that an employer violates the NLRA if it effects a unilateral change of an existing term or condition of employment without bargaining to impasse. This extends to cases in which an existing agreement has expired and negotiations on a new one have yet to be completed. However, after a collective bargaining agreement expires, an arbitration clause does not continue in effect unless the dispute at issue arises under the expired agreement.**

A corporation operated a check-printing plant in California. After the expiration of the collective bargaining agreement (CBA) between the corporation and the union, ten employees were laid off. The union filed grievances, claiming a violation of the CBA. The corporation refused to process the grievances or submit to arbitration. The National Labor Relations Board determined that the corporation had violated the NLRA and ordered it to process the grievances and to bargain with the union over the layoffs, but it refused to order arbitration. The U.S. Court of Appeals enforced the board's order except that it found the layoff grievance arbitrable, and the corporation petitioned for a writ of certiorari from the U.S. Supreme Court. The Court held that the layoff dispute was not arbitrable. It refused to impose a statutory duty on the corporation to arbitrate a post-expiration dispute. Arbitration will not be imposed if to do so would go beyond the scope of the parties' consent. Further, since the layoff dispute did not arise under the CBA, the arbitration provisions of the CBA could not be used to force arbitration. *Litton Financial Printing v. NLRB*, 501 U.S. 190, 111 S.Ct. 2215, 115 L.Ed.2d 177 (1991).

No public policy reason required a court to overturn an arbitration award reinstating a truck driver who failed two drug tests in a 16-month time period, according to the Supreme Court. The arbitration award constituted an agreement of the parties and its rehabilitation provisions were consistent with federal labor law.

The employer sought to discharge the driver on two occasions after drug tests indicated marijuana use. Arbitrators ordered his reinstatement on both occasions, with provisions for suspension without pay, participation in substance abuse programs and continued random drug testing. The second arbitrator included a provision requiring the driver to reimburse the employer for the costs of both arbitration proceedings and to furnish the employer with a signed, undated letter of resignation to take effect if he tested positive again within the next five years. The arbitrator held that there was no "just cause" to discharge the driver, as required by the applicable collective bargaining agreement.

The employer brought a federal district court action against the driver's collective bargaining association to vacate the second arbitration award, arguing that it violated a strong public policy against the operation of dangerous machinery by drug users. The court held that the driver's conditional reinstatement did not violate that policy and the U.S. Court of Appeals, Fourth Circuit, affirmed the decision.

The Supreme Court initially noted that the parties' collective bargaining agreement granted the arbitrator the authority to interpret the meaning of the agreement's language, including the term "just cause." Because the parties had bargained for the arbitrator's construction of their agreement, the decision would only be set aside in the rare case in which it did not "draw its essence from the contract."

The employer did not contest that the arbitrator had acted outside the scope of his contractual authority, but asserted that the federal policy interest in transportation industry safety required a court to vacate the arbitration award because the collective bargaining agreement would be itself contrary to public policy. The Supreme Court noted that the public policy exception is narrow. Although U.S. Department of Transportation regulations and federal transportation laws require the testing of those in safety-sensitive jobs for drug use, they do not prohibit the reinstatement of a person in such a position for failing random drug tests on one or even two occasions. Moreover, the award's rehabilitative aspects were consistent with the federal transportation law regime, since it required the driver to participate in substance abuse treatment and continue undergoing testing. The Supreme Court affirmed the lower court decisions, allowing the arbitration award to stand. *Eastern Associated Coal Corp. v. United Mine Workers of America, District 17 et al.*, 531 U.S. 57, 121 S.Ct. 462, 148 L.Ed.2d 354 (2000).

The Supreme Court interpreted the Federal Arbitration Act in a manner permitting the enforcement of mandatory arbitration clauses in employment contracts other than in the transportation industry. An employee was required to arbitrate his discrimination claims under the terms of his employment contract, instead of pursuing his claims under the California Fair Employment and Housing Act.

Under the employee's contract, he agreed to settle any claims against the employer through final and binding arbitration. The contract explicitly included employment claims arising under federal anti-discrimination laws such as Title VII of the Civil Rights Act of 1964, the Age Discrimination in Employment Act and the Americans with Disabilities Act. After two years of employment, the employee filed a state court action alleging discrimination and state tort law violations. The employer obtained a federal district court order enjoining the state action and compelling arbitration under the Federal Arbitration Act. However, the U.S. Court of Appeals, Ninth Circuit, held that the FAA does not apply to employment contracts. Observing that no other federal circuit court had ever reached this conclusion, the U.S. Supreme Court agreed to review the case.

The Court held that the FAA requires judicial enforcement of a wide range of written arbitration agreements and was enacted pursuant to Congress' substantive power to regulate interstate commerce. Congress exempted from FAA coverage "contracts of employment of seamen, railroad employees, or any other class of workers engaged in foreign or interstate commerce." The employee argued that the Ninth Circuit had correctly interpreted this provision as exempting all employment contracts from FAA coverage, which would allow his state discrimination and tort claims to proceed.

The Supreme Court rejected this view, which would require a finding of congressional intent to regulate all employment contracts under the full extent of Congress' commerce power. The explicit reference to "seamen" and "railroad employees" in the section made it unlikely that all employment contracts were excluded. Construing the usual meaning of the statutory language as applied to interstate commerce and the pro-arbitration purposes of the FAA, the act foreclosed the conclusion reached by the Ninth Circuit excluding all employment contracts from FAA coverage. The Court held that the act excluded only the contracts of employment for transportation workers. Accordingly, the Ninth Circuit's decision was reversed and remanded. *Circuit City Stores, Inc. v. Adams*, 532 U.S. ___, 121 S.Ct. 1302, 149 L.Ed.2d 234 (2001).

A decision of the U.S. Court of Appeals, Ninth Circuit, that resulted in a former professional baseball player being awarded $3 million in a dispute over free agency was overturned in the following case. A majority of the justices of the Supreme Court concluded that the circuit court had usurped the role of an outside arbitrator by awarding the player the money.

The player was trying to collect a share of a $280 million settlement that baseball owners agreed to pay in 1990 after arbitrators found that they had worked together to hold down free-agent players' salaries. The player alleged his shared should be $3 million. When the player's claim was denied by the Major League Baseball Players Association, he requested arbitration. The arbitrator also denied the player's claim, and a district court upheld this decision. The Ninth Circuit reversed, and the MLBPA appealed.

In an 8–1 decision, the Supreme Court agreed with the MLBPA that the Ninth Circuit violated federal labor arbitration law by rejecting an arbitrator's findings and making its own decision. "Because the court's determination conflicts with our cases limiting review of an arbitrator's award entered pursuant to an agreement between an employer and a labor organization and prescribing the appropriate remedy where vacation of the award is warranted, we grant [the MLBPA's] petition for review and reverse," the majority wrote in an unsigned opinion. In examining the circuit court opinion, the Supreme Court concluded that the Ninth Circuit disagreed with the arbitrator's factual findings, which is not a legitimate basis for overturning an arbitrator's decision, especially when the decision is made pursuant to an agreement between the parties, as existed under the circumstances of this case. The Court noted that the Ninth Circuit erred when it ordered an award to the player, finding the appropriate remedy in the event of "serious error" by an arbitrator is to vacate the arbitrator's decision and remand for further arbitration. The circuit court decision in favor of the player was reversed, and the case was remanded. *Major League Baseball Players Association v. Garvey,* 532 U.S. ___, 121 S.Ct. 1724, 149 L.Ed.2d 740 (2001).

CHAPTER SIX

Employment Practices

I. EMPLOYMENT PRACTICES

A. Hiring Practices

The Tucker Act allows a federal contract employee to sue the United States for damages resulting from a breach of the contract in federal court. However, federal courts lack jurisdiction to hear claims for money damages by an employee not hired pursuant to an express or implied contract.

While employed in a data processing position with the Army and Air Force Exchange Service (AAFES), an employee was selected for participation in the Executive Management Program (EMP). A regulation provided that EMP status could be withdrawn for "conduct off the job reflecting discredit on the AAFES." Subsequently, the employee was arrested off the base for possession of controlled substances. He pled guilty to four misdemeanor counts of violating state drug laws. The AAFES then discharged him. After his administrative appeal was denied, he sued in federal court, alleging that his due process rights and his right to a free and impartial appeal pursuant to AAFES regulations were infringed. The district court dismissed the case, but the U.S. Court of Appeals reversed, finding that the Tucker Act (which gives federal courts jurisdiction over certain suits against the United States founded upon express or implied contracts) provided a basis for jurisdiction. The U.S. Supreme Court granted review.

The Supreme Court held that the Tucker Act did not confer jurisdiction over the ex-employee's claim for money damages. The ex-employee had not worked for the AAFES under an express contract. Rather, he had been appointed to his positions. Thus, the court of appeals had erred by implying a contract based on the AAFES regulations. Tucker Act jurisdiction could not be imposed as a result of those regulations. The Court reversed the appellate court's decision, holding that the ex-employee was not allowed to sue in federal court over his termination. *Army and Air Force Exchange Service v. Sheehan*, 456 U.S. 728, 102 S.Ct. 2118, 72 L.Ed.2d 520 (1982).

The Privileges and Immunities Clause allows discrimination against citizens of another state if the governmental body doing the discriminating has a substantial reason for the difference in treatment and if the degree of discrimination bears a close relationship to the reason.

Acting pursuant to a statewide affirmative action program, the Camden, New Jersey, City Council adopted an ordinance setting minority hiring goals on all public works contracts. In addition, the ordinance required at least 40 percent of the employees of contractors and subcontractors working on city construction projects to be Camden residents. After the state treasury department approved the ordinance, an association of labor organizations filed an appeal. The New Jersey Supreme Court rejected the unions' challenges to the ordinance's validity. The court held that the Privileges and Immunities Clause of the Constitution did not apply because the ordinance only discriminated on the basis of municipal residency, not state residency.

On appeal to the U.S. Supreme Court, the Court noted that the municipal ordinance was properly subject to the restrictions and commands of the Privileges and Immunities Clause. A municipality is merely a political subdivision of a state; what the state cannot do directly, the municipality cannot do by derived authority. Even though the ordinance mostly affected New Jersey residents who lived outside Camden (who could not bring a Privileges and Immunities Clause challenge because that was only for citizens of other states), there were some out-of-state residents affected to bring the challenge. The Court reversed and remanded for a determination of whether the city's justification for the ordinance was sufficient to allow the difference in treatment for out-of-state residents. *United Building & Construction Trades Council v. Mayor and Council of City of Camden,* 465 U.S. 208, 104 S.Ct. 1020, 79 L.Ed.2d 249 (1984).

B. Wages and Compensation

In 1978, the Court suspended a Georgia county education board rule that would have required county employees to forego their salaries when running for political office. The rule violated § 5 of the Voting Rights Act.

A black administrator of student personnel services for a county board of education announced his candidacy for the Georgia House of Representatives. Less than a month later, the board unexpectedly adopted a rule, without federal approval, requiring that any board employee running for office would have to take a leave of absence without pay. As a result, the administrator was forced to take three leaves of absence, losing approximately $11,000 in salary. The administrator sued in a federal district court, alleging that the rule was invalid because it was a standard in regard to voting and therefore required federal clearance under § 5 of the Voting Rights Act of 1965. The administrator also pointed out that he was the first black from the county to run for the Georgia legislature since the Reconstruction Era. The district court held that the rule should obtain federal approval before it was implemented. However, the court declined to decide whether the rule itself had a discriminatory purpose or effect, refusing to rule on its compliance with § 5 of the Voting Rights Act. The U.S. Supreme Court agreed to hear the case.

The Supreme Court agreed that the rule was a voting procedure, thus subject to compliance with § 5. The Court noted that previous decisions had given § 5 a broad interpretation, in order to encompass any state enactments altering its election law. The rule in question imposed substantial economic disincentives for public employees seeking office. The Court ruled that although the leave of absence rule was established by a school board which itself did not conduct elections, the rule became subject to Voting Rights Act requirements because it affected the electoral process. The Court affirmed the district court's decision and the rule was suspended, pending its clearance of § 5 of the Voting Rights Act. *Dougherty County Bd. of Educ. v. White,* 439 U.S. 32, 99 S.Ct. 368, 58 L.Ed.2d 269 (1978).

If an agency has determined that contract work is not subject to the Davis-Bacon Act (which regulates the amount of wages owed and payable on certain construction contracts), then an employee has no private right of action on the contract for back wages under the act.

The Davis-Bacon Act provides that the advertised specifications for all federal construction contracts in excess of $2,000 must contain a provision stating the minimum wages to be paid laborers and mechanics—such wages to be based on the Secretary of Labor's determination of the prevailing rates in the locality. Also, the Act requires the contracts to contain a stipulation that the contractor will pay at least those wages. In 1967, a not-for-profit consortium of universities entered into a contract with the Atomic Energy Commission to provide scientific and management services to the government in connection with the construction, alteration and repair of a physics research facility. The contract stated that the consortium would not be using its employees to perform work subject to the Act; thus, it did not contain a prevailing wage stipulation. Subsequently, an employee of the consortium sued it in a federal court for violating the Act by failing to pay prevailing wages. The district court ruled for the consortium, but the U.S. Court of Appeals reversed.

On further appeal to the U.S. Supreme Court, the Court held that the Davis-Bacon Act did not confer upon an employee a private right of action for back wages under a contract which had been administratively determined not to call for work subject to the Act, and which did not contain prevailing wage stipulations. If there had been such stipulations in the contract, a suit against the consortium might have been possible. However, there were no such stipulations in the contract at issue. Accordingly, as no private right of action existed, the Court reversed the court of appeals' decision and remanded the case. *Universities Research Ass'n, Inc. v. Coutu*, 450 U.S. 754, 101 S.Ct. 1451, 67 L.Ed.2d 662 (1981).

In the case below, the Supreme Court held that public employees who were promoted to General Schedule positions from Wage System positions were not entitled to a "two-step" pay increase.

Six civilian employees of the Department of the Navy were paid pursuant to the WS (prevailing rate wage system applicable primarily to federal "blue collar" workers) until they were promoted to positions covered by the GS (general schedule applicable primarily to "white collar" workers). After their promotions, an administrative hearing was conducted at which it was determined that the employees were only entitled to pay increases under the "highest previous rate" rule rather than to the greater pay increases under the "two-step increase" rule. They appealed, filing an action with the Court of Claims. The court upheld their claim and invalidated the regulation that construed the "two-step increase" rule as applying only to transfers or promotions within the GS. The U.S. Supreme Court granted certiorari.

The Supreme Court held that the "two-step increase" rule did not apply to WS employees promoted to GS positions. Here, the regulation in question clearly allowed the two-step increase in pay only when employees were transferred or promoted to higher-grade positions within the GS system. Congress did not intend to include employees promoted from WS to GS positions when it enacted the governing statute. Further, the Civil Service Commission had consistently construed the regulation in question as granting two-step pay increases only to promotions within the GS. As a result, the employees were only entitled to the lower "highest previous rate" increase. The Court reversed the decision of the Court of Claims. *United States v. Clark*, 454 U.S. 555, 102 S.Ct. 805, 70 L.Ed.2d 768 (1982).

In the following case, the Court found that the California prevailing wage statute did not reference or have a connection with an ERISA plan.

California's prevailing wage law is based on the federal Davis-Bacon Act, 40 U.S.C. §§ 276a to 276a–5, and requires contractors working on public works projects to pay their employees at least the general prevailing wage rate for similar work being performed in the locality. Both laws allow public works contractors to pay apprentices less than the prevailing journeyman wage where they participate in approved programs complying with the National Apprenticeship Act. The California Apprenticeship Council approves apprenticeship programs in the state under the act. It charged a subcontractor working on a Sonoma County construction project with improperly paying apprentices who worked in a non-approved program the apprentice wage rather than the appropriate prevailing journeyman wage. It ordered the County of Sonoma to withhold payments to the contractor for the violation. The contractor filed a petition in a federal district court claiming that the prevailing wage act was preempted by the Employee Retirement Income Security Act. The court agreed with the contractor that the joint apprenticeship training system under which the apprentices worked was an employee welfare benefit plan under ERISA and that the prevailing wage statute related to it. However, it held that the state wage act was not preempted. The U.S. Court of Appeals, Ninth Circuit, reversed the district court decision, and the U.S. Supreme Court agreed to review the case.

The Court recited its test from earlier ERISA preemption cases under which a state law is held to relate to a covered employee benefit plan if it has a connection with or reference to such a plan. In this case, the California prevailing wage statute referred to approved apprenticeship programs that did not necessarily have to be ERISA plans. Because an apprenticeship plan could be approved whether or not its method of funding brought it under ERISA, California's prevailing wage statute did not make reference to an ERISA plan. The court also held that the California law did not have a connection with an ERISA plan. Here, the prevailing wage statute merely offered economic incentives to apprenticeship programs to comport with the state's requirements. It did not dictate the choices facing ERISA plans. The Supreme Court reversed and remanded the court of appeals' decision. *California Div. of Labor Standards Enforcement v. Dillingham Construction, N.A., Inc.*, 519 U.S. 316, 117 S.Ct 832, 136 L.Ed.2d 791 (1997).

The withholding of money due a subcontractor because of the subcontractor's violations of California labor law regarding prevailing wage payments did not violate due process, as the subcontractor could

bring a state law claim against either the state defendants or the contractor who withheld the money.

A subcontractor hired to work on several California public works projects was deemed to have violated the California Labor Code (Code) by not paying the state determined prevailing wage and failing to comply with the Code provisions regarding payroll records. As a result, the California Division of Labor Standards Enforcement directed the parties who awarded the contracts to withhold over $135,000 from the contractors. The contractors then paid the subcontractor an amount that reflected the withheld amount. In an attempt to get the full amount owed to it, the subcontractor sued the DLSE and various other state entities, claiming the withholding violated the Due Process Clause of the 14th Amendment of the Constitution, because the subcontractor's property (the withheld money) was taken without a hearing. A federal district court agreed with the subcontractor, and concluded that several sections of the California Labor Code were unconstitutional. On appeal, the U.S. Court of Appeals, Ninth Circuit, the circuit court agreed, finding the lack of a provision in the Code for a hearing violated due process. The state defendants appealed, and the Supreme Court granted certiorari.

The Court reversed, finding the Code provided the subcontractor with a means to pursue its claims in state court. Under the California Labor Code, a contractor or a contractor's assignee can sue the awarding body over alleged breaches of the contract or to recover wages or penalties imposed based on the contract. Because the contractor has the right of assignment, it could have assigned the subcontractor the right to bring a claim against the state regarding the withheld wages and penalties. Further, the Supreme Court determined that even if the contractor would not assign the right to sue the awarding body to the subcontractor, the subcontractor could bring a state law breach of contract suit against the contractor in order to recover the disputed amount. Since no deprivation of property without due process occurred, the Supreme Court reversed the circuit court decision. *Lujan, et al. v. G&G Fire Sprinklers, Inc.,* 532 U.S. ___, 121 S.Ct. 1446, 149 L.Ed.2d 391 (2001).

Federal taxes on back wages are to be calculated based on the year the back wages are paid, not the year the wages should have been paid.

The Supreme Court ruled that back pay awards won by professional baseball players after a 1980s labor dispute were subject to federal taxes based on the year the money was paid out, not the year that it should have been paid. The Court unanimously agreed that more than $2 million in back wages the Cleveland Indians Baseball Co. paid to 22 players in 1994 was attributable to that year for the purposes of Social Security, Medicare and federal unemployment taxes. According to the opinion, the IRS reasonably interpreted the law when it held that taxes are owed on the back wages for the year in which they were actually paid. *United States v. Cleveland Indians Baseball Co.,* 532 U.S. ___, 121 S.Ct. 1433, 149 L.Ed.2d 401 (2001).

C. Collective Bargaining

The Supreme Court upheld the constitutionality of an Ohio law placing the teaching workload of state university faculty outside the purview of collective bargaining.

In 1993, the Ohio legislature passed a law to ensure that teaching standards remained consistent among state universities. The law directed each state university to develop workload standards that took precedence "over any conflicting provisions of any collective bargaining agreement." In 1994, Central State University adopted its policy and notified the faculty's union (AAUP) that the policy would not be subject to bargaining. The AAUP sued in state court to stop the policy from being enforced, arguing that the law violated the Equal Protection Clauses of both the Ohio and the U.S. constitutions by creating a class of public employees not entitled to bargain regarding their workload.

Finding no evidence linking "collective bargaining with the decline in teaching over the last decade," the Ohio Supreme Court concluded that there was no rational basis for singling out faculty members and that the law violated both constitutions. The Supreme Court, reviewing only the federal issue, reversed. The Ohio court misconstrued the rational basis test, the Supreme Court explained. Even though it had not been shown that (past) collective bargaining had led to the decline in classroom time for faculty, that did not detract from the rationality of the legislative decision. *Central State Univ. v. American Ass'n of Univ. Professors, CSU Chapter*, 526 U.S. 124, 119 S.Ct. 1162, 143 L.Ed.2d 227 (1999).

D. Veterans

In the following case, the Supreme Court struck down as unconstitutional a New York veteran's preference statute granting preferential treatment for state residents. As the case demonstrates, government action will be strictly scrutinized when persons are treated differently.

The state of New York granted a civil service employment preference to residents who were veterans of the armed forces during a time of war, and who had been residents of the state when they entered military service. Two men who met all the criteria except the last one took and passed civil service examinations, but were denied the veterans' preference. They sued in federal court, challenging the residency requirement as violative of the Equal Protection Clause and of the constitutionally protected right to travel. The district court dismissed their complaint, but the U.S. Court of Appeals reversed. The U.S. Supreme Court granted certiorari. The Court first noted that the right to travel includes the freedom to enter and reside in any state. The state law here implicated that right by using a classification that penalized the exercise of that right. Under the heightened scrutiny advocated by the Court, the law did not overcome the burden imposed on it. The state did not meet its burden of showing that it had selected a means of rewarding service that did not unnecessarily impinge on constitutionally protected interests. The Court struck down the law as unconstitutional and affirmed the appellate court's decision. *Attorney General of New York v. Soto-Lopez*, 476 U.S. 898, 106 S.Ct. 2317, 90 L.Ed.2d 899 (1986).

An employer must permit an employee to take a leave of absence to perform active duty for the Armed Forces under the Veterans' Reemployment Rights Act. There is no requirement that leave requests be reasonable; they can be for terms of three years or longer.

A National Guard member in Alabama worked for a private hospital until he accepted a three-year full-time appointment with the Guard. He then requested a leave of absence from his hospital job. The hospital denied his request and brought suit in a federal district court, seeking a declaratory judgment that the Veterans' Reemployment Rights Act did not provide re-employment rights after tours of duty as long as the employee's. The court ruled in the hospital's favor, holding that the leave requests had to be reasonable for re-employment rights to be protected, and finding that the request for a three-year leave was *per se* unreasonable. The U.S. Court of Appeals affirmed, and appeal was taken to the U.S. Supreme Court.

The Supreme Court stated that the Act, codified at 38 U.S.C. § 2024(d), did not limit the length of military service after which a member of the Armed Forces retained a right to civilian re-employment. The Act provided that any covered employee "shall ... be granted a leave ... for the period required to perform active duty [and] [u]pon ... release from ... such duty ... shall be permitted to return to [his or her] position." By reading the statute as a whole, the Court concluded that the unqualified nature of this protection was deliberate. Accordingly, there was no requirement that leave requests be "reasonable," and the employee was entitled to re-employment at the expiration of his tour of service. The Court reversed the lower courts' decisions. *King v. St. Vincent's Hospital*, 502 U.S. 215, 112 S.Ct. 570, 116 L.Ed.2d 578 (1991).

E. Investigations

Although an employee may refuse to answer an employer's investigatory questions if the answers could expose him or her to criminal prosecution, the employee may be sanctioned for making false statements regarding the charged conduct.

Federal employees who were subjected to adverse actions by their employer agency made false statements to federal investigators regarding alleged misconduct. In addition to the misconduct charges, the agency also included the false statements as a ground for adverse action. The employees appealed to the Merit Systems Protection Board, which upheld the penalties on the misconduct charges but overturned the false statement charges. The Director of the Office of Personnel Management appealed the board's decision to the U.S. Court of Appeals, Federal Circuit. The appellate court agreed with the board that no penalty could be imposed based upon a false denial of the misconduct charges. The court held that the Fifth Amendment Due Process Clause prohibits a federal agency from charging an employee with falsification based on the employee's denial of another charge. It further held that an employee's false statement may not be considered for the purpose of impeachment.

On appeal, the U.S. Supreme Court reversed. It noted that neither the Due Process Clause nor the Civil Service Reform Act precluded the government from sanctioning an employee for making false statements to it regarding alleged misconduct by the employee. Even though due process requires notice and an opportunity to be heard, it does not include the right to make false statements with respect to charged conduct. If answering an agency's investigatory question could expose an employee to prosecution, the employee can exercise his Fifth Amendment right to remain silent. However, if the employee chooses to make a false statement regarding the charged conduct, the government is not prohibited from taking adverse action against him based upon those statements. *LaChance v. Erickson*, 522 U.S. 262, 118 S.Ct. 753, 139 L.Ed.2d 695 (1998).

In the case below, the Supreme Court found that no exception to the prohibition on lying to government investigators exists under 18 U.S.C § 1001.

Federal agents suspected a New York union officer of accepting prohibited cash payments from an employer whose employees were represented by the officer's union. During the course of an interrogation by the agents, the officer denied receiving any cash or gifts from the employer while he was a union officer. He was later indicted for accepting unlawful cash payments from the employer in violation of federal labor law and for making a false statement within the jurisdiction of a federal agency in violation of 18 U.S.C. § 1001. The U.S. District Court for the Southern District of New York found him guilty of the charges, and the conviction was affirmed by the U.S. Court of Appeals, Second Circuit. The U.S. Supreme Court agreed to hear the officer's appeal.

On appeal, the officer asserted that 18 U.S.C. § 1001 excluded a suspect's "exculpatory no" from coverage and applied only to statements that perverted a governmental function. He also claimed that a literal reading of the statute violated the Fifth Amendment prohibition on compelled criminal testimony. The Court rejected these arguments, finding that there was no exception in § 1001 to the prohibition on lying to government investigators. The Fifth Amendment does not create a privilege to lie, and Congress could properly find the obstruction of a legitimate investigation to constitute a serious separate offense from the underlying wrongdoing of accepting cash from the employer. Finding no exception to the statute's language, the Court affirmed the conviction. *Brogan v. U.S.*, 522 U.S. 398, 118 S.Ct. 805, 139 L.Ed.2d 830 (1998).

F. Governmental Enactments

When the government operates a private corporation for profit, such as Amtrak, the corporation will be considered a government entity by the courts and its actions will generally be deemed to constitute government action. Here, the government established a reimbursement scheme for railroad employee travel privileges.

After Congress enacted the Rail Passenger Service Act to revive the failing intercity passenger train industry, Amtrak (a private, for-profit corporation) was authorized to operate, or contract with private railroads for the operation of, intercity rail passenger service. In the agreements entered into between Amtrak and the railroads, Amtrak had discretion to determine railroad employees' privileges to travel on Amtrak trains for free or at reduced fares. However, protests by the railroads at Amtrak's decision to limit and reduce such privileges resulted in the restoration of such privileges (as they existed before Amtrak) by act of Congress. The act also required the railroads to reimburse Amtrak for its costs in providing these services. Eventually, a set figure was determined by Congress as the reimbursement amount. The railroads sued in federal court, claiming that the reimbursement requirement of the act violated due process. The court held for Amtrak and the government, but the U.S. Court of Appeals reversed in part, finding that the part of the act that required the railroads to pay more than the incremental cost of carrying the pass riders violated the Due Process Clause.

On further appeal, the U.S. Supreme Court held that Congress did not violate due process by requiring the railroads to reimburse Amtrak for the rail travel privileges that Amtrak provided to railroad employees and retirees. Even if the railroads had a private contractual right not to pay more than the incremental cost of the pass privileges, Congress was not limited by the Due Process Clause with respect to choosing a different reimbursement scheme. Accordingly, the Court reversed the appellate court's decision. *National Railroad Passenger Corp. v. Atchison, Topeka & Santa Fe Railway Co.*, 470 U.S. 451, 105 S.Ct. 1441, 84 L.Ed.2d 432 (1985).

The Fifth Amendment to the U.S. Constitution prohibits the government from taking private property for public use without just compensation. Government entitlements such as social security payments have been construed by the Court to be property rights that must be subject to the same analysis as private property. Accordingly, when an entitlement is threatened, the Court will inquire into the due process rights of the recipient.

In 1950, Congress amended the Social Security Act (SSA) to authorize voluntary participation by the states in the Social Security System. They could obtain coverage for state and local employees by executing an agreement with the Secretary of Health and Human Services. Also, they could terminate their agreements upon two years' notice to the secretary. When the increasing rate of state withdrawals threatened the integrity of the system, Congress amended the act in 1983 to provide that no agreements could be terminated after the effective date of the amendment. California, which had previously filed notices of termination, instituted proceedings attacking the validity of the amendment. A federal court found that the amendment was unconstitutional, and appeal was taken to the U.S. Supreme Court.

The Supreme Court reversed the district court's holding. It found that the amendment did not violate the constitutional prohibition against the taking of property without due process of law. Since Congress had the right to alter, amend or repeal any provision of the SSA, the amendment did not take a property right away from the state. Congress could amend not only the SSA, but also the agreements entered into in conformity with the act. Accordingly, the Court reversed and remanded the case, holding that states could be prevented from withdrawing from the Social Security System. *Bowen v. Public Agencies Opposed to Social Entrapment*, 477 U.S. 41, 106 S.Ct. 2390, 91 L.Ed.2d 35 (1986).

National security is a paramount interest that supersedes any other in Supreme Court balancing tests. However, the government must be clear in stating its policies and employment practices by defining terms such as "classified information."

Over half of the federal government's civilian and military personnel were required to sign nondisclosure agreements in order to obtain access to classified and "classifiable" information. The nondisclosure agreements were standard forms describing confidentiality obligations and penalties for unauthorized disclosure. Congress enacted a resolution prohibiting federal fund expenditures for enforcing the use of the forms, which were designed by the Information Security Oversight Office (ISOO) and the Central Intelligence Agency (CIA). Following the congressional action, the ISOO's director issued a regulation defining the term "classifiable" as information that was in the process of becoming classified. However, the Director of Central Intelligence (DCI) continued to require employees to sign the CIA form for an additional three months. The DCI then issued a form which eliminated the term "classifiable." The American Foreign Service Association sued the ISOO's director and the DCI in the U.S. District Court for the District of Columbia claiming that use of the forms violated the resolution. The district court dismissed the association's claim on grounds that the congressional action unconstitutionally interfered with presidential authority to protect national security. The employee association appealed to the U.S. Supreme Court, which agreed to hear the matter.
The Supreme Court observed that the ISOO's regulations remedied the vagueness in the term "classifiable." The DCI had deleted the word "classifiable" from the documents and replaced it with the definition given in the ISOO's regulation. The court ordered the directors to notify their employees that the term classifiable had been defined. The Court ruled that at least for current employees, the controversy was now moot. However, the Court remanded the case on the issue of the definition of "classified information," which the association argued did not comply with the congressional resolution. *American Foreign Service Ass'n v. Garfinkel*, 490 U.S. 153, 109 S.Ct. 1693, 104 L.Ed.2d 139 (1989).

II. SEARCH AND SEIZURE

A. Drug Testing

Individual rights to be free from searches and seizures do not outweigh the right of the government to protect the public safety. In such cases, there is an identifiable "special need" which transcends law enforcement and the standard inquiry into probable cause.

Railway labor organizations sued the U.S. Secretary of Transportation in a federal district court for an order that would prevent enforcement of regulations under the Federal Railroad Safety Act of 1970. The regulations required testing after major train accidents and permitted railroads to administer breath or urine tests after serious incidents and where supervisors had reasonable suspicion from observing individual behavior. A U.S. district court concluded that the public and governmental interest in safety outweighed the labor organization members' interest in privacy. The U.S. Court of Appeals, Ninth Circuit, held that the testing was unconstitutional. It reversed the district court decision, ruling that government action was not sufficient to implicate the Fourth Amendment for the permissive tests, and that the required tests failed to use particularized suspicion to confine the tests to actual detection of currently impaired employees.

The Supreme Court ruled that even private railroads acting with the government's encouragement in taking of blood and urine samples were performing searches and seizures under the Fourth Amendment. The appeals court had failed to balance the interests among the employers, employees and the public. The public interest was strong enough to constitute a "special need" beyond normal law enforcement and justified departure from the usual warrant and probable cause requirements. Obtaining a warrant was likely to frustrate the government effort to reveal drug use, and privacy interests were minimal. The Court reversed the appeals court and affirmed the district court's decision for the secretary. *Skinner v. Railway Labor Executives' Ass'n,* 489 U.S. 602, 109 S.Ct. 1402, 103 L.Ed.2d 639 (1989).

Under the Supreme Court's reasoning, the taking of urine samples constitutes a search or seizure under the Fourth Amendment. The government has such a strong interest in controlling drug abuse that it was permitted to take employee urine samples in the following case even though there was no reasonable suspicion of drug use by the employees.

U.S. Customs Service employees contested the service's right to implement a drug testing program for employees seeking transfer or promotion to some positions. Employees seeking jobs requiring direct involvement in drug interdiction and enforcement, use of firearms, or handling of classified material were to be tested under the program. The testing required applicants to give urine samples under observation by a same-sex monitor. Employees who tested positive were subject to dismissal from the service but would not be turned over to agencies for criminal prosecution without written consent by the employee. The employees' union sued the Customs Service in a federal district court, claiming that the testing program violated the Fourth Amendment. The court ruled in the employees' favor and the Service appealed to the U.S. Court of Appeals, Fifth Circuit. The appeals court vacated the lower court's order prohibiting enforcement of the testing program. The union appealed to the U.S. Supreme Court.

The Supreme Court followed the *Skinner* case in finding that the taking of urine constituted a search or seizure under the Constitution. The customs service testing program served a special government need beyond normal law enforcement. The program was designed to deter drug use among persons eligible for sensitive positions. The special need to keep drug abusers from these positions justified departure from the usual warrant and probable cause requirements. The government's need to conduct searches without reasonable suspicion outweighed the employee privacy interest for employees engaged in drug interdiction and suggested for employees the need to carry firearms. However, the record was insufficient to assess the government's reasonable interest in testing employees required to handle classified material. The Court affirmed the appeals court decision in part and remanded for a determination of the necessity to test employees who handled classified material. *National Treasury Employees Union v. Von Raab,* 489 U.S. 656, 109 S.Ct. 1384, 103 L.Ed.2d 685 (1989).

In the case below, the Supreme Court found that a state statute requiring candidates for certain state offices to submit to drug testing was unconstitutional.

The Georgia legislature enacted a statute requiring certain candidates for state office to certify that they had taken a urinalysis drug test and that the result was negative. Anyone who declined to take the test, or who tested positive, was barred from holding office. Testing could, at the option of the candidate, be performed at an approved medical testing laboratory or at the office of the candidate's physician. The test was designed to reveal the presence or absence of five illegal drugs. Libertarian Party candidates challenged the statute in a U.S. district court, alleging violations of their constitutional rights. The district court held for the state, and the candidates appealed to the U.S. Court of Appeals, Eleventh Circuit. The Eleventh Circuit affirmed, and the U.S. Supreme Court granted certiorari.

To be reasonable under the Fourth Amendment, a search ordinarily must be based on individualized suspicion of wrongdoing. However, exceptions based on "special needs" are sometimes warranted. Here, the Court found that there was no special need to justify the drug testing. Since the candidate would provide a urine specimen in the office of his or her private physician and would control the dissemination of the results, the statute did not identify candidates who violated anti-drug laws, nor did it deter illicit drug users. Rather, the statute merely served to meet a symbolic need wherein the state could display its commitment to the struggle against drug abuse. The state did not assert any evidence of a drug problem among its elected officials; those officials do not typically perform high-risk, safety-sensitive tasks; and the certification would not immediately aid an interdiction effort. Therefore, the Court reversed the lower courts' judgments. *Chandler v. Miller,* 520 U.S. 305, 117 S.Ct. 1295, 137 L.Ed.2d 513 (1997).

B. Search and Seizure

An agency may enter into an area open to the public to serve a subpoena that directs the production of documents without violating the Fourth Amendment.

The Fair Labor Standards Act (FLSA) authorizes the Secretary of Labor to investigate and gather data regarding wages, hours, and other conditions of employment to determine possible FLSA violations. In January 1982, an official with the Department of Labor began an investigation of a restaurant-motel. Seeking payroll records, the official went to the employer's premises, and while in the public lobby, served a subpoena *duces tecum* (order for the production of documents) on an employee. The subpoena directed any employee with custody and personal knowledge of the records to appear before the Department of Labor with those records. The employer refused to comply with the subpoena, claiming that it constituted an unlawful search and seizure in violation of the Fourth Amendment because a judicial warrant had not previously been obtained. A federal district court agreed with the employer, and appeal was taken to the U.S. Supreme Court, which held that the subpoena *duces tecum* did not violate the Fourth Amendment. Here, the official had gone to the employer's premises, waited in a public lobby for a particular employee to appear, and then served the subpoena. This was not the sort of governmental act that was forbidden by the Fourth Amendment. The subpoena did not authorize either entry or inspection of the employer's premises; it only directed the employer to produce certain wage and hour records. There was no entry by the official into areas closed to the public. The Court reversed the lower court's decision and held the warrant to be valid. *Donovan v. Lone Steer, Inc.,* 464 U.S. 408, 104 S.Ct. 769, 78 L.Ed.2d 567 (1984).

The Fourth Amendment protects people from unreasonable governmental search and seizure. Who conducts the search and the context in which the search takes place defines the reasonableness of the search. Police have to meet the *probable cause* standard in conducting searches. In the following case, the Supreme Court held school officials to a lower standard than probable cause, ruling that a search by school officials need only be reasonable at its inception and its scope may not exceed that which is necessary under the circumstances.

A teacher at a New Jersey high school found two girls smoking in the lavatory in violation of school rules. She brought them to the assistant vice principal's office where one of the girls admitted to smoking in the lavatory. However, the other denied even being a smoker. The assistant vice principal then asked the latter girl to come to his private office where he opened her purse and found a pack of cigarettes. As he reached for them he noticed rolling papers and decided to thoroughly search the entire purse. He found marijuana, a pipe, empty plastic bags, a substantial number of one dollar bills and a list of "people who owe me money." He then turned her over to the police. A juvenile court hearing was held and the girl was adjudged delinquent. She appealed the juvenile court's determination, contending that her constitutional rights had been violated by the search of her purse. She argued that the evidence against her obtained in the search should have been excluded from the juvenile court proceeding.

The U.S. Supreme Court held that the search did not violate the Fourth Amendment prohibition against unreasonable search and seizure. The Court stated: "The legality of a search of a student should depend simply on the reasonableness, under all the circumstances, of the search." Two considerations are relevant in determining the reasonableness of a search. First, the search must be justified initially by reasonable suspicion. Second, the scope and conduct of the search must be reasonably related to the circumstances that gave rise to the search, and school officials must take into account the student's age, sex and the nature of the offense. The Court upheld the search of the student in this case because the initial search for cigarettes was supported by reasonable suspicion. The discovery of the rolling papers then justified the further searching of the purse since such papers are commonly used to roll marijuana cigarettes. The "reasonableness" standard was met by school officials in these circumstances, and thus the evidence against the girl was properly obtained. *New Jersey v. T.L.O.*, 469 U.S. 325, 105 S.Ct. 733, 83 L.Ed.2d 720 (1985).

The Fourth Amendment guarantees the right of citizens to be free from unreasonable searches and seizures by government agents. In determining the reasonableness of government searches and seizures, the Court employs a balancing of interests approach. In public employment cases, the interests balanced include employee privacy rights and the public employer's interest in operating an efficient workplace. The following case utilizes the balancing of interests test and explains that Fourth Amendment jurisprudence (primarily a criminal law area) does not entirely apply to public employment cases.

A physician and psychiatrist at a California state hospital was primarily responsible for training young physicians in psychiatric residency programs. He occupied the same office for 17 years, when hospital officials became concerned about possible improprieties in his management policies. The officials were concerned that the doctor had sexually harassed two female hospital employees, had taken inappropriate disciplinary action against a resident, and had acquired a personal computer for use in the residency program under questionable circumstances. The hospital's executive director asked the psychiatrist to take paid administrative leave during an investigation of the charges. The director then formed an investigative team composed of an accountant, a physician, a hospital security officer and a hospital administrator. The administrator decided to make a search of the doctor's office, allegedly in compliance with the hospital policy of conducting routine inventory of state property in terminated employee offices. However, when the search was conducted, the psychiatrist remained on administrative leave and had not yet been terminated. The search involved several entries into the office and seizure of items from the doctor's desk and file cabinets, including personal items such as photos and a valentine's card. The investigators put the remainder of the doctor's personal property in storage and placed it at the psychiatrist's disposal. The employer used the seized items in a proceeding before a state personnel hearing officer to impeach the psychiatrist's credibility.

The psychiatrist filed a separate lawsuit against the hospital administrators in a federal district court for violation of his Fourth Amendment rights. The court granted the administrator's motion for summary judgment, ruling that the search was proper. However, the U.S. Court of Appeals, Ninth Circuit, reversed and remanded this decision, ruling that the psychiatrist had a reasonable expectation of privacy in his office. The U.S. Supreme Court granted the administrator's petition for certiorari. The Court considered the case in view of *New Jersey v.*

T.L.O., finding that the Fourth Amendment governed the conduct of public employees making searches. The court of appeals was correct in ruling that public employees had an expectation of privacy in their offices, a standard which warranted a case by case analysis. Offices were not private enclaves and the government had the right to make reasonable intrusions in its capacity as an employer. Some government offices also were so open to fellow employees or the public as to involve no expectation of privacy. In this case, the psychiatrist had occupied the same office by himself for 17 years and had a reasonable expectation of privacy in his desk and file cabinets.

However, the psychiatrist's reasonable expectation of privacy was to be balanced against the public employer's interest in supervision, control and efficient operation of the workplace. The Court refused to impose a search warrant requirement for public employers, because such a requirement would frustrate the governmental purpose behind the search. Under *T.L.O.,* exceptional circumstances going beyond the normal need for law enforcement made the warrant and probable cause requirements impracticable. The warrant requirement would unduly interfere with work-related searches by public employers and should only be imposed in searches that were not work-related. This was because obtaining a warrant would disrupt the daily work routine of government business and would require officials to become familiar with probable cause standards. The governmental interest in efficiency outweighed the psychiatrist's privacy expectation.

The probable cause standard was rooted in criminal investigations and had little meaning in the context of public employment. Instead, the reasonableness standard established in *New Jersey v. T.L.O.* was the appropriate standard for work-related non-investigatory intrusions of work-related misconduct. The reasonableness of such a search involved inquiry into whether the action was justified at its inception and reasonably related in scope to the circumstances that justified the interference in the first place. Generally, a search could be justified at its inception when there were reasonable grounds for suspecting that it would turn up evidence that a public employee was guilty of work-related misconduct, known as "individualized suspicion." Both the district court and the court of appeals were in error and summary judgment was inappropriate. The court reversed and remanded the case to the court of appeals to resolve factual disputes about the reasonableness of the search. *O'Connor v. Ortega,* 480 U.S. 709, 107 S.Ct. 1492, 94 L.Ed.2d 714 (1987).

Fourth Amendment analysis frequently involves the definition of what constitutes a search or seizure. The following case illustrates that these terms may be construed broadly in order to scrutinize the reasonableness of actions by government agents.

A car thief was killed when he crashed into a police roadblock during a high-speed chase. The administrator of his estate then brought a lawsuit against the county and the police, alleging that they violated the decedent's Fourth Amendment rights by placing the roadblock in such a way that he would likely be killed. Allegedly, a semi was placed completely across the highway, behind a curve, with a police car's headlights aimed so as to blind the thief on his approach.

A federal court dismissed the action, finding that the roadblock was reasonable under the circumstances, and the U.S. Court of Appeals affirmed on the ground that no Fourth Amendment seizure had occurred. On appeal, the U.S. Supreme Court held that a seizure occurs when governmental termination of a person's movement is effected through means intentionally applied. Here, the administrator alleged that the decedent was stopped by an instrumentality put in place to stop him. Thus, a Fourth Amendment seizure claim had been stated. The Court reversed the lower courts' decisions and remanded the case for a determination of whether the district court had properly found the seizure to be reasonable. *Brower v. County of Inyo*, 489 U.S. 593, 109 S.Ct. 1378, 103 L.Ed.2d 628 (1989).

CHAPTER SEVEN

Termination and Suspension

I. TERMINATION

The Due Process Clause of the Fourteenth Amendment to the U.S. Constitution prohibits states from depriving persons of life, liberty, or property without due process of law. In the context of public employment, due process generally means notice and an opportunity to be advised of the reason for employment termination, suspension or demotion. The contract of employment, whether by collective bargaining agreement, state law or otherwise, determines the precise procedural guarantees that must be provided. Due process is not an inflexible legal standard. It simply requires fundamental fairness in view of the legal rights described in the employment contract.

A. Property or Liberty Interests

Two 1972 Supreme Court cases help to define the concept of due process in public employment. In *Perry v. Sindermann* and *Bd. of Regents v. Roth*, below, the Court held that liberty and property rights are *created* by contract or state law, and *protected* by the U.S. Constitution. Tenured teachers enjoy property interests in continued employment under state tenure laws. However, untenured teachers have no more than "a unilateral expectation" of reemployment.

The Wisconsin state university system hired an assistant professor under a one-year contract. As the year drew to a close, the university notified the teacher that his contract would not be renewed. The notice conformed to university rules, which did not require any reason for nonretention or any hearing for the teacher. Wisconsin tenure law required teachers to have four years of service before becoming "permanent" employees. The teacher sued the state college board in a federal district court, alleging that he was being terminated for making critical statements about university administrators. The teacher also claimed that the failure of university officials to give any reason for nonretention violated his procedural due process rights. The court held for the teacher on his due process claim and the U.S. Court of Appeals, Seventh Circuit, affirmed this decision. The U.S. Supreme Court agreed to hear the university board's petition.

In dismissing the teacher's due process claims, the Supreme Court stated that no liberty interest was implicated because in declining to rehire the teacher, the university had not made any charge against him such as incompetence or immorality. Such a charge would have made it difficult for the teacher to gain employment elsewhere and thus would have deprived him of liberty. As no reason was given for the nonrenewal of his contract, the teacher's liberty interest in future employment was not impaired and he was not entitled to a hearing on these grounds. The Court declared that because the teacher had not acquired tenure he possessed no property interest in continued employment at the university. The teacher had a property interest in employment during the term of his one-year contract, but upon expiration the interest ceased to exist. The Court stated: "To have a property interest in a benefit, a person clearly must have more than an abstract need or desire for it. He must have more than a unilateral expectation of it. He must, instead, have a legitimate claim of entitlement to it." Because the teacher's contract secured no interest in reemployment for the following year, he had no property interest in reemployment. The Court reversed the lower court decisions and remanded the case. *Bd. of Regents v. Roth*, 408 U.S. 564, 92 S.Ct. 2701, 33 L.Ed.2d 548 (1972).

A fair and impartial hearing, conducted in accordance with procedural safeguards, must be given to a dismissed teacher if there is a property or a liberty interest involved or if the dismissal involves a stigma upon the character of the teacher.

The *Sindermann* case involved a teacher employed at a Texas university for four years under a series of one-year contracts. When he was not rehired for a fifth year he brought suit contending that due process required a dismissal hearing. The Supreme Court held that "a person's interest in a benefit is a 'property' interest for due process purposes if there are such rules and mutually explicit understandings that support his claim of entitlement to the benefit that he may invoke at a hearing." Because the teacher had been employed at the university for four years, the Court felt that he may have acquired a protectable property interest in continued employment. The case was remanded to the trial court to determine whether there was an unwritten "common law" of tenure at the university. If so, the teacher would be entitled to a dismissal hearing. *Perry v. Sindermann*, 408 U.S. 593, 92 S.Ct. 2694, 33 L.Ed.2d 570 (1972).

Applying many of the principles of the *Roth* case, above, the Court found no protectable property interest in the following case involving a police officer who was an at-will employee. The employee also had no liberty interest to protect because the reasons for dismissal remained confidential.

A policeman in a North Carolina city was dismissed by the city manager upon the recommendation of the chief of police. A city ordinance allowed for the termination of a permanent employee, such as the officer, if he failed to perform work up to the standard of his classification. Upon being discharged, the officer sued, asserting that he had a constitutional right to a pretermination hearing. He also argued that he had been deprived of property and liberty interests by his dismissal. The district court ruled against the officer and the court of appeals affirmed. The officer then appealed to the U.S. Supreme Court. The Court held that the district court had correctly concluded that the officer "held his position at the will and pleasure of the city." It also ruled that no liberty interest had been violated because no stigma attached through a public communication. The reasons for the officer's dismissal had been kept private. Since he was an at-will employee, he also had no property interest to be protected. The Court affirmed the lower court decisions, and held that no pretermination hearing had been necessary. *Bishop v. Wood*, 426 U.S. 341, 96 S.Ct. 2074, 48 L.Ed.2d 684 (1976).

The Supreme Court held that an at-will employee could sue for damages under 42 U.S.C. § 1985(2) on claims that two company officials targeted him for termination for cooperating with federal agents in a criminal investigation against the company.

An at-will employee for a Georgia-based health care company cooperated with federal agents investigating the company for Medicare fraud. The employee attended the grand jury proceedings and was expected to appear as a witness in a criminal trial after the company was indicted. After being fired, he sued in federal court under 42 U.S.C. § 1985(2), alleging that three of the company's officers conspired to intimidate him and to retaliate against him for attending the grand jury proceedings and to keep him from testifying at the criminal trial. Section 1985(2) prohibits people from entering into conspiracies to "deter, by force, intimidation or threat," any witness from testifying in court. It provides a cause of action when parties to a conspiracy cause the witness to be "injured in his person or property."

The district court dismissed the lawsuit, holding that an at-will employee has no constitutionally protected property interest in continued employment. Therefore, an employee who loses his job pursuant to a conspiracy theory proscribed by § 1985(2) has not suffered an actual injury.

The U.S. Court of Appeals, Eleventh Circuit, affirmed, and the Supreme Court accepted the case for review. The Court reversed the Eleventh Circuit's decision, holding instead that the sort of harm alleged by the employee— "essentially third-party interference with at-will employment relationships"— states a claim for relief under § 1985(2). The harm has long been recognized under tort law as a compensable injury; Georgia, for example, provides a cause of action against third parties for wrongful interference with employment relations, and the Supreme Court refused to ignore that tradition.

Moreover, "[t]he gist of the wrong at which § 1985(2) is directed is not deprivation of property, but intimidation or retaliation against witnesses in federal-court proceedings." Therefore, the fact that at-will employment is not "property" for purposes of the Due Process Clause does not mean that an at-will employee who loses his job does not suffer injury to his "person or property" as contemplated by § 1985(2). *Haddle v. Garrison*, 525 U.S. 121, 119 S.Ct. 489, 142 L.Ed.2d 502 (1998).

B. Procedural Safeguards

School boards derive their authority from state laws, and are generally authorized to make employment decisions including hiring, firing and negotiating employment contracts. The fact that school boards must negotiate with collective bargaining representatives as adversaries in contract negotiations does not deprive school boards of their status as impartial decision makers in employment matters. Without a showing of actual bias, boards are presumed to be impartial when they conduct hearings for employment termination.

Wisconsin education law prohibited strikes by teachers. Under state law, school boards had sole authority to make hiring and firing decisions and were required to negotiate employment terms and conditions with authorized collective bargaining representatives. When contract negotiations between teachers and their local school board became protracted, the teachers called a strike. The board attempted to end the strike, noting that it was in direct violation of state law. When the teachers refused to return to work, the board held disciplinary hearings and fired the striking teachers. The teachers appealed to the Wisconsin courts, arguing that the school board was not an impartial decision maker and that their discharges had violated their due process rights. The Wisconsin Supreme Court ruled that due process under the Fourteenth Amendment required that the teachers' conduct and the board's response to that conduct be evaluated by an impartial decision maker and that the board itself was not sufficiently impartial to make the decision to discharge the teachers. The board appealed this decision to the U.S. Supreme Court.

The Supreme Court reversed the Wisconsin Supreme Court decision and held that there was no evidence that the board could not make an impartial decision in determining to discharge these teachers. The mere fact that the board was involved in negotiations with the teachers did not support a claim of bias. The board was the only body vested with statutory authority to employ and dismiss teachers. Moreover, participation in negotiations with the teachers was also required by law. This involvement prior to the decision to discharge the teachers was not a sufficient showing of bias to disqualify the board as a decision maker under the Due Process Clause of the Fourteenth Amendment. *Hortonville Joint School Dist. No. 1 v. Hortonville Educ. Ass'n*, 426 U.S. 482, 96 S.Ct. 2308, 49 L.Ed.2d 1 (1976).

Public employees are vested by state law with the right to notice and a hearing at some point in the termination process. The Court upheld an Ohio statute in which employees were limited to notice and an informal hearing in termination matters, but had no full administrative hearing rights until after the termination.

Ohio law protected all civil service employees from dismissal except for "misfeasance, malfeasance, or nonfeasance in office." Employees who were terminated for cause were entitled to an order of removal stating the reasons for termination. Unfavorable orders could be appealed to a state administrative board whose determinations were subject to state court review. A security guard hired by a school board stated on his job application that he had never been convicted of a felony. Upon discovering that he had in fact been convicted of grand larceny, the school board dismissed him for dishonesty in filling out the job application. He was not afforded an opportunity to respond to the dishonesty charge or to challenge the dismissal until nine months later. In a second case, a school bus mechanic was fired because he had failed an eye examination. The mechanic appealed his dismissal after the fact because he had not been afforded a pretermination hearing. A federal district court rejected both of the employees' claims and they appealed to the U.S. Court of Appeals, Sixth Circuit, which reversed the district court's decisions. The U.S. Supreme Court consolidated the appeals by the school districts.

The Supreme Court held that the employees possessed a property right in their employment and were entitled to a pretermination opportunity to respond to the dismissal charges against them. The pretermination hearing, stated the Court, need not resolve the propriety of the discharge, but should be a check against mistaken decisions—essentially a determination of whether there are reasonable grounds to believe that the charges against the employee are true and support the proposed action. The Supreme Court upheld that portion of the lower court decisions that found the delay in the guard's administrative proceedings did not constitute a separate constitutional violation. The Due Process Clause requires a hearing "at a meaningful time," and here the delay stemmed in part from the thoroughness of the procedures afforded the guard. On the matter of the right to a pretermination hearing, however, both cases were remanded for further proceedings consistent with the Court's decision. *Cleveland Bd. of Educ. v. Loudermill*, 470 U.S. 532, 105 S.Ct. 1487, 84 L.Ed.2d 494 (1985).

The following case illustrates the importance of the employment contract (or a statute that addresses the employment relationship) in determining what process is due the employee. The Due Process Clause may be invoked by private employers, when a government agency issues an order determining employee-employer rights.

A trucking company discharged one of its drivers, alleging that he had disabled several lights on his assigned truck in order to obtain extra pay while awaiting repairs. The driver filed a grievance, asserting that the discharge had been in retaliation for having complained of safety violations. He also filed a complaint with the Department of Labor, alleging that his firing violated § 405 of the Surface Transportation Assistance Act, which forbids such action. A field investigator obtained statements substantiating the driver's claim, and offered the company the opportunity to submit a written statement detailing the basis for the employee's discharge, but it was not allowed to examine the substance of the investigator's evidence. A preliminary administrative order called for the employee's temporary reinstatement, and the company filed suit in a federal court, challenging the constitutionality of the department's order. The company charged that reinstatement prior to an evidentiary hearing violated its due process rights. The court ruled for the company, and appeal was taken directly to the U.S. Supreme Court.

The Supreme Court affirmed in part and reversed in part the district court's decision. It stated that due process required pre-reinstatement notice of the employee's allegations, notice of the substance of the relevant supporting evidence, an opportunity to submit a written response, and an opportunity to meet with the investigator and present statements from rebuttal witnesses. Due process did not require employer confrontation and cross-examination before preliminary reinstatement if a prompt post-reinstatement evidentiary hearing was available. *Brock v. Roadway Express, Inc.*, 481 U.S. 252, 107 S.Ct. 1740, 95 L.Ed.2d 239 (1987).

Even in a case involving national security, public employees are entitled to have appropriate procedures for employment actions. Statutes and regulations describing appropriate procedures must be obeyed.

The National Security Agency (NSA) terminated the employment of a cryptographic technician for engaging in homosexual relationships with foreign nationals. The NSA proposed terminating the employee according to its personnel regulations. The termination letter noted that the employee's "indiscriminate personal conduct" made his continued access to classified information impossible. After a hearing, the employee's security clearance was revoked and because this was a condition to NSA employment, his termination became final. The employee then requested a hearing before the Secretary of Defense, claiming that the 1959 NSA Act did not authorize termination without a hearing before the defense secretary. The secretary's response was that the removal was for cause under the NSA's regulations and did not require the secretary's authority. The employee sued the secretary in the U.S. District Court for the District of Columbia, claiming that the Act did not delegate authority to remove employees to the NSA's director. The district court granted the secretary's motion for summary judgment. The U.S. Court of Appeals, District of Columbia Circuit, reversed the district court's decision, ruling that the Act applied. The defense secretary appealed to the U.S. Supreme Court.

The Supreme Court noted that the NSA Act authorized the defense secretary or his designee to establish positions and make necessary appointments to carry out the function of the agency. The authority to appoint also implied a power to remove. The Act was not the exclusive means to remove NSA employees for national security reasons. The alternative selected by the NSA director was a correct procedure for removal because of permissive language in the Act. The secretary had broad discretion to terminate employees consistent with national security, just as discretion was present in the selection of NSA employees. The termination procedure selected by the NSA director provided a hearing equivalent to that provided under the NSA Act. The Court reversed the appeals court, permitting the secretary to terminate the technician's employment. *Carlucci v. Doe,* 488 U.S. 93, 109 S.Ct. 407, 102 L.Ed.2d 395 (1988).

C. Other Considerations

In the case below, the nonrenewal of a tenured teacher's contract because of her failure to earn continuing education credits was held constitutionally allowable and not a deprivation of her substantive due process and equal protection rights.

A tenured Oklahoma teacher failed to earn required continuing education credits. This violated her school district's policy, and she forfeited salary increases to which she would have been otherwise entitled. The state legislature then mandated salary raises for teachers regardless of compliance with continuing education requirements. The district threatened to terminate the teacher's employment unless she fulfilled the continuing education requirements. When she refused, the district refused to renew her contract. She sued the district in a federal district court, which dismissed her case. However, the U.S. Court of Appeals, Tenth Circuit, reversed the district court's decision, and the district appealed to the U.S. Supreme Court.

Regarding the Due Process Clause part of the teacher's claim, the Court said that the district's rule was endowed with a presumption of legislative validity and the teacher failed to rebut that presumption. The desire of the district to provide well-qualified teachers was not arbitrary—especially when it made every effort to give this specific teacher a chance to meet the requirements. The rule was reasonable and the teacher's interest in continued employment did not outweigh the compelling state interest in public education. Nor was there a deprivation of equal protection since all teachers were obligated to obtain the same credits. The sanction of contract nonrenewal was rationally related to the district's objective of enforcing the continuing education obligation of its teachers. The Court reversed the court of appeals' decision, finding the district sanctions constitutional on both Due Process and Equal Protection Clause grounds. *Harrah Independent School Dist. v. Martin*, 440 U.S. 194, 99 S.Ct. 1062, 59 L.Ed.2d 248 (1979).

Where an employer takes improper action against an employee, and a union refuses to process the employee's grievance, both the union and the employer can be held liable for damages to the employee.

A U.S. Postal Service employee was suspended without pay for fighting with a coworker. He was a member of the American Postal Workers Union. After the employee was formally terminated, he filed a grievance with the union as provided by the collective bargaining agreement (CBA). The union chose not to take his grievance to arbitration, and he then sued the union and the Postal Service in a federal district court, asserting that the Postal Service had violated the CBA by dismissing him without just cause, and that the union had breached its duty of fair representation. A jury found for the employee and against both defendants and apportioned the damages between the two. On appeal to the U.S. Court of Appeals, Fourth Circuit, the court affirmed except for the award of damages against the union. The Postal Service then appealed to the U.S. Supreme Court.

The Supreme Court held that where damage had been caused by both the employer and the union, it was proper to apportion liability between the two according to the damage each had caused. Here, requiring the union to pay damages would not impose on it a burden inconsistent with national policy, but rather would provide an additional incentive to unions to process members' claims where warranted. The Court thus reversed the court of appeals' decision, and allowed apportionment of the damages between the Postal Service and the union. *Bowen v. United States Postal Service*, 459 U.S. 212, 103 S.Ct. 588, 74 L.Ed.2d 402 (1983).

The paramount interest of national security prevails over individual due process rights, as shown in the following case involving a work-related security clearance.

The Navy hired a veteran's-preference civilian employee to work at its refit facility, which worked on the Trident submarine. All employee positions at the facility were classified as sensitive. While waiting for a security clearance, the employee performed only limited duties. His security clearance was denied after he had been at the facility for more than a year because the Navy discovered that he had several felony convictions. He was dismissed for cause after administrative proceedings were held and he appealed. He argued that because he had been removed for cause and not for national security reasons, he had not been afforded sufficient procedural protections. The U.S. Court of Appeals agreed, and the Navy appealed to the U.S. Supreme Court. The Supreme Court held that the employee received sufficient procedural due process. It stated that the employee had been dismissed for cause because he did not have the necessary security clearance. The decision not to issue a security clearance was not reviewable in this case, where national security granted broad discretion to the Navy to determine who should have access to classified information. The Court held that since a security clearance was a requirement for employment at the facility, the clearance-denied employee had been dismissed for just cause. The Court reversed the court of appeals' decision. *Dep't of Navy v. Egan,* 484 U.S. 518, 108 S.Ct. 818, 98 L.Ed.2d 918 (1988).

In the case below, the Supreme Court found that a termination agreement could not prevent a former employee from testifying against his former employer. Despite a termination agreement, the state's court order could not extend beyond the parties' controversy to control proceedings brought in other states by other parties.

A longtime General Motors (GM) employee who worked on fuel line designs frequently testified for GM in product liability cases. In one Georgia case, he testified that a GM truck fuel system was an inferior product. He was then fired and he filed a Michigan trial court action against GM for wrongful discharge and other claims. GM counterclaimed for breach of a fiduciary duty not to disclose privileged and confidential information and for misappropriating documents. The parties reached a settlement agreement under which the former employee received payment in return for a permanent injunction prohibiting him from testifying as an expert witness in other GM product liability cases without prior written consent. However, the order did not affect the still pending Georgia litigation. A separate settlement agreement permitted the employee to testify in other cases if another tribunal ordered his appearance. Six years later, the former employee was subpoenaed to testify in a Missouri wrongful death action involving a GM vehicle fire. GM resisted his appearance, asserting that the Michigan court order barred his testimony. A federal district court allowed the employee to be deposed and to testify and a jury awarded the victim's estate over $11 million in damages. The U.S. Court of Appeals, Eighth Circuit, reversed the district court judgment under the Full Faith and Credit Clause of the Constitution.

The Supreme Court accepted the estate's petition for review and found no public policy exception permitting a state court to resist the recognition of a foreign state court judgment. However, the Michigan court order could not extend beyond the parties' controversy to control proceedings brought in other states by other parties. Because the Michigan court had no power over the Missouri parties, it could not prevent the employee from testifying in the Missouri action. Moreover, the parties' agreement allowed the employee to testify where ordered by another court. The Court reversed the judgment and remanded the case. *Baker v. General Motors Corp.*, 522 U.S. 222, 118 S.Ct. 657, 139 L.Ed.2d 580 (1998).

A person may not bring suit under the federal Racketeer Influenced and Corrupt Organizations Act for injuries caused by an overt act that is not an act of racketeering or otherwise unlawful under the statute.

Robert A. Beck II was a former president, CEO, director and shareholder of Southeastern Insurance Group (SIG). Beck discovered that several former senior officers and directors of SIG conspired to and engaged in racketeering. After Beck contacted regulators, he claimed the officers and directors (respondents) orchestrated a scheme to remove him from the company. After being terminated, Beck sued, asserting, among other things, a § 1964(c) cause of action for respondents' alleged conspiracy to violate §§ 1962(a), (b), and (c) of the Racketeer Influenced and Corrupt Organizations Act. Beck alleged that his injury was proximately caused by an overt act — the termination of his employment — done in furtherance of the respondents' conspiracy, and that § 1964(c), therefore, provided him with a cause of action under RICO. The district court dismissed Beck's RICO conspiracy claim, agreeing with the respondents that employees who are terminated for refusing to participate in RICO activities, or who threaten to report RICO activities, do not have standing to sue under RICO for damages resulting from their loss of employment. In affirming, the U.S. Court of Appeals, 11th Circuit, held that, because the overt act causing Beck's injury was not an act of racketeering, it could not support a § 1964(c) cause of action.
The Supreme Court affirmed in a majority opinion written by Justice Clarence Thomas. "As at common law," the justice said, "a civil conspiracy plaintiff cannot bring suit under RICO based on injury caused by any act in furtherance of a conspiracy that might have caused the plaintiff injury. Rather, consistency with the common law requires that a RICO conspiracy plaintiff allege injury from an act that is analogous to an 'act of a tortious character,' ... meaning an act that is independently wrongful under RICO. The specific type of act that is analogous to an act of a tortious character may depend on the underlying substantive violation the defendant is alleged to have committed." "However," Justice Thomas added, "respondents' alleged overt act in furtherance of their conspiracy is not independently wrongful under any substantive provision of the statute." Because the termination of Beck was not independently wrongful under the disputed RICO provision, Beck could not bring suit under § 1964(c) in an attempt to recover damages resulting from the loss of his position with SIG. *Beck v. Prupis et al.*, 529 U.S. 494, 120 S.Ct. 1608, 146 L.Ed.2d 561 (2000).

II. SUSPENSION

The following case demonstrates that a determination of the appropriate procedure in a particular case can also determine the substantive outcome of the case.

The U.S. Fish and Wildlife Service (FWS) hired a man as an administrative officer for a youth conservation camp. His position was to last for the duration of the program. Prior to that time, however, the FWS advised him that it intended to dismiss him for, among other things, his unauthorized use of a government vehicle. After he replied to the charges, the FWS dismissed him, but failed to advise him of his right to a formal hearing. Over a year later, the FWS concluded that it should only have suspended him for 30 days, and offered him back pay from the time the suspension would have ended to the time when the program had ended. He elected to sue in the claims court, asserting that the suspension was unwarranted. The claims court ruled that under the Civil Service Reform Act (CSRA) there should be no review of the personnel action. The employee successfully appealed to a federal district court, and the U.S. Court of Appeals denied the government's request for a rehearing. The case came before the U.S. Supreme Court, which held that the claims court had been correct in denying the employee a review of the personnel action taken against him. The Court stated that the CSRA had deliberately excluded employees in the nonpreference "excepted service" category from judicial review for a suspension action. It ruled that the employee's action could only be heard by either the Merit Systems Protection Board or the FWS. The Court reversed the appellate court's decision, and denied judicial review to the employee. *U.S. v. Fausto*, 484 U.S. 439, 108 S.Ct. 668, 98 L.Ed.2d 830 (1988).

The NCAA has been held not to be a state actor by the Supreme Court. In a 1988 Nevada case, the Court concluded that the NCAA did not have the power to discipline a school's coach, and thus could not be liable for sanctions imposed against him.

Following a lengthy investigation of allegedly improper recruiting practices by the University of Nevada, Las Vegas (UNLV), the NCAA found 38 violations, including 10 by the school's head basketball coach. The NCAA proposed a number of sanctions and threatened to impose more if the coach was not suspended. UNLV decided to suspend the coach. Facing an enormous pay cut, the coach sued the NCAA under 42 U.S.C. § 1983 for violating his due process rights. The Nevada Supreme Court held that the NCAA's conduct constituted state action for constitutional purposes. It upheld a Nevada trial court's dismissal of the suspension and award of attorneys' fees. The NCAA appealed to the U.S. Supreme Court.

The Supreme Court held that the NCAA's participation in the events that led to the suspension did not constitute state action within the meaning of § 1983. The NCAA was not a state actor on the theory that it misused the power it possessed under state law because UNLV (and not the NCAA) had suspended the coach. UNLV's decision to suspend the coach in compliance with the NCAA's rules and recommendations did not turn the NCAA's conduct into state action. This was because UNLV retained the power to withdraw from the NCAA and establish its own standards. The NCAA could not directly discipline the coach, but could threaten to impose additional sanctions against the school. It was the school's decision and not the NCAA's decision to suspend the coach. *NCAA v. Tarkanian*, 488 U.S. 179, 109 S.Ct. 454, 102 L.Ed.2d 469 (1988).

In the case below, the Supreme Court held that refusal to pay a suspended police officer (who had been charged with a felony) pending a hearing did not violate due process.

A police officer employed by a Pennsylvania state university was arrested in a drug raid and charged with several felony counts related to marijuana possession and distribution. State police notified the university of the arrest and charges, and the university's human resources director immediately suspended the officer without pay pursuant to a state executive order requiring such action where a state employee is formally charged with a felony. Although the criminal charges were dismissed, university officials demoted the officer because of the felony charges. The university did not inform the officer that it had obtained his confession from police records and he was thus unable to fully respond to damaging statements in the police reports. He filed a federal district court action against university officials for failing to provide him with notice and an opportunity to be heard before his suspension without pay. The court granted summary judgment to the officials, but the U.S. Court of Appeals, Third Circuit, reversed and remanded the case.

The Supreme Court agreed to review the case, and stated that the court of appeals had improperly held that a suspended public employee must always receive a paid suspension under *Cleveland Bd. of Educ. v. Loudermill*, 470 U.S. 532 (1985). The Court held that the university did not violate due process by refusing to pay a suspended employee charged with a felony pending a hearing. It accepted the officials' argument that the Pennsylvania executive order made any pre-suspension hearing useless, since the filing of charges established an independent basis for believing that the officer had committed a felony. The Court noted that the officer here faced only a temporary suspension without pay, and not employment termination, as was the case in *Loudermill*. The Court reversed and remanded the court of appeals' judgment for consideration of the officer's arguments concerning a post-suspension hearing. *Gilbert v. Homar*, 520 U.S. 924, 117 S.Ct. 1807, 138 L.Ed.2d 120 (1997).

III. UNEMPLOYMENT COMPENSATION

A. Religious Convictions

In *Sherbert v. Verner*, the Supreme Court held that a state's disqualification of a claimant from the receipt of benefits was improper because the claimant was being forced to choose between her religion and

work. There must be a compelling state interest, held the Court, to justify the burden on the claimant's free exercise rights.

An employee was discharged by her employer because she refused to work on Saturday. She was a Seventh-day Adventist and Saturday was a Sabbath day. When she was unable to find other employment because of her religious refusal to work on Saturdays, she filed a claim for unemployment compensation benefits. The South Carolina Employment Security Commission denied her benefits because she failed, "without good cause," to accept suitable work which had been offered. The denial of benefits was affirmed by a trial court, and by the Supreme Court of South Carolina. The case then came before the U.S. Supreme Court. The Court held that the denial of benefits imposed a burden on the claimant's free exercise of religion in violation of the First Amendment. Here, the claimant was being forced to choose between following the precepts of her religion (and thus forfeiting benefits) and abandoning the precepts of her religion to accept work. The Court reversed the state supreme court's decision and remanded the case, holding that the claimant was entitled to be paid unemployment compensation benefits. *Sherbert v. Verner,* 374 U.S. 398, 83 S.Ct. 1790, 10 L.Ed.2d 965 (1963).

In *Thomas,* the Supreme Court noted that a state could not deny a benefit because of conduct mandated by religious belief—thereby putting substantial pressure on the claimant to modify his behavior and to violate his beliefs—unless there was a compelling state interest to justify such action.

An employee of a foundry and machinery company worked in the roll foundry, fabricating sheet steel for a variety of industrial uses. When the roll foundry closed, the company transferred the employee to a department that fabricated turrets for military tanks. The employee, a Jehovah's Witness, believed that working on weapons would violate the principles of his religion. Because there were no "nonweapons" jobs in the company and because the company refused to lay him off, he quit. He then applied for unemployment compensation, which was denied. The Indiana Court of Appeals awarded benefits, but the state supreme court reversed. Further appeal was taken to the U.S. Supreme Court.

The Supreme Court held that the denial of benefits violated the applicant's First Amendment right to the free exercise of his religion. It did not matter that another Jehovah's Witness was willing to work on tank turrets. The religious belief in question need not be shared by all the members of a religious sect. The important consideration was that the employee had quit for religious reasons. The Court stated that a person may not be compelled to choose between the exercise of a First Amendment right and participation in an otherwise available public program. It thus reversed the lower court and granted benefits to the applicant. *Thomas v. Review Bd. of Indiana Employment Security Div.,* 450 U.S. 707, 101 S.Ct. 1425, 67 L.Ed.2d 624 (1981).

In the case below, the Court held that an employee's conversion to a religion that   prohibited work on a particular day of the week was not misconduct so as to deprive her of unemployment compensation benefits after her discharge.

A Florida jeweler hired a woman to work at a retail jewelry store. Subsequently, the woman became baptized in the Seventh-day Adventist Church. She informed her supervisor that she could no longer work from sundown on Friday to sundown on Saturday, due to her religious beliefs. After initially accommodating her, the jeweler discharged her. When she filed for unemployment compensation benefits, the jeweler contested payment, asserting that "misconduct" connected with her work was the reason for the discharge. Benefits were denied. Following the Florida District Court of Appeal's affirmance of no benefits, the applicant appealed to the U.S. Supreme Court. The Supreme Court held that the denial of benefits violated the Free Exercise Clause of the First Amendment. Under a strict scrutiny analysis, the rejection of benefits failed. First, even though Florida law only disqualified applicants for a limited time, rather than making them completely ineligible, the denial could not be justified. Second, it did not matter that the employer did not change the conditions of employment so as to conflict with the employee's religious beliefs, or that the employee converted to the religion during the course of the employment. Benefits had to be paid. Finally, the Court noted that paying benefits here would not foster religion in violation of the Establishment Clause. *Hobbie v. Unemployment Appeals Comm'n of Florida,* 480 U.S. 136, 107 S.Ct. 1046, 94 L.Ed.2d 190 (1987).

In *Frazee*, the Supreme Court held that a claimant could refuse a job that conflicted with his religious beliefs, and still be eligible for unemployment benefits.

An Illinois man was offered a temporary retail position by a temp placement agency. He refused the position because the job would have required him to work on Sunday, a day he considered to be "the Lord's day." He then applied for unemployment compensation benefits, claiming that there was good cause for his refusal to work on Sunday. The Illinois Department of Economic Security denied his application, and a board of review upheld that decision. It found that the applicant's refusal to work was based solely on an entirely personal belief which was not a tenet or dogma of a church, sect or denomination. The Illinois courts also upheld the denial of benefits, and appeal was taken to the U.S. Supreme Court.

The applicant charged that the denial of benefits violated his free exercise of religion, as guaranteed by the First Amendment to the U.S. Constitution. The Court agreed. So long as the applicant had a sincere belief that required him to refrain from the work offered, it did not matter that the belief was not in response to the commands of a particular religious organization. Further, the state had not shown any justification for burdening the applicant's beliefs by denying employment benefits. The granting of benefits was not likely to cause a mass movement away from Sunday employment by others. The Court reversed the lower courts and granted benefits to the applicant. *Frazee v. Illinois Dep't of Economic Security*, 489 U.S. 829, 109 S.Ct. 1514, 103 L.Ed.2d 914 (1989).

In 1990, the Supreme Court essentially overruled prior decisions regarding the free exercise of religion by holding that a law of general applicability (which had an incidental burden on the free exercise of religion) was not violative of the First Amendment. In the case below, two unemployment benefits claimants were denied benefits because they ingested peyote, and the Court upheld the denial of benefits because peyote is a controlled substance.

A drug rehabilitation organization fired two employees because they ingested peyote for sacramental purposes at a Native American church ceremony. Peyote is a hallucinogenic drug. When the two men applied for unemployment compensation benefits, their applications were denied on the ground that they had committed work-related misconduct. The Oregon Court of Appeals reversed that determination, finding that the denial of benefits violated the Free Exercise Clause of the First Amendment. The state supreme court affirmed, and the case reached the U.S. Supreme Court which held that a remand was required to determine whether religious use of peyote was legal in Oregon. *Employment Div., Dep't of Human Resources v. Smith*, 485 U.S. 660, 108 S.Ct. 1444, 99 L.Ed.2d 753 (1988).

On remand, the Oregon Supreme Court held that the applicants' religious use of peyote was against the law in Oregon because no exception was made for sacramental use of the drug. However, the court then decided that the prohibition against use of the drug was invalid under the Free Exercise Clause. Thus, the state could not deny unemployment benefits to the applicants. The case again came before the U.S. Supreme Court.

The Supreme Court stated that Oregon could prohibit sacramental peyote use without violating the Free Exercise Clause and, accordingly, could deny unemployment benefits to persons discharged for such use. Here, a law of general applicability, which was religiously neutral, prohibited the possession of controlled substances (including peyote) without making exceptions for religious use. This was permissible. It only incidentally affected religion. The Court reversed the state supreme court's decision, and held that unemployment benefits could be denied. *Employment Div., Dep't of Human Resources v. Smith*, 494 U.S. 872, 110 S.Ct. 1595, 108 L.Ed.2d 876 (1990).

B. Strikes and Leaves of Absence

In 1979, the Supreme Court upheld a New York law that allowed striking employees to collect unemployment compensation benefits after eight weeks of unemployment.

A New York statute allowed striking employees to collect unemployment compensation benefits after eight weeks of unemployment. Several companies' employees began collecting benefits after being on strike for eight weeks. Because New York's system was financed primarily by employer contributions based on the amount of benefits paid to former employees of each employer in past years, a large part of the cost of these benefits was ultimately imposed on the companies. They sued, seeking a declaration that the New York law was invalid because it conflicted with federal law. A federal district court ruled in their favor, but the U.S. Court of Appeals reversed.

On further appeal, the U.S. Supreme Court affirmed the court of appeals' decision. The Court held that the New York law was one of general applicability, and that it did not involve any attempt by the state to regulate conduct in the private sector labor-management field. Congress left it to the states to fashion their own unemployment compensation programs (and especially their own eligibility criteria); thus, the New York statute had to be treated with deference. The Court also noted that Congress, in enacting the National Labor Relations Act and the Social Security Act, did not intend to preempt a state's power to pay unemployment compensation benefits to strikers. *New York Telephone Co. v. New York State Dep't of Labor*, 440 U.S. 519, 99 S.Ct. 1328, 59 L.Ed.2d 553 (1979).

In the following case, the Supreme Court held that a state statute that disallowed unemployment benefits to employees who "financed" strikes was not preempted by federal labor law. Unemployment compensation requires that the recipient be unemployed involuntarily. The financing of the strikes was deemed to be voluntary unemployment.

A Michigan statute made employees ineligible for unemployment compensation benefits if they provided "financing," by means other than the payment of regular union dues, for a strike that caused their unemployment. Employees of General Motors were required by their union to pay "emergency dues" to augment the union's strike insurance fund. Subsequently, several local unions went on strike, curtailing operations at other plants. Strike fund benefits were paid to all the workers who were idle. They then sought unemployment compensation, but were denied such benefits by the Michigan Supreme Court. They appealed to the U.S. Supreme Court. The Court agreed with the lower court that the employees' payment of emergency dues amounted to "financing" of the strikes, which caused the unemployment. Even though federal labor law protects employees' rights to authorize a strike, it does not prohibit a state from deciding to disallow unemployment benefits to employees who cause their own unemployment— either by financing a strike or by directly participating in the strike. The decision to participate in the strike amounted to causing the unemployment in this case; it was voluntary rather than involuntary. The Court affirmed the Michigan Supreme Court's decision denying benefits. *Baker v. General Motors Corp.*, 478 U.S. 621, 106 S.Ct. 3129, 92 L.Ed.2d 504 (1986).

In 1987, the Supreme Court held that a woman who had left work to have a baby was not entitled to unemployment benefits after the company notified her that there were no positions available. This was not discrimination on the basis of pregnancy, because the state statute involved was neutral toward pregnancy.

A Missouri woman worked for a company for about three years; she then requested a leave of absence due to pregnancy. The company granted her a "leave without guarantee of reinstatement" which meant that she would only be rehired if a position was available when she was ready to return to work. When she later notified the company of her willingness to return, no positions were available. She then filed a claim for unemployment compensation benefits, which was denied. A trial court held that the Missouri statute—which disqualifies a claimant who has left work voluntarily without good cause attributable to the work or the employer—was inconsistent with the Federal Unemployment Tax Act (FUTA). The court of appeals affirmed, but the state supreme court reversed. Further appeal was taken to the U.S. Supreme Court.

The Court held that the Missouri statute was consistent with FUTA. Congress only intended to prohibit states from singling out pregnancy for unfavorable treatment when it decreed that no state could deny any compensation "solely on the basis of pregnancy or termination of pregnancy." Here, the Missouri statute was neutral toward pregnancy. Since the employee had left work for a reason that had no causal connection to either her work or her employer, she was not entitled to unemployment compensation benefits. She had not been denied benefits "solely" because of her pregnancy. The Court affirmed the state supreme court's decision against the employee. *Wimberly v. Labor and Industrial Relations Comm'n,* 479 U.S. 511, 107 S.Ct. 821, 93 L.Ed.2d 909 (1987).

CHAPTER EIGHT

Workers' Compensation

I. WORKERS' COMPENSATION

A. Federal Statutes

The Federal Employees' Compensation Act (which is essentially a workers' compensation statute) does not bar a third party from bringing suit against the government for indemnification where multiple tortfeasors cause employee injury.

In 1975, an airplane operated by the U.S. Air Force and manufactured by a private corporation crashed near Saigon, South Vietnam, during a mission to evacuate over 250 orphans shortly before the fall of Saigon. A civilian employee of the U.S. Navy died in the crash. The United States paid death benefits to her survivors under the Federal Employees' Compensation Act (FECA). The administrator of the employee's estate filed suit against the corporation, seeking damages for wrongful death and for the injuries suffered by the employee prior to her death. The corporation sought indemnification from the government under the Federal Tort Claims Act, and settled the lawsuit brought by the administrator. The government moved to dismiss the lawsuit against it on the ground that FECA's exclusive liability provisions barred the third-party claim. The district court granted summary judgment to the corporation, but the U.S. Court of Appeals reversed.

On further appeal to the U.S. Supreme Court, the Court held that FECA's exclusive liability provision, 5 U.S.C. § 8116(c), did not bar the corporation's indemnity action against the government. FECA is essentially a workers' compensation statute designed to guarantee employees the right to receive immediate, fixed benefits, regardless of fault (and without having to sue for them), in return for which they give up the right to sue the government. Section 8116(c) was intended to govern only the rights of employees, their relatives, and people claiming through them or on their behalf. It was not intended to bar an indemnity action by a third party against the United States. Accordingly, the Court reversed the court of appeals' decision and remanded the case. *Lockheed Aircraft Corp. v. United States*, 460 U.S. 190, 103 S.Ct. 1033, 74 L.Ed.2d 911 (1983).

Despite the fact that the government is not liable for losses such as pain and suffering under FECA, if the employee recovers for such losses against a third party, the government can be reimbursed for the FECA money it has paid out for economic losses like medical expenses and lost wages.

A special agent for the FBI was injured in an automobile accident in Philadelphia while on official business. As such, he was entitled to FECA benefits for his medical expenses and lost wages. However, FECA did not have to provide money for such losses as pain and suffering. After receiving money under FECA, the FBI agent sued the other driver for his pain and suffering losses. The lawsuit settled, and the United States then sought to be reimbursed for its FECA payments out of the settlement. The agent refused to pay the money to the government, instead filing suit to obtain a declaration that the government was limited to recovering for economic losses of the sort covered by FECA. A federal district court ruled for the government, but the U.S. Court of Appeals reversed.

On further appeal to the U.S. Supreme Court, the Court noted that § 8132 of FECA entitled the United States to be reimbursed for compensation out of any damages award or settlement made in satisfaction of third party liability, even if the award or settlement was not for medical expenses or lost wages. FECA does not confine the rights of the government to those of a subrogee; it simply creates a general right of reimbursement that prevails even where the employee's recovery from a third party includes losses that are excluded from FECA coverage (like pain and suffering). Accordingly, the Court reversed the court of appeals' decision and held that the government could recover the FECA money it had paid to the FBI agent. *United States v. Lorenzetti*, 467 U.S. 167, 104 S.Ct. 2284, 81 L.Ed.2d 134 (1984).

Private workers' compensation insurers are not "state actors" under the Fourteenth Amendment so as to trigger an employee's right to a hearing over an insurer's decision to withhold payments for disputed treatment.

In 1993, Pennsylvania amended its workers' compensation laws to create a procedure under which the reasonableness and necessity of an employee's medical treatment could be reviewed before the bill was paid. Under this system, if an insurer disputed the treatment, it could request a review and withhold payment to a health care provider pending resolution of the dispute by a utilization review organization (URO). The URO had to issue a determination within 30 days of review request. An employee could appeal an unfavorable determination, but the insurer did not have to pay for the treatment unless and until the determination was overturned. If the URO found in the employee's favor, the insurer had to pay the disputed bill immediately.

A group of employee organizations and individual employees who had medical bills withheld pursuant to the new procedure sued several private insurers, claiming that in withholding worker's compensation benefits without predeprivation notice and a hearing, the insurers acted "under color of state law" by depriving them of a property right under 42 U.S.C. § 1983 and the Fourteenth Amendment. The district court dismissed the complaint, and the U.S. Court of Appeals, Third Circuit, reversed. The Supreme Court held that that a private insurer's decision to withhold medical payments and seek review of disputed treatments was not fairly attributable to the state so as to trigger the Fourteenth Amendment right to notice and a hearing. Nor did the decision to withhold payments deprive the plaintiff employees of any constitutionally protected property right.

The mere fact that a business is subject to extensive regulation does not, by itself, convert the business' action to state action. Nor was the employee's right to medical payments for work-related injuries a state-created property right. This is because an employee is not entitled to payment for *all* medical treatment once the employer's liability is established. The employee is entitled only to payment for medical treatment that is "reasonable and necessary." Any dispute over the treatment's reasonableness and necessity must be resolved before the employee's right to receive payment arises. Here, the individual employees had proven only that they suffered work-related injuries. To be entitled to payment, they still had to prove that the treatment they sought was reasonable and necessary. *American Manufacturers Mutual Ins. Co. v. Sullivan*, 526 U.S. 40, 119 S.Ct. 977, 143 L.Ed.2d 130 (1999).

Federal maritime law allows a cause of action for negligence that results in wrongful death, according to the following decision.

While conducting sandblasting work on a U.S. Naval ship, an individual was injured and subsequently died from his injuries. At the time of the injury, the individual was working for a subcontractor of Mid-Atlantic Coatings, which was a subcontractor for Norfolk Shipbuilding & Drydock Corporation. His mother then brought a lawsuit under federal maritime law in federal district court, seeking damages for wrongful death under general maritime law. A U.S. district court dismissed the mother's action, finding no cause of action exists for negligence under general maritime law when the deceased was a nonseaman and the injury occurred in state territorial waters. The U.S. Court of Appeals, Fourth Circuit, reversed, finding a maritime cause of action for negligence leading to a wrongful death exists under *Moragne v. States Marine Lines,* 398 U.S. 375 (1970). Norfolk's petition for certiorari was accepted by the Supreme Court.

The Court affirmed, finding no prohibition against recognizing a federal maritime cause of action for wrongful death resulting from negligence. The Court noted that a cause of action already existed under federal law for wrongful death if a breach of the maritime duty of seaworthiness occurs, and found no barriers to allowing a cause of action for wrongful death arising from negligence.

This conclusion was a logical extension of the holding in *Moragne*, which allowed a maritime cause of action for death caused by a violation of the maritime duty of seaworthiness. In examining potential federal statutory bars to such an action, the Supreme Court analyzed the language of the Jones Act, the Death on the High Seas Act and the Longshore and Harbor Workers' Compensation Act, and concluded that none of these statutes preempted the mother's negligence claim. *Norfolk Shipbuilding & Drydock Corp. v. Garris*, 532 U.S.___, 121 S.Ct. 1927, ___ L.Ed.2d ___ (2001).

B. State Workers' Compensation Statutes

In *Wengler*, the Supreme Court held that a state statute that denied a widower death benefits unless he was incapacitated or dependent on his wife's earnings violated the Equal Protection Clause of the U.S. Constitution's Fourteenth Amendment because the statute granted death benefits to widows without providing the same restrictions.

The wife of a Missouri man died in a work-related accident in the parking lot of her employer. Her husband filed a claim for death benefits under Missouri's workers' compensation law. However, the law provided that a widower could not receive death benefits unless he was either mentally or physically incapacitated from wage earning, or unless he could show actual dependency on his wife's earnings. His claim was denied because he did not fit into the statutory parameters, but a state trial court reversed on equal protection grounds. After the Missouri Supreme Court reversed, finding that the substantive difference in the economic standing of working men and women justified the advantage that the law gave to a widow, the U.S. Supreme Court granted certiorari.

The Supreme Court held that the Missouri law indisputably mandated gender-based discrimination. Further, the discriminatory means employed was not substantially related to the achievement of the important governmental objective of providing for needy spouses. Either all widows and widowers could be paid or only dependent surviving spouses could be paid. The discriminatory law, then, simply did not stand up under the scrutiny of the Court. The claim that it was administratively more convenient to have the law structured in this way was not sufficient to justify the different treatment for men. The Court reversed the lower court's decision and remanded the case. *Wengler v. Druggist Mutual Ins. Co.,* 446 U.S. 142, 100 S.Ct. 1540, 64 L.Ed.2d 107 (1980).

In the following case, the Supreme Court held that an employee could obtain a supplemental workers' compensation award from another state where he would have been eligible for an award in the first place.

A resident of the District of Columbia was hired there by a company, but also worked for the company in the state of Virginia. He sustained a back injury while working in Virginia, and received benefits under Virginia's workers' compensation law. Subsequently, he received a supplemental award under the District of Columbia's workers' compensation law. His employer and its carrier challenged this second award because Virginia law excluded any other recovery "at common law or otherwise." Thus, the District of Columbia should have given the first award "full faith and credit." An administrative order upholding the second award was reversed by a U.S. Court of Appeals, and the case came before the U.S. Supreme Court.

The Court held that the U.S. Constitution's Full Faith and Credit Clause did not preclude successive workers' compensation awards where the second state would have had the power to apply its workers' compensation law in the first place. Here, since the employee could have sought a compensation award from the District of Columbia in the first place, the employer and its insurer would have had to measure their liability exposure by the more generous workers' compensation scheme anyway. Accordingly, the first state's interest was not enough to prevent the second state from making the supplemental award. The Court reversed and remanded the case. *Thomas v. Washington Gas Light Co.,* 448 U.S. 261, 100 S.Ct. 2647, 65 L.Ed.2d 757 (1980).

In 1988, the Supreme Court determined that a state could apply an additional award provision for the employer's violation of a state safety regulation to a private contractor operating a federally owned facility. The Supremacy Clause did not bar the application of workers' compensation laws to the premises.

An Ohio man worked at a nuclear production facility owned by the United States, but operated by a private company. He fractured his ankle when he fell from scaffolding, caused when his glove caught on a protruding bolt. After receiving workers' compensation benefits, he sought an additional award on the ground that his injury had resulted from the company's violation of a state safety requirement. The industrial commission denied his claim for a supplemental award because of federal preemption, but the state court of appeals ordered the commission to consider the application, and the state supreme court affirmed. On further appeal, the U.S. Supreme Court held that the Supremacy Clause did not bar the state from applying its additional award provision of the workers' compensation law to a private contractor operating a federally owned nuclear production facility which performs a federal function. Here, Congress had provided clear and unambiguous authorization for the application of the provision in 40 U.S.C. § 290—which provided that states could apply workers' compensation laws to federal facilities the same as to private facilities. The Court thus affirmed the state court decisions. *Goodyear Atomic Corp. v. Miller,* 486 U.S. 174, 108 S.Ct. 1704, 100 L.Ed.2d 158. (1988).

In the case below, the Supreme Court held that the exclusivity provisions in state workers' compensation laws did not bar migrant workers from availing themselves of a private right of action under the Migrant and Seasonal Agricultural Worker Protection Act.

Several migrant farm workers sustained severe injuries in an automobile accident while they traveled to work in a fruit company's van. They received workers' compensation benefits as a result. Subsequently, they filed suit against the fruit company, alleging that their injuries had been caused in part by the company's intentional violations of the Migrant and Seasonal Agricultural Worker Protection Act's motor vehicle safety provisions. The company sought summary judgment which was granted by the district court, but the U.S. Court of Appeals reversed. The U.S. Supreme Court granted certiorari. It held that the exclusivity provisions in the state workers' compensation laws did not bar the migrant workers from asserting a claim under the act. Section 1854 of the act established a private right of action that provided for both actual and statutory damages in cases of intentional violations. This federal remedy was not precluded by state law. Thus, even though an award of actual damages under the act could be offset from workers' compensation benefits, the claim itself was not precluded. The Court affirmed the court of appeals' decision denying summary judgment. *Adams Fruit Co. v. Barrett,* 494 U.S. 638, 110 S.Ct. 1384, 108 L.Ed.2d 585 (1990).

The Supreme Court upheld a 1987 Michigan statute which required employers who had coordinated benefits for disabled workers under an earlier law to reimburse the workers for the benefits which had been withheld.

Michigan workers' compensation law has been subject to continuing debate and study for almost two decades. In 1981, a statute that allowed "benefit coordination" was enacted, allowing employers to decrease benefits to those disabled employees who were eligible to receive wage-loss compensation from other employer-funded sources. Certain employers then attempted to apply the law to employees injured prior to 1982. The legislature subsequently enacted a law disapproving this practice. The employers sought judicial relief (partly because the new statute required them to reimburse disabled employees nearly $25 million). The controversy eventually reached the U.S. Supreme Court.

The employers argued that the reimbursement provision violated the Contract Clause and the Due Process Clause of the U.S. Constitution. The Court disagreed. With respect to the Contract Clause, there was no contractual relationship that had been impaired by the new statute under the circumstances of this case. Although employment contracts existed prior to the new law's enactment, they did not address the specific workers' compensation terms at issue. Further, there was no due process violation because the reimbursement provision was a rational means of meeting a legitimate objective—preserving injured workers' rights to their full benefits. The Court thus held that the Michigan statute did not violate the Constitution. *General Motors Corp. v. Romein,* 503 U.S. 181, 112 S.Ct. 1105, 117 L.Ed.2d 328 (1992).

Section 2(c)(2) of the District of Columbia Workers' Compensation Equity Amendment Act of 1990 required employers who provided health insurance for their employees to provide equivalent health insurance coverage for injured employees who were eligible for workers' compensation benefits. The Supreme Court held that this section was preempted by ERISA because it related to a covered benefit plan.

A District of Columbia workers' compensation act required employers who provide health insurance for their employees to provide equivalent health insurance coverage for injured employees eligible for workers' compensation benefits. An employer filed an action in the U.S. District Court for the District of Columbia against the locality and its mayor, claiming that the act was preempted by the Employee Retirement Income Security Act, which superseded state laws that related to any employee benefit plan covered by ERISA. The court granted the locality's motion to dismiss. On appeal, the U.S. Court of Appeals reversed, holding that preemption was within ERISA's structure and plain meaning. The locality appealed.

The U.S. Supreme Court affirmed the judgment of the court of appeals. It stated that a law "relates to" a covered employee benefit plan if it has a connection with or reference to such a plan. ERISA preempts any state law that refers to or has a connection with covered benefit plans that do not fall within its exceptions — even if 1) the law is not specifically designed to affect such plans, 2) the effect is only indirect, and 3) the law is consistent with ERISA's substantive requirements. The Court held that employer-sponsored health insurance programs are subject to ERISA regulation, and any state law imposing requirements by reference to such covered programs must yield to ERISA. Even though the act's requirements "related to" an ERISA-exempt workers' compensation plan, ERISA's exemptions do not limit its preemptive sweep once it is determined that a law "relates to" a covered plan. The court held that ERISA's broad coverage superseded the workers' compensation act because the act related to a covered plan. The locality could not require employers to provide equivalent health insurance coverage for injured employees who were eligible for workers' compensation. *Dist. of Columbia v. Greater Washington Bd. of Trade*, 506 U.S. 125, 113 S.Ct. 580, 121 L.Ed.2d 513 (1992).

II. LONGSHORE AND HARBOR WORKERS' COMPENSATION ACT (LHWCA)

A. "Maritime Employment"

The Longshore and Harbor Workers' Compensation Act provides compensation for the death or disability of any person engaged in "maritime employment," if the disability or death resulted from an injury incurred upon the navigable waters of the United States or any adjoining pier or other area customarily used by an employer in loading, unloading, repairing, or building a vessel. In the following case, land-based employees who were involved in part of the activity of loading or unloading cargo were deemed to be "maritime employees" who were eligible for LHWCA benefits.

Two Texas men were injured in the course of their employment: one, while fastening military vehicles onto railroad flatcars on a public dock (he hit his own hand with a hammer), and the other, while unloading a bale of cotton from a dray wagon into a pier warehouse. Even though both men were injured while working on land, they applied for workers' compensation under the Longshore and Harbor Workers' Compensation Act (LHWCA), 33 U.S.C. § 901 *et seq.* They were denied benefits because the administrative law judges decided that "maritime employment" included only the part of the unloading process that takes place before the stevedoring gang places cargo onto the dock, and the part of the loading process that takes place to the seaside of the last point of rest on the dock. The Benefits Review Board reversed the decisions, and the U.S. Court of Appeals affirmed.

On further appeal, the U.S. Supreme Court held that coverage under the LHWCA was not limited to workers who were assigned to work over the water itself. Both workers were the kind of land-based employees that Congress intended to encompass within the term "maritime employment." They performed the same type of duties as longshoremen—and this was the crucial factor in determining coverage. A worker responsible for some portion of the activity of moving cargo directly from ship to land transportation is as much an integral part of the process of loading or unloading a ship as a person who participates in the entire process. Thus, the workers here had been engaged in maritime employment and were entitled to recover benefits under the LHWCA. The Court affirmed the appellate court's decision. *P.C. Pfeiffer Co., Inc. v. Ford,* 444 U.S. 69, 100 S.Ct. 328, 62 L.Ed.2d 225 (1979).

For the purposes of the LHWCA, a worker performing his or her job upon actual navigable waters of the United States will be deemed to be "engaged in maritime employment" even if performing a job which would not qualify the worker for benefits if it was performed on docks or piers.

A company contracted to build the foundation of a sewage treatment plant that would extend about 700 feet over the Hudson River, a navigable waterway of the United States. An employee of the company, while working on a cargo barge in the river directing a crane operator, was injured when a line used to keep caissons (large, hollow circular pipes) in position snapped. He filed a claim for compensation under the LHWCA. If the injury had occurred prior to 1972—when the LHWCA was amended—the employee would clearly have been covered. However, the 1972 amendments added a status requirement that employees covered by the act be "engaged in maritime employment" within the meaning of the act. The employee's claim was denied. The U.S. Court of Appeals upheld the denial of benefits because the claimant's employment lacked a "significant relationship to navigation or to commerce on navigable waters." The U.S. Supreme Court granted certiorari.

The Supreme Court held that the claimant, as a marine construction worker injured while performing his job upon actual navigable waters, was "engaged in maritime employment" within the meaning of the act and was thus covered under the LHWCA. The Court examined the legislative history of the 1972 amendments and found that Congress did not intend to exclude "employees traditionally covered" under the LHWCA. So long as the employee is working on the actual navigable waters of the United States, he need not show that his employment possesses a significant relationship to navigation or to commerce. That requirement is for employees injured on the adjoining land covered by the act. The Court reversed the court of appeals' decision, finding that the claimant was entitled to benefits. *Director, Office of Workers' Compensation Programs v. Perini North River Associates*, 459 U.S. 297, 103 S.Ct. 634, 74 L.Ed.2d 465 (1983).

In 1985, the Supreme Court noted that not every person involved in every task that is part of offshore drilling can be considered a "maritime employee." If the employee is not on navigable waters at the time of the injury, then he or she must be involved in one of the essential elements of the loading, unloading, repairing or building of a vessel.

While working as a welder on a fixed platform oil rig, an employee of a welding company was injured. The platform was located in Louisiana territorial waters. He accidentally burned through the bottom of a gas flow line, and an explosion occurred. When his employer's workers' compensation carrier denied him LHWCA benefits, he filed a complaint with the Department of Labor. An administrative law judge held for the employer and its carrier, but the Benefits Review Board reversed. It found that even though the injury had occurred in state waters, the employee could recover by virtue of the Outer Continental Shelf Lands Act because his injury occurred as a result of operations on the shelf. The U.S. Court of Appeals affirmed, but relied on the LHWCA to do so.

On further appeal, the U.S. Supreme Court held that the employee was not entitled to LHWCA benefits because his employment was not "maritime." Not everyone involved in every task that is part and parcel of offshore drilling can be considered a maritime employee. Congress' purpose under the LHWCA was to cover those workers on a covered situs who are involved in the essential elements of the loading, unloading or construction of vessels. The welding work involved here was far from the traditional work covered by the LHWCA. Further, even though the employee would have been eligible for LHWCA benefits if he had been injured on the continental shelf, such was not the case here. Accordingly, the appellate court's decision was reversed and the employer was only entitled to recover state workers' compensation benefits. *Herb's Welding, Inc. v. Gray*, 470 U.S. 414, 105 S.Ct. 1421, 84 L.Ed.2d 406 (1985).

B. "Person Entitled to Compensation"

Section 33(g) of the LHWCA provides that a person "entitled to compensation" must obtain prior written approval from the employer and its insurer of any settlement of a third-party claim, upon penalty of forfeiture of all rights under the act. The Supreme Court held that this forfeiture provision applied to a worker whose employer was neither paying benefits yet, nor subject to an order to pay.

An employee of a drilling company injured his hand while working on an oil drilling platform owned by an exploration company. The platform was located on the Outer Continental Shelf, an area subject to the LHWCA. The worker's employer and its insurer paid him temporary disability benefits for 10 months. The Department of Labor notified the insurer that the worker was entitled to permanent partial disability payments, but none were made. Meanwhile, the worker settled an action against the exploration company. The employer funded the settlement under an indemnification agreement with the exploration company. However, the worker never secured a formal, prior, written approval of the settlement from his employer. When the worker then sought disability payments from his employer, it denied liability on the grounds that the employee had forfeited his benefits under the LHWCA by failing to obtain approval of the settlement as required by § 33(g) of the act. An administrative law judge awarded benefits to the worker, and the Benefits Review Board affirmed. The U.S. Court of Appeals, Fifth Circuit, reversed.

The U.S. Supreme Court affirmed the denial of benefits to the worker. It held that § 33(g)'s forfeiture provision applied to a worker whose employer, at the time the worker settles with a third party, was neither paying compensation to the worker nor subject to an order to pay under the act. The language of the act was clear and could not support the award of benefits to the worker. Since the employee was "entitled to compensation" under the LHWCA, he fell within the strictures of § 33(g). Though the result here was harsh, it was for the legislature to change the statute, not the courts. *Estate of Cowart v. Nicklos Drilling Co.*, 505 U.S. 469, 112 S.Ct. 2589, 120 L.Ed.2d 379 (1992).

The LHWCA requires a "person entitled to compensation" to obtain the employer's approval before entering into settlements. For purposes of death benefits, the Supreme Court held that a surviving spouse does not constitute a "person entitled to compensation" before the injured worker's death. Therefore, the spouse does not have to obtain the employer's approval.

A Mississippi shipbuilding company employee was exposed to asbestos at work. He was later diagnosed as suffering from asbestosis, chronic bronchitis and possible malignancy in his lungs. He filed a claim for disability benefits under the LHWCA and his employer admitted liability. He then sued 23 manufacturers and suppliers of asbestos and entered into settlement agreements with eight of them. His wife joined in the settlements and released any cause of action she might have for wrongful death. None of these settlements were approved by the employer. After the employee died, the wife filed a claim for and was granted death benefits under the LHWCA. The employer contested the claim on the ground that the wife had been a "person entitled to compensation" under the LHWCA who was required to obtain the employer's approval before entering into the settlements. Thus, because she had failed to do so, she forfeited her eligibility for death benefits. The U.S. Court of Appeals, Fifth Circuit, affirmed the grant of death benefits to the wife. The U.S. Supreme Court held that before the injured worker's death, his wife had not been a "person entitled to compensation" for death benefits. Thus, she did not have to obtain the employer's approval of the settlements and did not forfeit her right to collect death benefits under the LHWCA. *Ingalls Shipbuilding, Inc. v. Director, OWCP*, 519 U.S. 248, 117 S.Ct. 796, 136 L.Ed.2d 736 (1997).

C. Procedural Issues

The LHWCA provides that "in any proceeding for the enforcement of a claim for compensation under [the LHWCA] it shall be presumed, in the absence of evidence to the contrary ... that the claim comes within the provisions of [the LHWCA]." However, unless a *claim* is filed, the presumption does not attach.

An employee, covered by the LHWCA, filed a claim for disability benefits after he awoke in the early morning hours of November 20, 1975, with severe pains in his neck, shoulders and arms. He asserted that he had suffered an injury at work on the previous day while attempting to lift duct work weighing approximately 500 pounds with a co-worker. Physicians later attributed the pain to an exacerbation of an arthritic condition. An administrative law judge determined that the accident never occurred, and denied the claim; the Benefits Review Board affirmed. The U.S. Court of Appeals vacated the board's decision, holding that the employee had suffered an "injury" when he awoke in pain, and that there was a presumption (which had not been rebutted) that the injury was "employment-bred." The U.S. Supreme Court granted review.

The Supreme Court held that the court of appeals had erred in holding that the employee was entitled to the presumption that his injury was compensable. The employee here had asserted that he was injured at work, not that he was injured at home. Because he had never made a *claim* that the injury occurred at home, there could be no presumption that his injury was compensable; the presumption attaches to the claim. The appellate court also erred in its use of the term "injury." The mere existence of a physical impairment, held the Court, was insufficient to shift the burden of proof to the employer that the injury was not "employment-bred." The employee had not stated a *prima facie* case of compensability under the LHWCA, so the Court reversed the court of appeals' decision. *U.S. Industries/Federal Sheet Metal, Inc. v. Director, Office of Workers' Compensation Programs*, 455 U.S. 608, 102 S.Ct. 1312, 71 L.Ed.2d 495 (1982).

Section 7(c) of the Administrative Procedure Act provides that the proponent of a rule or order has the burden of proof. This section applies to adjudications under the LHWCA and the Black Lung Benefits Act. The Supreme Court held that the true doubt rule—which allowed claimants under the acts to win when the evidence was evenly balanced—used in administrative hearings was inconsistent with § 7(c).

The U.S. Department of Labor applied the "true doubt" rule to resolve claims under the Black Lung Benefits Act and the LHWCA. The rule shifted the burden of persuasion to a party opposing a claim for benefits so that in cases in which the evidence was evenly balanced, the claimant prevailed. In two separate cases arising under these federal acts, administrative law judges awarded benefits to the claimants. However, in the case involving benefits under the Black Lung Act, the U.S. Court of Appeals, Third Circuit, vacated a benefit review board's decision, finding the true doubt rule inconsistent with Department of Labor regulations. In the LHWCA case, the Third Circuit court reversed the award, ruling that the true doubt rule violated § 7(c) of the Administrative Procedure Act (APA). The U.S. Supreme Court agreed to hear the cases and consolidated them on appeal.

The Court found a dispute in the interpretation of the term "burden of proof" under the APA. The Department of Labor argued that "burden of proof" applied only to the burden of going forward with evidence (in other words, the burden of production). The employers argued that "burden of proof" included the ultimate burden of persuasion. The dispute was significant because it would change the result reached by the administrative law judges in both cases. The Court determined that at the time of the passage of the APA, the term "burden of proof" meant "burden of persuasion." Under the Department of Labor's true doubt rule, where evidence was evenly balanced, the claimant always won. However, because the APA required that a claimant must lose in the case of evenly balanced evidence, the true doubt rule violated the APA. The department of labor's analysis was incorrect and the employers prevailed. *Director, Office of Workers' Compensation Programs v. Greenwich Collieries*, 512 U.S. 267, 114 S.Ct. 2251, 129 L.Ed.2d 221 (1994).

Section 921(c) of the LHWCA permits "[a]ny person adversely affected or aggrieved by" an order of the Benefits Review Board to appeal to a U.S. Court of Appeals. The Supreme Court held that the Director of the Office of Workers' Compensation Programs, U.S. Department of Labor, did not have standing to appeal an order entered adverse to a claimant.

A shipbuilding and drydock worker was injured in an on-the-job accident and sought benefits under the LHWCA. He was fired because of medical restrictions that made him unable to perform his former job duties. An administrative law judge determined that the worker was partially disabled and therefore entitled to only partial disability benefits during his period of unemployment. The federal Benefits Review Board affirmed the judgment and held that the company was entitled to discontinue making disability payments after 104 weeks, when the LHWCA special fund would become liable for further payments. The worker did not seek further review, but the director of the Office of Workers' Compensation Programs appealed the findings of partial disability and special fund liability. The U.S. Court of Appeals, Fourth Circuit, held that the director had no legal standing to appeal the board's order, and the director appealed further to the U.S. Supreme Court.

The Supreme Court found no support for the director's argument that she had standing as "a person adversely affected or aggrieved" under the LHWCA. The statute did not specify that the director was a person under the act, and federal agencies were not automatically presumed to have standing in cases of such an omission. The director retained rulemaking power under the LHWCA and maintained the ability to alter rules under which the board operated. The director was unable to demonstrate how an erroneous board ruling would interfere with the performance of her assigned duties. She was not assigned to further the interests of employees. Rather, the act required the director to encourage informal settlements between employers and employees. The director's argument that she must ensure adequate remedies for disabled workers was contrary to the statute. The Court affirmed the judgment of the court of appeals. *Director, Office of Workers' Compensation Programs, Dep't of Labor v. Newport News Shipbuilding and Dry Dock Co.*, 514 U.S. 122, 115 S.Ct. 1278, 131 L.Ed.2d 160 (1995).

D. Benefit Awards

In the following case, the Supreme Court held that employees who would be eligible for LHWCA benefits could apply for more generous state law workers' compensation benefits. The LHWCA did not preempt the state laws, but rather supplemented them.

Five employees of a shipbuilding and repair company were injured while involved in shipbuilding or ship repair activities. Although the LHWCA applied to the injuries sustained, they applied for benefits under Pennsylvania's workers' compensation law. The employer asserted that the LHWCA was the exclusive remedy, but the state administrative agency ruled that the LHWCA did not preempt state workers' compensation laws. After this decision was affirmed in the state courts, the U.S. Supreme Court granted review. The Court noted that the 1972 amendments to the LHWCA, which extended federal jurisdiction landward beyond the shoreline of the navigable waters of the United States, supplemented, rather than supplanted, state workers' compensation law. The idea was to provide complete coverage to maritime laborers so that they would not have to guess which jurisdiction they were supposed to be in before filing a claim. Here, by filing under state law, the workers may have gotten better benefits than under an exclusively federal system, but the LHWCA was enacted to raise awards to a federal minimum because state compensation laws were generally less generous. Thus, the concurrent jurisdiction provided by the LHWCA was not inconsistent with this idea, and the workers were entitled to state benefits. The Court affirmed the state court decisions. *Sun Ship, Inc. v. Pennsylvania*, 447 U.S. 715, 100 S.Ct. 2432, 65 L.Ed.2d 458 (1980).

Where the LHWCA schedule provides for specified benefits for specific injuries, workers may not recover under the more general provision that grants compensation in "all other cases."

A District of Columbia worker was injured in the course of his employment, sustaining a knee injury that resulted in a loss of use of between 5 and 20 percent of one leg. Because he worked in the District of Columbia, he was entitled to compensation under the LHWCA. His injury was classed as one of "permanent partial disability." A question arose as to whether the worker should be compensated according to the specific schedule set out in the LHWCA, or whether he was entitled to the "all other cases" compensation award (which was larger). An administrative law judge granted him the larger recovery, the Benefits Review Board affirmed, and the U.S. Court of Appeals also affirmed. On further appeal to the U.S. Supreme Court, the Court held that workers' compensation had to be limited by the statutory schedule because the worker's injury was of a kind specifically identified in the schedule. The "all other cases" larger award was not intended by Congress to be an alternative where specific injuries were provided for in the schedule. Rather, it was meant to apply where the injuries received did not fall into the schedule. Even though this result yielded less benefits to the worker, the Court noted that the LHWCA was not set up to guarantee a completely adequate remedy for all covered disabilities, but rather was designed as a compromise between the competing interests of disabled workers and their employers. *Potomac Electric Power Co. v. Director, Office of Workers' Compensation Programs,* 449 U.S. 268, 101 S.Ct. 509, 66 L.Ed.2d 446 (1980).

The Supreme Court held that a deceased worker's rights in his union trust funds had been too speculative to meet the definition of "wages" in the LHWCA. Accordingly, when determining how much money was owed to his widow, the employer's contributions to the trust funds did not have to be included.

A construction company employee was fatally injured while working on the District of Columbia Metrorail System. He was covered by the District's workers' compensation statute that incorporated the LHWCA. The employer began to pay the widow and minor children two-thirds of the workers' "average weekly wage" as required by the LHWCA. The widow disputed the amount of benefits owed her, claiming that her husband's average weekly pay included not only his take-home pay, but also the $.68 per hour in contributions which the employer was required to make to union trust funds under the terms of a collective bargaining agreement. An administrative law judge rejected the widow's contention, and the Benefits Review Board affirmed. The U.S. Court of Appeals reversed, and the U.S. Supreme Court agreed to hear the case.

The Supreme Court held that employer contributions to union trust funds are not "wages" under the LHWCA. Wages must be identifiable and calculable. Remuneration like board, rent, housing and lodging has a present value that can readily be converted into a cash equivalent on the basis of market value. Here, the worker's rights in his union trust funds had been too speculative to meet the definition of "wages." The Court further noted that Congress had not intended to expand the definition of wages to include fringe benefits. And even though fringe benefits make up an increasing amount of a worker's wages, the Court noted that it was for Congress to decide whether to change the LHWCA to expand the term "wages" to include employer contributions to trust funds. *Morrison-Knudsen Constr. Co. v. Director, Office of Workers' Compensation Programs,* 461 U.S. 624, 103 S.Ct. 2045, 76 L.Ed.2d 194 (1983).

In *Bath Iron Works*, below, the Supreme Court held that claims for hearing loss under the LHWCA, whether filed by current workers or retirees, are claims for a scheduled injury and must be compensated under the section of the act that provides benefits regardless of whether earning capacity has been impaired.

A man worked for an iron works corporation for many years. After he retired, he learned that he suffered from a work-related hearing loss. Upon filing a claim for disability benefits under the LHWCA, an administrative law judge awarded him benefits under a combination of compensation systems set forth under pertinent provisions of the act. The decision was affirmed by the Benefits Review Board. Upon appeal by the corporation, the U.S. Court of Appeals affirmed the decisions of the lower tribunals. The corporation appealed further.

The U.S. Supreme Court held that claims for hearing loss filed by either current workers or retirees were claims for scheduled injuries which had to be compensated under the system of scheduled injury compensation, rather than under the system providing compensation for retirees who suffered from occupational diseases that did not become disabling until after retirement. As a scheduled injury type of loss, the worker is presumptively disabled simultaneously with the injury. The court reasoned that the loss could not be compensated under the system that termed the hearing loss as a latent occupational disease which did not become manifest until after retirement, since the hearing loss resulted in immediate disability. It did not matter that the worker did not notice the hearing loss until after he retired. The Court affirmed the decision of the court of appeals. Disability benefits had to be awarded under the statutorily scheduled injury plan, and not under a combination of compensation systems. *Bath Iron Works v. Director, OWCP*, 506 U.S. 153, 113 S.Ct. 692, 121 L.Ed.2d 619 (1993).

A disability award under the LHWCA may be modified where there is a change in an employee's wage-earning capacity, even when there is no change in the employee's physical condition.

The LHWCA is a comprehensive federal statute that compensates land-based maritime workers for disabilities and deaths resulting from work-related injuries. The act allows the modification of awards on the grounds of a change in conditions or a mistake in a determination of fact. An injured longshore worker suffered a permanent partial disability of over 20 percent and received a permanent partial disability award under the LHWCA. He returned to work at a reduced wage, but began attending trade school for training as a crane operator. He was then re-employed at an average weekly wage that was three times greater than his preinjury pay rate. His physical condition remained unchanged. His former employer sought to modify the disability award in view of his increased wage-earning capacity, asserting that there had been a change in conditions under the LHWCA. An administrative law judge determined that the modification should take place due to his increased wage-earning capacity despite the absence of a change in physical condition. The employee appealed the termination of his disability payments to the U.S. Court of Appeals, Ninth Circuit, which reversed the decision, ruling that the LHWCA authorizes the modification of awards only on the basis of a change in the claimant's physical condition.

The U.S. Supreme Court agreed to hear the employer's appeal. It found no statutory language that limited the modification of an award to cases in which there was a change in physical condition. The applicable conditions could include increased wage-earning capacity because the LHWCA defined disability as an economic concept and not a medical concept. A disability award under the LHWCA could be modified whenever there was a change in the employee's wage-earning capacity, despite the lack of change in the employee's physical condition. The Supreme Court reversed and remanded the court of appeals' decision. *Metropolitan Stevedore Co. v. Rambo*, 515 U.S. 291, 115 S.Ct. 2144, 132 L.Ed.2d 226 (1995).

On remand, the Ninth Circuit reversed the order to discontinue compensation payments and the U.S. Supreme Court again accepted review. It observed that the uncertain nature of an employee injury and the need for swift resolution of compensation issues prohibited the complete foreclosure of an LHWCA remedy even where an employee's wage-earning capacity was not currently diminished. The employee was entitled to nominal compensation, which would hold open the possibility of future modification should his earnings later fall below his preinjury level. An injured employee's disability is not necessarily reflected in actual wages earned after an injury, and an LHWCA fact-finder must make a determination that takes the future effect of a disability into account. The Court vacated the Ninth Circuit's judgment. *Metropolitan Stevedore Co. v. Rambo*, 521 U.S. 121, 117 S.Ct. 1953, 138 L.Ed.2d 327 (1997).

E. Suits Against Third Parties

The Supreme Court stated that a stevedore who had obtained a lien against any judgment its injured longshoreman recovered did not have to reduce the lien by contributing to the costs of recovery.

A longshoreman who worked for a stevedore was injured while working on board a vessel. He received $17,000 in workers' compensation, then filed suit against the vessel's owner for negligence in creating hazardous conditions on board the vessel. During settlement negotiations, his attorney gave the stevedore notice of the pending action and requested it to reduce its $17,000 lien by a share of the costs of recovery. The stevedore had obtained a lien against any recovery the longshoreman might receive from the vessel owner. When the stevedore refused to reduce its lien amount, and the lawsuit settled for $60,000, the longshoreman sought summary judgment on the reduction of the lien. The district court denied the motion, the U.S. Court of Appeals affirmed, and the case reached the U.S. Supreme Court, which held that the LHWCA supported the conclusion that the stevedore's lien could not be reduced. Since the stevedore could recover all its costs if it sued in the longshoreman's place, the act implied a similar distribution of expenses where the longshoreman himself was bringing the suit. Accordingly, the Court affirmed the lower courts' decisions and held that the lien could not be reduced. *Bloomer v. Liberty Mutual Ins. Co.,* 445 U.S. 74, 100 S.Ct. 925, 63 L.Ed.2d 215 (1980).

Under the LHWCA, injured workers who accept compensation under an award in a compensation order have only six months in which to begin an action against the third party who allegedly caused their injuries. After that time, any right to sue is completely transferred to the employer, who may choose not to sue.

Three longshoremen, who had been injured aboard ship in the course of their employment, accepted compensation from their stevedore employers pursuant to an award in a compensation order. More than six months later, the longshoremen sued the owners of the ships, alleging negligence. The federal district courts granted summary judgment to the ship owners on the ground that the causes of action had been assigned to the stevedore employers (because the longshoremen had failed to bring suit within six months of the compensation awards). The U.S. Court of Appeals affirmed, and the U.S. Supreme Court granted certiorari.

The LHWCA provides that a longshoreman's acceptance of compensation from his or her employer, pursuant to an award in a compensation order, will operate as an assignment to the employer of the longshoreman's rights unless the longshoreman brings an action against the third person within six months after the award. The Supreme Court noted that this language was both mandatory and unequivocal. Accordingly, the longshoremen were precluded by the LHWCA from pursuing their third-party claims against the ship owners regardless of the fact that the stevedores had failed to pursue the assigned claims. The Supreme Court affirmed the lower courts' decisions. *Rodriguez v. Compass Shipping Co., Ltd.*, 451 U.S. 596, 101 S.Ct. 1945, 68 L.Ed.2d 472 (1981).

Where an injured worker who is eligible for benefits under the LHWCA accepts compensation "under an award in a compensation order," the worker has only six months in which to file a lawsuit against a third party. After that time, the right to sue is irrevocably assigned to the employer. However, if there has been no compensation order, the six-month period does not begin to run.

A longshoreman fell from a ladder and was injured while working aboard a chartered vessel. His employer (who was not the charterer) did not contest his right to receive compensation benefits, filling out the necessary forms and making payments for 23 months, at which time the employer terminated benefits. The longshoreman then filed suit against the vessel charterer for negligence. A federal district court dismissed the claim for lack of jurisdiction, but the U.S. Court of Appeals reversed. Further appeal was taken to the U.S. Supreme Court.

The Supreme Court noted that § 33(b) of the LHWCA only gave an injured longshoreman who accepted compensation "under an award in a compensation order" six months in which to file a negligence action against a third party. After that time, the longshoreman's cause of action is irrevocably assigned to his or her employer. However, in this case, no administrative proceedings had taken place and the mere filing of forms by the employer was not the equivalent of an "award in a compensation order." Accordingly, the longshoreman's claims against the charterer were not irrevocably assigned to the employer. The Court noted that this interpretation did not frustrate the act's purpose (ensuring prompt payment to injured workers and relieving parties of the expense of litigating compensation claims) because employers could make voluntary payments to workers and then seek indemnification for those payments. The Court thus affirmed the court of appeals' decision in favor of the longshoreman. *Pallas Shipping Agency, Ltd. v. Duris*, 461 U.S. 529, 103 S.Ct. 1991, 76 L.Ed.2d 120 (1983).

An employee injured on a vessel, who is entitled to LHWCA benefits, may also be able to sue the vessel's owner for additional damages if his or her injury was "caused by the negligence of the vessel."

A longshoreman worked for 19 years loading and unloading barges for the owner of a fleet of barges which acted as its own stevedore. In January 1978, while carrying a heavy pump, the longshoreman slipped and fell on snow and ice that the owner had negligently failed to remove from the funnels of a barge. He sustained an injury that made him permanently unable to return to his job. His employer compensated him for his injury. He then brought suit against his employer, however, asserting that his injury had been "caused by the negligence of the vessel" within the meaning of § 5(b) of the LHWCA. The district court awarded him $275,000 in damages, holding that the receipt of compensation payments did not bar his lawsuit. The court failed to increase the award to take inflation into account, and also failed to discount the award to reflect its net present value. The U.S. Court of Appeals affirmed, and the employer sought review from the U.S. Supreme Court.

The Supreme Court held that the longshoreman could bring a separate negligence action against the owner/employer after receiving benefits if the injury was caused by the negligence of the owner of the vessel in its "owner" capacity. However, the Court also stated that the district court had erred in its damages calculation. It should not have used the "total offset rule" (where inflation is offset by a discount for net present value). Instead, the court should have figured in both values when making its award of damages. The Court vacated and remanded the case for further proceedings with respect to ascertaining the proper damages amount. *Jones & Laughlin Steel Corp. v. Pfeifer*, 462 U.S. 523, 103 S.Ct. 2541, 76 L.Ed.2d 768 (1983).

If a general contractor purchases workers' compensation insurance to cover employees of its subcontractors, then it will be immune to liability from suit under the LHWCA.

A government agency was charged with the construction and operation of a rapid transit system for the District of Columbia area. It hired subcontractors to work on various aspects of the construction project. The LHWCA made general contractors liable for workers' compensation unless the subcontractor has made such a payment. Rather than wait to see if its subcontractors were going to obtain such insurance, the agency arranged for workers' compensation insurance on its own. Subsequently, several employees of subcontractors were hurt; they obtained workers' compensation benefits for respiratory injuries sustained as a result of high levels of silica dust and other industrial pollutants. They then sued the agency (general contractor), seeking to supplement their compensation awards. A federal court granted summary judgment to the agency, but the U.S. Court of Appeals reversed because the agency had "unilaterally" purchased the workers' compensation policy rather than waiting until after the subcontractors had failed to do so.

On further appeal, the U.S. Supreme Court held that the immunity provided by the LHWCA, for contractors who secure payment of compensation, applied to the agency. The LHWCA merely placed a contingent obligation on contractors to secure compensation whenever subcontractors failed to do so. It did not grant immunity to contractors only when they waited to purchase workers' compensation insurance until after subcontractors affirmatively defaulted. So long as the contractor purchased the coverage, it was entitled to the LHWCA's grant of immunity. The Court reversed the appellate court's decision, and granted immunity to the agency. *Washington Metropolitan Area Transit Authority v. Johnson*, 467 U.S. 925, 104 S.Ct. 2827, 81 L.Ed.2d 768 (1984).

The turnover duty of the LHWCA requires a vessel to exercise ordinary care under the circumstances to turn over the ship and its equipment in such condition that an experienced expert stevedore will be able to carry on cargo operations with reasonable safety. However, the vessel's duty to warn of latent defects in the cargo stow is narrow.

A longshoreman was injured when he jumped three feet to the deck of a cargo hold and slipped on a sheet of plastic that had been placed under the cargo by the stevedore who had loaded it. He filed suit against the owner and operator of the ship under the LHWCA. Under § 5(b) of the act, 33 U.S.C. § 905(b), a shipowner must exercise ordinary care to maintain the ship and its equipment in a condition so that an expert and experienced stevedore can load and unload cargo with reasonable safety. A shipowner must also warn the stevedore of latent hazards that are known or should be known to the shipowner. A Pennsylvania federal district court granted summary judgment to the shipowner, and the U.S. Court of Appeals, Third Circuit, affirmed. The U.S. Supreme Court granted certiorari.

The Supreme Court held that a vessel's duty to warn of latent defects in the cargo stow, upon turning the vessel over to a stevedore, was narrow. A vessel is not required to supervise the ongoing operations of the loading stevedore, or inspect the completed stow, to discover hazards in the cargo stow. However, the district court had improperly granted summary judgment on the ground that the vessel had no actual knowledge of the hazard leading to the longshoreman's injury. Some crew members, in positions where their knowledge could be imputed to the vessel, might have observed the plastic being placed under the cargo during the loading process. Further, the plastic might not have been visible during unloading, triggering the duty to warn. The Court vacated and remanded the case for further proceedings. *Howlett v. Birkdale Shipping Co.*, 512 U.S. 92, 114 S.Ct. 2057, 129 L.Ed.2d 78 (1994).

III. JONES ACT

In *Wilander*, below, the Supreme Court held that one need not aid in the navigation of a vessel in order to qualify as a "seaman" under the Jones Act. The LHWCA excludes from its coverage "masters or members of a crew of any vessel," or "seamen," but it does not indicate that members of a crew are required to navigate to be considered "seamen."

A paint foreman was inspecting a pipe on an oil drilling platform when a bolt, serving as a plug in the pipe, blew out under pressure and injured him. He sued his employer under the Jones Act, seeking to recover for its negligence. In a federal district court, the jury entered an award for the foreman, finding that he was a "seaman" under the Jones Act. The U.S. Court of Appeals affirmed, holding that the employee did not have to aid in the navigation of a vessel to be considered a seaman. The U.S. Supreme Court granted certiorari.

The Court noted that when the Jones Act was passed in 1920, general maritime law required only that a seaman be employed on board a vessel in furtherance of its purpose to be classed as a "seaman." Although some courts had required that a seaman aid in navigation to be able to bring a suit under the Jones Act, the Court rejected this approach. Further, under the LHWCA (which is mutually exclusive of the Jones Act), no coverage is provided for "a master or member of a crew of any vessel." This term was the equivalent of a "seaman." Accordingly, the foreman was not precluded from seaman status even though he did not perform transportation-related functions on board the vessel. The Court affirmed the court of appeals' decision, allowing the foreman to recover for his injuries. *McDermott International, Inc. v. Wilander*, 498 U.S. 337, 111 S.Ct. 807, 112 L.Ed.2d 866 (1991).

In 1991, the Supreme Court held that a maritime worker who was covered by the LHWCA could also be a "seaman" under the Jones Act, and thus entitled to bring a lawsuit for his injuries. Despite the fact that the two acts are mutually exclusive, an employee who receives voluntary payments under the LHWCA can still sue under the Jones Act. Any recovery would be credited against liability imposed by the LHWCA; thus, there could be no double recovery.

A rigging foreman employed by a ship repair company rode to vessels on floating platforms so that repair services could be performed. He sometimes acted as a lookout during the towing process. When a thin wooden sheet covering a hole in the deck of a platform gave way, the foreman suffered disabling leg and back injuries. He sought and received benefits from the company under the LHWCA. Later, he brought suit under the Jones Act, alleging that he was a seaman injured as a result of his employer's negligence. The federal district court granted summary judgment to the company, finding first that the employee was not a "seaman" and, second, that the exclusive remedy provisions of the LHWCA barred the employee's suit. The U.S. Court of Appeals reversed, and the company petitioned for a writ of certiorari. The U.S. Supreme Court held that a maritime worker whose occupation was one of those enumerated in the LHWCA could still be a seaman within the meaning of the Jones Act pending final agency determinations that the injured employee was a crew member. Further, the fact that the employee had received benefits under the LHWCA did not mean that he was barred from litigating his employer's liability under the Jones Act. Since issues of fact existed regarding the employee's seaman status, the court of appeals had properly reversed the district court. *Southwest Marine Inc. v. Gizoni*, 502 U.S. 81, 112 S.Ct. 486, 116 L.Ed.2d 405 (1991).

The Supreme Court stated a test for determining the "employment-related connection to a vessel in navigation" required for seaman status under the Jones Act. First, the worker's duties must contribute to the function of the vessel or to the accomplishment of its mission, and second, the worker must have a connection to a vessel in navigation that is substantial in both its duration and its nature.

The Jones Act provides a negligence cause of action for any seaman injured in the course of employment. The act does not define the term "seaman." A supervising engineer employed by a cruise ship company was based in a Miami office but his duties included supervising ship engineering departments at sea. While at sea, a ship's doctor diagnosed the engineer with a detached retina, but postponed treatment for two days. As a result, the engineer lost 75 percent of his vision in one eye. After returning to work, the engineer sailed to Germany for six months to work on the ship in drydock. The following year the engineer's employment was terminated and he filed a lawsuit against the company in the U.S. District Court for the Southern District of New York for compensatory damages under the Jones Act. The court instructed the jury that the engineer could be deemed a seaman within the meaning of the act if it was determined that he was either permanently assigned to the ship or performed a substantial part of his work on board. The court also instructed the jury not to consider the time during which the ship was in drydock. Following a verdict in favor of the engineer, the shipping company appealed to the U.S. Court of Appeals, Second Circuit, which vacated the district court judgment and remanded the case for a new trial. The U.S. Supreme Court granted further review.

The Court observed that the Jones Act and the Longshore and Harbor Workers' Compensation Act (LHWCA) established mutually exclusive compensation systems for seamen and land-based maritime workers, respectively. In order to cope with the lack of a statutory definition for the term "seaman," the Court stated that a status-based standard must be utilized by courts to inquire into the employee's connection to a vessel in navigation. The test had two components, under which the employee's duties must contribute to and have a connection to a vessel in navigation that is substantial in both duration and nature. In this case, the district court had improperly instructed the jury to disregard the time the ship had spent in drydock and the Court directed the district court to reevaluate the case consistently with its new test. *Chandris, Inc. v. Latsis*, 515 U.S. 347, 115 S.Ct. 2172, 132 L.Ed.2d 314 (1995).

Under the Jones Act, "seaman status" exists where the employee's duties contribute to the function of a vessel or the accomplishment of its mission. The seaman must also have a connection to the vessel in navigation that is substantial in terms of duration and nature.

A deck hand worked on various vessels in the San Francisco Bay area through a union hiring hall. On several occasions, a tugboat company hired him through the hiring hall to perform maintenance and deck hand duties. On one such occasion, he was injured in a fall while painting a docked tugboat. Rather than submitting a workers' compensation claim, the deck hand filed a federal district court lawsuit against the tugboat operator for negligence under the Jones Act, unseaworthiness under general maritime law and additional claims. The court granted the tugboat operator's summary judgment motion, agreeing that the deck hand was not a seaman who was entitled to Jones Act coverage. The court denied the deck hand's motion for reconsideration, and he appealed to the U.S. Court of Appeals, Ninth Circuit, which reversed and remanded the case. The tugboat operator appealed to the U.S. Supreme Court.

The Court observed that it had previously announced a rule for determining seaman status under the Jones Act based on the employee's duties. Jones Act seaman status exists where the employee's duties contribute to the function of a vessel or the accomplishment of its mission, and the seaman has a connection to a vessel in navigation that is substantial in terms of duration and nature. In this case, the deck hand had been hired to paint the vessel while it was docked and he was not expected to sail with it after completing the job. Because his duties did not involve seagoing work and had only a transitory connection to a vessel, he did not qualify for seaman status and the district court had properly granted summary judgment to the tugboat operator. *Harbor Tug and Barge Co. v. Papai*, 520 U.S. 548, 117 S.Ct. 1535, 137 L.Ed.2d 800 (1997).

APPENDIX A

United States Constitution

Relevant Provisions with respect to Employment Law

ARTICLE I

Section 1. All legislative Powers herein granted shall be vested in a Congress of the United States, which shall consist of a Senate and House of Representatives.

* * *

Section 8. The Congress shall have Power To lay and collect Taxes, Duties, Imposts and Excises, to pay the Debts and provide for the common Defence and general Welfare of the United States; but all Duties, Imposts and Excises shall be uniform throughout the Unites States;

To borrow money on the credit of the United States;

To regulate Commerce with foreign Nations, and among the several States, and with the Indian Tribes;

To establish an uniform Rule of Naturalization, and uniform Laws on the subject of Bankruptcies throughout the United States;

* * *

To promote the Progress of Science and useful Arts, by securing for limited Times to Authors and Inventors the exclusive Right to their respective Writings and Discoveries;

* * *

To make all Laws which shall be necessary and proper for carrying into Execution for the foregoing Powers, and all other Powers vested by this Constitution in the Government of the United States, or in any Department or Officer thereof.

* * *

Section 9. * * * No Bill of Attainder or ex post facto Law shall be passed.

* * *

Section 10. No State shall * * * pass any Bill of Attainder, ex post facto Law, or Law impairing the Obligation of Contracts, or grant any Title of Nobility.

339

ARTICLE II

Section 1. The executive Power shall be vested in a President of the United States of America. * * *

ARTICLE III

Section 1. The judicial Power of the United States, shall be vested in one supreme Court, and in such inferior Courts as the Congress may from time to time ordain and establish. The Judges, both of the supreme and inferior courts, shall hold their Offices during good Behaviour, and shall, at stated Times, receive for their Services a Compensation, which shall not be diminished during their Continuance in Office.

Section 2. The judicial Power shall extend to all Cases, in Law and Equity, arising under this Constitution, the Laws of the United States, and Treaties made, or which shall be made, under their Authority; - to all Cases affecting Ambassadors, other public Ministers and Consuls; - to all Cases of admiralty and maritime Jurisdiction, - to Controversies to which the United States shall be a party; - to Controversies between two or more States; - between a State and Citizens of another State; - between Citizens of different States; - between Citizens of the same State claiming Lands under the Grants of different States, and between a State, or the Citizens thereof, and foreign States, Citizens or Subjects.

* * *

ARTICLE IV

Section 1. Full Faith and Credit shall be given in each State to the public Acts, Records and judicial Proceedings of every other State. * * *

Section 2. The Citizens of each State shall be entitled to all Privileges and Immunities of Citizens in the several States.

* * *

Section 4. The United States shall guarantee to every State in this Union a Republican Form of Government, and shall protect each of them against Invasion; and on Application of the Legislature, or of the Executive (when the Legislature cannot be convened) against domestic Violence.

ARTICLE V

The Congress, whenever two thirds of both Houses shall deem it necessary, shall propose Amendments to this Constitution, or, on the Application of the Legislatures of two thirds of the several States, shall call a Convention for proposing Amendments, which, in either Case, shall be valid to all Intents and Purposes, as part of this Constitution, when ratified by the Legislatures of three fourths of the several States, or by Conventions in three fourths thereof, as the one or the other Mode of Ratification may be proposed by the Congress; Provided that no Amendment which may be made prior to the Year One thousand eight hundred and eight shall in any Manner affect the first and fourth Clauses in the Ninth Section of the first Article; and that no State, without its Consent, shall be deprived of its equal Suffrage in the Senate.

ARTICLE VI

* * *

This Constitution, and the Laws of the United States which shall be made in Pursuance thereof; and all Treaties made, or which shall be made, under the Authority of the United States, shall be the supreme Law of the Land; and the Judges in every State shall be bound thereby, any Thing in the Constitution or Laws of any State to the Contrary notwithstanding.

The Senators and Representatives before mentioned, and the Members of the several State Legislatures, and all executive and judicial Officers, both of the United States and of the several States, shall be bound by Oath or Affirmation, to support this Constitution; but no religious Test shall ever be required as a Qualification to any Office or public Trust under the United States.

* * *

AMENDMENT I

Congress shall make no law respecting an establishment of religion, or prohibiting the free exercise thereof; or abridging the freedom of speech, or of the press; or the right of the people peaceably to assemble, and to petition the Government for a redress of grievances.

* * *

AMENDMENT IV

The right of the people to be secure in their persons, houses, papers, and effects, against unreasonable searches and seizures, shall not be violated, and no Warrants shall issue, but upon probable cause, supported by Oath or affirmation, and particularly describing the place to be searched, and the persons or things to be seized.

AMENDMENT V

No person shall be held to answer for a capital, or otherwise infamous crime, unless on a presentment or indictment of a Grand Jury, except in cases arising in the land or naval forces, or in the Militia, when in actual service in time of War or public danger; nor shall any person be subject for the same offence to be twice put in jeopardy of life or limb; nor shall be compelled in any criminal case to be a witness against himself, nor be deprived of life, liberty, or property, without due process of law; nor shall private property be taken for public use, without just compensation.

AMENDMENT VI

In all criminal prosecutions, the accused shall enjoy the right to a speedy and public trial, by an impartial jury of the State and district wherein the crime shall have been committed, which district shall have been previously ascertained by law, and to be informed of the nature and cause of the accusation; to be confronted with the witnesses against him; to have compulsory process for obtaining witnesses in his favor, and to have the Assistance of Counsel for his defense.

AMENDMENT VII

In Suits at common law, where the value in controversy shall exceed twenty dollars, the right of trial by jury shall be preserved, and no fact tried by jury, shall be otherwise re-examined in any Court of the United States, than according to the rules of the common law.

AMENDMENT VIII

Excessive bail shall not be required, nor excessive fines imposed , nor cruel and unusual punishments inflicted.

AMENDMENT IX

The enumeration in the Constitution, of certain rights, shall not be construed to deny or disparage others retained by the people.

AMENDMENT X

The powers not delegated to the United States by the Constitution, nor prohibited by it to the States, are reserved to the States respectively, or to the people.

AMENDMENT XI

The Judicial power of the United States shall not be construed to extend to any suit in law or equity, commenced or prosecuted against one of the United States by Citizens of another State, or by Citizens or Subjects of any Foreign State.

* * *

AMENDMENT XIII

Section 1. Neither slavery nor involuntary servitude, except as a punishment for crime whereof the party shall have been duly convicted, shall exist within the United States, or any place subject to their jurisdiction.

Section 2. Congress shall have power to enforce this article by appropriate legislation.

AMENDMENT XIV

Section 1. All persons born or naturalized in the United States, and subject to the jurisdiction thereof, are citizens of the United States and of the State wherein they reside. No State shall make or enforce any law which shall abridge the privileges or immunities of citizens of the United States; nor shall any State deprive any person of life, liberty, or property, without due process of law; nor deny to any person within its jurisdiction the equal protection of the laws.

* * *

Section 5. The Congress shall have power to enforce, by appropriate legislation, the provisions of this article.

APPENDIX B

GLOSSARY

Age Discrimination in Employment Act (ADEA) - The ADEA, 29 U.S.C. § 621 *et seq.*, is part of the Fair Labor Standards Act. It prohibits discrimination against persons who are at least 40 years old, and applies to employers which have 20or more employees and which affect interstate commerce.

Americans with Disabilities Act (ADA) - The ADA, 42 U.S.C. § 12101 *et seq.*, went into effect on July 26, 1992. Among other things, it prohibits discrimination against a qualified individual with a disability because of that person's disability with respect to job application procedures, the hiring, advancement or discharge of employees, employee compensation, job training, and other terms, conditions and privileges of employment.

Bona fide - Latin term meaning "good faith." Generally used to note a party's lack of bad intent or fraudulent purpose.

Class Action Suit - Federal Rule of Civil Procedure 23 allows members of a class to sue as representatives on behalf of the whole class provided that the class is so large that joinder of all parties is impractical, there are questions of law or fact common to the class, the claims or defenses of the representatives are typical of the claims or defenses of the class, and the representative parties will adequately protect the interests of the class. In addition, there must be some danger of inconsistent verdicts or adjudications if the class action were prosecuted as separate actions. Most states also allow class actions under the same or similar circumstances.

Collateral Estoppel - Also known as issue preclusion. The idea that once an issue has been litigated, it may not be retried. Similar to the doctrine of *Res Judicata* (see below).

Due Process Clause - The clauses of the Fifth and Fourteenth Amendments to the Constitution which guarantee the citizens of the United States "due process of law" (see below). The Fifth Amendment's Due Process Clause applies to the federal government, and the Fourteenth Amendment's Due Process Clause applies to the states.

Due Process of Law - The idea of "fair play" in the government's application of law to its citizens, guaranteed by the Fifth and Fourteenth Amendments. Substantive due process is just plain *fairness*, and procedural due process is accorded when

345

the government utilizes adequate procedural safeguards for the protection of an individual's liberty or property interests.

Employee Retirement Income Security Act (ERISA) - Federal legislation which sets uniform standards for employee pension benefit plans and employee welfare benefit plans. It is codified at 29 U.S.C. § 1001 *et seq.*

Enjoin - (see Injunction).

Equal Pay Act - Federal legislation which is part of the Fair Labor Standards Act. It applies to discrimination in wages which is based on gender. For race discrimination, employees paid unequally must utilize Title VII or 42 U.S.C. § 1981. Unlike many labor statutes, there is no minimum number of employees necessary to invoke the act's protection.

Equal Protection Clause - The clause of the Fourteenth Amendment which prohibits a state from denying any person within its jurisdiction equal protection of its laws. Also, the Due Process Clause of the Fifth Amendment which pertains to the federal government. This has been interpreted by the Supreme Court to grant equal protection even though there is no explicit grant in the Constitution.

Establishment Clause - The clause of the First Amendment which prohibits Congress from making "any law respecting an establishment of religion." This clause has been interpreted as creating a "wall of separation" between church and state. The test now used to determine whether government action violates the Establishment Clause, referred to as the *Lemon* test, asks whether the action has a secular purpose, whether its primary effect promotes or inhibits religion, and whether it requires excessive entanglement between church and state.

Ex Post Facto Law - A law which punishes as criminal any action which was not a crime at the time it was performed. Prohibited by Article I, Section 9, of the Constitution.

Exclusionary Rule - Constitutional limitation on the introduction of evidence which states that evidence derived from a constitutional violation must be excluded from trial.

Fair Labor Relations Authority (FLRA) - The authority charged with interpreting collective bargaining agreements between federal employers and employees, and with preventing and remedying unfair labor practices by federal employers.

Fair Labor Standards Act (FLSA) - Federal legislation which mandates the payment of minimum wages and overtime compensation to covered employees. The overtime provisions require employers to pay at least time-and-one-half to employees who work more than 40 hours per week.

Family and Medical Leave Act - Federal legislation that grants eligible employees (those working at least 1,250 hours during the preceding 12-month period) the right to take up to 12 weeks of unpaid leave per year under specified circumstances related to family health care, and childbirth or adoption.

Federal Employers' Liability Act (FELA) - Legislation enacted to provide a federal remedy for railroad workers who are injured as a result of employer or co-employee negligence. It expressly prohibits covered carriers from adopting any regulation, or entering into any contract, which limits their FELA liability.

Federal Tort Claims Act - Federal legislation which determines the circumstances under which the United States waives its sovereign immunity (see below) and agrees to be sued in court for money damages. The government retains its immunity in cases of intentional torts committed by its employees or agents, and where the tort is the result of a "discretionary function" of a federal employee or agency. Many states have similar acts.

42 U.S.C. §§ 1981, 1983 - Section 1983 of the federal Civil Rights Act prohibits any person acting under color of state law from depriving any other person of rights protected by the Constitution or by federal laws. A vast majority of lawsuits claiming constitutional violations are brought under § 1983. Section 1981 provides that all persons enjoy the same right to make and enforce contracts as "white citizens." Section 1981 applies to employment contracts. Further, unlike § 1983, § 1981 applies even to private actors. It is not limited to those acting under color of state law. These sections do not apply to the federal government, though the government may be sued directly under the Constitution for any violations.

Free Exercise Clause - The clause of the First Amendment which prohibits Congress from interfering with citizens' rights to the free exercise of their religion. Through the Fourteenth Amendment, it has also been made applicable to the states and their sub-entities. The Supreme Court has held that laws of general applicability which have an incidental effect on persons' free exercise rights are not violative of the Free Exercise Clause.

Immunity (Sovereign Immunity) - Federal, state and local governments are free from liability for torts committed except in cases in which they have consented to be sued (by statute or by court decisions).

Incorporation Doctrine - By its own terms, the Bill of Rights applies only to the federal government. The Incorporation Doctrine states that the Fourteenth Amendment makes the Bill of Rights applicable to the states.

Injunction - An equitable remedy (see Remedies) wherein a court orders a party to do or refrain from doing some particular action.

Issue Preclusion - (see Collateral Estoppel).

Jurisdiction - The power of a court to determine cases and controversies. The Supreme Court's jurisdiction extends to cases arising under the Constitution and under federal law. Federal courts have the power to hear cases where there is diversity of citizenship or where a federal question is involved.

Labor Management Relations Act (LMRA) - Federal labor law which preempts state law with respect to controversies involving collective bargaining agreements. The most important provision of the LMRA is § 301, which is codified at 29 U.S.C. § 185.

National Labor Relations Act (NLRA) - Federal legislation which guarantees to employees the right to form and participate in labor organizations. It prohibits employers from interfering with employees in the exercise of their rights under the NLRA.

Negligence Per Se - Negligence on its face. Usually, the violation of an ordinance or statute will be treated as negligence per se because no careful person would have been guilty of it.

Occupational Safety and Health Act (OSH Act) - Federal legislation which requires employers to provide a safe workplace. Employers have both general and specific duties under the OSH Act. The general duty is to provide a workplace which is free from recognized hazards that are likely to result in serious physical harm. The specific duty is to conform to the health and safety standards promulgated by the Secretary of Labor.

Overbroad - A government action is overbroad if, in an attempt to alleviate a specific evil, it impermissibly prohibits or chills a protected action. For example, attempting to deal with street litter by prohibiting the distribution of leaflets or handbills.

Per Curiam - Latin phrase meaning "by the court." Used in court reports to note an opinion written by the court rather than by a single judge or justice.

Preemption Doctrine - Doctrine which states that when federal and state law attempt to regulate the same subject matter, federal law prevents the state law from operating. Based on the Supremacy Clause of Article VI, Clause 2, of the Constitution.

Prior Restraint - Restraining a publication before it is distributed. In general, constitutional law doctrine prohibits government from exercising prior restraint.

Pro Se - A party appearing in court, without the benefit of an attorney, is said to be appearing pro se.

Remand - The act of an appellate court in returning a case to the court from which it came for further action.

Remedies - There are two general categories of remedies, or relief: legal remedies, which consist of money damages, and equitable remedies, which consist of a court mandate that a specific action be prohibited or required. For example, a claim for compensatory and punitive damages seeks a legal remedy; a claim for an injunction seeks an equitable remedy. Equitable remedies are generally unavailable unless legal remedies are inadequate to address the harm.

Res Judicata - The judicial notion that a claim or action may not be tried twice or relitigated, or that all causes of action arising out of the same set of operative facts should be tried at one time. Also known as claim preclusion.

Section 504 of the Rehabilitation Act of 1973 - Section 504 applies to public or private institutions receiving federal financial assistance. It requires that, in the employment context, an otherwise qualified individual cannot be denied employment based on his or her handicap. An otherwise qualified individual is one who can perform the "essential functions" of the job with "reasonable accomodation."

Section 1981 & Section 1983 - (see 42 U.S.C. §§ 1981, 1983).

Sovereign Immunity - The idea that the government cannot be sued without its consent. It stems from the English notion that the "King could do no wrong." This immunity from suit has been abrogated in most states and by the federal government through legislative acts known as "tort claims acts."

Standing - The judicial doctrine which states that in order to maintain a lawsuit a party must have some real interest at stake in the outcome of the trial.

Statute of Limitations - A statute of limitation provides the time period in which a specific cause of action may be brought.

Summary Judgment - Federal Rule of Civil Procedure 56 provides for the summary adjudication of a case if either party can show that there is no genuine issue as to any material fact and that, given the facts agreed upon, the party is entitled to judgment as a matter of law. In general, summary judgment is used to dispose of claims which do not support a legally recognized claim.

Supremacy Clause - Clause in Article VI of the Constitution which states that federal legislation is the supreme law of the land. This clause is used to support the Preemption Doctrine (see above).

Title VII, Civil Rights Act of 1964 (Title VII) - Title VII prohibits discrimination in employment based upon race, color, sex, national origin, or religion. It applies to any employer having 15 or more employees. Under Title VII, where an employer intentionally discriminates, employees may obtain money damages unless the claim is for race discrimination. For those claims, monetary relief is available under 42 U.S.C. § 1981.

Tort - A tort is a civil wrong, other than breach of contract. Torts include negligence, assault, battery, trespass, defamation, infliction of emotional distress and wrongful death.

U.S. Equal Employment Opportunity Commission (EEOC) - The EEOC is the government entity which is empowered to enforce Title VII (see above) through investigation and/or lawsuits. Private individuals alleging discrimination must pursue administrative remedies within the EEOC before they are allowed to file suit under Title VII.

Vacate - The act of annulling the judgment of a court either by an appellate court or by the court itself. The Supreme Court will generally vacate a lower court's judgment without deciding the case itself, and remand the case to the lower court for further consideration in light of some recent controlling decision.

Void-for-Vagueness Doctrine - A judicial doctrine based on the Fourteenth Amendment's Due Process Clause. In order for a law which regulates speech, or any criminal statute, to pass muster under the doctrine, the law must make clear what actions are prohibited or made criminal. Under the principles of the Due Process Clause, people of average intelligence should not have to guess at the meaning of a law.

Writ of Certiorari - The device used by the Supreme Court to transfer cases from the appellate court's docket to its own. Since the Supreme Court's appellate jurisdiction is largely discretionary, it need only issue such a writ when it desires to rule in the case.

INDEX